SUMMER JOBS ABROAD

2004

D1783874

SOUTH TYNESIDE LIBRARIES
WITHDRAWN FROM STOCK

Date   Price
3·1·2005   40P

PAID

SUMMER JOBS ABROAD 2004

EDITORS

David Woodworth
Victoria Pybus

Distributed in the USA by
The Globe Pequot Press, Guilford, Connecticut

Published annually by
Vacation Work, 9 Park End Street, Oxford
www.vacationwork.co.uk

Thirty fifth edition

SUMMER JOBS ABROAD

Copyright (c) Vacation Work 2004
No part of this publication may be reproduced or transmitted in any form
or by any means without the prior written permission of the publisher.

ISBN 1-85458-302-6 (hardback)
ISBN 1-85458-301-8 (softback)
ISSN 0308 7123

Statement for the purposes of
The Employment Agencies Act 1973:
The price of the Directory of Summer Jobs Abroad is £16.95 (hardback)
or £10.99 (softback) and is for the book and the information contained
therein; it is not refundable.

South Tyneside Libraries

B21 116 2542.

208678

Askews	08-Dec-2003
Cover design by mccdesign	£10.99
Typeset by Brendan Cole	

CNL

331.34

Cover design by mccdesign

Typeset by Brendan Cole

Printed and bound in Italy by Legoprint, SpA, Trento

Contents

Summer Jobs Available

Country-Specific Vacancies

USEFUL PUBLICATIONS

**THIS EDITION IS VALID FOR
THE 2004 SUMMER SEASON ONLY.**

N.B. The author and publishers have every reason to believe in the accuracy
of the information given in this book and the authenticity and correct
practices of all organisations, companies, agencies etc. mentioned: however,
situations may change and telephone numbers etc. can alter, and readers are
strongly advised to check facts and credentials for themselves.

We have made every effort to make this book as useful as possible for you.
We would appreciate any comments that you may have concerning
the employers listed. Any comments will be treated in strict confidence.

Introduction

We are delighted that this new edition of *Summer Jobs Abroad* for 2004 not only includes details of more employers than ever before but also contains the widest possible range of jobs with something to interest everyone from a would-be bar pianist to a computer geek as well as the usual range of workcamps, hotels, campsites, harvests, couriers etc.

Much of this book consists of individual entries for specific employers and agencies, which are able to offer work overseas: the information in these entries has been supplied by the organisations themselves, and is included at their request. Entries covering opportunities in a wide distribution of countries or continents are in the *Worldwide* chapter at the beginning of the book; while those with a distribution in three or more European countries are in the *Organisations with Vacancies Across Europe* chapter; others are listed in the relevant country chapter. At the start of each country chapter there are some general notes on employment prospects and regulations on work permits, visas etc.

The European Union which allows inter-state mobility of workers who are nationals of EU member countries is due to enlarge prodigiously on 1 May 2004 when eight former eastern bloc countries (Czech Republic, Estonia, Hungary, Latvia, Lithuania, Poland, Slovakia and Slovenia) plus Malta and Cyprus are expected to join the EU. These are mostly countries where unemployment is high (18% in Poland) and earnings are an eighth of other EU countries' citizens. It is understandably predicted that more people will move from these countries to western ones to work for higher pay once they are granted free mobility to do so, than vice versa.

Where there are few opportunities for paid employment in eastern Europe and developing countries, we have given details of voluntary organisations willing to accept unskilled workers for short periods of time. Even in those countries where paid employment is available, voluntary work has a number of advantages. Hours of work are likely to be shorter, leaving more time available for recreational and cultural activities, which are generally regarded to be an integral part of workcamp life. In most cases, volunteers are drawn from a number of countries, so that contact is made not only with local residents, but also with young people from all over the world.

Only brief details have been given on opportunities in the USA. Opportunities there are so numerous that they are included in a separate annual volume entitled *Summer Jobs in the USA 2004*, which includes details of jobs in resorts, theatres, hotels, business, national parks, etc, and is available in Britain from Vacation Work at the price of £12.99 plus £1.50 post and packing.

The publishers cannot undertake to contact individual employers or to offer any assistance in arranging specific jobs.

Victoria Pybus
David Woodworth
Oxford October 2003

Opting for a Summer Job Abroad

The reasons why young people look for alternatives to the conventional summer job in their hometown are many and varied. Often it is just a case of itchy feet. Travelling abroad to do a holiday job is one of the best ways to shake off the boredom and routine of living at home and working locally. Whereas months of slogging at a local burger bar will allow you to save some money, time spent working abroad may alter your view of where you are headed in life.

Many students cite positive reasons for choosing to work abroad: to experience a foreign culture from the inside rather than as an onlooker, to fill a gap in their life's timetable in a productive way, **to improve their knowledge of foreign languages** and cultures, to **gain practical skills**. Usually there is an element of all these at work.

Working abroad is one of the means by which students and others can afford to stay overseas for an extended period, to have a chance to **absorb a foreign culture**, to meet foreign people on their own terms and to gain a better perspective on their own culture and habits. Sweeping generalisations about the valuable cultural insights afforded by working in a foreign land should be tempered with a careful consideration of the reality of doing a job abroad. In most cases, the expression 'working holiday' is an oxymoron like 'cruel kindness'. Jobs are jobs wherever you do them, and there is little scope for developing a social life and exploring museums if you are stranded in an obscure industrial town teaching English six days a week or manning reception in a damp caravan for a camping holiday operator. After perusing the jobs listed in this volume, it will be necessary to ask yourself whether you think you are sufficiently adaptable to work for a season in a Swiss hotel, Latvian summer camp, Danish strawberry farm or whatever catches your eye.

Earning and saving during the summer vacation have become crucially important to the vast majority of students since grants for higher education have been whittled away. A secondary consideration for some is that a summer job might **enhance a future CV** and allow you to gain useful experience or new skills. Jobs abroad can fulfil both these requirements. Some areas of career interest can just as easily be served by a summer job abroad as at home in fields as diverse as archaeology and social services, teaching and agriculture.

Employers have been shown to favour candidates who have demonstrated initiative and spent their time productively using a broad range of skills and working abroad will help you to fulfil these criteria. This does not necessarily mean finding an internship with a New York investment bank. Increasingly, employers are becoming open-minded to the fact that high-flying summer work is hard to come by and that transferable skills are what matter. For instance, those people who attain the position of barge manager on the French waterways will have demonstrated language and communication skills, leadership abilities, client service and a hardy stomach. Someone who works as a bar attendant may well have demonstrated these same skills plus a degree of numeracy and a faculty for working long hours under pressure.

Undoubtedly there are some drawbacks as well. It is more difficult to land a job when you are not available for interview and when you are not fluent in the dominant language of the region. Then there is the hassle and cost of getting abroad and possible administrative formalities such as visas and insurance. You will have to sever yourself temporarily from your commitments at home (boyfriends/girlfriends, pets, teams and clubs). One of the main drawbacks of a summer job abroad is that if anything goes wrong, you are a long way from the safety net of home. Job descriptions may sound more glamorous than the reality (as is true with jobs anywhere) so that a job serving cocktails in paradise may turn out to be clearing ashtrays in a seedy discotheque.

Certain obstacles in the mind of the irresolute must be overcome: Can I possibly afford it? What jobs can I get? Do I need specific skills? What if I only speak English? This introductory section sets out to allay anxieties and to encourage readers to peruse details of the thousands of summer jobs available. Those who have shed their unrealistic expectations are normally exhilarated by the novelty and challenge of finding and doing a summer job abroad.

Finding a summer job abroad may strike you as a daunting task. However this book leads you through the process in a systematic way and provides sufficient listings to help you find a job suited to your needs. Some jobs listed pay very well and come with room and board; others are voluntary and therefore unpaid. Some last for the whole season (June to September or longer); others are just for a couple of weeks. Working abroad for a short period will enable the dream to become a reality, of being immersed in a different culture, meeting new friends and earning money at the same time.

Where to Go and What to Do

At the risk of oversimplifying the choices, the seeker of a summer job abroad must either fix up a definite job before leaving home or take a gamble on finding something on arrival. There is a lot to recommend prior planning, especially for people who have seldom travelled abroad on their own and who feel some trepidation at the prospect.

If you have no predisposition to choose one country over another based on previous holidays, language studies at school or information from friends or relatives who live abroad, you are free to consider any job listed in this book. It will soon become apparent that there are far fewer listings in developing countries, simply because paid work in the developing world is rarely available to foreigners. Yet many students arrange to live for next to nothing doing something positive (see the section on Volunteering below).

Some organisations and employers listed in this directory accept a tiny handful of individuals who satisfy stringent requirements; others accept almost anyone who can pay the required fee, for example agencies that recruit paying volunteers for conservation work in exotic places or to teach English. Some work schemes and official exchanges require a lot of advance planning since it is not unusual for an application deadline to fall three to six months before departure.

The kind of job you find will determine the stratum of society in which you will mix and therefore the content of the experience. The traveller who spends a few weeks picking olives for a Cretan farmer will get a very different insight into Greece from the traveller who looks after the children of an Athenian shipping magnate. And both will probably have more culturally worthwhile experiences than the traveller who settles for working at a beach café frequented only by his or her partying compatriots.

The more unusual and interesting the job the more competition it will attract. For example it can be safely assumed that only a small percentage of applicants to the American Scandinavian Foundation is accepted as engineering trainees in Finland

and only a few of the many British students who would like to spend the summer working in a British embassy abroad actually get to participate in the Foreign Office scheme. On the other hand, less glamorous options can absorb an almost unlimited number of people, for example working as a counsellor on an American children's summer camp or volunteering to work on a kibbutz in Israel. All these possibilities are included in this book.

The question of work permits and visas must be tackled by British students who plan to work in a country outside Europe. The standard situation among all European Union countries (plus Iceland, Liechtenstein and Norway) is that nationals of any member state have the right to work (or look for work) for up to three months. Before the end of that period they should apply to the police or the local authority for a residence permit, showing their passport and job contract, a process that can be more bureaucratic and difficult than the legislation would indicate.

On May 1 2004, the European Union is set to welcome ten new member countries: Poland, Hungary, Latvia, Lithuania, Estonia, The Czech Republic, Slovakia, Slovenia, Cyprus and Malta. Some years will be required for the economies of most of these countries to be comparable to those of most of Western Europe and most countries (except Britain) will bar citizens of these countries to full EU working rights in their countries for several years and vice versa (unemployment in some of these countries is nearly 20%).

Work permits and residence visas outside Europe or for North American job-seekers worldwide are not readily available in many countries and for many kinds of job. In most cases, the job-seeker from overseas must find an employer willing to apply to the immigration authorities on his or her behalf well in advance of the job's starting date, while they are still in their home country. A more accessible alternative is to join an organised exchange programme like the ones administered by the CIEE and BUNAC, where the red tape is taken care of by a sponsoring organisation (see the introduction to the Worldwide chapter). Britons and other EU citizens who want to work outside Europe must investigate possibilities country-by-country (see sections on Red Tape Visas and Work Permits in the country chapters).

Seasonal Work Available

The Tourist Industry

The tourist industry is a mainstay of summer job seekers. The seasonal nature of hotel and restaurant work discourages a stable working population, so that hotel proprietors often rely on foreign and student labour during the busy summer season. Also, many tourist destinations are in remote places; young people have ended up working in hotels in some of the most beautiful corners of the world from high in the Alps to national parks in the USA.

In a few cases, agencies can place eligible British students in continental hotels for the season but mostly it is a case of applying to individual hotels. Only in a few cases can agencies and leisure groups place people without any relevant experience (e.g. in a café or takeaway in your hometown) or knowledge of the relevant language.

The earlier you decide to apply for seasonal hotel work the better are your chances. Hotels often recruit months before the summer season, and it is advisable to write to as many hotel addresses as possible by March, preferably in their own language. A knowledge of more than one language is an immense asset for work in

Europe. If you have an interest in working in a particular country and want to cast your net wider than the hotels listed in this directory, get a list of hotels from their tourist office in London or from the internet and contact the largest ones.

If you secure a hotel job without speaking the language of the country and lack relevant experience, you will probably be placed at the bottom of the pecking order, e.g. in the laundry or washing dishes. Reception and bar jobs are usually the most sought after and highly paid. However, the lowly jobs have their saving graces. The usual hours of chamber staff (7am-2pm) allow plenty of free time and of course you do not have to deal with guests. The same complaints crop up again and again among people who have worked in hotel kitchens: long and unsociable hours, low wages, dodgy accommodation and food, and hot working conditions.

But there are benefits as well. The vast majority of hotels provide their staff with accommodation and meals; a deduction may be made from wages for living expenses but in most cases this will not be unreasonable. Excellent camaraderie and team spirit, the opportunity to learn a foreign language, beautiful surroundings and the ease with which wages can be saved, including the possibility of an end-of-season bonus, are further incentives to consider a season in a foreign hotel.

Resorts and Holiday Centres

Camping tour operators employ a huge number of students and young people for the summer season. The Holidaybreak group (see entry in *Vacancies Across Europe* section), which includes Eurocamp and Keycamp, alone recruits up to 1,500 campsite couriers and children's couriers. The courier's job is to clean the tents and caravans between visitors, greet clients and deal with difficulties (particularly illness or car breakdowns) and introduce clients to the attractions of the area or even arrange and host social functions and amuse the children. All of this will be rewarded with on average £90-£100 a week in addition to free tent accommodation. Many companies offer half-season contracts April to mid-July and mid-July to the end of September. Setting up and dismantling the campsites in March/April and September (known as *montage* and *démontage*) is often done by a separate team. The work is hard but the language requirements are nil. The majority of vacancies are in France, though the major companies employ people from Austria to Denmark.

Successful couriers make the job look easy, but it does demand a lot of hard work and patience. Occasionally it is very hard to keep up the happy, smiling, never-ruffled courier look, but most seem to end up enjoying the job since it provides accommodation, a guaranteed weekly wage and the chance to work with like-minded people.

The big companies interview hundreds of candidates and have filled most posts by the end of January. But there is a high dropout rate and vacancies are filled from a reserve list, so it is worth ringing around the companies later on for cancellations. Despite keen competition, anyone who has studied a European language and has an outgoing personality stands a good chance if he or she applies early and widely enough.

Many specialist tour companies employ leaders for their clients (children and/or adults) who want a walking, cycling, watersports holiday, etc. Any competent sailor, canoeist, diver, climber, rider, etc. should have no difficulty marketing their skills abroad. A list of special interest and activity tour operators (to whom people with specialist skills can apply) is available from AITO, the Association of Independent Tour Operators (133A St Margaret's Road, Twickenham TW1 1RG). In the US, consult the *Specialty Travel Index* (305 San Anselmo Ave, San Anselmo, CA 94960; www.specialtytravel.com); the directory is issued twice a year at a cost of $10 in the

US, \$22 abroad.

For people who are pursuing a career in travel and tourism, it would be worth looking at another Vacation Work Publications title *Working in Tourism* (£11.95).

Agriculture

Farmers from Norway to Tasmania (with the notable exception of developing countries) are unable to bring in their harvests without assistance from outside their local community and often reward their itinerant labour force well. Finding out where harvesting jobs can be found is a matter of doing some research (for example in the book *Work Your Way Around the World*) and asking around for instance at hostels and the pubs frequented by farmers. Small-scale farmers are less inclined to publicise vacancies in a directory like this one than hoteliers, though this book contains details of interesting farm work schemes in Switzerland and Norway, and some large Danish and Dutch farms are listed.

The organic farming movement is a very useful source of agricultural contacts. Organic growers everywhere take on volunteers to help them minimise or abolish the use of chemicals and heavy machinery. Various co-ordinating bodies go under the name of WWOOF - World Wide Opportunities on Organic Farms. National WWOOF co-ordinators compile and sell a worklist of their member farmers willing to provide free room and board to volunteers who help out and who are genuinely interested in furthering the aims of the organic movement. Each national group has its own aims, system, fees and rules but most expect applicants to have gained some experience on an organic farm in their own country first. WWOOF is an exchange: in return for your help on organic farms, gardens and homesteads, you receive meals, a place to sleep and a practical insight into organic growing. (If the topic arises at immigration, avoid the word 'working'; it is preferable to present yourself as a student of organic farming organising an educational farm visit or a cultural exchange.)

WWOOF has a global website *www.wwoof.org* with links to the national offices in the countries that have a WWOOF co-ordinator. WWOOF organisations exist in many countries worldwide – developed and developing. Individual farm listings in other countries, i.e. those with no national organisation, are known as WWOOF Independents. It is necessary to join WWOOF before you can obtain addresses of these properties. If you are starting in Britain, send an s.a.e. to the UK branch of WWOOF (PO Box 2675, Lewes, Sussex BN7 1RB) who will send you a membership application form. Membership costs £20 per year and includes a subscription to their bi-monthly newsletter which contains small adverts for opportunities both in Britain and abroad or just £15 for online membership and online updates.

Teaching English

There are areas of the world where the boom in English language learning seems to know no bounds, from Ecuador to Slovenia, Lithuania to Vietnam. In some private language institutes, being a native speaker and adopting a professional manner are sometimes sufficient qualifications to get a job. But for more stable teaching jobs in recognised language schools, you will have to sign a contract (minimum three months, usually nine) and have some kind of qualification which ranges from a university degree to a certificate in education with a specialisation in ELT (English Language Teaching is now the preferred label).

To fix up a job in advance, make use of the internet and check adverts in the Education section of the *Guardian* every Tuesday. In a few cases, a carefully crafted

CV and enthusiastic personality are as important as EFL training and experience. There is also increasing scope for untrained but eager volunteers willing to pay an agency to place them in a language teaching situation abroad (for example, see the entry for i-to-i in the *Worldwide* chapter).

Native speaker teachers are nearly always employed to stimulate conversation rather than to teach grammar. Yet a basic knowledge of English grammar is a great asset when more advanced pupils ask awkward questions. The wages paid to English teachers are usually reasonable, and in developing countries are quite often well in excess of the average local wage. In return you may be asked to teach some fairly unsociable hours since most private English classes take place after working hours, and so schedules split between early morning and evening are commonplace.

Most language institutes operate throughout the academic year and close for the summer though some run summer courses or more commonly are affiliated with residential summer language camps where English and sports are taught to children and teenagers. These create jobs for monitors and counsellors as well as for EFL teachers. (See, for example, entries for A.C. Link in Italy chapter, Village Camps in the France and Switzerland chapters and APASS in the Poland chapter).

A good source of information about the whole topic of English teaching is the latest edition of *Teaching English Abroad* by Susan Griffith, available from Vacation Work Publications £12.95.

Au Pairs, Nannies & Mothers' Helps

Young women and (increasingly) young men can arrange to live with a family, helping to look after the children in exchange for pocket money. The terms au pair, mother's help and nanny are often applied rather loosely, since all are primarily live-in jobs concerned with looking after children. Nannies may have some formal training and take full charge of the children. Mother's helps work full-time and undertake general housework and/or cooking as well as childcare. Au pairs are supposed to work fewer hours and are expected to learn a foreign language (except in the USA) while living with a family. The Council of Europe guidelines stipulate that au pairs should be aged 18-27 (though these limits are flexible), should be expected to work about five hours a day, five days per week plus a couple of evenings of babysitting, must be given a private room and full board, health insurance, opportunities to learn the language and weekly pocket money of £40 to £50 in most cases plus board and lodging.

A number of agencies both in the UK and in the destination countries are described in this book. A list of agencies can be found at *www.europa-pages.com/au-pair*. After satisfying an agency that you are a suitable candidate for a live-in childcare position, you will have to wait until an acceptable match can be made with a family abroad. Make enquiries as early as possible, since there is a shortage of summer-only positions. In the first instance contact several agencies to compare terms and conditions. If your requirements are very specific as regards location or family circumstances, ring around some agencies and ask them to be blunt about their chances of being able to fix you up with what you want. In the UK agencies are permitted to charge a fee of up to £40 plus VAT only after a placement has been verified.

The advantage of a summer placement is that the au pair will accompany the family to their holiday destination at the seaside or in the mountains; the disadvantage is that the children will be out of school and therefore potentially a full-time responsibility.

Anyone interested in finding out about all aspects of live-in childcare should consult *The Au Pair & Nanny's Guide to Working Abroad* (Vacation Work Publications, £11.95).

Volunteering

Charities and aid organisations offer a range of structured and unstructured voluntary opportunities around the world. For example, enterprising summer workers have participated in interesting projects from helping a local native settlement to build a community centre in Arctic Canada, to working with hill tribes in the state of Haryana in northern India.

Every year the international workcamps movement mobilises thousands of volunteers from many countries to join a programme of conflict resolution and community development. As well as providing volunteers with the means to live cheaply for two to four weeks in a foreign country, workcamps enable unskilled volunteers to become involved in what is usually useful work for the community (e.g. building footpaths, working with disabled people), to meet people from many different backgrounds and to increase their awareness of other lifestyles and social problems.

When starting your research for a longer stint abroad as a volunteer, it is important to maintain realistic expectations. Ideally, your research should begin well in advance of your intended departure so that applications can be lodged, sponsorship money raised, language courses and other preparatory courses attended, and so on. When you receive the literature or check the website of voluntary organisations, consider the tone as well as the content. For example, profit-making commercial companies that charge high fees for participating in their programs are more likely to produce glossy brochures that read almost like a tour operator's, whereas underfunded charities or small grassroots organisations with no publicity budget will probably duplicate their information on an ancient photocopier.

Many voluntary agencies require more than idle curiosity about a country; they require a strong wish to become involved in a specific project and in many cases an ideological commitment to a cause. Almost without exception, volunteers must be self-funding, which serves to deter all but the committed.

For anyone with a green conscience, numerous conservation organisations throughout the world welcome volunteers for short or long periods. Projects range from tree planting to gibbon counting. Unfortunately, the more glamorous projects such as helping to conserve a coral reef or accompanying scientific research expeditions into wild and woolly places charge volunteers a great deal of money for the privilege of helping.

For a specialist directory of opportunities, consult *Green Volunteers: The World Guide to Voluntary Work in Nature Conservation* and *Archaeo-Volunteers* a guide to international possibilities for heritage-related voluntary work, both published in Italy and distributed by Vacation Work Publications in Europe (£10.99 each plus £1.75 postage). Related titles from the Vacation Work are *Working with the Environment* and *Working with Animals;* a new edition of the latter was published in 2003. Also look at the website for the Ecovolunteer Programme of wildlife and conservation projects worldwide (*www.ecovolunteer.org.uk*). *The International Directory of Voluntary Work* contains advice and listings of all types of voluntary work worldwide.

Several organisations assist scientific expeditions by supplying fee-paying volunteers. For details of scientific expedition organisations which use self-financing volunteers, see entries for Coral Cay Conservation, Earthwatch and Trekforce among others in the Worldwide chapter.

Maximise Your Chances

Plan of Attack

1. Remember that most employers prefer to take on a person to work for the whole of the season rather than several people to work for shorter periods. If you are able to work for longer than the minimum period quoted, let the employer know at an early stage since this is often a deciding factor.

2. Most employers like to make their staff arrangements in good time so try to apply early, but not earlier than the date mentioned in the job details or later than the closing date for applications, if given. Some of the biggest employers may maintain reserve lists to cover late staff cancellations, so it might pay off to apply after the deadline, but don't be disappointed if you receive no reply.

3. Apply as widely as possible. If more than one job seems to be suitable or appeals to you, apply for all of them. Make sure that you are qualified for the position for which you are applying. Check minimum age and work period requirements and any special qualifications needed, particularly if a good knowledge of another language is called for. If there is any shortfall, emphasise other skills and qualifications that may be useful.

4. Compose a short formal letter, explaining which position interests you, when you are available and why you think you are suitable. If possible produce this letter on a computer; if not, take care to make it legible. Always mention that the job has been seen in this book: employers can be wary as to the origin of information about themselves but most of them have a long-standing and trusting relationship with Vacation Work and its publications.

5. Try to address the potential employer in his or her language. It is not only polite to do so, but there is a possibility that he or she is unable to speak English.

6. Enclose with your letter a standard *Curriculum Vitae* (CV or résumé) on a single A4 sheet covering the following points and any other details you consider relevant:
   - Personal details (name, address, nationality, age, date of birth, marital status)
   - Previous work experience, especially of similar type of work.
   - Special qualifications, especially when they have some relevance to the job in question, e.g. canoe instructor's certificate, typing speeds or fluency in another language
   - Education (brief details of type of education, examinations passed).

7. Enclose a small recent passport-sized photo of yourself. (This may not be necessary when applying to a voluntary organisation.)

8. Employers are more likely to reply promptly if you enclose an international reply coupon, available at any post office. This will not guarantee a reply, but it will make one more likely.

9. If there is no reply from the employer within a reasonable period of time (say two weeks), it may be advisable to follow up the written application with a telephone call or an e-mail. The employer may be impressed by your initiative and perseverance

if it is matched by enthusiasm and politeness. Otherwise, he/she may feel hassled. In a few cases it is expected that applicants should make themselves available for an interview or visit the employer in person. Where this is the case, the applicant is likely to find more success if he can back up claims of suitability with a written CV and references.

10. When a job is offered to you, check details of wages, hours and other conditions of work with the employer. Do not be afraid to negotiate; you are always entitled to ask whether or not different terms are possible.

12. Please note that wages are normally quoted in sterling but will usually be paid in foreign currency: exchange rates may vary. The details given in the Directory have been supplied by the employer and will normally be correct, but it is wise to obtain written confirmation of them before taking up the position. You should insist that you receive a contract of employment before you set off for your job if the journey involves any great expense, or if the employer seems at all vague about the details of the work you will do.

13. When you are offered a job, please confirm acceptance or otherwise as quickly as possible. Do not accept more than one job. If you need to juggle possible outcomes, keep the prospective employers informed of your intentions and the expected timescale. If plans change and you do not want to take up a job you have already accepted, it is only fair to let the employer know immediately.

14. If you are offered more than one job, decide quickly which one you prefer and inform both employers of your decision as promptly as possible.

15. Those who contact employers and apply for positions via e-mail should ensure that if a CV is attached, that it is written in a programme that is readable and receivable by the receiver and that it contains no viruses.

The Internet

An increasing number of job vacancies (summer or permanent) is now available on the internet. Yet the plethora of resources can be bewildering and not infrequently disappointing - the number and range of jobs posted often fall short of the claims. No employer looking for two waitresses and a bellhop for the summer wants to publicise this fact through cyberspace since they are bound to be inundated with SPAM and applications from Merseyside to Mongolia. The internet as a job-finding tool works best for those with specific experience and skills, for example people looking for TEFL jobs abroad.

Still, internet surfers will find a host of potentially useful links on the web. Many websites promise to provide free on-line recruitment services for travellers. These include *www.hotrecruit.co.uk*, *Jobs Abroad Bulletin* (*www.payaway.co.uk*), *www.coolworks.com* (recommended for seasonal work in the North American tourist industry), *www.anyworkanywhere.com*, *www.summerjobseeker.com* (travel, leisure, tourism), *ww.travelrecruit.com*, *www.jobmonkey.com* and so on. Those looking for work in France can peruse opportunities posted on *www.AnnuairEmploi.com*. Elsewhere on the web, committed individuals around the world manage non-commercial sites on everything from kibbutzim to bar-tending. The Vacation Work website (*www.vacationwork.co.uk*) has a regularly updated section listing job vacancies for travellers both in Britain and abroad and an excellent links page.

BEFORE YOU GO:
Essential Preparation

Travel

Student travellers can take advantage of a comprehensive range of special discounts both at home and abroad which enable them to go almost anywhere in the world on the cheap. To qualify for a range of discounts on train, plane and bus fares, on selected accommodation, admission to museums, etc., you need an International **Student Identity Card (ISIC)** which is recognised all over the world. The card is obtainable for £6 or by post for £6.50 from ISIC Mail Order, PO Box 48, Horndean, Waterlooville, Hants, PO8 0FJ. The ISIC card is valid for 16 months from September 1st. All full-time students are eligible (though some flight carriers do not offer discounts to students over the age of 31). An alternative card is the **International Youth Card** for those aged under 26.

Both cards are available from STA Travel (☎1-800-781-4040; www.sta-travel.com – to find your nearest outlet, use their websites or the telephone directory), Student Flights (Students Union, Keele University, Staffordshire ST5 5BJ; ☎tel 752-715215; fax 01752-715915) and some other student travel outlets. The ISIC card and the Youth Card are available to persons of all nationalities; applications should include proof of student status, a passport photo, full name, date of birth, nationality, address and a cheque or postal order. The ISIC fee of $22 comes with a basic accident/sickness insurance package. An alternative card is the International Student Exchange Identity Card available from ISE Cards, 5010 East Shea Blvd, A-104, Scottsdale, AZ 85254 (☎1-800-255-8000; www.isecard.com) at a cost of $25. Valuable discounts are also available for air travel. Student and youth discount flights are operated by the major student travel organisations under the umbrella of the Student Air Travel Association – these include STA travel and Student Flights, mentioned above. Most of the flights are open to ISIC card holders under 30 (some have different age restrictions) together with their spouses and dependent children travelling on the same flight or to young persons with a valid EURO<26 or Go 25 card.

Specialist youth and student travel agencies are an excellent source of information for just about every kind of discount. Staff are often themselves seasoned travellers and can be a mine of information on budget travel in foreign countries. But check out your High Street, local independent travel agent and no-frills airlines as well to compare prices before making a final decision.

The leading youth and budget travel specialist in the UK is STA Travel which can organise flexible deals, domestic flights, overland transport, accommodation and tours. It publishes brochures-cum-magazines which survey travel options for students; pick up STA's *The Guide*. STA (STA Travel, 6 Wrights Lane, London W8 6TA; ☎0870 1600599; www.statravel.co.uk) is a major international travel agency with 250 branches worldwide. As well as worldwide airfares, they sell discounted rail and coach tickets, budget accommodation and insurance and many other packaged products.

In America, in addition to the major student travel agencies CIEE and STA Travel mentioned above in the context of student cards, discount tickets are available online on a standby basis from agencies like Air-Tech at 588 Broadway, Suite 204, New York, NY 10012 (☎212-219-7000; e-mail fly@airteck.com; www.airtech.com), Air Treks (442 Post St, Suite 400, San Francisco, CA 94102; ☎1-800-350-0612;

www.AirTreks.com) and Air-hitch (☎1-877-247-8735; www.airhitch.org). The cheapest fares from the US are available to people who are flexible about departure dates and destinations; the passenger chooses a block of possible dates (up to a five-day 'window') and preferred destinations. The company then tries to match these requirements with empty airline seats being released at knock-down prices.

From the UK to Europe it is often cheaper to fly on one of the new no-frills ticketless airlines shuttling between Stansted or Luton and many European destinations than it is by rail or bus. Note that quoted prices do not include taxes that can add up to £30 to the fare. These airlines do not take bookings via travel agents so it is necessary to contact them directly – they fly to and from various European cities:

- *Easyjet* –☎0870 607 6543; www.easyjet.com.
- *Ryanair* – ☎ 0871 246 0000; www.ryanair.com.
- *Virgin Express* –☎ 020-7744 0004; www.virgin-express.com.

Cheap rail travel is dependent chiefly upon age and is generally open to everyone under the age of 26. Inter-Rail is available on a zonal basis - from £119 for a 12-day 1 zone pass to £249 for a month long all-zones pass covering all 28 countries on the network as well as entitling you to discounts on *Eurostar* and cross-Channel travel. Inter-Rail passes are available from youth travel agencies and from Rail Europe (178 Piccadilly, London W1J 9AL; ☎08705 848848; www.raileurope.co.uk).

Eurolines, the UK's largest scheduled coach operator to Europe and Ireland with over 500 destinations, offers a 10% discount to passengers under 26. Return prices to Paris, Amsterdam, Brussels and Dublin start from £99. To book or plan a journey visit www.eurolines.co.uk or call 08705 143 219. It pays to compare prices between coach and rail because the differences are sometimes more than you would expect. Book 7 days before the date of travel to get the lowest possible coach fares.

One of the most interesting revolutions in independent and youth travel has been the explosion of backpackers' bus services which are hop-on hop-off coach services following prescribed routes. These can be found in New Zealand, Australia, USA, Canada, South Africa and Russia as well as on the European continent and in Britain and Ireland. For example a month long coach pass on *Busabout Europe* (258 Vauxhall Bridge Road, London SW1V 1BS; ☎020-7950 1661; www.busabout.com) costs £279 for those under 26. Alternatively you can buy a Flexi-pass; for example 15 days of travel in two months costs £329. In North America trips run by *Green Tortoise* (494 Broadway, San Francisco, California 94133; 800-867-8647; www.greentortoise.com) use vehicles converted to sleep about 35 people and make interesting tours, detours and stopovers around the Americas.

What to Pack

Even if you are travelling directly to your place of work, don't load yourself down with excess baggage. Most people who go abroad for a summer job want to do at least some independent travelling when their job ends and will find themselves seriously hampered if they are carrying around a 30-kilo rucksack. When you're buying a backpack/rucksack in a shop try to place a significant weight in it so you can feel how comfortable it might be to carry on your back, otherwise you'll be misled by lifting something usually filled with foam.

While aiming to travel as lightly as possible you should consider the advantage of taking certain extra pieces of equipment. For example a Swiss army knife is often invaluable (if only for its corkscrew) and a comfortable pair of shoes is essential since most summer jobs will involve long hours on your feet whether in a hotel dining room or in a farmer's field. Ideally, talk to someone who has done the job before who might recommend an obscure piece of equipment you'd never think of, for example a pair of fingerless gloves for cold-weather fruit-picking or dental floss which can be used as strong twine for mending backpacks, hanging up laundry, etc.

You might allow yourself the odd lightweight luxury, such as a favourite CD, a short-wave radio or a jar of peanut butter. You can always post some belongings on ahead, with the employer's permission. Try to leave at home anything of either monetary or sentimental value.

Good maps and guides always enhance one's enjoyment of a trip. If you are in London or Bristol, visit the famous map shop Edward Stanford Ltd (12-14 Long Acre, Covent Garden, WC2E 9LP;☎020-7836 1321 and in Bristol at 29 Corn Street, Bristol BS1 1HT; ☎0117-929-9966) and Daunt Books for Travellers (83 Marylebone High Street, W1M 4DE; ☎ 020-7224 2295). The Map Shop (15 High St, Upton-on-Severn, Worcestershire WR8 0HJ; ☎ 01684 593146/ themapshop@ btinternet.com; www.themapshop.co.uk) does an extensive mail order business and will send you the relevant catalogue. Two other specialists are the Inverness-based Traveller's Companion (www.travellerscompanion.co.uk) and Maps Worldwide, Daytum Hours, Lancaster Road, Bowerhill, Melksham, Wilts. SN12 6XJ (☎ 01225 707004/www.mapsworldwide.com).

There are dozens of travel specialists throughout North America, including the *Complete Traveller Bookstore* (199 Madison Ave, New York, NY 10016; ☎ 212-685-9007/fax 212-481-3253/completetraveller@worldnet.att.net) which also issues a free mail-order catalogue and, in Canada, *Wanderlust* (1929 West 4th Avenue, Kitsilano, Vancouver, BC, V6J 1M7; ☎ 604-739-2182/fax 604-733-9364/ wanderlust@uniserve.com/www.pilipalapress.com/namericastockists.html).

Visas and Red Tape

Up-to-date visa information is available from national consulates in London/ Washington or on the internet. For example the visa agency *Thames Consular Services* in London (Thames Consular Services Ltd, Unit 4, The Courtyard, Swan Centre, Fishers Lane, London W4 1RX; www.thamesconsular.com) allows you to search visa requirements and costs for individual countries and specialise in providing UK residents with visas for most countries.

As mentioned earlier, the free reciprocity of labour within the European Union means that the red tape has been greatly simplified for European nationals wanting to work in Europe. **The standard situation among all the established EU countries (ie excepting those due to join in 2004) (plus Norway and Iceland which belong to the European Economic Area or EEA) is that nationals of any EU state have the right to work without a work permit and to look for work in another member state for up to three months. At the end of that period they should apply to the police or the local authority for a residence permit, showing their passport and job contract.**

Outside Europe, obtaining permission to work is next to impossible for short periods unless you are participating in an approved exchange programme where the red tape is taken care of by a sponsoring organisation. The same applies to non-European students looking for seasonal jobs in Europe. Established organisations which run work abroad programmes are invaluable for guiding students and other young people through the red tape problems and for providing a soft landing for first time travellers.

For example *BUNAC* (16 Bowling Green Lane, London EC1R 0BD; ☎ 0207-

251-3472; www.bunac.org) is a student club that helps British students to work abroad while BUNAC USA (PO Box 430, Southbury, CT06488; www.bunac.org) assists a large number of Americans to work in Britain for up six months and in the Antipodes. BUNAC in the UK has a choice of programmes in the United States, Canada, Costa Rica, Australia, New Zealand, South Africa and Ghana, and in all cases assists participants to obtain the appropriate short-term working visas. In some programmes, participants have jobs arranged for them, for instance as counsellors or domestic staff at American children's summer camps; in others, it is up to individuals to find their own summer jobs once they arrive at their destination.

The CIEE (Council on International Educational Exchange; www.councilexcha nges.org.uk) in London oversees work abroad programmes for Britons in the USA, Canada, Australia, New Zealand, Thailand, Japan and China (52 Poland St, London W1F 7AB; ☎ 020-7478 2020. The CIEE in the US does likewise for American students who want to work in Ireland, France, Germany, Canada, Australia, New Zealand, Japan or China: see their entry under the heading *Other Employment Abroad* in the *Worldwide* chapter.

Many other youth exchange organisations and commercial agencies offer packages which help students to arrange work or volunteer positions abroad. For example *Camp America* and *Camp Counselors USA* are major recruitment organisations which arrange for thousands of young people to work in the US mostly on summer camps (see chapter on the USA). Other agencies specialise in placing young people (both women and men) in families as au pairs, as voluntary English teachers or in a range of other capacities – see the enties for individual countries.

The Schengen Visa. This is a visa for entry and in no way supportive or indicative of individual states' work permit regulations. Some member states of the European Union, namely Austria, Belgium, Denmark, Finland, France, Germany, Greece, Iceland, Italy, Luxembourg, the Netherlands, Norway, Portugal, Spain and Sweden, all being signatories of The Schengen Convention, issue a new type of uniform Visa, called the Schengen Visa.

The Schengen Visa issued by an Embassy or Consulate of the above mentioned countries allows the holder to move freely in all these countries within the validity of the visa. To obtain this type of visa you will be required to hold a passport or travel document that is recognised by all of the Schengen member states and valid at least three months beyond the validity of the visa. If your passport or travel document is valid only for certain Schengen states then the validity of your visa will be restricted to those states.

If you intend to visit only one schengen country, you must apply for a visa at the Embassy or Consulate of that country. If you intend to visit several schengen countries, you must apply for a visa at the Embassy or Consulate of the country in which your main destination is situated. If you intend to visit several schengen countries without having a main destination, you should apply for a visa at the Embassy or Consulate of the first country of entry.

A Schengen Visa is not the appropriate visa if you wish to remain in a Schengen member state for longer than 3 months or take up employment or establish a business or trade or profession. The list of countries whose citizens do not require a visa to enter any schengen member state for a period of up to 90 days is as follows:

All member countries of the European Union, Plus Andorra, Argentina, Australia, Bolivia, Brazil, Brunei, Bulgaria, Canada, Chile, Costa Rica, Croatia, Cyprus, Czech Republic, Ecuador, El Salvador, Estonia, Guatemala, Holy See, Honduras, Hong Kong (Special Passport), Hungary, Israel, Japan, Latvia, Lithuania, Macao (Special Passport), Malaysia, Malta, Mexico, Monaco, New Zealand, Nicaragua, Panama,

Paraguay, Poland, Romania, San Marino, Singapore, Slovakia, Slovenia, South Korea, Switzerland, United States Of America, Uruguay, Venezuela. If you are a citizen of a country which has not been included in the above lists you will need a Schengen Visa.

Accommodation

Employers who regularly employ foreign young people will either provide accommodation or help their staff to arrange lodgings locally. The majority of jobs listed in this book come with accommodation. Always find out ahead of time what the deal is: how much do you lose from your wages to cover accommodation? What facilities (especially for self-catering) are provided? How close to your place of work is it? Will there be extra costs for food, utilities, etc.? Are staff allowed to move out if they find more congenial or cheaper accommodation?

Much of the accommodation provided by employers for staff is very basic indeed and you should be prepared for something a lot more rustic than you are used to at home or at university. The only job which might provide more luxurious accommodation is as an au pair or any live-in job where you live in the employer's own house which may come with its own drawbacks.

If accommodation is not provided with the job, try to arrange something in advance, and certainly for the first couple of nights. If necessary make the journey to your destination several days early to fix up a suitable room. In cities, try universities, which might rent out student accommodation that has been vacated for the summer or whose notice boards may include details of housing. In holiday resorts, accommodation may be at a premium and you will have to use your ingenuity to find something you can afford.

Membership of the *Youth Hostels Association* costs £13 if you're over 18, £6.50 if you're not; you can join at any YHA hostel or shop or at their HQ (Membership Department, YHA, Trevelyan House, Dimple Road, Matlock, Derbyshire DE4 3YH; ☎ 0870 7708868; www.yha.org.uk). Seasonal demand abroad can be high, so it is always preferable to book in advance if you know your itinerary. You can pre-book beds over the internet on www.iyhf.org or through individual hostels and national offices listed in the *Hostelling International Guides*: Volume I covers Europe and the Mediterranean, Volume II covers the rest of the world. They can be ordered by ringing Customer Services on the above number and cost £8.50 each including postage.

Hostels of Europe and Hostels of America offer membership to a network of more than 500 Hostels on the best-travelled routes. Members get discounts of 5%-15% on accommodation, internet access, tours, etc. Information and on-line bookings can be made through www.hostels.net which is a searchable database of independent hostels in Europe, America and downunder. A one-year membership costs $15.

Hostels worldwide employ young people for a variety of jobs during the summer. In exchange for their labour, staff normally receive free board and lodging and some pocket money. The wardens or managers of individual hostels normally recruit their own staff.

Money

The average budget of a travelling student is about £25 a day though many survive on half that. Whatever the size of your travelling fund, you should give some thought to how and in what form to carry your money. Travellers' cheques are much safer than cash, though they cost an extra 1% and banks able to encash them are not always near to hand. The most universally recognised brands are American Express, Thomas Cook and Visa. (Note that Thomas Cook travellers' cheques and foreign currency are sold free of commission on their website www.thomascook.co.uk.) It is advisable also to keep a small amount of cash. The easiest way to look up the exchange rate of any world currency is to check on the internet (e.g. www.xe.net/ucc or www.oanda.com) or to look at the Monday edition of the *Financial Times*.

Euro notes and coins were introduced across most of Europe from January 2002. The countries that have replaced their currencies with the Euro are Austria, Belgium, Finland, France, Germany, Greece, Ireland, Italy, Luxembourg, the Netherlands, Portugal and Spain. National currency notes and coins were withdrawn in these countries and replaced by the Euro. Please note that most wages etc in this book are quoted in English pounds sterling: exchange rates can fluctuate, so you are always advised to convert wages quoted at the current rate before accepting a job.

Ask your bank for a list of cash machines in the countries you intend to visit. Otherwise you can find these listed at www.mastercard.com or www.visaholiday-card.com.

Theft takes many forms, from the highly trained gangs of gypsy children who artfully pick pockets in European railway stations to more violent attacks on the streets of American cities. Risks can be reduced by carrying your wealth in several places including a comfortable money belt worn inside your clothing, steering clear of seedy or crowded areas, remaining particularly alert in railway stations and moderating your intake of alcohol. If you are robbed, you must obtain a police report (often for a fee) to stand any chance of recouping part of your loss from your insurer (assuming the loss of cash is covered in your policy) or from your travellers' cheque company. Always keep a separate record of the cheque numbers you are carrying, so you will know instantly the numbers of the ones that have been taken.

If you do end up in dire financial straits and do not have a credit card, you should contact someone at home who is in a position to send money. You may contact your bank back home and ask them to wire money to you, often through the Swift service. This can only be done through a bank in the town you're in – something you have to arrange with your own bank, so you know where to pick the money up. Sample charges might be £15-£20 through high street banks.

Western Union offers an international money transfer service whereby cash deposited at one branch can be withdrawn by you from any other branch or agency, which your benefactor need not specify. Western Union agents – there are 90,000 of them in nearly 200 countries – come in all shapes and sizes (e.g. travel agencies, stationers, chemists). The person sending money to you simply turns up at a Western Union counter, hands over the desired sum plus the fee, which is £8 for up to £25 transferred, £21 for £100-£200, £37 for £500 and so on. For an extra £7 your benefactor can do this over the phone with a credit card. In the UK, ring 0800 833833 for further details, a list of outlets and a complete rate schedule.

Thomas Cook, American Express and the Post Office offer a similar service called Moneygram. Cash deposited at one of their foreign exchange counters is available within ten minutes at the named destination or can be collected up to 45 days later. The fee for sending £500 (for example) is £33. Ring 0800 897198 for details.

Insurance and Health

The National Health Service ceases to cover British nationals once they leave the United Kingdom. If you are a national of the European Economic Area (UK, Ireland, Netherlands, Belgium, Liechtenstein, Luxembourg, Denmark, Germany, France, Italy, Spain, Portugal, Greece, Austria, Finland, Sweden, Norway and Iceland)

and will be working in another EEA country, you will be covered by the European Community Social Security Regulations. Advice and the leaflet SA29 *Your Social Security Insurance, Benefits and Health Care Rights in the European Community* may be obtained free of charge from the Inland Revenue, National Insurance Contributions Office, International Services, Benton Park View, Longbenton, Newcastle-upon-Tyne NE98 1ZZ (☎ 0845-9154811 or 0845-908459/fax 0845-9150067). Those intending to work abroad can obtain further details from the leaflet SA29 or by contacting International Services (on the details shown above) with details of their intended employment abroad.

Leaflet T6 (Health Advice for Travellers) available from post offices contains an application form to obtain form E111 (called the 'E-one-eleven') which is a certificate of entitlement to medical treatment in the EEA. The E-111 is not issued to EEA nationals who are going to work in another member country for less than 12 months and who continue to pay UK National Insurance contributions. Form E128 is now issued which gives entitlement to a full range of health care. This form also applies to students staying temporarily in another EEA country as part of their studies. For information on your entitlement to a certificate E128, please contact International Services on the details above.

When British nationals begin work abroad they may be required to pay foreign social security contributions in order to be eligible for health cover. Leaflet T6 gives details of the special health agreements that the United Kingdom has with non-EU countries including Australia, the Channel Islands, Malta, New Zealand and several Eastern European countries which enable visitors to use their health services. In countries outside the EEA and not listed in leaflet T6, British citizens can use the public health service only if they are contributing to its Social Security scheme: for example, in Switzerland they must be paid-up members of a Swiss sickness insurance fund.

Foreign health services rarely offer as comprehensive a free service as the NHS does; while some offer free treatment, others will only subsidise the cost. The cost of bringing a person back to the UK in the case of illness or death is never covered under the reciprocal arrangements so it is wise to purchase private insurance. Ordinary travel insurance policies cover only those risks that a holidaymaker can expect to face and will not cover work-related injuries such as treating backs damaged while grape-picking, or burns caused by an overboiling goulash in a restaurant kitchen.

The following companies should be able to arrange insurance cover for most people going to work abroad, as long as they are advised of the exact nature of the physical/manual job to be undertaken:

Extrasure Travel Insurance Ltd, 16 St. Helen's Place, London EC3A 6DF (☎ ☎020-7480 6871; fax 020-7480 6189; www.extrasureonline.co.uk). Specialist in travel policies; can arrange insurance for those working abroad for short or long periods (up to 12 months).

The Travel Insurance Agency, Suite 2, Percy Mews, 775B High Road, North Finchley, London N12 8JY (☎020-8446 5414; fax 020-8446 5417; www.travelinsurers.com). Policies only for travellers, including those working abroad.

Worldwide Travel Insurance Services Ltd, The Business Centre, 1 Commercial Road, Paddock Wood, Tonbridge, Kent TN12 6YT (☎01892-833338; fax 01892-837744; e-mail sales@worldwideinsure.com; www.worldwideinsure.com). Comprehensive policies for most work abroad from 5 days to 24 months. Manual labour cover can be purchased from overseas for an additional premium.

Endsleigh Insurance, Endsleigh House, Cheltenham, Glos GL50 3NR (01282-

451166; www.endsleigh.co.uk). Offices in most university towns. Twelve months of cover in Europe costs from £215, worldwide £338.

If you are planning to include developing countries on your itinerary, you will want to take the necessary health precautions, though this won't be cheap unless you are able to have your injections at your local NHS surgery where most injections are free or given for a minimal charge. Malaria poses an increasing danger and expert advice should be sought about which medications to take for the specific parts of the world you intend to visit.

Tap water is unsafe to drink in many parts of the world so it will be necessary to give some thought as to the method of water purification you will use (filtering, boiling or chemical additives). Remember that water used to wash vegetables, brush teeth or make ice cubes is also potentially risky. Tap water throughout Western Europe is safe to drink.

MASTA (Medical Advisory Service for Travellers Abroad) run a Travel Health Centre at 52, Margaret St, London W1 (for further information on this and other MASTA clubs nation-wide visit www.masta.org) and also maintains an up-to-date database on travellers' diseases and their prevention. You can ring their interactive Travellers' Health Line on 0906 822 4100 with your destinations (up to six countries) and they will send you a basic health brief by return, for the price of the telephone call (60p per minute).

Increasingly, people are seeking advice via the internet; check for example www.fitfortravel.scot.nhs.uk; www.tmb.ie and www.travelhealth.co.uk. The BBC's Health Travel Site www.bbc.co.uk/health/travel is a solid source of information about travel health ranging from tummy trouble to water quality to snake bites.

Many women are reluctant to travel alone though thousands do so with great pleasure. Sensible precautions include behaving with modesty and trusting your instincts about potentially suspect characters and situations. General advice on minimising the risks of independent travel is contained in the book *World Wise – Your Passport to Safer Travel* published by Thomas Cook in association with the Suzy Lamplugh Trust and the Foreign Office (www.suzylamplugh.org/worldwise; £6.99 plus £1 postage). Arguably its advice is over-cautious, advising travellers never to hitch-hike, ride a motorbike or accept an invitation to a private house. Travellers will have to decide for themselves when to follow this advice and when to ignore it.

THE EURO

At the time of going to press the following rates applied:

£1 = €1,45 €1 = 70p $1 = €0,92 €1 = $1.09

Where wages have been quoted in Euros by an employer we have put the sterling value in brackets afterwards converted at the above rates

Organisations with Vacancies Worldwide

Agricultural Work

IAEA/AgriVenture: Avenue M, NAC, Stoneleigh Park, Kenilworth, Warwickshire CV8 2LR (☎+ 44 (0) 2476 696578; fax: + 44 (0) 2476 696684; e-mail: uk@agriventure.com; www. agriventure.com).

Farming or Horticultural Working Programmes to Australia, New Zealand, Canada, USA and Japan are arranged by AgriVenture. Applicants must be aged 18-30, have no dependants, be British citizens, have a full driving licence and have good practical experience within agriculture or horticulture. Programmes depart all the year around (applications required approx 2 months minimum before departure).

Programme costs start at around £2000 and include: return flights (and transfer to host family), full travel and work insurance, work permits, job placement, departure information meeting, seminar in host country and full emergency back-up through offices in hosting country.

For a free brochure or more information *telephone* freephone 0800 783 2186 or e-mail with your name, address and post code.

Some European citizens can participate to the above countries. *Further information* from the European AgriVenture Office (in Denmark) on +45 59 51 15 25 or e-mail europe@agriventure.com

Canadian and USA citizens can *call* AgriVenture in Calgary on + 1 403 255 7799 or e-mail canada@agriventure.com and can visit Japan, Australia, New Zealand, UK and various other European destinations.

New Zealand citizens can *call* AgriVenture in Whakatane on + 64 7 307 0086 or e-mail nz@agriventure.com and can visit Japan, USA, Canada, UK and various European destinations.

Australian citizens can call AgriVenture in Sydney on + 61 2 92 99 53 00 or e-mail australia@agriventure.com and can visit Japan, USA, Canada, UK and various European destinations.

WWOOF (World Wide Opportunities on Organic Farms)

WWOOF exists to give people the opportunity of gaining first hand experience of organic farming and gardening in return for spending a weekend or longer helping on a farm. Since WWOOF began in England in 1971, similar schemes have developed in other countries around the world. Each national group has its own aims, system, fees and rules, e.g. WWOOF Australia, WWOOF Italy. They are all similar in that they offer volunteers the chance to learn in a practical way the growing methods of their host. Each group will supply a booklet listing WWOOF hosts to members from which volunteers can choose a farm. Most national organisations expect applicants to have gained experience on an organic farm in their own country. Where countries do not have a national WWOOF organisation, individual hosts are listed with WWOOF Independents.

Details of schemes in the USA can also be found in the publication *Educational and Training Opportunities in Sustainable Agriculture* available free from the Alternative Farming Systems Information Center, USDA, National Agricultural Library, Room 132, 10301 Baltimore Avenue, Beltsville MD 20705-2351, USA (☎301-504-6559;

fax 301-504-6927; e-mail: afsic@nal.usda.gov; www.nal.usda.gov).

For further information applicants should *contact* WWOOF (UK) (c/o Fran Whittle, P.O. Box 2675, Lewes, Sussex BN7 1RB; www.wwoof.org.uk), or WWOOF Independents in countries including including France, Spain, Portugal, Ireland, South America, South Africa and India (addresses from www.wwoof.org), for information on overseas projects and application forms: please send an S.A.E./ International Reply Coupon.

Hotel Work and Catering

SPECIALIST HOLIDAYS GROUP: King's Place, 12-42 Wood Street, Kingston-upon-Thames, Surrey, KT1 1SG (☎0870-888-0028; e-mail overseasrecruitment@s-h-g.co.uk; www.shgjobs.co.uk). The Specialist Holidays Group incorporates Crystal Holidays, Thomson Ski & Lakes, Simply Travel plus many more. They recruit for Winter Ski, Lakes & Mountains & Specialist Sun staff throughout the year in many exciting European, American & Canadian destinations.

Qualified Nannies & Children's Representatives, Resort Representatives, Chalet Hosts, Chalet Assistants, Hotel Chefs, Hotel Assistants, Maintenance Staff, Kitchen/Night Porters: to work in a variety of destinations throughout the year. Positions are available for qualified and unqualified staff with a flexible and friendly attitude. A good understanding of customer requirements and the ability to work within a busy team. All employees must be aged 18 and over.

Please *apply* online @ www.shgjobs.co.uk.

Volunteer with us . . . and you'll be working for change

Concordia needs young people to participate in short term community based volunteer projects in over 40 countries internationally. No experience, just motivation required.

Are you
* *between 16-30 years and interested in international exchange?*
* *available for 2-4 weeks during spring or summer?*
* *interested in the environment, conservation, renovation, construction or social work?*
* *a teamworker, keen to develop new skills and meet new people?*
* *willing to invest a small amount of your time, money and energy to contribute positively to international understanding and community development?*

If you can answer yes to all these questions and want to know more, write enclosing an sae to:
The International Volunteer Co-ordinator • Concordia • Heversham House
20-22 Boundary Road • Hove • BN3 4ET
Email: info@concordia-iye.org.uk or visit our website: www.concordia-iye.org.uk

---

Industrial and Office Work

FOREIGN AND COMMONWEALTH OFFICE: Room 2/98, Old Admiralty Building, Whitehall, London, SW1A 2PA. (☎020-7008 0764; Fax 020-7008 0638; e-mail OUAS@fco.gov.uk)

The Foreign and Commonwealth Office (FCO) promotes and protects British Interests Overseas; presenting a positive image of the UK, helping British citizens and assisting British exporters. They also advise and support government ministers in the formulation and implementation of foreign policy.

Short Term Attachments to Overseas Posts in a limited number are offered by the FCO for undergraduates in their penultimate year. The attachments can last between two weeks and two months over the summer vacation period, depending on the student's and the FCO's circumstances.

The Foreign and Commonwealth Office covers all costs of return flights/visas

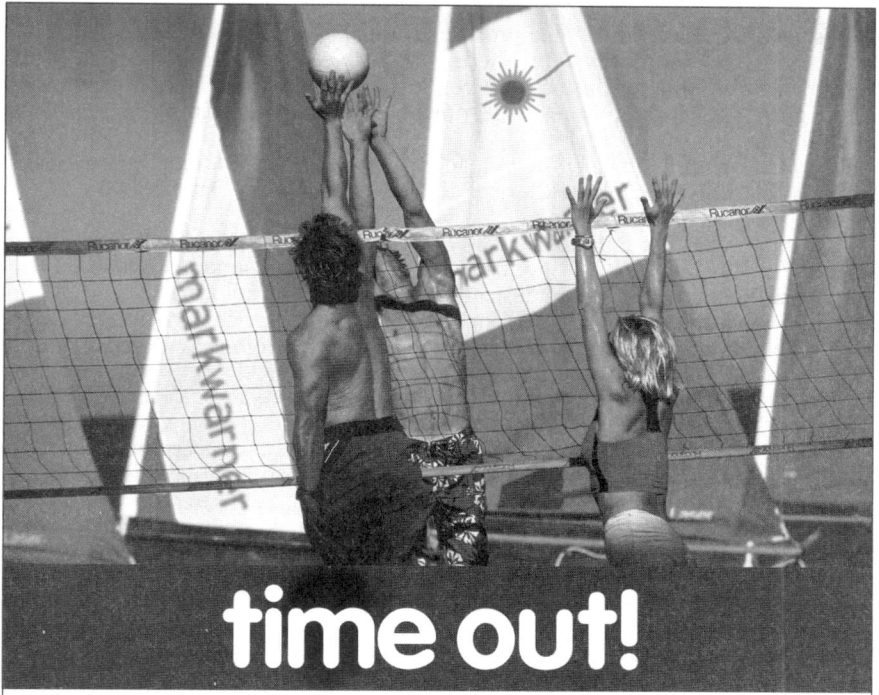

time out!

For Mark Warner's energetically elevated staff, time out usually means they're going to play as hard as they work.

This summer, we want **chefs, nannies, waiting & bar staff, activity and watersport instructors, kitchen porters** and more at our exclusive Resort Hotels in Corsica, Sardinia, Italy, Turkey and Greece.

What's in it for you? A positively rewarding season packed with tremendous fun, valuable experience and an attractive package.

For hot times ahead, call Mark Warner Resorts Recruitment on 020 7761 7300 or visit www.markwarner-recruitment.co.uk for details.

markwarner

to Posts. Accommodation is also provided. Students are asked to cover their living expenses while on placement, wherever possible Posts try to provide pocket money. To be eligible for this scheme you must be in your penultimate year of your first degree. Applicants must also be British Citizens and be seriously interested in a career in the diplomatic service.

Application forms can be downloaded from the Foreign and Commonwealth Office website www.fco.gov.uk, or call 020 7008 0764 from October 2003.

IMI PLC: Lakeside, Solihull Parkway, Birmingham Business Park, Birmingham B37 7X7 (☎0121-717 3700; fax 0121-717 3741; e-mail grad.recruit@imi.plc.uk; www.imiplc.com). This major international engineering group operates in the field of fluid control and is divided into four main business areas. Each of these is focused on market requirements and linked by common technology and manufacturing techniques. IMI has offices in over 60 countries worldwide but predominantly in the UK, Switzerland and Germany. **Vacation Placements** are offered by IMI each year (approx.12) to penultimate year students who are studying for a degree in Mechanical, Manufacturing, or Electronic and Electrical Engineering.

Overseas Placements can be offered dependent on individual language skills and placement availability. Successful candidates should be able to work for a period of 8-12 weeks. Applicants should have a good working knowledge of the country's language. During their placements students are required to attend a two day Management Skills training course. The salary for a placement is £770 per month. On completion of a successful placements students will be offered sponsorship through their final year at university and a place on the IMI Graduate Engineering Training Scheme.

Application forms available from the above address and on the company website: closing date for applications is 28th February.

INTERNATIONAL ASSOCIATION FOR THE EXCHANGE OF STUDENTS FOR TECHNICAL EXPERIENCE (IAESTE): See below for addresses.
IAESTE operate an exchange scheme whereby students in degree level scientific and technical studies are offered **course-related traineeships** in industrial, business, governmental and research organisations in over 80 countries. IAESTE selected trainees are employed on short term contracts, usually for up to 3 months, undertaking specific scientific, or professional tasks. Students are responsible for their own travel and insurance costs, but are paid a salary by the host employer to cover their cost of living.

Students should seek more information from the relevant address below. Special arrangements may be possible for sponsored students whose companies can arrange reciprocal placements for foreign students.

The British address for *applications* to this body is IAESTE UK, 10 Spring Gardens, London SW1A 2BN (☎020-7389 4114; www.iaeste.org.uk).

Sports, Couriers and Camping

AIRTOURS, DIRECT HOLIDAYS, PANORAMA & MANOS HOLIDAYS: Holiday House, Sandbrook Park, Sandbrook Way, Rochdale, Lancs OL11 5SA ☎☎0870-241 2642 or visit the website www.mytravelcareers.co.uk). All companies are UK tour operators and part of the My Travel group.
Customer Services Representatives based overseas, to look after one or more properties, visit customers on a daily basis to ensure they have the best holiday ever. Also responsible for airport transfers, welcome events, maximising the sale

of excursions and additional services offered in resort and handling any problems that may arise. Aged 20+. Must have minimum 12 months' experience working in a customer service or sales environment and be reliable, resilient, efficient and hard working.

Customer Service Assistants welcome customers at the companies' more popular resorts, care for them during the transfers and ensure that their holidays begins without a hitch. Also help to guide customers on excursions and assist the Customer Service Representatives with welcome events. Age 19+. Should have at least 6 months experience of working a customer service environment and be reliable, efficient, flexible and hard working. In addition needs bags of enthusiasm and stamina.

Escapades Rep are responsible for ensuring that 18-30 customers have the holiday of a lifetime. To organise and guide day and evening events such as beach parties, bar crawls and clubbing nights out and become the customers' best friend, inspiring them to live the Escapades holidays experience. Obligatory to work harder than you've ever worked before and provide a great service in a very highly pressured sales environment. Age 19+ with an affinity to the youth market, limitless energy, initiative and enthusiasm and bags of stamina.

Childrens' Representative responsible for the set up and day-to-day running of overseas children's clubs and the safety, welfare and enjoyment of younger customers, ensuring that the children you look after have a brilliant holiday. Age 18+ must possess experience of working with groups of children aged 3-10 along with at least three months' experience in a customer service environment.

Nursery Nurse to be resposible for the organisation and day-to-day running of nursery facilities, ensuring that the children are well-cared for so their parents can enjoy a well-earned break. Age 18+, must have experience of working with children aged 0-3 along with a CACHE/NNEB or equivalent qualification. In addition should have at least 3 months' experience of working in a customer service environment.

Escape Reps to be responsible for the organisation and day to day running of Escape Clubs delivering cool and funky fun-filled activities for the 11-15 age group. As the clubs only run throughout July and August, contracts last for only ten weeks. Suitable for university students wanting to work during the summer break. Age 18+, must have experience of working with the 11-15 age group and a minimum of 3 months' customer service experience. Candidates from a sports/coaching background also welcome, particularly those who are Lifeguard qualified or who have a Rescue Training certificate.

Entertainers to be responsible for providing a comprehensive day and evening entertainment programme in larger company hotels. Age 18+. Need not be professional entertainers but talent would be a distinct advantage. Should have at least 6 months experience in a customer service environment.

All the above posts can be *applied for on-line* at www.mytravel.careers.co.uk or call the recruitment line 0870 241642.

COSMOS: Wren Court, 17 London Road, Bromley, Kent, BR1 1DE (☎☎0208-695-4724; fax 0208-695-4409; e-mail cosmos@cosmos-uk.co.uk; www.cosmos-holidays.co.uk). Cosmos is an independent tour operator, providing holidays in the Mediterranean and further afield.

Overseas Representatives (200). Customer services, sales, guiding excursions. Wages £395

Children's Representatives (60) to organise activities for the children aged 3-11. Wages: £460.

Operations Assistant (10). To provide administrative support at the resort.

Minimum period of three months between March and October. Accommodation is provided. Knowledge of German is not essential but advantageous.

Applications to the above address.

DISCOVER ADVENTURE LTD: Throope Down House, Blandford Road, Coombe Bissett, Salisbury SP5 4LN; ☎ 01722-718444; fax 01722-718445; ww w.discoveradventure.com; e-mail darren@discoveradventure.com. Operates multi-activity, mountain-biking and trekking tours worldwide.

Tour Leaders. Applicants must have spoken English, be aged over 25 and hold a first aid certificate. An MBLA or MLA certificate is an advantage.

Applications should be made by sending a CV and covering letter to Darren Nicholson at the above address.

DRAGOMAN & ENCOUNTER: Camp Green, Kenton Road, Debenham, Suffok IP4 6LA (☎01728-861133; e-mail bels@dragoman.co.uk). Operates adventure tours worldwide.

Leaders for trips to Africa, Asia and the Americas. Aged 25 or over. Good spoken English required.

Applications and requests for further information should be made to the above address or email.

EXPLORE WORLDWIDE: 1 Frederick Street, Aldershot, Hants., GU11 1LQ (☎01252-760200; fax 01252-760207; e-mail info@explore.com; www.explore.com). Explore Worldwide is Europe's largest adventure tour operator.

Tour Leaders (110) to work 7 days per week for 3-6 months leading tour groups of 16 clients per group, to 96 countries around the world. Applicants with language skills and previous travel experience preferred. Wages by negotiation. Full training given.

Tour leaders are expected to be available all hours. Work is available throughout the year, with the minimum period of work being 3 months. Board and lodging are included. Must be aged 25 or over and hold a first aid certificate. Second language preferred.

Applications to the above address are accepted all year round.

FIRST CHOICE HOLIDAYS: London Road, Crawley, West Sussex, RH10 2GX (☎01293-588585; fax 01293-588-277; overseas.recruitment@firstchoice.co.uk; www.firstchoice4jobs.com). First Choice Holidays are a large, award-winning tour operator with worldwide destinations.

First Choice embraces a number of brand name holidays including JWT , Falcon and Sunsail. They need the following staff to work abroad across these companies: **Cabin** Crew for Ireland, **Overseas Resort Representatives** for First Choice, Falcon and JWT, **Various Staff** for Sunsail. Sovereign **Service Executives**.

Applicants should have excellent customer service skills, be attentive to detail in order to provide a high level of service to customers, previous experience beneficial. Applicants should be at least 21 years old. The above positions all require responsible people, willing to work long, unsociable hours. All applicants must be confident, able to speak publicly to groups of varying sizes, and be sociable, committed, self-motivators.

For all positions, the period of work is flexible between March and October. Accommodation is provided free of charge.

Recruitment takes place all year round: *EU applicants only*. Full details of all the above positions and how to apply can be found on the website www.firstchoice4jobs.com.

HALSBURY TRAVEL LTD: 35 Churchill Park, Colwick Business Estate, Nottingham NG4 2HF (☎0115-9404 303; fax 0115-9404 304; e-mail acorn@halsbury.com; www.halsbury.com). Halsbury Travel is an ABTA Bonded Tour Operator, specialising in School Group, European and Worldwide Tours. Established in 1986 they are one of the leading UK student group tour operators.

Group Leaders (100), **Language Tutors** (20). Required to work with touring groups in France, Germany or Spain. Wage £160 per week plus accommodation and meals.

Camp Supervisors (6). To work on camps in France or Spain. Wage £400 per month.

Tour Leaders and Couriers (50) to accompany History, Geography, Art and Business Studies, Sports and Travel, Leisure/Tourism Groups. Wages of £30 per day, plus accommodation and meals.

All applicants should be fluent in the native language of the country they wish to work in. Most positions involve 8 hour days 6 days per week, working for a minimum period of 1 week. Board and accommodation is provided.

Applications are invited to the above address in May/June for the winter season, (skiing jobs), and in January or February for jobs in the summer season.

THE IMAGINATIVE TRAVELLER: TL Jobs, The Imaginative Traveller, 1 Betts Avenue, Martlesham Heath, Nr Ipswich, Suffolk IP5 3RH, UK (e-mail tljobs@imtrav.net; www.imaginative-traveller.com). Operates small group, active journeys in the Middle East, Asia and Europe.

Tour leaders. Comprehensive training is provided for those willing to work at least 13 months overseas. Need to be responsible, self-reliant traveller with great people skills and a positive attitude. Good spoken English is required.

An *application form* and information pack is available from the above address: applicants should include a letter explaining why they would be suitable for the role.

INGHAMS TRAVEL: 10-18 Putney Hill, London SW15 6AX (☎020-8780 4400; fax 020-8780 8805; e-mail travel@inghams.com; www.inghams.co.uk). Inghams Travel is the largest independent operator of ski holidays in the UK with an excellent reputation built up over the last 70 years; they offer quality ski and lakes and mountains holidays to Europe and North America and aim to attract the best staff in the industry and our salaries and conditions of employment reflect this policy.

Representatives (approx.160) for client service, administration, sales, guiding of excursions and general problem solving. Salary £800-£1,200 per month including commission. Knowledge of French, German, Italian or Spanish is required. Minimum age 23.

Hotel Managers (5) for staff management, budgetary control, guest and supplier liaison, problem solving and menu planning. Wages £500-£800 per month. Applicants must have good man management and food and beverage experience within the hospitality industry. A good command of French or German is essential. Minimum age 24.

Hostesses (20) to waitress, clean and liaise with guests. Salary £200-300 per month. Experience in waitressing and chambermaiding is required. Minimum age 18.

Chefs and **Assistant Chefs** required to cater for up to 80 guests. Recognised cooking qualifications required and the ability to budget and menu plan. Salary £400-800 per month. Minimum age 20.

All staff to work 6 days a week in one of the following countries: Andorra, Austria, France, Italy and Switzerland. Minimum period of work 3-4 months from May to September. Free board and accommodation is provided. Applicants must be friendly, outgoing flexible team players with enthusiasm and a good sense of humour and must be customer care orientated and have a liking for the country and culture.

Applications all year round to the above address.

JOB-EXPRESS: Postbus 1459, Randstad 22-117, NL-1300 BL Almere, The Netherlands (☎+31-36-530 2000; fax +31-36-530 0300; e-mail postmaster@job express.nl; www.jobexpress.nl). Dutch recruitment and international employment agency specialising in international positions worldwide.
Campsite Workers, Animation Staff, Bar/Restaurant Staff, and **Other Positions** are frequently available for Dutch speakers as well as English speakers with a foreign language (preferably German).

Job Express often have permanent positions available for English speakers with fluency in French, German, Italian or Spanish. Several information packs are available at low cost. Please see their website or contact them for details.

This agency seeks staff for a number of temporary and permanent jobs around Europe. The hours of work vary but are generally over a 6 day week. Board and lodging is available for these jobs and will be either free or at cost price according to the job. *Applications* are invited all year round for these positions, contact Job-Express at the above address for more details.

KUMUKA EXPEDITIONS: c/o Brian Hamilton, 40 Earls Court Road, London W8 6EJ (e-mail humanresources@kumuka.com). Operates tours in Africa, South America, Asia, the Middle East and Europe.
Drivers and Tour Leaders. Wages on application. Good spoken English required. Must hold a Heavy Goods Vehicle driving licence, have a good mechanical knowledge and be over 25.

Applications should be made by e-mail to the above address.

ST PETER'S PILGRIMS: 87a Rushey Green, Catford, London, SE6 4AF (☎020-8244 8844; fax 020-8697 2466; e-mail info@stpeter.co.uk; website www.stpeter.co.uk)
Representatives/Pilgrimage Leaders (2) to look after pilgrims and arrange hotel bookings, transfers, excursions and daily programmes. Pilgrimages are arranged to most pilgrim destinations worldwide from Easter to October. A good knowledge of Christianity is required. Representatives will be paid c.£1000 and will have full board, uniform and other extras provided.
Applications to Bob Metcalf at the above address.

STEPPES LATIN AMERICA: The Travel House, 51 Castle Street, Cirencester, Gloucestershire GL7 1QD (01285-885333; fax 01295-885888; enquiry@steppesl atinamerica.co.uk; www.steppeslatinamerica.co.uk). Steppes Latin America is the specialist tour operator from Mexico down through Central America to Tierra del Fuego, covering the whole of Latin America.
Tour Guides (4) and **Representatives** (4) to look after clients in South America. £400 per month including board and accommodation. Minimum period of work is 6 months to a year, year round. Hours of work are flexible and there is a day off a week. Knowledge of Spanish/Portuguese required.
Apply to the Overseas Personnel department at the above address.

SUNSAIL LTD: The Port House, Port Solent, Portsmouth, Hampshire PO6 4TH (☎02392-222-308; 24 hrs 02392-334-600; www.sunsail.com; e-mail hr@sunsail.com). Sunsail are the leaders in worldwide sailing holidays with 34 bases worldwide employing around 1000 staff; of these two thirds are seasonal workers, although career progression and training within the company is also available.

Flotilla Skipper. Must be RYA Yachtmaster/Coastal Skipper/Commercially Endorsed professional sailor with unlimited patience and a friendly personality. To be responsible for the organisation/safety of guests aboard up to 13 cruising yachts. Duties include navigational briefings/assistance in all sailing matters and excellent organisational skills. Considerable yacht skippering and people skills essential.

Yacht Technicians capable of diagnosing/repairing ancillary systems aboard flotilla and base charter yachts. Knowledge of mechanics, woodwork, fibreglass and practical skills essential to carry out maintenance and yacht repair. Previous knowledge of marine systems and sailing an advantage.

Hostess to work as part of a team of three staff to look after flotilla guests. Duties include basic accounts, organisational skills, dealing with local suppliers, organising BBQs/events and customer care. Knowledge of German/French particularly valued.

All the above positions require staff who are flexible and used to dealing with people.

Diesel Mechanics, Electronics Specialists, Sailmakers, Storepersons to work on a seasonal and full time basis in Greece and Turkey. Relevant qualifications and experience essential in order to join teams of experts maintaining fleets of charter yachts in the Mediterranean.

The following staff are also required for seasonal vacancies (March-October) to run Watersports Hotels for up to 200 guests:

Hotel Managers, Front of House/Food and Beverage Managers, 706/1/2 Chefs, Commis Chefs, Catering Assistants, Barpersons, Receptionists, Waiting Staff, Childcare Assistants (NNEB, BTech, RGN), Activities Organisers. In addition to the specific roles staff commit a great deal of time to socialising with and looking after guests.

Sailing Managers, RYA Qualified Yacht/Windsurfing/Dinghy and BWSF Water-Ski Instructors qualified to instruct and provide rigging assistance and rescue cover for beach operations.

Bosun/Engineers required to maintain outboards and yacht engines. Woodwork, GRP repair and all yacht maintenance skills are desirable for this work.

All positions to work 6-day week. Salary up to £200 per week depending on position. Accommodation provided on yachts or sharing rooms ashore, where applicable. Food on site included, return flights on successful completion of contracted period. To work from March/April-October/November, certain vacancies also available for summer vacation periods. Minimum age, 19. Relevant qualifications and experience essential. Staff should be enthusiastic, hard working, loyal and honest with an outgoing personality.

Apply for a Recruitment Pack to the above address.

THOMAS COOK TOUR OPERATIONS: 29-31 Elmfield Road Bromley Kent BR1 1LT (☎0870-607 0309; e-mail overseas.jobs@thomascook.com). Thomas Cook Tour Operations is the country's leading name in the travel business, and part of the worldwide Thomas Cook Group. The company is looking for enthusiastic, responsible people to work overseas and help provide hassle-free enjoyable holidays to all customers for Thomas Cook, JMC, Sunset or Blue Sky Holidays Direct. As the face of Thomas Cook Tour Operations in resort, you must be hard working and approachable with real customer focus.

Overseas Representatives: to be responsible for ensuring that customers receive hassle-free holidays. Customer facing experience, a genuine desire to help and stamina to work long hours are all essential. Minimum age 20 years old.

Children's Representatives: to supervise and entertain groups of children aged 3-16 years. Experience of working with large groups of children is essential. Minimum age 19 years old.

Crèche Representatives: to look after and care for younger children aged between 6 months and 2 years, a qualification in childcare is essential. Minimum age 19 years old.

Overseas Administrators: the overseas offices are the nerve centre of Thomas Cook Tour Operations overseas operation. Office experience and people used to working under pressure are required. Sound knowledge of MS word, Excel and Outlook is essential. Minimum age 19 years old.

Contracts run from March to October with a possibility to continue through out the winter. All applicants must have a valid EEC or British passport.

To *apply* telephone 0870-607 0309 or e-mail overseas.jobs@thomascook.com.

It's time to leave the country!

If you share our spirit of adventure, passion for uncompromising customer service and our vision of being the best, Thomas Cook may well have the right opportunity for you in one of our overseas resorts.

The roles available include:

Resort Representative	KidsWORLD Representative
Overseas Office Administrator	KidsWORLD Crèche Representative
Transfer Representative	Entertainment Representative

Whichever position you choose requires 100% hard work and commitment, along with boundless energy and bags of enthusiasm. You will also need to be bursting with confidence, a skilled communicator, have a friendly personality and be a strong team player to join us.

To find out more, contact us for a recruitment pack on: 0870 60 70 309, e-mail our dedicated recruitment team on overseas.jobs@thomascook.com; or visit our website at www.thomascookjobs.com

Thomas Cook

THOMSON: Human Resources Overseas, Greater London House, Hampstead Road, London NW1 7SD (☎020-7383 1031; www.thomson-holidays.com/jobs). Thomson Holidays, Portland Direct, Skytours and Club Freestyle are all holiday products of Britain's No. 1 holiday company, Thomson Holidays, part of The World of Tui.

Representatives to be based abroad. The role involves meeting holiday makers on arrival, providing information about the resort and advice on how holiday makers can make the most of their holiday, including the recommending and selling of excursions. Other responsibilities include monitoring quality standards and providing excellent customer service whatever the situation.

Applicants should be 21+, willing to work in any destination, have at least a year's experience involving face to face customer contact and have a high standard of personal presentation. A second European language is desirable, but not essential. Package includes salary and commission paid monthly in the UK, accommodation, uniform and other benefits.

Childrens' Representatives are required to organise varied, imaginative and fun activities for 3-12 year olds. The role involves supervising daytime and evening activities. Aged 19+, applicants must hold a child care, infant teaching or nursing qualification, have at least 6 months practical experience working independently with large groups of children and a valid first aid certificate. Alternatively, an opportunity to study towards a child care qualification while working is available to those without a child care qualification. Additionally, a friendly outgoing personality and a genuine liking for children is essential. Package includes: salary paid monthly in UK, accommodation, meals, uniform and other benefits.

Entertainers to organise and present a 14-day entertainment schedule at one of Thomson's resort hotels, to delight customers and enhance their holiday enjoyment with a varied, polished and highly professional programme. This means actively attending rehearsals and promoting all the entertainment being organised and get all important feedback from the guests.

Multi-Sport Coaches to run sports programmes for those aged 12 years and over, of any standard. Working within Thomson superfamily hotels and apartments which are featured as Super Sports and have excellent sports facilities. The programme includes varied activities from football to tennis.

Applications for summer should be made between October and April. For further details and an application form send a large self-addressed envelope.

TUCAN: 316 Uxbridge Road, Acton, London W3 9QP, UK (☎0208-896 1600; nikki@toucantravel.com). Operates throughout Central and South America.

Tour Leaders to guide international groups. Good English and Spanish are required. Applicants should be aged over 24. Positions are normally held for a year minimum.

Applications should be made by CV and covering letter to the above address or e-mail.

VENTURE CO: The Ironyard, 64-66 The Market Place, Warwick (☎ 01926-411122; fax 01926-411133; mail@ventureco-worldwide.com; www.ventureco-worldwide.com). VentureCo is a Gap Year and Career Gap provider operating in Argentina, Chile, Costa Rica, Cuba, Guatemala, India and Mexico.

Expedition Leader (8) to lead groups for 4 months. £600 to £1,050 monthly, which includes all board and accommodation. Should be MLTB qualified, have a good knowledge of Spanish, at least 3 years' overseas travel/work experience and be minimum age 25 and be prepared to work 24/24. Period of work is from January to May. Must be group-oriented and enjoy working with 18-25 year olds.

Apply immediately to the above address or e-mail.

WORLD CHALLENGE EXPEDITIONS: The Leadership and Development Centre, Black Arrow House, 2 Chandos Road, London NW10 6NF (☎0208-728 7200; e-mail jpenney@world-challenge.co.ukk; www.world-challenge.co.uk). World Challenge Expeditions, the educational training specialists, run four flexible programmes. Each of the programmes works to raise motivation in young people through developing skills in leadership, team building, decision making and problem solving.

Expedition Leaders (300) World Challenge Expeditions requires male and female leaders for summer schools' educational expeditions to Central and South America, Africa, Himalayas and South East Asia.

Fee negotiable and all expenses paid. Periods of work are four weeks between late June and late August.

Apply to Leader Recruitment Team on the above details.

A WORLD OF EXPERIENCE EQUESTRIAN AGENCY: 52 Kingston Deverill, Warminster, Wiltshire (☎01985-844022; fax 01985-844102; e-mail angie@equijobshop.com; www.equijobshop.com). An advertising and introduction service established in 1988, which brings jobseekers and employers together in the horse world enabling them to contact each other. Overseas employers are all English-speaking and most jobs involve the care/exercise of valuable competition horses and travelling with them to national/international competitions.

Grooms, Head Grooms, Riding Instructors and **other stable staff** for vacancies all year round in about 20 countries in Europe and worldwide. Wages vary from £150-£250 or more per week plus free accommodation for an 8-12 hour day, 6 days per week.

Previous experience of full time employment with horses is strongly preferred; equine qualifications are essential for instructors but not for other posts. Jobseekers must be adaptable, aged at least 18, and preferably available for at least 3 months.

Jobseeker registration is free; *register* on the website www.equijobshop.com or *write* for a registration form enclosing an s.a.e..

Voluntary Work

Children

MONDO CHALLENGE: Galliford Building, Gayton Road, Milton Malsor, Northampton NN7 3AD; ☎01604-858225; fax 01605-859323; e-mail businesslin k@compuserve.com; www.yangrima.org.

Mondo Challenge is a new and rapidly expanding organisation that sends Volunteers to **Teach Children** in Tanzania, The Gambia, India, Nepal, Sri Lanka and Chile.

Volunteers need not be qualified teachers but must have an interest in children. Volunteers pay a joining fee of £800 per three months. The minimum stay is a month, but three months is recommended. It is also possible to go on more than one project consecutively. Volunteers pay all their own travel and living costs including board and accommodation. These are however very cheap in Africa, India etc. By the end of 2003, Mondo Challenge expect to have sent about 150 volunteers in that year. All ages are welcome. The oldest so far is in his 60s. Mondo Challenge also send volunteers to carry out business support. These volunteers must have a business background.

Further information from the above address.

SCRIPTURE UNION: 207-209 Queensway, Bletchley, Milton Keynes, Bucks MK2 2EB.(☎01908-856177; fax 01908-856012; e-mail: holidays@scriptureunion. org.uk; www.scriptureunion.org.uk). Scripture Union activities include programmes for Bible reading, missions and **residential holidays for children and young people, work in schools, youth work and the publishing of Christian resources. Activity Holiday Voluntary Instructors** (4,000) to work a minimum of one week throughout the summer. Volunteers are expected to **help organise Christian activity holidays for young people** and **carry out residential work**. Volunteers work on sites for up to 24 hours per day in Britain and overseas. Applicants must be in sympathy with the aims of Scripture Union, committed Christians and over 18 years old. There is always a need for those who have qualifications or interests in outdoor activities, sports, working with the disabled, first aid or life saving.

Applications from December onwards to the Holidays Administrator, at the above address.

Conservation & Environment

AFRICAN CONSERVATION EXPERIENCE: PO Box 9706, Solihull, West Midlands, B91 3FF (☎0870-241 5816; e-mail: info@ConservationAfrica.net;

www.ConservationAfrica.com).
Voluntary Conservation Work Placements: lasting 4-12 weeks around the year for young people on game reserves in Southern Africa, including South Africa, Botswana and Zimbabwe. Tasks may include darting rhino for relocation or elephant for fitting tracking collars. **Game capture, tagging, assisting with wildlife veterinary work, game counts and monitoring** may be part of the work programme. Marine projects involve **dolphin and whale research, seal and sea bird monitoring. Alien plant control and** the **re-introduction of indigenous plants** is often involved. Applicants must have reasonable physical fitness and be able to cope mentally. Enthusiasm for conservation is essential. The programme may be of special interest to students of environmental, zoological and biological sciences, veterinary science and animal care.

Applicants are invited to attend Open Days at various venues across the UK. Costs vary depending on reserve and time of year; support and advice are given on fund-raising. *Applications* to Lisa Hewston at the above address.

CORAL CAY CONSERVATION LTD.: The Tower, 13th Floor, 125 High Street, Colliers Wood, London SW19 2JG (☎0870-7500688; fax 0870-7500667; e-mail info@coralcay.org; www.coralcay.org). Coral Cay Conservation recruits paying volunteers to help alleviate poverty through research, education, training and alternative livelihood programmes worldwide. Volunteers are provided with full training; no previous experience required.
Expedition Leaders to oversee running of marine or forest expeditions. Must have proven leadership experience. Plus, for marine expeditions scuba diving qualifications and for forest expeditions a Mountain Leader qualification is preferable.
Science Officers to oversee coral reef and/or tropical forest scientific training and survey programmes. Minimum qualification: degree and/or proven field research experience.
Scuba Instructors to provide scuba training for expedition personnel and host country counterparts. PADI OWSI and EFRI as minimum.
Medical Officers to oversee all aspects of expedition medical health. Minimum qualification: paramedic, registered nurse or GP with A & E experience.

The above are needed to work for Coral Cay Conservation (CCC), a non-profit organisation **established in 1986 to provide support for the conservation and sustainable use of tropical and marine resources.** CCC maintains full-time expedition projects in the Philippines, Malaysia, Fiji, Mexico and Honduras. No wage is paid and expedition staff are required to cover the costs of their flights and insurance. CCC covers accommodation, food and other subsistence costs. To work 12 hours per day, 6 days per week. Minimum period of work is four months in any given year.

Either e-mail, or send *applications* to Susan Gluck at the above address.

EARTHWATCH: 267 Banbury Road, Oxford, OX2 7HT and 57 Woodstock Road, Oxford OX2 6HJ (☎01865-318831; fax 01865-311383; www.earthwatch.org/europe; e-mail vp@earthwatch.org.uk (volunteer project enquiries); info@earthwatch.org.uk (general enquiries).
Volunteers to work with scientists as part of a team conducting **research into a variety of conservation and heritage projects** in the UK, and all over the world. Project fees range from £120 to £2,500, over a period of two days or up to three weeks. No formal qualifications or experience are required.

For further details *contact* the above address.

ECOVOLUNTEER PROGRAM: Meyersweg 29, 7553 AX Hengelo, Netherlands (☎+31-74 250 8250; fax +31-74 250 6572; e-mail info@ecovolunteer.org; www.ecovolunteer.org or for Britons www.ecovolunteer.org.uk). The Ecovolunteer Program organises wildlife conservation projects and wildlife research projects operated by local conservation organisations worldwide.

Volunteers: (500-600) work varies from **practical fieldwork** to **production and support jobs in wildlife rescue centres**, to **visitor education, maintenance work, and household duties**, dependent on each individual project.

Volunteers are recruited for projects lasting from 1-4 weeks. The minimum age of volunteers is 18; participants must be in good physical health. Accommodation is provided.

A list of the national agencies can be found on the Ecovolunteer website or obtained from the above address as there are offices in Austria, Belgium, Brazil, France, Germany, Hungary, Italy, the Netherlands, Spain, Switzerland the UK and Thailand. Their latest projects include a wildlife sanctuary in Thailand and a Kiwi bird project in New Zealand.

Applications should be made to the national Ecovolunteer agency of the country in which the applicant is resident.

EXPLORATIONS IN TRAVEL: 2458 River Road, Guilford, Vermont. 05301 USA (☎1-802-257-0152; fax: 1-802-257-2784; e-mail: explore@volunteertravel.com; www.volunteertravel.com). Explorations in Travel arrange volunteer placements around the world, throughout the year, with placements arranged individually.

Volunteers to work with **wildlife and domestic animal rescue organizations, rainforest reserves, organic farms, environmental and conservation projects, sustainable tourism and schools.** Placements are in Australia, Belize, Costa Rica, Ecuador, Guatemala, Mexico and Puerto Rico. Periods of work etc. by arrangement; most placements are available throughout the year. Volunteers most often pay a local family for room and board. Minimum age 18.

For further details *contact* John Lee, Program Director, at the above address.

FRONTIER: 50-52 Rivington Street, London EC2A 3QP (☎020-7613 2422; e-mail info@frontier.ac.uk; www.frontier.ac.uk). Frontier is an ideal starting point: 62% of Frontier volunteers now have a career in this area. Frontier provide unique opportunities for tropical research training, field experience and the chance to work on official aid-funded projects overseas.

Frontier conduct vital **conservation research into some of the world's most threatened wildlife and habitats.** Expeditions are currently focused on biodiversity conservation and management issues in dry forests, tropical forests, savanna and coral reefs. Each expedition is operated in association with host country institutions, typically a university or natural resource management authority.

Volunteers are needed to carry out **baseline biological surveys and socio-economic research** in these areas during 4, 8, 10 or 20 week long expeditions to the Andamen Islands, Madagascar, Nicaragua, Tanzania and Vietnam. Frontier also recruits volunteers to participate in expeditions lasting 28 days, combining expedition and leadership skills with the **conservation of endangered wildlife and threatened habitats**. All survey data is collated into reports for use by host governments in the formulation of future natural resource use management plans.

No previous experience is necessary as training is provided in situ by highly qualified field scientists, leading to a BTEC qualification in Tropical Habitat Conservation or in Expedition Management. Expeditions run throughout the year. Volunteers are expected to raise from £1,500 for four weeks up to a maximum of

20 weeks (excluding flight costs). Costs cover local travel, food, accommodation, science equipment and vehicle maintenance, insurance and visa. Advice is given with fund raising.

Contact the above organisation for a free information pack and application form.

GREENFORCE
CONSERVATION EXPEDITIONS
Amazon, Africa, Fiji, Borneo, Bahamas

Join a wildlife research team working to preserve endangered species and wildlife habitat. 10 weeks All training provided inc dive training for marine volunteers.
Visit our website and find out how you can help:

www.greenforce.org info@greenforce.org Tel 0870 770 2646 Fax 0870 770 2647

GREENFORCE: 11-15 Betterton Street, Covent Garden, London WC2H 9BP (☎020-7470 8888; fax: 020-7470 8889; e-mail: info@greenforce.org; www.greenforce.org).

Volunteers (320 per year) required to 'Work on the Wild Side' on one of Greenforce's five wildlife research projects in the Peruvian Amazon, Zambia, Malaysian Borneo, Fiji and the Bahamas. Projects work to protect endangered species and habitats on behalf of a host country authority. Establishing new protection zones and managing wildlife resources are the main objectives of these long-term conservation projects. Placements last for 10 weeks, commencing in January, April, July and October, plus a limited number of 4-week placements in summer months.

Volunteers work as Fieldwork Assistants, carrying out tasks such as tracking animal movements and studying coral reef species over a 10-week project phase. All training is provided including diver training and rope access (Amazon project). Greenforce offers a traineeship to one member of each volunteer team; the selected trainee stays on camp for a further expedition as a staff assistant at no further cost. The position is aimed at those seeking to develop a career in conservation.

No previous experience is necessary; no qualifications required. Applicants must be over the age of 18. Applicants may attend one of the regular, informal open evenings. A briefing pack is provided, giving information about fund-raising and relevant medical advice, etc. Volunteers can attend a training weekend 6 weeks prior to joining the project (cost included in contribution). The first week of the expedition is spent undertaking further training and familiarisation with the project and host country. Costs are from £2,550 for 10 weeks in Peru and Zambia; £2,750 for the others. Summer expeditions cost £1,500 (Amazon and Africa), £1,600 for Borneo. These fees cover all training and instruction, food, accommodation, visas and medical insurance but not flights. Diving equipment and training are provided at no extra cost.

For further details *contact* the above address.

INKANATURA TRAVEL: Manuel Bañòn 461, San Isidro, Lima, Peru (☎014-402022; fax 014-229225; e-mail dm-ricalde@wayna.rcp.net.pe or jmelton@chavin.

rcp.net.pe). Two conservation organisations, Selva Sur and Peru Verde have formed a non-profit travel agency to **promote ecotourism** and assist **conservation work** in order to save Peru's unique biodiversity. Volunteers are also needed for projects in Bolivia and Brazil.

Resident Naturalists required for four lodges in southeastern Peru to **guide tourists and take on small research projects. Possible wildlife studies include tapirs, spider monkeys (and 5 other small monkey species), peccaries, macaws, bats, deer, large macaws and the endangered Giant River Otter.** Duration is 90 days, with an option to extend. After training and depending on experience, the applicant may be able to get a contract for guiding tourists. Free food and lodging will be provided as well as transport from Cusco. A deposit of £188/$300 will be required to cover the first month, which will be forfeited if the volunteer leaves before the end of the 90 day period without good cause. If a volunteer should abandon the project without good cause he/she will also have to pay for his/her own transport home.

Volunteers to assist research projects. Duration of stay is 4 weeks. Food and lodging costs of £12/$20 must be met by the volunteer as must insurance and the cost of travel to the project. US residents can obtain a tax break on these costs.

Some of the projects that volunteers can work on occur throughout the year, while others run from late October-January. There are also opportunities for independent research, to teach English and help train local residents/indigeneous people who are running ecotourism schemes near reserves in Manu, Tambopata, Lower Urubamba and Madidi.

Full details of these projects, costs and how to *apply* can be obtained from the above address or on the website.

INTERNATIONAL CONSERVATION HOLIDAYS: BTCV, Conservation Centre Booking Service, Balby Road, Doncaster DN4 ORH; ☎01302-572200; fax 01302-310167; e-mail natural-breaks@btcv.org.uk; www.btcv.org). BTCV is the UK's leading practical conservation charity. Founded in 1959, they help over 130,000 volunteers per year to take hands on action to improve urban and rural environments.

Volunteers to take part in **international conservation projects** in Australia, Bulgaria, Canada, Ecuador, France, Germany, Greece, Hungary, Iceland, Japan, Portugal, Romania, Turkey, Thailand, and the USA. Board, accommodation and insurance provided for from £240 per week. Projects take place throughout the year and last from 1-10 weeks. Minimum age 18: knowledge of languages not essential. Volunteers must pay their own travel expenses.

For full details of BTCV's Conservation Holiday programme, *contact* BTCV for an up-to-date brochure; full project details are also available on the BTCV website.

TREKFORCE EXPEDITIONS: 34 Buckingham Palace Road, London SW1W 0RE (☎020-7828 2275; e-mail info@trekforce.org.uk; www.trekforce.org.uk) .

Trekforce offers a once in a lifetime opportunity to play your part in international conservation and travel to some of the most beautiful and remote rainforests in the world. Trekforce sends adventurous volunteers on expeditions to the jungles of Central and South America and East Malaysia. Lasting from two to five months, the challenging team-based projects focus on **conservation of endangered rainforests**, working with scientists on vital research and local community projects. Trekforce's longer programmes involve a two-month conservation phase, up to a month learning new languages and two months teaching in rural communities. Trekforce is a registered charity (no. 1005452), so all costs can be fundraised in advance with extensive help and support from the UK staff.

Volunteers (aged 18-32) must be enthusiastic, hard-working and have a sense of adventure-no two days will be the same.

Trekforce regularly run Introduction Days, a chance to meet previous volunteers and find out more information about project work, jungle life and fundraising. Dates of Introduction Days and information on all aspects of the expeditions can be found on the website (see above).

Apply online for more information.

Gap Year/Year Out

AFRICA AND ASIA VENTURE: 10 Market Place, Devizes, Wilts., SN10 1HT (☎01380-729009; fax 01380-720060; e-mail av@aventure.co.uk; www.aventure.co.uk). 'AV' has nine years experience offering 18-23-year-old volunteers 4-5 month rewarding **projects in teaching, community and conservation** in Africa, the Indian Himalayas, Nepal and for those keen to improve their Spanish, Mexico. You can also take part in shorter vacation expeditions in Kenya that combine community work with travel and adventure.

Gap Year with AV will start with an in-country orientation course covering customs, country and TEFL, then experience of a rewarding project, followed by travel opportunities including a fantastic safari travelling in game reserves, deserts, or white water rafting. All this supported by excellent back-up enabling you to experience first hand countries away from the tourist trail.

Apply on the above number or online.

GAP ACTIVITY PROJECTS LIMITED: GAP House, 44 Queen's Road, Reading, Berkshire RG1 4BB (☎0118-9594914; fax 0118-9576634; e-mail volunteer@gap.org.uk; www.gap.org.uk). GAP is an educational charity based in Reading which organises voluntary work opportunities for 17-19 year olds in their 'year out' between school and higher education, employment or training. Successful volunteers undertake full-time work for between four and twelve months in return for which they receive food, accommodation and (usually) some pocket money.

Currently opportunities exist in Argentina, Australia, Brazil, Canada, Chile, China, (including Hong Kong), Costa Rica, Ecuador, the Falkland Islands, Fiji & the South Pacific, Germany, Hungary, India, Israel, Japan, Lesotho, Malaysia, Mexico, Morocco, Nepal, New Zealand, Paraguay, Poland, Romania, Russia, South Africa, Swaziland, Thailand, Trinidad and Tobago, the USA, Vietnam and Zambia. A wide variety of projects is on offer including **teaching English as a foreign language, general duties in schools, assisting on community projects or caring for the sick and people with disabilities, outdoor activities and sports coaching, conservation work and scientific surveys.**

GAP has no closing date for applications, although you stand a better chance of being placed on your first choice project, if you apply early. GAP welcomes applications at any time from year 12 onwards. Every applicant is invited to interview with interviews taking place from the middle of October onwards in Reading, Leeds, Dublin, Edinburgh, Glasgow and and other regional locations. Brochures are available each year from August onwards for placements starting a year later.

To receive a copy of the GAP brochure and application form students should *contact* careers staff at their school or college, or telephone, e-mail or write to the GAP office, stating clearly for which year they will be applying.

INVOLVEMENT VOLUNTEERS ASSOCIATION INC (IVI): PO Box 218, Port Melbourne, Victoria 3207, Australia (☎+61 9646-9392; fax +61 396465504; e-mail: ivworldwide@volunteering.org.au). Involvement Volunteers Association Inc. (IVI) was established in 1988 with the aim of making voluntary work available to people who wish to assist others and to learn from their volunteer experiences.

IV volunteers participate as individuals or groups of individual volunteers in Networked International Volunteering as unpaid participants. The aim of Involvement Volunteering is to enable volunteers to assist non-profit **projects related to the natural environment (at farms, national or zoological parks, animal reserves or historic places) or social service in the community (at homes, camps or schools for disadvantaged people, orphanages, villages).**

Placements of 2-12 weeks are currently available in Argentina, Armenia, Australia, Bangladesh, Belgium, Cambodia, China, Denmark, Ecuador, England, Fiji, Finland, Germany, Greece, India, Italy, Japan, Kenya, Korea, Lebanon, Macau, Mexico, Mongolia, Nepal, New Zealand, Philippines, Poland, Russia, Sabah (Malaysia), Samoa, South Africa, Spain, Thailand, Turkey, Ukraine, USA, Vietnam and Venezuela. **Single Placement Programs or Trip Programs (as many placements as can be fitted in a 12 month period travelling the world) can provide valuable practical experience related to potential tertiary education, completed degree courses or completed careers (for early retirees).** Some placements have food and accommodation provided while some can cost up to about £35 per week for food and accommodation, depending on the economy of the country and the host organisation.

Involvement Volunteers Association Inc. is a registered non-profit making organisation which charges fees to cover administration cost for a programme of any number of Networked International Volunteering; placements with suggested travel arrangements in any number of the countries in a period of up to 12 months. IV Associates support the volunteers in Australia, England, Fiji, Germany, New Zealand Sabah (Malaysia), Thailand, Korea, Nepal, South Africa and South American Countries. Where appropriate, IV volunteers are met on arrival at the airport and provided with a communications base during their visit. Advice is given on banking, specially discounted internal travel, special trips, eco trips, discounted scuba diving courses, sea kayaking, snorkelling and sailing in suitable areas.

European applicants can *contact* Involvement Volunteers UK, 7 Bushmead Avenue, Kingkerswell, Newton Abbot, Devon, TQ12 5EN (☎01803-872594; e-mail ivengland@volunteering.org.au) or Involvement Volunteers-Germany, Volksdorfer Strasse 32, 22081 Hamburg, Germany (☎+49 40 41269450; fax +49 40 5113229; e-mail ivgermany@volunteering.org.au.

THE PROJECT TRUST: The Hebridean Centre, Ballyhough, Isle of Coll, Argyll PA78 6TE (☎01879-230-444; fax 01879-230-357; e-mail info@projecttrust.org.uk). The Project Trust arranges for volunteers to spend a whole year in an exciting country, becoming part of a community and learning another language.

The Project Trust is an educational trust, which sends 200 school leavers overseas every year to over twenty countries around the world. At present these are: Bolivia, Botswana, Brazil, Chile, China, Dominican Republic, Guyana, Hong Kong, Honduras, Japan, Jordan, Malawi, Malaysia, Morocco, Namibia, Niger, Peru, South Africa, Sri Lanka, Swaziland, Tanzania, Thailand, Uganda and Vietnam. There are a wide variety of projects on offer, from **teaching** to **development work**, **outward bound activities, and child and health care**. Placements are for twelve months.

All volunteers attend a selection course on the Isle of Coll in the autumn before they go overseas. Week-long training courses take place on the Isle of Coll after final exams in the summer, and following a year overseas the volunteers assemble again on the Isle of Coll to debrief on the their experiencesl before dispersing to university or their future careers.

The cost is £3,550 for the year which includes insurance and travel, full support overseas, food and accommodation. Fundraising workshops are held throughout the country to help volunteers raise the necessary finance.

Apply as early as possible to avoid disappointment.

QUEST OVERSEAS: 32 Clapham Mansions, Nightingale Lane, London SW4 9AQ (☎020-8673 3313; fax 020-8673 7623; e-mail e-mailus@questoverseas.com / jon@questoverseas.com; www.questoverseas.com). Quest Overseas run projects and expeditions in South America and Africa for gap year students, university students and graduates.

Gap year students can apply to join a 3-month combined project and expedition.. The 3-month Quests in South America consists of 3 weeks one-to-one Spanish course, 4 weeks on a conservation or community project, and a six-week expedition trekking, mountain-biking and white-water rafting through Peru, Bolivia and Chile. **Projects in Africa** need volunteers to work for 6 weeks either on game reserves in Swaziland (ecological surveys, trail building) or in coastal villages in Tanzania (building schools, medical facilities). Both projects are followed by an adventurous six-week expedition and a scuba-diving course in Mozambique.

Volunteers of all ages can join the **Project Quest** expeditions, voluntary work placements either for individuals or as part of a team. Project Quest runs throughout the year in both South America and Africa.

Expedition Quest consists of two- and six-week Expeditions exploring some of the best and most adventurous parts of South America and Africa - an assault on the senses!

Projects cost between £1,345 and £4,620 for the three-month combined expeditions – this includes all board and accommodation as well as support on the project. Flights and insurance are not included.

Applications should be made either through the website or to the above address as early as possible in order to allow you to get your first choice of project.

RALEIGH INTERNATIONAL: Raleigh House, 27 Parsons Green Lane London SW6 4HZ (☎020-7371 8585; e-mail info@raleigh.org.uk; www.raleighinternational. org). Raleigh International is a charity that aims to inspire and develop people through challenging community, conservation and adventure projects on expeditions around the world. Opportunities available for Volunteers aged 17-25 and staff aged 25+.

Expedition destinations in 2004/2005 include Chile, Ghana, Namibia, Costa Rica/Nicaragua and Borneo. Projects range form **building schools** in Borneo, trekking across Costa Rica from the Caribbean to the Pacific, **conservation work** in National Parks in Namibia, **health projects** in Ghana and bio-diversity research in glacier rich southern Chile.

If you are interested, come and attend an Introduction Day. These are full of team challenges and information sessions about the fantastic opportunities with Raleigh International. The day is a chance for you to discover what you can expect from a Raleigh expedition as well as what will be expected from you. Volunteers are asked to fundraise £3,500 on behalf of Raleigh International. On expedition all costs are covered and a six month return ticket is provided allowing the option of independent travel after expedition. Fundraising for Raleigh International is great fun with regional and national events provided and many years of advice and experience.

Contact the above address for further information.

TEACHING & PROJECTS ABROAD: Gerrard House, Rustington, West Sussex, BN16 1AW (☎+44-(0)1903-859911; fax 01903-785779; e-mail info@teaching-abroad.co.uk; www.teaching-abroad.co.uk). Provides an opportunity to combine adventurous foreign travel with a worthwhile job. You will gain experience in **teaching, medicine, conservation** and much more. Volunteer placements are available worldwide.

Voluntary Placements (2,000) mostly for teaching work, in Bolivia, Chile, China, Ghana, India, Mexico, Mongolia, Nepal, Peru, Russia, Romania, South Africa, Thailand, Togo and Ukraine. Dates and duration are usually flexible. Volunteers are usually 17-25, but older candidates are welcome. In selected areas there are voluntary work experience programmes in business, conservation and other professions; most popular are those for medical subjects (around 250), media/journalism and supervised dissertations for degree courses. Applications are invited from anyone with good spoken English, irrespective of nationality.

All placements are self-funded and the placement fees, which vary according to location, cover insurance, supervision and support, local board and lodging; fees are from £795 for a 3- month placement. Paid staff work in all locations to vet placements, accommodation and work supervisors. They meet volunteers on arrival and remain available to deal with any queries.

Details of the projects can be found on the above website or in the full brochure available from the above address.

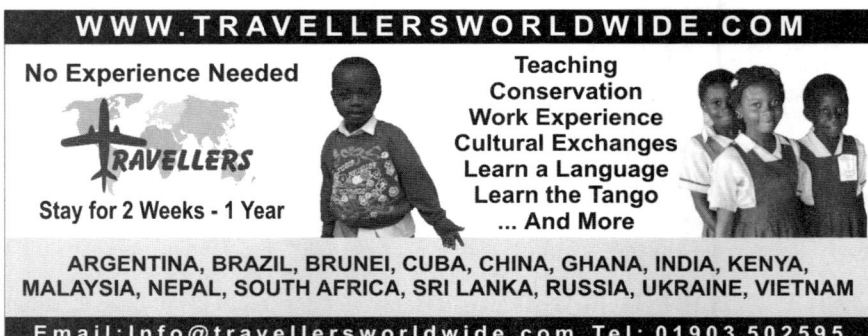

TRAVELLERS: 7 Mulberry Close, Ferring, West Sussex BN12 5HY (☎01903-502595; fax 01903 500364; e-mail info@travellersworldwide.com; www.travellers worldwide.com). A Founder Member of the Year Out Group.

Voluntary placements (1,000+ per year) involving **teaching conversational English (also music, sports, drama and other subjects), conservation (with Orang-Utans, Elephants, Lion, dolphins, etc.), language courses, structured work experience (journalism, law, medicine, etc.) and cultural courses (photography, tango, etc.)** in Argentina, Brazil, Brunei, China, Cuba, Ghana, Guatemala, India, Kenya, Malaysia, Nepal, Russia, South Africa, Sri Lanka, Ukraine and Vietnam. Placements last from a month to a year, with flexible start dates all year round. Hundreds of projects are available worldwide and are described in detail on their website. Travellers will also attempt to arrange schemes not currently offered on request.

No formal qualifications required. Sample charges for 3 months in Sri Lanka are £1.345 and Ukraine £895. Prices include food and accommodation, meeting at the nearest airport, plus support and back-up from local staff in destination countries, but exclude flights, visa costs and insurance. (Travellers can arrange the latter but many volunteers prefer the flexibility of organising their own.)

Applications should be made to Philip Perkes, Director, at the above address.

Social & Community Schemes

AFS INTERCULTURAL PROGRAMMES UK: Leeming House, Vicar Lane, Leeds LS2 7JF; ☎0113-242 6136; fax 0113-243 0631; e-mail info-unitedkingdom@afs.org; www.afsuk.org). AFS is an international non-profit association of 54 national organisations and is one of the world's largest voluntary organisations providing over 10,000 participants with an intercultural learning experience each year.

Volunteers for 6 month placements with AFS International Volunteer Programmes in Latin America or Africa on voluntary projects dedicated to **healthcare, education, social welfare, environmental protection and other pressing human issues such as homelessness among urban poor, (with a special emphasis on meeting the needs of children).** Participants live with a local volunteer host family and are provided with an excellent support structure. Applicants must be aged 18-29 and no language skills or qualifications are required. Departures from the UK are in January and July. Cost £3,300.

School Programme. A unique opportunity for young people aged 16-18 to spend an academic year studying in one of over 20 countries. Participants live with a local host family and enrol in the local school/college system. Departures from the UK are between July and September. Must be able to fundraise.

Applications to the above address.

CIEE: (Council on International Educational Exchange), 3 Copley Place, Suit A, Boston MA 02116 (☎1-888-Council; fax1-212-822-2649; e-mail info@councilexchanges.org; www.councilexchanges.org).

The CIEE is a non-profit organisation that, in affiliation with co-operative organisations in North and West Africa, Europe, North America and Japan, which sponsors 2-4 week voluntary service projects for young people in the USA and abroad. Participants on these projects work and live as part of an international group of 10-20 volunteers and have a chance to **learn about the host community as well as to explore cross-cultural perspectives on global issues such as environmental protection, cultural preservation and development.**

The types of work include nature conservation, construction, renovation, historical preservation, archaeology and work with children and the elderly. Participants' costs are a $300 placement fee plus transportation. Room and board are provided during the project. Current project listings can be found on the website www.ciee.org

For more information please *contact* CIEE at the above address. Please note that it places American residents only; residents of other countries should contact a voluntary organisation in their home country.

CROSS-CULTURAL SOLUTIONS: US Head Office: ☎+1- 800- 380-4777 / +1- 914- 632- 0022; fax +1- 914- 632- 8494; email info@crossculturalsolutions.org; www.crossculturalsolutions.org. UK Information Office: ☎0845- 458- 2781 / 2782; email infouk@crossculturalsolutions.org; www.crossculturalsolutions.org.uk (see website for postal addresses)

Cross-Cultural Solutions is a recognised leader in the international volunteer field, sending hundreds of volunteers overseas every year. Volunteer programmes operate all year round in South and Central America, Africa, Asia and Eastern Europe and range from 2 to 12 weeks. Volunteers **work side-by-side with local people on locally designed and driven projects,** enabling them to participate in meaningful community development and see a country from a whole new perspective.

Cross-Cultural Solutions' programmes have a unique three-part design. Part one is the Volunteer Placement, which is assigned by matching the skills and interests of the volunteer to the needs of the community. The volunteer work is on sustainable community development projects with infants and children, teenagers, adults, the elderly, people living with HIV/AIDS or the mentally or physically disabled. Part two is the Perspectives Programme, which includes an in-depth orientation, insight into cultural norms, language assistance, guest speakers and special events. Part three is free time. Through each of these elements volunteers are able to immerse themselves into the culture of the country and fully realise their experience

Programme fees including accommodation, meals, ground transportation, full staff support and travel medical insurance start at $1,985 (approx. £1240). For more information *contact* Cross-Cultural Solutions' US or UK Office using the contact details above.

GLOBAL CITIZENS NETWORK: 130 N. Howell Street, St Paul, Minnesota 55104, USA (☎651-644-0960; e-mail info@globalcitizens.org; www.globalcitizens.org).
Volunteers for projects in Kenya, Tanzania, New Mexico, Arizona, Guatemala, Nepal, Peru and Mexico. Volunteer trips last 1, 2, or 3 weeks and are ongoing throughout the year. Programmes involving volunteers include **building a health centre, teaching in school and renovating a youth centre.** Volunteers pay a programme fee of $650-$1950 (£400-£1100), which includes most in-country costs (food, lodging, transportation etc.); the airfare is extra. No special qualifications are required but volunteers should be aged at least 18. Volunteers under 18 years must be accompanied by parent or guardian.

For more information *contact* the Program Director at the above address.

HABITAT FOR HUMANITY GREAT BRITAIN: 11 Parsons Street, Banbury, Oxon OX16 5LW (☎01295-264240; fax 01295-264230; e-mail globalvillage@hfhgb.org; www.hfhgb.org).
Global Village Mission Teams are small groups of people (7-15) who travel to one of 46 countries **to help build simple decent houses alongside local residents.** Costs include a contribution towards building costs, travel expenses, food, insurance and sight-seeing activities during rest days.

Trips are for 1-3 weeks for those who are interested in both travel and a Habitat for Humanity volunteer experience; the trips are designed to promote cross-cultural understanding and to raise awareness of the urgent worldwide issue of substandard housing. Applicants should be over 18; no experience or building skills is necessary.

For further information on Global Village and details of volunteering opportunities within Britain *contact* the above address.

OUTREACH INTERNATIONAL: Bartletts Farm, Hayes Road, Compton Dundon, Somerset TA11 6PF (tel/fax 01458 274957; e-mail gap@outreachinterna tional.co.uk; www.outreachinternational.co.uk. A specialist placement organisation with carefully selected projects with enough variety to ensure that the interests and skills of individual volunteers can be put to good use.
Volunteers needed **to participate in local initiatives in Mexico, Cambodia**

and Ecuador allowing them to live in communities and work alongside local people. Cambodian placements include working with young land mind and polio victims and children who have become victims of human trafficking. Volunteers teach English, computer skills and art skills. Physiotherapists, and volunteers with therapy skills would be appreciated in Cambodia. Other professional people with experience in computers, marketing, art & craft or teaching would be particularly sought after to help local initiatives; however on many of the projects no formal qualifications are needed. Enthusiasm and energy are more important attributes. Mexican projects are on the Pacific coast in traditional villages. The projects are with orphans, disabled children, teaching in local schools or working with giant sea turtles. In Ecuador, volunteers work in an orphanage and also carry out conservation work in the Amazon rainforest. Placements are for 3+ months and can be tailored to fit into a long summer holiday. Applicants will be invited to interview within 3 weeks of applying. Cost of £3,100 for 3 months includes air tickets, full insurance, language course, in-country support, food, accommodation and all project costs. Additional months are approximately £400 per month. Applicants should be confident young people with a desire to travel, learn a language and offer their help to a damaged society.

Applications to James Chapman, UK Director, at the above address.

Outreach International

GAP Year and Voluntary Projects in **Cambodia, Mexico** and **Ecuador**

Volunteers are needed to work on the following projects for three to nine months:

- Orphanages and Street Children
- Rehabilitation centres for land mine and polio victims
- Disabled children centres
- Special needs school
- Teaching English and sport in Pacific coast villages
- Art and craft. Dance
- Conservation work in the Amazon
- Work with whales, dolphins and giant sea turtles

Do you have an interest in immersing yourself in a fascinating foreign culture whilst working on an important, locally initiated, grass roots project?

Gap@Outreachinternational.co.uk www.Outreachinternational.co.uk Tel/Fax James Chapman on: 01458 274957

QUAKER VOLUNTARY ACTION: Friends Meeting House, 6 Mount Street, Manchester M2 5NS (tel/fax 0161-819 1634; e-mail qva@quakervolaction.freeserv e.co.uk; www.qva.org.uk).

QVA runs short-term (2-3 weeks) volunteer projects in Britain, Northern Ireland, Europe (including Eastern Europe and Turkey), Japan, the USA and elsewhere. There are many types of projects to choose from, including **building/renovation, environmental protection, archaeology, work with children, disabled people or the elderly.** Most projects run in the summer and last from 1 to 4 weeks. Some medium and long-term opportunities are now being developed. Please phone or e-mail for details. There are usually between 10 and 15 volunteers per project. **The aims of QVA are to promote co-operation and international understanding between people and to support community initiatives.**

Food and basic accommodation is provided free of charge for the duration of the project. Volunteers pay a registration fee : UK projects, unwaged £140, waged £65; projects abroad, unwaged £75, waged £100) and their travel to the project and their personal insurance.

For a free brochure (available from April) *send* a large £0.33 s.a.e. and a covering letter to the address above.

STUDENTS PARTNERSHIP WORLDWIDE (SPW): 17 Dean's Yard, London SW1P 3PB (☎020-7222 0138; fax 020-72330008; e-mail: spwuk@gn.apc.org; www.spw.org). SPW is an international youth development charity working with and for young people. It provides comprehensive in-country training and full support.

SPW offers 18-28 year olds the opportunity to **work in rural communities** in South Africa, Tanzania, Uganda, India and Nepal. **Overseas and local volunteers work together on either Health Educational or Environmental Programmes** for between 4 and 9 months. Projects start between September and April. SPW is a non-profit making charity – this means that volunteers are only asked to cover their own costs (£2,600-£2,950).

Contact the above address for further details or visit their website.

TEARFUND TRANSFORM INTERNATIONAL PROGRAMME: 100 Church Road, Teddington, Middlesex TW11 8QE (☎0845 355 8355; e-mail: transform@tearfund.org; www.tearfund.org/transform). Tearfund is an evangelical Christian development charity working with local partners to **bring help and hope to communities in need**. Last year Tearfund supported over 500 projects in 90 countries.

Volunteers to work for 4-6 weeks from early July to the end of August, to join teams of 8-12 people. Assignments are in a number of countries and include **practical work, renovation and work with children**.

A contribution of around £1,500 which includes orientation, travel, food and accommodation is required.

Applicants should be over 18 and committed Christians. Details are available from the Enquiry Unit at the above address and *applications* should be received by 1 February.

Workcamps

CONCORDIA: Heversham House, 20-22 Boundary Road, Hove, BN3 4ET (☎01273-422218; fax 01273 421182; e-mail info@concordia-iye.org.uk; www.concordia-iye.org.uk).

Concordia is a small not-for-profit charity committed to international youth exchange. Their International Volunteer Programme offers 16-30 year olds the opportunity to join international teams of volunteers working on **community based projects** in over 30 countries worldwide. Projects are diverse ranging from **nature conservation, restoration, archaeology, construction, art and culture** to projects that are socially based including **work with adults or children with special needs, children's play-schemes and teaching**. Projects last for 2-4 weeks with the main season from June to September and smaller winter/spring programme. Generally the work doesn't require specific skills or experience, though real motivation and commitment to the project are a must.

Volunteers pay a registration fee of £85-£125 depending on the country (£60 for projects in the UK) and fund their own travel. Board and accommodation is free of charge. Concordia also recruits volunteers (20+) to act as Group Co-ordinators on UK based projects, for which training is provided and all expenses are paid. Details of projects will be published in April. Early application is advised.

Concordia can only place volunteers who are resident in the UK. Volunteers applying from abroad should contact a volunteer organisation in their own country or country in which they are based.

For further information on volunteering or co-ordinating *write* (enclosing a stamped addressed A5 envelope) or *e-mail* the International Volunteer Co-ordinator at the address above or visit our website.

INTERNATIONAL VOLUNTARY SERVICE (BRITISH BRANCH OF SERVICE CIVIL INTERNATIONAL): IVS Field Office, Old Hall, East Bergholt, Colchester C07 6TQ (e-mail ivsgbn@ivsgbn.demon.co.uk; www.ivs-gb/org.uk).
International Voluntary Service sends volunteers to international workcamps and short-term projects across a choice of 25 countries in eastern and western Europe including the former Soviet Union, as well as Japan, North Africa, Turkey, the US and Australia. Volunteers work for two to four weeks in an international team of 10-20 people, sharing domestic and social life as well as the work. The projects include **work with children, work with people with physical or mental disabilities, solidarity work with people of other countries, and manual work, often connected with ecology or conservation.** The projects are not holidays. The work can be hard and demands commitment.

Most workcamps are between June and September. Volunteers must pay for membership of IVS, a registration fee and their own travel costs. Free board and accommodation are provided on the project. For certain countries previous experience of voluntary work is required or preferred. English is the language of most projects, but other languages are an advantage. IVS is working towards equal opportunities, and welcomes applications from women, black people, people with disabilities, people from ethnic minorities, gay men and lesbians. IVS can only accept applications from people with an address in Britain. The address of the American branch of Service Civil International for volunteers living in the USA, or US nationals is 5474 Walnut Level Road, Crozet, VA 22932, USA; e-mail scitalk@sci-ivs.org; www.sci-ivs.org

Applications should be sent with a stamped addressed envelope, for more information to the address above or to IVS North, 21 Otley Road, Headingley, Leeds LS6 3AA: £4.00 postage and packing is only necessary for the listing of summer workcamps (available from April): enquiries from January will be put on a mailing list to receive the listing when it is ready.

SERVICE CIVIL INTERNATIONAL/SCI-INTERNATIONAL: see the entry for International Voluntary Service above.

UNA EXCHANGE: Temple of Peace, Cathays Park, Cardiff CF10 3AP (☎ 029-20-223088; e-mail info@unaexchange.org; www.unaexchange.org).
Arranges international voluntary projects in Wales and sends volunteers to projects abroad for 2-4 weeks mostly between the months of April and September but also at other times of year. Projects include: **social, environmental and renovation work, and play-schemes.** UNA Exchange also operates a 'North-South' programme in 32 countries in Africa, Latin America and Asia, volunteers for this need to attend training weekends in Cardiff. There is a registration fee of £50 for the Welsh camps and between £100 and £140 for the camps abroad, depending on the country, but food and accommodation is provided.

There are longer term (6-12 month) projects available, mainly in Europe, through the European Voluntary Service (EVS) and MTV (Medium Term Volunteer) programmes.Volunteers applying from abroad should go through a workcamp organisation in their own country. Board and accommodation free.
Further details on the website: please enclose an A4 stamped addressed envelope with enquiries.

VOLUNTEERS FOR PEACE (VFP): 1034, Tiffany Road, Belmont, Vermont 05730, USA (☎802-259-2759; fax 802-259-2922; e-mail vfp@vfp.org; www.vfp.org).

Co-ordinates **International Workcamps** lasting 2-3 weeks in 70 countries in western and eastern Europe, North and West Africa and North, South and Central America. Work includes **construction, environmental, agricultural and social work**. A full listing of VFP's programmes can be found in the VFP's *International Workcamp Directory* ($20 post-paid in the USA).

For further details phone, write or e-mail for a free Newsletter.

YOUTH ACTION FOR PEACE: 8 Golden Ridge, Freshwater, Isle of Wight, P040 9LE (☎01983-752557; fax 01983-756900; e-mail yapuk@ukonline.co.uk; www.yap-uk.org).

Volunteers needed to take part in voluntary work projects (workcamps) organised by YAP in the UK and its sister organisations in forty countries in Europe, the Americas, Africa and Asia. The work undertaken may consist of tasks such as restoration, entertaining handicapped children or environmental work. Projects generally last for two to three weeks each, and take place all year round.

Participants will usually be working for around 35 hours per week with volunteers from different countries and local people; food, accommodation and leisure activities are provided. No particular qualifications are necessary, but applicants must normally be aged at least 18. A brochure with a complete list of projects is published at the beginning of April each year.

For further details *contact* Cedric Medland, Secretary, at the above address.

Work at Sea

GLOBAL CREW NETWORK: 145 Bracklyn Court, London N1 7EJ (☎ 07773-361959; e-mail info@globalcrewnetwork.com; www.globalcrewnetwork.com).

Crew recruited for tall ships, traditional boats and luxury yachts worldwide. Discounts on membership available for students.

For details see www.globalcrewnetwork or *contact* the above address.

Jobs on Luxury Yachts & Tall Ships, Worldwide!

www.globalcrewnetwork.com
info@globalcrewnetwork.com Tel: 07773 361 959
Vacancies for Professional & Novice Crew
Call us for a chat or visit our web site.

GOLDEN STAR CRUISES 85, Akti Miaouli Piraeus 185 38 Greece. (☎(00 3010) 4290650-5; fax (00 3010) 4290660; fax (Vera Devourou) (00 3010) 4290658 e-mail gscruz@goldenstarcruises.com; www.goldenstarcruises.com).

Wine Stewardesses to serve in restaurants and lounges (in cruise ships): 10 hours per day, 7 days a week. Wage approximately €400/£280 (plus commission) per month, plus insurance. Free accommodation on board. Requested period: from March to November for at least 5 months. Pleasant personality and knowledge of one (at least) European language.

Hostesses for passengers entertainment (office work, reception etc) Wage €700-€1000 (£490-£700) per month. 10 hours per day, 7 days per week. Requested period from March-November. Excellent knowledge of at least 2 European languages. Personality needed: Pleasant, energetic. The knowledge of Japanese language will be an advantage.

Applications from December to the above address, attn. Mrs Devourou,

P&O CRUISES: Richmond House, Terminus Terrace, Southampton, SO14 3PN, UK (☎023-8053 4200; e-mail ben.larkin@pocruises.com).

Port Presenters are required to promote shore excursions in the Caribbean and Americas. Work periods spent on board will be extensive.

Applications should be made by CV and covering letter to Martin Young at the above address.

OPENWIDE INTERNATIONAL LTD: 7 Westmoreland House, Cumberland Park, London NW10 6RE (☎020-8962 3400; fax 020-8962 3440; e-mail recruitment@openwideinternational.co.uk; www.openwideinternational.com). Europe's largest entertainment consultancy and the leaders on providing innovative entertainment to the leisure and tourism industry. Working with Openwide is an excellent way to develop professional and creative skills as an entertainer; over 150 people are recruited annually to work on cruise ships.

Cruise Staff Entertainers and Performers to work on ships in the Mediterranean and Caribbean.

Dancers, Vocalists, Presenters, DJs and Childrens Entertainers required to deliver daytime and evening entertainment programmes.

Excellent PR skills essential; knowledge of a Scandinavian language desirable. Salaries from £200+ per week plus meals, accommodation and flight. Full training given. Positions are available all year round. Contracts approx. 6 months.

All *applicants* are invited to send a CV and photographs to the Recruitment Department at Openwide International and also to visit their website: auditions held all year round.

Au Pairs, Nannies, Family Helps & Exchanges

A-ONE AU-PAIRS and NANNIES: Top Floor, Union House, Union Street, Andover, Hants SP10 1PA (☎01264-332500; fax 01264-362050; e-mail info@aupairsetc.co.uk).

Au Pairs/Au Pairs Plus required for light housework and childcare 5 days per week in a variety of countries. Wages, board and accommodation vary according to country of placement. Applicants should be 17-27 years old.

Contact Karen Hopwood, Proprietor, for details.

ACADEMY AU PAIR AND NANNY AGENCY: 42 Milsted Road, Rainham, Kent ME8 6SU (☎01634-310808; e-mail academy4aupairs@hotmail.com; website www.academyagency.co.uk).

Au Pairs: pocket money around £45 per week for 25 hours work. Should be aged 18-27.

Au Pairs Plus: pocket money £60 per week. Should be aged 18-27.

Nannies: wages £200 or more per week. Minimum age 18; must have NNEB or B-Tech qualifications and be able to produce references.

Mothers' Helps: wages £150 or more per week. Need not be qualified, but previous experience and references are essential.

All the above are needed for positions in Europe, including Britain; au pair positions can also be arranged in Australia. Positions are available throughout the year. Applicants should have some knowledge of the language of the country chosen.

Applications for summer placements should be made before March: for further details send a stamped addressed envelope or International Reply Coupon to the above address, stating which type of work is of interest.

AMICIZIA: Maria De Angelis: Via A. Doria 4/b/9 – 16126 Genova GE, Italy (tel/fax 010-246-4428; mobile 340-6464-191; deangelis@mamicizia.it; www.mamicizia.it). Amicizia have thirty years' experience in placing au pairs in Italy.

Au Pairs, Mothers' Helps, Domestic Nannies to stay with children and help with household duties. Applicants must be experienced with children, be flexible and willing. Wages from approx. £155-£186 monthly for au pairs and approx. £310/£370 monthly for Mothers' Helps, and more for other kinds of duties. Minimum period of work three months although nine months is preferred. Knowledge of Italian and English is usually essential, but is not essential if with families who know English and/or other languages. Placements available in Italy and across Europe, through Amicizia or through Amicizia correspondent agencies, and in Canada. See the website for details of stays in different countries in hotel and restaurant work, and for **shorter placements** with Italian families. Please Note: *under Italian law, Amicizia can only accept EU applicants, male or female.* Maria De Angelis requires at least €50 (£35) for postage/e-mail expenses, which is not refundable.

Applications to Mrs Maria de Angelis at the above address.

L'AQUILONE AU PAIR BUREAU: Via Giovanni Pascoli 15, I-20129 Milan, Italy (☎0039-2-29 52 96 39; fax 0039-2-29 52 21 75; e-mail: aquilone@azienda.net; www.s.snf.it/aquilone).

Au Pairs to work 30 hours a week. Salary £35 per week.

Au Pair Plus to work 36 hours a week. Salary £45 per week.

Mother's Help to work 48 hours a week. Salary £73 per week.

Italian applicants are placed in the following countries: Austria, Belgium, Denmark, France, Germany, Great Britain, Greece, Holland, Norway, Spain and Switzerland. Non-Italian applicants placed in Italy, Australia and New Zealand. Period of work varies from country to country but is usually 8-9 months during the academic year and 2-3 months during the summer. Applicants must have childcare experience and be aged between 18 and 28.

For more information about agency fees and details *contact* the above address.

CLUB TELI: 7 rue Blaise Pascal, F-74600 Seynod, France (☎0033-4-5052-2658; fax 4-5052-1016; e-mail clubteli@wanadoo.fr; www.teli.asso.fr). The Association Club TELI is a non-profit organisation founded in 1992, that offers monthly, several hundred international offers from employers, non-profit organisations, families and au pair agencies from around the world.

Apply by e-mail to Dominique Girerd, Director.

CHILDCARE INTERNATIONAL: Childcare International Ltd., Trafalgar House, Grenville Place, London NW7 3SA (☎020-8906 3116; fax 020-8906 3461; e-mail:

office@childint.co.uk; www.childint.co.uk).

Childcare Europe, Childcare Canada, Childcare South Africa, and Childcare Australia offer au pair/au pair plus, mother's help and nanny positions with associate agencies overseas: provides the opportunity to live abroad in a secure family environment caring for children and helping in the home. Opportunities to learn a language and experience different cultures through both study and everyday life. Salary provided according to age and experience. Full support available from a local representative to assist with language course and meeting friends. Placements in Canada require a one year minimum stay; applicants must have a nanny qualification and/or good childcare experience.

Applications to the above address.

INTER-SEJOURS: 179 Rue de Courcelles, F-75017 Paris, France (☎01-47 63 06 81; fax 01-40 54 89 41; e-mail marie.inter-sejours@libertysurf.fr; http://asso.inters ejours.free.fr).

Inter-Sejours is a non-profit making organisation with 36 years' experience. An immediate start is possible.

Au Pairs placed in Australia, Austria, Canada, Denmark, France, Germany, Ireland, Italy, the Netherlands, New Zealand, Spain, Sweden the USA and the UK. Working hours 15 to 30 hours a week depending on country. Pocket money minimum £200 per month. Some summer stays of 2-3 months available, but normal minimum stay 6-9 months; applicants who can stay for the whole school year preferred. Applicants should be aged 18-30, 17 in Spain and England; previous childcare experience an advantage.

Paying Guest stays also arranged with lessons and activities, around the year. Inter-Sejours also organise work placements in hotels and restaurants throughout England, Ireland and Spain, and also strawberry picking in Denmark, and language and humanitarian work programmes in Guatemala, and linguistic stays in Costa Rica.

For *further details* contact the above address

LAURENCE CHERIFAT PROGRAMMES AU PAIR: 95 Avenue Général Leclerc, Bat. B, F-94700 Maisons Alfort, France (tel/fax +33-(0)1-43-76-48-61).

Au Pairs aged 18-27 placed in England, Ireland, Spain, Greece and one year stays in the USA. Free board and lodging, medical insurance and pocket money £30-60 per week in exchange for 25-40 hours of help (childcare, light housework and language tuition). Minimum stay normally 6 months, except for Greece (12-18 months) but there are some summer stays in England and Spain.

Basic knowledge of the destination language not compulsory for Spain and Greece, applicants do not need any special qualifications apart from babysitting/childcare experience. Good back-up service and social programmes in each country.

Mother's Help/Nanny positions for native speakers of English, French or German, in Greece. Monthly salary £300-£500 with free board and lodging, medical/accident insurance and return airfare.

Applications to Miss Laurence Chérifat, at the above address.

LORRAINE BUSHELL: 5 Parklands, Blossomfield Road, Solihull B91 1NG (☎07973 886979; e-mail lorraine@au-pairs4u.com; www.au-pairs4u.com; www.100s-aupairs.co.uk). Based in Birmingham, Lorraine regularly travels to London and can arrange interviews all over the UK and in Ireland. Established some 37 years ago Lorraine has vast experience in the placement of au pairs.

Au Pairs. Pocket money £180.00 to £240.00 per month placed in major European countries:- France, Italy, Spain are the most popular countries and pocket money is paid in euros. Mainly working with overseas contacts to locate excellent host families.

AuPairCare. Round-trip airfare from your home country to the USA. 5 day/4 night training session in a Central New York Hotel. Medical insurance provided plus private room and full board with carefully screened host family. A local Area Director lives nearby and regular social and cultural activities are arranged with other au pairs. Approximately $500 towards education and two weeks paid vacation. 24 hour telephone helpline. Opportunity to travel in the 13th month. Comprehensive training and support.

Lorraine will deal with all visa requirements, tickets and arrange interview and paperwork. For this American programme, you must be aged 18 - 26 and be able to drive, have a good knowledge of English and be able to commit to a 12 month stay.

Applications to the above address.

MUM'S ARMY: The Torrs, Torrs Close, Redditch, B97 4JR (☎01527-402266; fax 01527-403990; e-mail marion@mumsarmy.u-net.com; www.mumsarmy.u-net.com).
Au Pairs placed in France, Germany, Italy, Spain, Western Europe, the USA and the United Kingdom. Minimum stay 2-3 months in the summer or 9 months plus at any other time of year. Applicants must be over 18 years old.

For further details contact *Marion Farr* at the above address.

NEILSON: Locksview, Brighton Marina, Brighton, East Sussex BN2 5HA (☎0870-2412901 fax 0870-9099089; www.neilson.com/recruitment; e-mail recruitment@neilson.com). Neilson is a holiday company committed to providing excellent quality activity holidays. They pride themselves on having a high staff/client ratio and the exceptional calibre of their overseas staff.
Child Minders (10) (NNEB, BTEC or equivalent preferred) to care for 0-5 year olds in the resorts. Summer and winter (ski) work is available. Working 6 days a week. Pay from £95 per week. Flights paid to and from resort, accommodation, insurance and uniform provided. Applicants should be at least 18 years old with experience of working with children, a sense of fun, and be creative team players.

Contact The Overseas Recruitment Team, at the above address or on recruitment@neilson.com .

TRAVEL ACTIVE: PO Box 107, 5800 AC Venray, The Netherlands (☎478-551900; fax 478-551911; e-mail info@travelactive.nl).
Au Pairs for placements in Europe and the USA. Wages of approx. £70 per week in the USA and Switzerland, £120 per month elsewhere. To work minimum 30 hours per week and maximum 45 hours per week. Minimum length of stay 6-12 months or 2 months as a summer au pair. Applicants need a basic knowledge of the language of the country of placement and/or of English.

For further information *contact* the above address. Applicants must be Dutch or Belgian.

UK AND OVERSEAS AGENCY LTD: Suite 21-23 (Kent House), 87 Regent Street, London W1R 7HF (☎0207-494-2929; fax 0207-494-2922; e-mail london@nannys.co.uk; www.nannys.co.uk). This agency was established over thirty years ago, and place live-in nannies and au pairs in locations worldwide.
Au Pairs, Nannies, Mothers' Helps, Domestics: The Agency offer jobs throughout the UK, Europe and in the Middle East, Australia, Japan, Singapore and the USA, as well as many other countries. Currently available jobs are listed on the agency's

website.

Applicants must speak English. The agency employs both experienced and inexperienced staff. The only stipulated requirements are good references. Conditions vary, as do hours of work. The minimum period for summer work is three months. The usual period of stay is one year. All positions provide board and lodging free of charge.

Recruitment is ongoing. It will normally take between two and ten weeks to find a suitable overseas placement.

Apply through the website: completed applications with photos and references must be sent by post.

Other Employment Abroad

ALLIANCE ABROAD INTERNATIONAL, INC: 702 West Avenue, Austin, TX 78701, USA or 2423 Pennsylvania Avenue NW, Washington, DC 20037, USA (☎202-467-9467; fax 202-467-9460; e-mail INFO@alliancesabroad.com / cgeorge@alliancesabroad.com; www.alliancesabroad.com). Organises a variety of employment including placements in both paid and voluntary positions. Schemes have included:

Outbound Program Director, Volunteer, Internship and Youth Programs

Internships and Work Experience Placements with employers across the United States. Wages paid; accommodation with families or American students.

Teaching Opportunities, many of which require no prior teaching experience and professional certification in Brazil, China, Taiwan, Mexico, and Thailand.

Pub/Hotel/Restaurant Placements in Ireland and Canada for 2-6 months. Wages £40 per week plus tips and full board.

Volunteer Internships with employers in or near major cities in Germany, France and Spain for 1-3 months; no wage, room and board provided with families.

Voluntary Work on social, medical, developmental and educational placements in Africa, Costa Rica, Mexico and Asia for 2-12 months.

For all the above application fees of approx. £46 are payable plus varying programme fees to cover accommodation, insurance, local back-up etc.

Contact the above address or e-mails for details.

Advertising Casual, Seasonal, Temporary & Even Long-Term Job Opportunities Worldwide ! AnyworkAnywhere.com

Anywork Anywhere: www.anyworkanywhere.com. This organisation provides a free source of information to people looking for work throughout the UK and worldwide via their web site.

Tour Guides, Overland Drivers, Ski / Board Instructors & Guides, Chalet Chefs

& Hosts, All levels of Hotel & Pub Staff, Nannies, Barge & Yacht Crew, Care Workers, Teachers, Nurses, Holiday & Theme Park, Campsite and Summer Resort Staff are amongst the jobs described as well as a wide and changing variety of many others. Interested candidates can simply contact their chosen advertiser and apply direct, with no registration necessary.The site also provides a broad range of other resources for work and travel worldwide.

For further information *consult* www.anyworkanywhere.com.

BUNAC: 16 Bowling Green Lane, London EC1R OQH (☎020-7251 3472; fax 020-7251 0215; e-mail enquiries@bunac.org.uk; www.bunac.org).
BUNAC, a non-profit organisation, has enabled over 250,000 Gap Year and full time students to work overseas since 1962. BUNAC is a national club whose members are able to obtain jobs, work permits and affordable flight packages. There are a great variety of programmes on offer including summer camp counselling in the USA and work and travel programmes to the USA, Canada, Australia, New Zealand, South Africa, Ghana and Costa Rica.

BUNAC also offers an internship programme, OPT USA, enabling students and non-students to undertake course or career-related training in the USA.

BUNAC provides help and advice on jobs, accommodation and travel as well as providing back-up services while working and travelling.

For *further information* contact the above address.

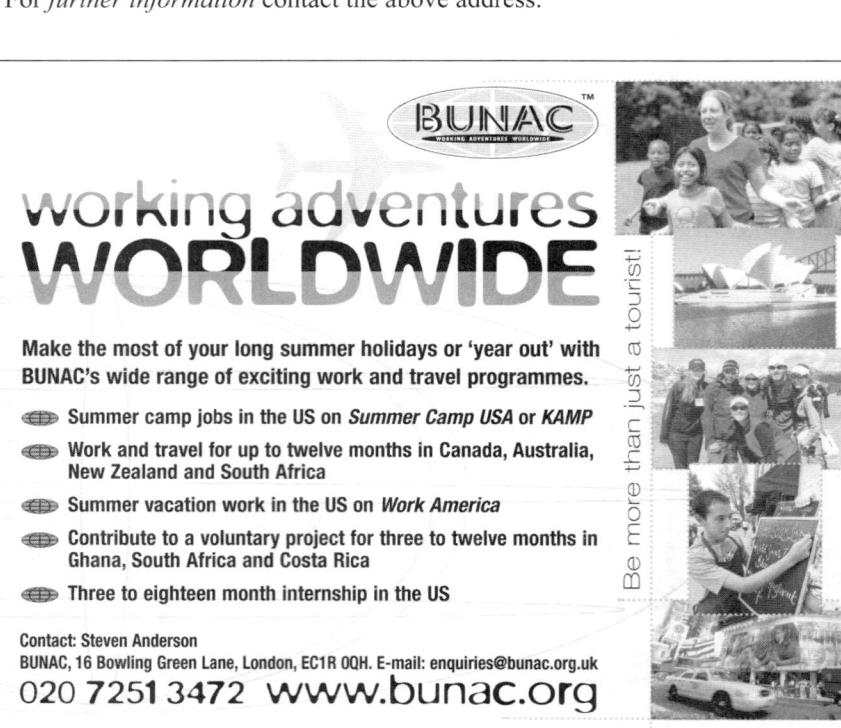

CIEE: (Council on International Educational Exchange), 3 Copley Place, Suit A, Boston MA 02116; 1 –888-268-6245 e-mail info@councilexchanges.org; www.cou ncilexchanges.org).

The CIEE (Council on International Educational Exchanges) in the US administers a Work Exchange programme that enables *US citizens* (with some exceptions for permanent residents of the US) who are college students over 18 years of age to work legally in the following countries for the following lengths of time:

○ *Australia:* for up to 4 months at any time of year;
○ *Canada:* at any time of year for up to 5 months;
○ *France:* any time of year for up to 3 months;
○ *Germany:* summer option from May 15-October 15 for up to 3 months; internship option any time of year for up to 6 months;
○ *Ireland:* any time of year for up to 4 months;
○ *New Zealand:* Up to six months, anytime from April 1-October 31.

The cost of participating in this programme varies according to destination and includes work documentation, a programme handbook, an orientation upon arrival in the country of destination and a resource office which students can make use of during their stay. Applicants must be either full time students (enrolled for at least eight credits) or within one semester of study at an accredited college or university and matriculated towards a degree (Australian participants DO NOT need to be students, they only need to be between the ages of 18 and 30). Applications must be made from inside the USA. CIEE also offers more than 800 International Volunteer Projects in 30 countries open to all team-minded individuals. CIEE's *Teach in China and Thailand* programmes enables Bachelors degree holders to spend a semester or full academic year teaching English to Chinese/Thai college students of all ages. Wages and room and board provided.

US applicants *contact* 1-888-COUNCIL; UK & Australian Applicants contact the British office on 020-7478 2000.

INTEREXCHANGE: 161 Sixth Avenue, New York, NY 10013, USA (☎212-924-0446; fax 212-924-0575; e-mail info@interexchange.org; www.interexchange.org). Inter-Exchange is a private non-profit organisation that can help US citizens to find short term jobs, au pair, internship, voluntary and English teaching opportunities throughout Europe. Various schemes exist in Belgium, Bulgaria, France, Germany, Italy, Netherlands, Norway, Poland, Russia, Spain, Ukraine and the UK.

For further details contact Inter-Exchange at the above address.

i-to-i: 261 Low Lane, Leeds LS18 5NY (☎0870-333 2332; fax 0113-2054619; e-mail: info@i-to-i.com; www.i-to-i.com). i-to-i is a volunteer travel and TEFL training organisation specialising in teaching, conservation and work placements in Latin America, Africa, Australia and Asia. i-to-i also offers weekend and online TEFL (Teach English as a Foreign Language) training for those who want to combine teaching as part of their travel. Over 2,000 volunteers are trained and placed each year. All projects are thoroughly researched and volunteers are met and supported whilst away by in-country co-ordinators. All prices include pre-departure training (TEFL for teaching placements), comprehensive insurance and 24 hour support from the UK. Food and accommodation included on most projects and some also offer local language courses on arrival. i-to-i projects are suitable for anyone from

Find yourself here

COMMUNITY WORK
CONSERVATION
TEACHING
BUILDING
HEALTH
MEDIA

To be part of it, visit i-to-i.com or call 0870 333 2332   Volunteer travel & TEFL training

18-80 to 70: gap year and university students, graduates, career breakers and older volunteers with a sense of adventure.

Ventures: Voluntary teaching, conservation, business, journalism, media and health placements abroad. Current projects include an elephant orphanage in Sri Lanka, sea turtle conservation in Costa Rica, newscasting on a radio station in Ghana, and teaching English in a Nepalese Buddhist monastery amongst many others. Accommodation varies from homestays with local families to camping, guesthouses, and apartments. Projects are available all year round from one month to the complete year out.

Escapes: Two week projects in Croatia, Bolivia, Brazil, Costa Rica, Dominican Republic, Ecuador, El Salvador, Guatemala, Kenya, Nepal, Sri Lanka, Peru, Honduras, South Africa, India and Mongolia for those with a desire to travel with purpose but without the time for a full Venture. Also suitable for groups. Inclusive price for pre-departure training, full board, airport pickup and comprehensive insurance.

TEFL Training: i-to-i offers intensive weekend TEFL courses in the UK and Ireland. There is also an optional 20 hour home-study grammar module. Fees are £195. An online TEFL course is also available at www.onlineTEFL.com allowing study from any location worldwide. Both courses are designed for travellers and include a module on finding work abroad.

For *further details* contact the above address.

TRAVEL ACTIVE: PO Box 107, N-5800 AC Venray, The Netherlands (☎+31-478 551900; fax +31-478 551911; e-mail info@travelactive.nl; www.travelactive.nl). Travel Active is Holland's largest youth exchange organisation, offering work exchange, au pair and high school programmes on a global scale.

Travel Active also receives students from all over the world on its incoming high school, au pair and work exchange programmes. For these programmes Travel Active also offers its own, tailor-made insurance. Dutch and Belgian youngsters may choose from a variety of work programmes, with or without job placement. Internships are also available. Several programmes combine a language course with a job placement. Travel Active is member of FIYTO, ALTO, IAEWEP and a founding member of IAPA.

For *further details* contact the above address.

WWW.VOOVS.COM: 26 Vine Close, Welwyn Garden City, Hertfordshire AL8 7PS (☎01707-396511; e-mail info@voovs.com. A recruitment website offering the following positions.

Beach Resort/Camping/Activity Jobs from April to October. Vacancies for instructors, nannies, couriers, chefs, bar and hotel staff etc. Wages start at £50 per week, with accommodation and transport provided. To work a 6-day week.

Cruise Ship/Yachting Jobs available around the year. Varied contracts. Wages from £500 a month.

Ski Resort Jobs including work in chalets, hotels and bars and as reps, instructors, nannies and technicians. Wages start at £50 per week; ski pass, transport to resort and accommodation provided. To work a 6-day week.

All applicants must be aged over 18. Other types of work covered include TEFL and voluntary work.

For *further details* see www.voovs.com.

Organisations with Vacancies Across Europe

Agricultural Work

APPELLATION CONTROLEE: Ulgersmaweg 26c, 9731 BT Groningen, The Netherlands (☎+31 (0)50 5492434; fax +31 (0)50 5492428; e-mail project2@bart.nl; www.apcon.nl). An organisation organising working holidays in several European countries.

The Netherlands Programme offer participants the opportunities to spend periods of two weeks or longer working with Dutch farmers, with likely duties including fruit picking and packing. Wages at the Dutch minimum of £3.25 per hour for 8 hours' work a day; extra for overtime. Accommodation in your own tent either on the farm or on a nearby campsite.

France Fruit Picking Programme taking place in the Maine et Loire Department of Western France. The job involves picking various fruits beginning with strawberries in May and followed by raspberries, bilberries and melons later on. Wages either at piece work rates (average earnings £25-£40 per day) or at an hourly rate (approx. £30 for an 8 hour day). The normal minimum stay on a farm is 3 weeks. Accommodation will be either camping or the farmer may provide clean but basic accommodation.

Grape picking in France takes place in the Beaujolais, Maconais and Bourgogne regions in September. Wages around £28 a day plus board and lodging. To work 7 days a week; period of work 1-4 weeks.

Denmark Programme involves work on the Danish strawberry harvest which lasts for 3-8 weeks in the summer and takes place throughout the country. Payment at piece work rates; accommodation will consist of camping.

Fruit Picking in England: this programme involves working for at least one month in a season which runs from April to November. The farms involves are mainly Kent, West Sussex, Essex and Suffolk. Payment at national minimum rates. Accommodation may be camping or basic accommodation provided by the farmer.

A registration fee is payable. For further details of the above schemes *contact* the above address.

Boats

EUROPEAN WATERWAYS: 35 Wharf Road, Wraysbury, Staines, Middlesex TW19 5JQ (fax 01784-483072; e-mail sales@GoBarging.com; www.GoBarging.com).

European Waterways are in their 29th year of designing, building and operating a fleet of fully crewed luxury hotel barges in England, France, Germany, Ireland and Scotland.

Cordon Bleu Chefs (4). Wages £1,000-£1,200 per month. Must have training to Cordon Bleu standard, hold a driving licence and be at least 25 years old.

Skippers (2). £1,200-£1,400 per month. Applicants must be over 25, speak French, have a driving licence and have some mechanical experience.

Deckhand Mechanics (4). £600 per month. Must have suitable experience and a driving licence.

Stewards/Stewardesses (4). £500 per month. Cleaning, ironing waitressing etc.

Must be hard workers.

Period of work from April to October for work on 12 hotel barges. Must speak French for French positions.

Application forms to Mrs I Price at the above address.

Hotel Work and Catering

CHOICE HOTELS EUROPE: 112 Station Road, Edgware, HA8 7BJ (☎020-8233 2001; fax 020-8233 2080; e-mail FBernardon@ChoiceHotelsEurope.com). Owns, manages and franchises over 500 hotels in 13 European countries. Positions are primarily for the UK and Ireland, but guidance and advice can be given for other countries.

Receptionists, Chefs, Waiter/Waitresses, Bar Persons. Minimum period of work 6 months, 1 year in front office. 39 hours per week spread over 5 days. Salary in accordance with minimum wages regulations. Applications are considered all year round. Applicants should have a smart appearance, pleasant customer oriented personality and be over 18 years old. Priority given to those with hotel qualifications and/or experience and good English or French (fluent for front office).

Applications in writing to Francoise Bernardon, Human Resources Officer, at the address above.

FIRST CHOICE SKI, LAKES & MOUNTAINS: First Choice Holiday, London Road, Crawley, West Sussex (☎01293-588531; fax 01293-588277; e-mail skijobs@firstchoice.co.uk). As well as being a tour operator First Choice has a Hotels Divison which leases and runs 25 Clubhotels and 55 Chalets in European ski lakes and mountain resorts.

Hotel Managers/Assistant Managers, Chefs (all grades), **Chalet Cooks** and **General Assistants**, (500 in all). A job with First Choice provides an opportunity to travel, meet and make new friends, improve language skills and gain experience. Staff are encouraged to expand their knowledge of the Catering and Hospitality industry, and many current Hotel Managers have been bar or kitchen staff in previous seasons. An attractive package including travel to and from the resort, medical insurance, personal belongings insurance, food and accommodation is offered. Applicants must have a National Insurance number and either EU passport or relevant EU work visa/permit.

For more information *please send an S.A.E.* to Overseas Recruitment Dept, First Choice Ski Lake & Mountains Division at the above address.

OPENWIDE INTERNATIONAL LTD.: 7 Westmoreland House, Cumberland Park, London NW10 6RE (☎020-8962 3400; fax 020-8962 3440; e-mail recruitment@openwideinternational.com; www.openwideinternational.com). Openwide International is Europe's largest independent supplier of entertainers and all-round personalities to the mainstream leisure and tourism industry. Working with Openwide is an excellent way to develop professional skills and over 100 people are recruited annually to work in hotels.

Entertainers with bright, enthusiastic personalities and excellent PR and communication skills to work in hotels in Spain, Cyprus, Greece, Balearics, Turkey and the Canaries. A knowledge of Spanish, German or French would be an advantage but not essential. All successful applicants will be given full training on the running of daytime and evening entertainment programmes.

Positions are available all year round; minimum period of work 6 months with salaries between £130 and £225 per week plus meals, accommodation and flight.

Main season is May to November.

All applicants are invited to send CVs and *applications* to the Overseas Recruitment Department at Openwide International and also visit their website.

SCOTT DUNN: 12 Noyna Rd, London, SW17 7PH (☎0208-682-5087; fax 020-8682-5090; e-mail antonia.laws@scottdunn.com). A small, very professional company, which provides beautiful villas and chalets in stunning locations all over Europe.

Chalet and Villa Chefs/Cooks (20) required to plan the menu and cook to a very high standard for the clients in their exclusive villas and chalets. Applicants must have completed a six month cooking course, or have extensive experience and flair. Must be organised and outgoing.

Chalet and Villa Hosts (20) required to assist the chef, look after the guests, supervise the local maid and maintain the villa/chalet. No formal qualifications necessary, but applicants must be outgoing, organised and good with people.

Nannies (20) Required to care for our younger guests. Must have a recognised childcare qualification, at least one year's childcare experience and be organised, confident and outgoing.

Board and accommodation are provided free of charge. Wages and hours to be discussed at interview. Work is available during the winter and summer season. Knowledge of French, Spanish, Italian or Portugese useful, but not mandatory.

For summer positions *apply* in January, or for winter positions apply from July.

Industrial and Office Work

THE AMERICAN SCANDINAVIAN FOUNDATION (ASF): Scandinavia House, 58 Park Avenue, New York, NY 10016, USA (☎212-879-9779; fax 212-249-3444; e-mail trainscan@amscan.org; www.amscan.org). A non-profit organisation set up in 1910 to promote educational and cultural exchange between the USA and Denmark, Finland, Iceland, Norway and Sweden. Through ASF reciprocal training programme young Americans aged over 21 are able to live and work in Scandinavia on a temporary basis.

ASF offers short term training placements to American students in the fields of: engineering, computer science, chemistry and business studies. Placements, primarily in Finland and Sweden, last from 8 weeks and occur from late Spring through to the Autumn. Work Placements last 2 to six months. Applicants should be full-time students majoring in the field in which training is sought, with at least three years undergraduate study completed and some previous relevant work experience. Knowledge of a Scandinavian language is not required. Work permits are arranged by ASF. Trainees receive sufficient income from trainers to cover living expenses during their stay, but are expected to cover the cost of the round-trip airfare.

While some trainees may arrange a place for themselves outside of the ASF scheme, ASF offers help with arranging work permits. All that is required is written confirmation from the training firm specifying the dates of training, the income, type of work and the name of the training supervisor. A non-returnable application fee of $50 (£33 approx.) is charged but this includes a one year membership of the foundation.

Those interested should *contact* ASF at the above address.

JOBCENTRE PLUS: International Jobsearch Advice, Jubilee House, 33-41 Park Place, Leeds LS1 2RE (☎0845 60 60 234 for jobsearch helpline; www.jobcentrep lus.gov.uk).

Jobcentre Plus handles a selection of vacancies for work abroad, which can be accessed from the job search facility on the website or via touch point screens called Jobpoints available in all Jobcentres and Jobcentre Plus offices. You can ask an advisor for an overseas job search at one of these offices or call the dedicated job search helpline above.

As part of the European Employment Services (EURES) network, Jobcentre Plus receives new jobs from Europe on a daily basis.

Jobcentre Plus also publish a series of fact sheets for each of the EEA countries (see Useful Publications).

To find out more about the EURES network and get information on living and working in EEA countries *visit* the EURES website http:/europa.eu.int/eures: this site has a European job bank and a facility to post CVs so they can be viewed by potential employers throughout Europe.

Sports, Couriers and Camping

ACORN ADVENTURE: 22 Worcester Street, Stourbridge, DY8 1AN. (☎01384-446057; fax 01384-378866; e-mail topstaff@acornadventure.co.uk; www.acorn-jobs.co.uk). Adventure Activity Holiday company offering groups multi-activity camping holidays in North Wales, the Lake District, Spain and Italy as well as France.

Instructors, Village Representatives, Catering Supervisor, Catering Assistant. 300 seasonal staff needed mid-April to September (some shorter contracts). Activities include sailing, canoeing, kayaking, climbing, abseiling and caving. Excellent rates of pay, plus supplement/bonus subject to centre and position.

All positions are available in the UK, France and Italy. Instructor and village respresentative positions also available in Spain.

Applications by post should be marked for the attention of Recruitment and a full information pack will be sent to you, or *apply* online.

AMERICAN COUNCIL FOR INTERNATIONAL STUDIES (ACIS): AIFS (UK), 38 Queen's Gate, London SW7 5HR (☎020-7590 7474; fax 020-7590 7475; e-mail tmdepartment@acis.com; www.acis.com). ACIS has been offering quality educational travel for 20 years. Tour managers are vital to the success of the company, and are given unequalled training and support.

Tour Managers (100) to lead American high school teachers and students on educational trips through Europe. The length of trips varies from one to two 2 weeks and may visit one or several countries. All trip details and itineraries are pre-arranged. Busiest periods are March/April and June/July. Tour Managers for both short and long periods are needed; minimum is 9 days. Tour Managers meet groups on arrival, travel with them, act as commentators and guides, keep accounts, direct bus drivers, troubleshoot etc. Fluency in French, Italian, German or Spanish is essential for trips outside the UK and Ireland. Applicants must be over 21, and either have or be studying for a university degree. Daily salary, accommodation provided with the groups in 3/4-star hotels, generous tips, insurance and back-up provided.

Apply online via the website where there is an application form. .

BOMBARD BALLOON ADVENTURES: Château de Laborde, Laborde Au Chateau 21200 Beaune, France. (www.bombardsociety.com/jobs). Since 1977, Bombard Balloon Adventures has provided complete luxury travel programs built around hot-air ballooning. During our summer season (May-Oct), our team travels to France, Tuscany, Switzerland, Austria, and the Czech Republic; and to the Swiss

Alps in winter (Jan-Feb).

Ground Crew (15) to assist in preparation and packing of ballooning equipment, driving, and general household chores. Complete job description is on www.bombardsociety.com/jobs . Requires a clean driving licence, excellent physical fitness, a cheerful personality, responsible driving skills, the ability to live with others, and a neat, clean-cut appearance. Language skills are a plus but not required. Period of work by arrangement.

Applicants should send a CV including height, weight, and nationality; a scanned ID photo and copy of driving licence; and dates of availability to Michael Lincicome by e-mail (preferred) at mike@bombardsociety.com or to the address above.

CANVAS HOLIDAYS: East Port House, 12 East Port, Dunfermline, Fife KY12 7JG (☎01383-629018; fax 01383-629071; www.canvasholidays.com). Canvas Holidays are looking for enthusiastic, resourceful people who enjoy a challenge and love the outdoor life. Main positions include:

Campsite Courier. Varied responsibilities. Involves cleaning and preparation of customer accommodation, welcoming and looking after customers during their holiday and ensuring that they have the best holiday ever. As a campsite courier you will have new challenges every day which can lead to one of the most enjoyable summers you will ever have. Variable working hours.

Children's Courier. As a Canvas Holidays Children's Courier you will have had formal experience of working with children. You will organise and carry out a six day programme which involves five hours a day of Children's Club for children between the ages of 4 and 11. You will be expected to help out with courier duties as and when requried. For many customers, the Children's Club is one of the main parts of the holiday. You will need to have the energy of a seven year old and the imagination of an eleven year old to succeed!

Remuneration package includes tented accommodation, medical insurance, full uniform and return coach travel to and from a UK port of entry. Positions are available from March until October.

Applications are invited from individuals and couples. Contact Sandy, Karen or Nina at the above contact details for an application pack.

CASTERBRIDGE TOURS LTD: Salcombe House, Long Street, Sherborne, Dorset DT9 3BU (☎01935-810810; fax 01935-815815; e-mail tourops@casterbridge-tours.co.uk). Casterbridge operate customised Group Tours throughout Britain and Europe. They have three specialist divisions: Student Educational Study Tours; Concert Tours for Performing Choirs, Orchestras and Bands; Adult Special Interest Tours.

Tour Managers/Guides to escort groups in Europe. Wages from £280 per week, with board and lodging provided. To work all hours necessary, seven days per week. Period of work by arrangement between March and June. Applicants are expected to attend a training course; knowledge of languages useful.

Applications to the above address.

CLUB CANTABRICA HOLIDAYS LTD: 146/148 London Road, St. Albans, Herts AL1 1PQ (☎01727-866-177; fax 01727-843766 www.cantabrica.co.uk). Club Cantabrica is an independent tour operator with 28 years' experience. Offering luxury coach, air and self-drive holidays on excellent sites in Corfu, French Alps, Italy and Spain. Opportunities also available for ski season positions in the Austrian Tyrol and the French Alps.

Resort Manager (14) to manage sites varying in size from 25-100 units. Must have previous campsite rep. experience and French, German, Italian or Spanish language skills. Wages between £200 and £220 per week, plus bonus.

Campsite Couriers (30) to work on camp sites in Corfu, France, Italy, and Spain. Work involves looking after clients, setting up and closing down site, tent and mobile home cleaning and maintenance, paperwork and excursion sales. Wages £100 per week plus commission, including bonus.

Peak Season Courier (15) to cover same tasks as couriers but for June-September only. Minimum period of work 3 months. Wages £100 per week. Including bonus.

Childrens' Courier (13) to run Kids' Club on campsites, must have experience of working with children. Wages £100 per week plus commission and bonus.

Maintenance Staff (13) to carry out maintenance and upkeep work on tents and mobile homes. Applicants should have excellent practical skills. Wages £95-£125 per week.

Hotel Staff (32) including **General Duties Rep.** and **Chef** to help run the Club Hotel in Chamonix Valley and Val Cenis - fluent French and Italian speakers required.

Free accommodation provided. To work approximately 40 hours per 6 day week, from April to October, except Peak Season staff. Couriers should be enthusiastic and have plenty of stamina, with knowledge of languages an advantage. Applicants should be over 18 years old. Experience preferable.

Applications with curriculum vitae and stamped addressed envelope to the above address from December; applicants can also e-mail iona.mccabe@cantabrica.co.uk.

ESPRIT ALPINE SUN: 185 Fleet Road, Fleet, Hants GU51 3BL (☎01252-618318; fax 01252-618328; e-mail recruitment@esprit-holidays.co.uk; www.esprit-holidays.co.uk) Esprit Alpine Sun run Alpine holidays (France, Italy and Austria) for families in catered chalets and hotels and provide childcare in nurseries and Alpine adventure clubs for children aged 4 months to 12 years old. They are looking for enthusiastic staff who are interested in a career in travel.

Resort Managers. Minimum age 23: should be French, German or Italian speakers, with some management, customer care and accountancy experience.

Chalet Hosts for various grades of responsibilities: minimum age 18, Cordon Bleu/City and Guilds 706/HND/OND or equivalent or experience in cooking professionally required.

Nannies: should be aged 18 or over with NNEB, NVQ3, BTECH or RGN qualification.

Alpies Rangers with experience as play scheme leaders, children's sports coaches or trained teachers required to run adventure activity clubs. Minimum age 21. Should have a mature, fun loving personality.

All staff must be EU passport holders available from mid-June to mid-September. Ideal for anyone who has an interest in alpine activities, i.e. mountain walking and biking, white water rafting etc.

All staff assist with chalet cleaning, babysitting and hosting guests. Weekly wage, with food and accommodation, uniform, swimming pool pass and transport provided.

Applications to the above address.

EQUITY LIMITED: Dukes Lane House, 47 Middle Street, Brighton, BN1 1AL (☎+44 (0)1273-886901; fax +44 (0)1273-203212; e-mail recruitment@equity.co. uk). Equity is a direct sell tour operator, organising educational tours, sports tours, ski courses and weekend breaks with the emphasis on customer service, quality and value for money.

Resort Representatives (5) to work with school groups on cookery, language or sports tours in France, Germany, Italy and Spain. Reps have a briefing at the Brighton office before travelling and a day in resort to set up prior to the group's arrival. Duties include liaison between the group, hotelier and coach driver; organisation of course-related excursions and interviews; translating during demonstrations and helping pupils with course-related work. Wages of £20-25 per day plus full board, accommodation, travel expenses, insurance and uniform. Positions are available for periods varying from one week to one month between February and October. Minimum age 21.Applicants must be fluent in French, German, Italian or Spanish, well organised and able to work on their own initiative. They must be able to relate to children and will ideally have some experience of working with school groups or in a public service industry. A driving licence is required for some tours.

Apply with a CV and a covering letter to Carrie Husband at the above address.

EUROCAMP: Overseas Recruitment Department (Ref SJ/04) (☎01606-787525). Eurocamp is a leading tour operator in quality self-drive camping and mobile home holidays in Europe. Each year the company seeks to recruit up to 1,500 enthusiastic people for the following positions:

Campsite Courier: job involves cleaning and preparing customer accommodation, providing assistance, acting as an information service and performing some administrative duties. Couriers need to be flexible to meet the needs of the customer to provide them with excellent service. Minimum age 18 years. Applicants should be independent with plenty of initiative and relish a challenging and rewarding position. They should also possess a friendly and helpful personality. Previous customer service experience would be an advantage. Applicants should be available to work from April/May to September.

Children's Courier: work involves organising a wide range of exciting activities for children aged 4-13. Applicants should possess initiative, imagination and enthusiasm along with good safety awareness. Previous childcare experience is essential. Minimum age is 18 years and applicants should be available from April/ May to September. Languages are not a requirement but would be an advantage (in particular German). Successful candidates will be asked to apply for an Enhanced Disclosure.

Senior Couriers: required to work alongside a team of Campsite Couriers and organise their daily workload, as well as carrying out the normal day to day duties of a Campsite Courier. Applicants should have good language skills and experience of leading a team.

Site Managers: required to lead a large team of Campsite Couriers, organising their daily workloads and ensuring they provide the very best customer service. Applicants should be 21 or over, have proven managerial experience, excellent communication skills and language ability.

Comprehensive training is provided together with a competitive salary, insurance, return travel and accommodation. Applications are accepted from September/ October and *can only be accepted from UK/EU passport holders*. Interviews will be conducted in Hartford, Cheshire between October and April.

Applicants should apply on-line at www.holidaybreakjobs.com or telephone 01606-781525 for an Application Pack.

EUROPEAN SERVICES LTD: 54 Oakland Road Trading Estate, Rodley, Leeds, LS13 1LQ, England. (☎0113-236 1577; fax 0113-236 1875; e-mail europserv@aol.com).
Staff to help with the installation and maintenance of mobile homes, tents and their storage and distribution. European Services operate in nine countries, with most

work being in France, Italy (a growing market) and Spain. Wages and period of work by arrangement.

Applicants must be over 21 and must have a valid driving licence. *To apply* or to obtain more information contact Marcus Edwards at the above address.

HAVEN EUROPE: HR Department, 1 Park Lane, Hemel Hempstead, Herts. HP2 4YL (☎01442-203970; fax: 01442-241473; www.haveneurope.com). Haven Europe is a market leader with over 25 years experience in providing family holidays. They are the owner and lead operator of eight parks in France, as well as providing holidays on many selected parks throughout France, Spain & Italy. Haven Europe offer the following varied roles in an Anglo-French working environment.
Park/Assistant Park Representatives, Children's Club Representatives, Reception Team Members (must be fluent in French), **Accommodation and Facility Team Members, Lifeguards** (must be NPLQ qualified), **Bar Servers** (must have conversational French), **Entertainers, Maintenance/Grounds Team Members.** Team Members will receive a competitive salary, accommodation on site, a free uniform, medical insurance and travel to site. Working as part of a team, your main aim will be to provide excellent customer service. Applicants must be over 18 and preferably available from March to September (some high season positions are available).

Those interested should *ring or write* to the above address.

HOLIDAYBREAK: Ref SJ/04, Hartford Manor, Greenbank Lane, Northwich, Cheshire, CW8 1HW (☎01606-787525; fax 0870-3667640; www.holidaybreakjo bs.com).
Couriers to welcome customers, clean customer accommodation, provide local information and deal with any problems. There is also some basic accounting and administration.
Children's Couriers to organise a wide range of exciting activities for children aged 4-13. Applicants must have experience of working with groups of children and possess initiative, imagination and enthusiasm along with safety awareness. Successful candidates will be asked to apply for an Enhanced Disclosure from the CRB. (See www.disclosure.gov.uk) for further details.
Montage/Demontage Assistants to assist with preparing the campsites and erecting tents at the beginning of the season and also to dismantle tents and store equipment at the end of the season. Must be prepared to work in all weathers. Successful candidates will be asked to apply for an Enhanced Disclosure from the CRB as above.
Area Assistant to assist and support the Area Manager in both administrative and on site duties. Duties include basic accounts, marketing reports, Health and Safety audits and travel organisation. Other duties would include collecting couriers from the local stations/airports, taking couriers shopping, gathering local information and other Courier duties. Must be aged 21+.

All staff will be provided with accommodation, return travel, training, competitive salary, uniform and subsidised insurance. Must be aged 18+ and an EU passport holder. Interviews are held in Cheshire in the UK.

For further details *apply online or phone* the above number for an Application Pack.

KEITH AND SHANAN MILLER: 53 Horsepool, Bromham, Chippenham, Wiltshire SN15 2HD (☎01380-850383; fax 01380-859159 e-mail ksmillerbrom@b tconnect.com). Organisers of adventure holidays worldwide for over 25 years, Keith and Shanan Miller now operate walking and cycling holidays on behalf of two major UK companies on a sub-contract basis.

Tour Leaders/Support Drivers to accompany groups of up to 16 adults on mountain walking holidays in the Alps and Provence, low level walking holidays in Tuscany and Switzerland and cycling holidays along the Loire. Food and accommodation are provided plus a wage of £150 per week. To work 7 days a week, but with free time built into itineraries. Period of work from mid-May to the end of September.

Applicants for the role of tour leader should be aged at least 23 and need some knowledge of French, or Italian language and culture as relevant plus experience/qualification in mountain walking and current first aid certificate.

Applications to Shanan Miller, Partner, at the above address or e-mail ksmillerb rom@btconnect.com.

MARK WARNER: telephone 020-7761-7300 (24 hour) or 020-7761 7340 for childcare recruitment.
Managers, Accountants, Receptionists, Watersports Instructors, Tennis and Aerobics Instructors, Chefs, Kitchen Porters, Waiting and Bar Staff, Nannies, Handymen, Nightwatchmen and more are required to work in hotels in Corsica, Greece and Turkey during the summer from April to October. Wages from £50 per week plus full board, medical insurance, travel expenses and free use of watersport and activity facilities. Some reserve staff also needed throughout the season. Requirements for languages, age, experience, qualifications etc. vary according to the job applied for.

For further details, please call the Resorts Recruitment Department on the above number.

POWDER BYRNE: 250 Upper Richmond Road, London SW15 6TG (☎020-8246 5342; fax 020-246 5321; www.powderbyrne.com). Powder Byrne is an exclusive tour operator offering tailor-made holidays, working alongside 4 and 5 star luxury hotels, to provide a top of the range holiday package. They are looking for highly motivated customer-focused team players to work in their summer resorts programme in exotic Mediterranean holiday destinations

Resort Managers required to manage a team of staff in resort, to provide a high calibre of services to Powder Byrne clients and to liaise with head office. Applicants should be 24+, have previous management experience, a professional approach and have the ability to think on their feet.

Drivers required to transport guests in exclusive company minibuses and assist the Resort Manager in providing a high level of customer service to Powder Byrne clients. Applicants should be 21+, good time-keepers, reliable and have customer service experience. Full, clean driving licence essential.

Nursery Nurses required to manage resort crèches for children aged six months to four years. Applicants should have relevant experience and be NNEB qualified or equivalent. (Non-qualified assistants are also required).

Children's Club Co-ordinators to organise and run our kids' clubs for four to 14 year olds. Applicants must have child care experience and lots of energy (would suit teachers during the school holidays). Sports orientated candidates preferred.

Accommodation, food, transport to resort insurance, uniform and competitive salary provided. Duration of contracts vary from six months to two weeks between April and October.

Applications are taken on-line at www.powderbyrne.co.uk.

SIMPLY TRAVEL & SIMPLY SKI: Kings Place, 12-42 Wood Street, Kingston-upon-Thames, Surrey, KT1 1SG (☎0870 888 0028; e-mail overseasrecruitment@s-h-g.co.uk; www.shgjobs.co.uk. Simply Travel and Simply Ski are part of the S Specialist Holidays Group a division of TUI UK, one of the top specialist tour operators in the UK. They offer a selection of top Mediterranean destinations as well as a winter ski programme in the top ski destinations.

Resort Representatives for the summer programme. All employees must be aged 21 and over, hold a clean driving licence and speak a second EU language. Simply Travel representatives need to be very independent and have a thorough understanding of customer requirements as they will often be working independently and alone.

Simply Ski recruits Resort Representatives, Cooking Chalet Hosts, Non-Cooking Chalet Assistants and Chalet Chefs, Hotel Chefs, Hotel Assistants for the winter ski season.

Applications to the above address.

SPECIALISED TRAVEL LTD: 12-15 Hanger Green, London, W5 3EL (☎020-8799 8360; fax 020-8998 7965; e-mail admin@stlon.com) Established in 1955, a tour operator specialising in concert tours of mainland Europe and the UK for both amateur and professional musical groups (choirs, bands and orchestras).

Couriers/Tour Leaders(1-2 per tour) to escort choirs, bands and orchestras from the USA on concert tours throughout the UK and Europe. To be responsible for all daily events, confirming accommodation, transportation, concert arrangements and leading sight-seeing excursions. Knowledge of touring and musical background is an advantage. Excellent organisational skills, leadership qualities and initiative required.

Work is available for a minimum of one tour in Spring and Summer. Work will be full time for the duration of each tour (usually 10-20 days). Board and accommodation is included for the duration of each tour. Wage level depends on the particular tour. Confidence in the native language of the country being toured is required.

Applications from EU nationals only are invited throughout the year to the above address.

TALL STORIES: Brassey House, New Zealand Avenue, Walton on Thames, Surrey KT12 1QD (☎01932-252002; fax 01932-252970; e-mail: info@tallstories.co.uk; www.tallstories.co.uk). Tall Stories offer adventure sports holidays in France, Spain, Austria, Mallorca and Corsica for people with no previous experience. Activities include rafting, mountain biking, trekking, kayaking, paragliding, snowboarding and many many more.

Representatives to work as sports reps for an adventure sports holiday company, acting as hosts to small groups of 8-16 clients in Austria, Corsica, France, Mallorca and Spain. Duties include airport transfers, organising hotels and sports as well as organising evening entertainment, and generally making the holidays of guests as good as possible. Reps are needed from mid-May to mid-September. Applicants should have outdoor sporting interests, speak French, Spanish or German, hold a clean driving licence (PSV licence an advantage) and get on with people. Must have experience of working with people: those with previous experience of rep work preferred. Must be aged 23 or over.

Chalet Person to cater for groups of 10-16 people in France and Austria; work includes cooking breakfast and evening meals, budgeting, cleaning, and looking after the running of a chalet. Period of work from mid-May to to mid-September.

Wages for above positions from £120 per week, plus food, accommodation and travel.

Applications should be sent to the Personnel Manager at the above address.

TRACKS TRAVEL LTD: The Flots, Brookland, Romney Marsh, Kent TN29 9TG (☎01797-344164; fax 01797-344135; e-mail info@tracks-travel.com; www.tracks-travel.com). A coach tour operator operating throughout the UK and Europe.

Drivers with a valid UK PCV Licence required.

Tour Managers must be good with a microphone, and confident in dealing with large groups.

Cooks: Must be able to cook for large groups. Relevant experience preferred.

Wage for all positions to be confirmed. Board and accommodation is available. Work is available throughout the year, but all applicants should be prepared to work for a minimum of 2 full seasons. Hours of work vary, depending on the nature of the tour. Knowledge of languages other than English is not required.

Applications should be made to the above address at any time of year.

VENUE HOLIDAYS: 1 Norwood St, Ashford, Kent TN23 1QU (☎01233-629950; fax 01233-634494; e-mail info@venueholidays.co.uk). Venue Holidays are a medium sized family run business supplying package camping and mobile home holidays. They offer the opportunity to live in a new environment, meet interesting people, travel and perhaps catch a tan.

Supervisors required for the period March to October. Must possess a clean driver's licence. Wages £700 per month.

Campsite Representatives (30) for work in Italy, France and Spain. Duties to include cleaning and maintaining holiday units, welcoming clients and looking after them during their stay, sorting out any problems, and liaising between the campsite's management and the UK office. Wage of £450 per month, with accommodation provided. To work hours as required. Minimum period of work June-August; the complete season runs from March to October. Applicants need to be fit, cheerful and to be able to work under pressure. Knowledge of French, German, Italian or Spanish would be advantageous but are not essential.

Applications should be sent to the above address from November.

Voluntary Work and Archaeology

ATD FOURTH WORLD: 48 Addington Square, London SE5 7LB (tel; 020-7703 3231; fax 020-7252 4276; e-mail atd@atd-uk.org; www.atd-uk.org).

ATD Fourth World is an international organisation which adopts a human rights approach to tackling extreme poverty, supporting the efforts of very disadvantaged and excluded families in fighting poverty and taking an active role in the community. As part of their work ATD organises workcamps, street workshops and family stays all over the European Union.

The workcamps are a **combination of manual work** in and around ATD's buildings, **conversation and reflection on poverty**. The street workshops take a festival atmosphere, involving artists, craftsmen, sportsmen and volunteers to underprivileged areas. The family stays allow families split by poverty with children in care and/or adults in homes to come together for a break.

The camps, street workcamps and family stays take place from July to September, and most last two weeks: participants must pay for their own travel costs, plus a contribution towards food and accommodation.

For further information *write*, enclosing a stamped addressed envelope or International Reply Coupon, to the above address or ATD Quart Monde, Summer Activities Team, 107 avenue du General Leclerc, 95480 Pierrelaye, France or email engage.ete@atd-quartmonde.org.

BRIDGES FOR EDUCATION INC: 94 Lamarck Drive, Buffalo, New York 14226, USA (☎+1 716 839-0180; fax +1 716 939-9493; e-mail jbc@buffalo.edu; www.bridges4edu.org).
Volunteer English Teachers. The purpose of Bridges for Education (BFE) is to promote tolerance and understanding using English as a bridge. BFE sends Canadian and American volunteer teachers, educated adults and college students to **teach conversational English in the summer in Eastern and Central Europe.**

Since 1994, BFE has organised 66 camps in eight countries serving 8,500 students from 33 countries. High School students whose parents or teachers are participants may also join a BFE team. About 130 volunteers are placed each year. Those skilled in teaching English as a Second Language are preferred but teachers who are certified in any area are welcome. College professors, educated adults, and college students are trained in basic ESL prior to departure. Applicants must be in good health.

Volunteers are required during the summer for three weeks teaching and an additional week of travel within the host country. Free room and board as well as a stipend equivalent to what a local teacher is paid for three weeks, are provided.

Applications from US or Canadian citizens only should be sent to the above address or made online.

THE DISAWAY TRUST: 34 Wade Close, Langley Point, Eastbourne, East Sussex BN23 6AW (☎01323-640289). The Disaway Trust relies on helpers to enable them to provide holidays for adults who otherwise would not be able to have a holiday. Young helpers can apply for funding.

About 60 volunteers are required for 8-14 day periods during the year to **help disabled people on holiday**. The organisation usually arranges two or three holidays a year which take place between May and October. A 50% contribution is required toward cost of travel, accommodation, board and entertainment.

No special qualifications or experience are required. The holiday venues are in the British Isles and in the Mediterranean.

Apply to Mark Hammersely for further details including information on dates and locations. The information pack for 2004 will be available in mid January.

EMMAUS INTERNATIONAL: Boite Postale 91, F-94143 Alfortville, France (☎-1-48-93-29-50; fax -1-43-53-19-26; e-mail contact@emmaus-international.org; www.emmaus-international.org).
Volunteers to take part in summer camps in several European countries. The work consists of **rag-picking and recycling materials to raise money for the poor.** Applicants must pay for their own travelling costs but receive free food and accommodation.

For *further details* contact the above address.

EUROPEAN VOLUNTARY SERVICE: EVS Unit, EIL Cultural and Educational Travel, 287 Worcester Road, Malvern, WR14 1AB (☎ ⬚ ⬚ ⬚; e-mail k.morris@eiluk.org). EIL is an approved Sending and Hosting organisation for the European Commission's new European Voluntary Service scheme.
EVS is for 18-25 year old EU citizens who want to work for 6-12 months in a **community-based project** in another European country. Travel, food, accommodation and an allowance are provided.

For more details *contact* the above address.

GEC/APARE: 41 Cours Jean Jaures, F-84000 Avignon, France (☎33-(0)4-90-27-08-61; fax 33-(0)4-90-86-82-19; e-mail gec@apare-gec.org; www.apare-gec.org).
The GEC is a NGO which promotes transnational co-operation by bringing together professionsals, local participants and young volunteers from around Europe and the Mediterranean region. Its objective is to carry out projects that contribute to the protection and enhancement of the environment and local heritage. The GEC develops voluntary efforts in favour of the environment and heritage preservation across Europe and the Mediterranean regions.
Euro-Mediterranean Campuses: The campuses are intended for students from Europe and Mediterranean countries. They take the form of workshops with about fifteen participants working in multi-disciplinary international groups for three to five weeks, during the students' summer holidays. They include **field studies and surveys that use professional skills in the areas of heritage preservation and the environment (in the widest possible sense):** architecture, history of art, regional development, sociology, law etc.)
 RIVE: The International Network of Volunteers for the Environment, Heritage and Sustainable Development: RIVE programmes (carried out in the context of the European Voluntary Service) allow participants to invest their skills in voluntary projects abroad, to the benefit of local communities. This programme is designed for young people from 18 to 25 years old, of whatever nationality or professional training, as long as they reside in a participating country of Europe, Eastern Europe or the Mediterranean. The projects last from six to twelve months. They can be held in urban or rural settings. The teams are made up of one to three young volunteers, preferably from different disciplines and cultural backgrounds.
 Applications to the above address.

INTERNATIONALE BOUWORDE (INTERNATIONAL BUILDING COMPANIONS): for addresses see below.
Recruits volunteers for **construction work** camps **on behalf of the socially, physically and mentally underprivileged**. The camps take place in Austria, Belgium, the Czech Republic, France, Germany, Hungary, Italy, Lithuania, the Netherlands, Poland, Romania, Slovakia, Switzerland and the Ukraine.
 Volunteers work for 8 hours per day, 5 days per week. Free board, accommodation and liability and accident insurance are provided: travel costs and insurance (approx. £60) are the responsibility of the volunteer. Camps last for 2-3 weeks and take place between June and September; Bouworde in Belgium and Italy operates workcamps around the year. Individual country branches are as below:

○ *Netherlands*: Internationale Bouworde, St Annastrat 172, NL-6524 GT Nijmegen (☎31-24-3226074; fax 31-24-3226076; e-mail info@bouworde.nl www.bouworde.nl). Represents IBO as a whole.
○ *Belgium*: (Flemish speaking): Bouworde, Tiensesteenweg 145, B-3010 Kessel-Lo (☎016 25 91 44; fax 016 25 91 60).
○ *France:* Compagnons Batisseurs, Secrétariat International, Ferme de la Capelanie, 39, Chemin de Verdun, 81100, Castres, France (☎33 5-63 72 59 64; fax 33-5-63 72 59 81).
○ *Germany:* Internationaler Bauorden, Liebigstrasse 23, D-67551 Worms-Horchheim (☎06241-37900; fax 06241-37902; e-mail bauorden@t-online.de; www.home.t-online.de/home/ibo-d/).
○ *Italy:* IBO Associazione Italian Soci Costruttori, Via Montebello, 46/A 551 00 Ferrara (☎0532-243279; fax 0532-245-689; e-mail info@iboitalia.org; www.iboitalia.org).
○ *Switzerland:* Internationaler Bauorden, Sekretariat Schweiz, Bahnhofstr. 8,

CH-9450 Altstälku (☎+41-71-755 1671; e-mail info@bayordeuich).
Applications, mentioning the country preferred, should be sent to the relevant address listed above.

TEJO (TUTMONDA ESPERANTISTA JUNULARA ORGANIZO): Nieuwe Binnenweg 176, 3015 BJ Rotterdam, the Netherlands (☎31 10 436 1044: fax 31 10 436 1751).
Volunteers to join **work camps** in various European countries arranged by TEJO, the World Organisation of Young Esperantists. Work to be done may be on **reconstruction projects**. Accommodation provided. Period of work normally from 1 to 2 weeks.

Applicants should be aged between 16 and 30. No previous experience necessary: all camps include Esperanto lessons for beginners, and a few are limited to Esperanto speakers.

For details *contact* the above address including an International Reply Coupon.

Au Pairs, Nannies, Family Helps & Exchanges

ANGLO CONTINENTAL PLACEMENTS AGENCY: 9 Wish Road, Hove, East Sussex, BA3 4LL (☎01273-776660; fax 01273-776634; e-mail sharon@angloconti nental.fsnet.co.uk; www.anglocontinentalplacement.co.uk). Established 1985.
Au Pairs recruited for Austria, Croatia, Czech Republic, Finland, France, Germany, Holland, Hungary, Iceland, Italy, Norway, Slovakia, Spain, Sweden, Switzerland and Turkey. Pocket money between £40 and £55 per week, plus board and lodging in own room, in exchange for around 5 hours' work a day. 12 months' long term stays for applicants from abroad can be arranged in the UK; pocket money £40-£55 per week.
Chefs, Receptionists, Waiters, Waitresses, Chambermaids, Kitchen Porters for hotel work UK and Spain. Applicants must be EU nationals, or must have a Visa for the appropriate country.

Applications enclosing 4 International Reply Coupons to Mrs Sharon Wolfe at the above address.

Anglo Continental Placements are also advertising for Chefs, Sous Chefs, Chefs de Partie, Commis Chefs, Wine Waiters, Receptionists, Waiters, Waitresses, Chambermaids, kitchen Porters, Porters, Jobs available in 2 star, 3 star, 4 star and 5 star hotels. Accommodation provided for all jobs.

Applications to the above address: *EU nationals, Austrians, and South Africans may apply.*

THE AU PAIR AGENCY: 231 Hale Lane, Edgware, Middlesex HA8 9QF (☎020-8958 1750; fax 020-8958 5261; e-mail: elaine@aupairagency.com; www.aupairagency.com). Established 1986.
Au Pairs from Britain mainly placed in France, Spain, Majorca, Italy and Germany.
Mothers' Helps placed in France.

Applicants should be aged between 18 and 25. Non-smokers preferred; drivers always welcomed. Summer stays of 12 weeks possible – early applicants receive priority. At all other times, a minimum commitment of 9-12 months is required. A reasonable knowledge of the language of the chosen country is needed. European au pairs and nationals of participating non-EU countries also placed in Britain. The Au-Pair agency does not place au-pairs in the USA. Although the agency works wth all the British government approved participating countries, it cannot place applicants from one country, via London, into another country. e.g. it cannot place au-pairs from Spain with families in Turkey.

All applicants receive pocket money plus full board and lodging. For *further details* contact Mrs Newman on the above number at least 12 weeks before preferred starting date.

AU PAIR CONNECTIONS: 39 Tamarisk Road, Wildern Gate, Hedge End, Hants SO30 4TN (☎01489-780438; fax 01489-692656; e-mail apconnectenthworld.com; www.aupair-connections.co.uk).
Au Pairs, Mothers' Helps placed in France, Spain, the Balearic Islands, Italy, Austria and elsewhere in Europe; applicants from overseas also placed in the UK. Pocket money approx. £50 per week. Minimum stays normally 6 months, but some summer stays of 10 weeks. Applicants must have experience of childcare, babysitting etc; a good knowledge of English is also useful as some families want their children tutored in English. The Agency also have 'homestay' for students. For further details contact Ms Denise Blighe at the above address.

All *applications* should be in writing enclosing a s.a.e.

AU PAIR IN EUROPE: P.O. Box 68056 Blakely Postal Outlet, Hamilton, Ontario, Canada L8M 3M7 (☎1-905 545 6305; fax 1 905-544 4121; e-mail aupair@princeent.com; www.princeent.com).
Au Pairs placed with families around the world. Au Pair in Europe helps applicants step by step through the whole process, including visa, medical insurance and travel arrangements. Countries available: Australia, Austria, Belgium, Bermuda, Denmark, England, Finland, France, Germany, Greece, Holland, Iceland, Italy, Monaco, New Zealand, Norway, Spain, Sweden, and Switzerland. Contracts range from 3 months to one year. Salary approximately $75-$120 per week plus free room and board.

Applicants should be aged 18-30. Childcare experience necessary. To work approximately 30 hours per week, plus some babysitting. Registration fee charged.
*Further information:*see the organisation's web page for further information.

AU PAIR INTERNATIONAL: Cherry Gardens, Nouds Lane, Lynsted, Kent ME9 0ES (01795-522544; fax 01795-522878; e-mail info@au-pairinternational.com; www.au-pairinternational.com). In business since 1981 Au Pair International is a member of REC. Friendly and thoroughly experienced.
Au Pairs recruited throughout the year for the UK and Europe. Live-in, £50 per week minimum pocket money or equivalent. 25 hours work per week, 2 days off. Unlimited number of posts available for 6-24 months stay, but some 10-week summer placements. Their families in the UK are mostly in London, London suburbs and the southern counties and South Coast. Vacancies in Europe are mainly in Cities and Coastal Towns.
Other services: au pair international has a sister company County Nannies which provides fully qualified **Nannies** and **Maternity Nurses.** Also babysitters (usually experienced or qualified) and **Mothers Helps** with some experience in childcare but usually with no professional qualifications. County nannies covers Kent, London, South East England and the Home Counties.
Applications to the above address in writing, by fax or e-mail.

BLOOMSBURY BUREAU: Marianne Dix, 3, Rokeby House, Long Yard, 86-90 Lamb's Conduit Street, London WC1N 3LX; (☎020-7430 2280; fax 020-74302325; e-mail bloomsburo@aol.com; www.bloomsburyaupairs.co.uk). This agency has been operating for thirty years, and every placement is personally supervised by the principal.
Au Pairs (300) for placements in EU countries throughout the year. Also unlimited

number of posts for long stays 6-12 months, especially in Austria, France, Germany, Ireland, Spain and throughout the UK. Pocket money £55 per week, in return for 30 hours help with childcare and light housework and helping with English.

There are also some hotel posts in Bavaria (20/30) for *EU nationals only* for the summer season May-October, approx. €600 (£420) per month live-in. Applicants should be aged at least 18 and supply a CV and one reference.

Applications to Marianne Dix, Principal, at the above address or online at www. bloomsburyaupairs.co.uk.

BUNTERS AU PAIR AGENCY: The Old Malt House, 6 Church Street, Pattishall, Towcester, Northants, NN12 8NB (☎01327-831144; fax 01327-831155; e-mail office@aupairnannies.com; www.aupairnannies.com).

Au Pair Jobs in Spain, France, Belgium, Austria, Italy, Holland and the UK; duties consist of light housework and assisting with children. Minimum stay 6-12 months; 10 week summer stays also arranged in Spain and France, but these must be applied for before May. Pocket money is a minimum of £45 per week depending on hours worked and location of placement.

Applicants should be aged 18-27, preferably be non-smokers, and should have experience with children (babysitting etc.), be able to provide references, and have some knowledge of the language of the country of placement.

For *further information* send a stamped addressed envelope to Caroline Jones at the above address.

EDGWARE AND SOLIHULL AU PAIR & NANNY AGENCY: PO Box 147, Radlett WD7 8WX (☎01923-289737; fax 01923-289739; e-mail info@the-aupair-shop.com; www.the-aupair-shop.com)..

Au Pairs needed for families all over Europe and the UK, placed in all the capital cities, e.g. London, Paris, Rome, Barcelona. Au pairs need a working knowledge of the country in which they wish to be placed. Good child-care experience and character references are essential.

For more information visit the website or *write* to the above address enclosing 2 Internatonal Reply Coupons.

EN FAMILLE OVERSEAS: 4 St Helena Road, Colchester CO3 3BA (☎01206-546741; fax 01206-546740; e-mail enfamilleoversea@btopenworld.com or marylou-toms@btinternet.com).

Paying Guest Stays Arranged in France, Germany, Italy and Spain. Also language courses with homestays arranged in France and Spain.

Applications to the above address.

EUROYOUTH ABROAD LTD: 301 Westborough Road, Westcliff, Southend-on-Sea, Essex SS0 9PT (☎01702-341434; fax 01702-330104). Established in 1961, Euroyouth have featured on Austrian and Italian TV programmes. They offer assistance during to each participant during their stay.

Paying Guest Holidays with or without language courses arranged around the year in Austria, France, Germany, Greece, Italy, Hungary, Portugal, Spain and Turkey for groups and individuals.

Holiday Guest Stays also arranged in Austria, France, Germany, Hungary, Italy, Spain and Turkey, mostly during the summer holiday period. Accommodation and food are provided in exchange for English conversation. Those interested must apply very early or consider a paying guest stay as an alternative.

In 2003 Italy was the most popular destination for applicants. Ages for both programmes 18-25 and in some cases for those over 25. Euroyouth charge a £100 application fee payable on registration.

Apply sending a stamped addressed envelope to the above address for details.

JOLAINE AU PAIR & DOMESTIC AGENCY: 18 Escot Way, Barnet, Hertfordshire EN5 3AN (☎020-8449 1334; fax 020-8449 9183; e-mail aupair@jol aine.prestel.co.uk; www.jolaine.com).
Au Pair/Mother's Help stays: Jolaine can arrange for applicants to be placed as au pairs/mother's helps with families in Europe. 6-12 month stays preferred (summer stays minimum 2 months). Paying guest stays also arranged in France, Belgium and Spain; minimum stay 1 week. Has a large network of reliable offices abroad, able to offer excellent support and help considered essential by the agency for its applicants.

Apply in writing enclosing large stamped addressed envelope for further details.

LUCY LOCKETTS & VANESSA BANCROFT DOMESTIC AGENCY: 400 Beacon Road, Wibsey, Bradford, BD6 3DJ (tel/fax 01274-402822; e-mail lucylocke tts@blueyonder.co.uk). Est. 1984.
Au Pairs and **Au Pairs Plus** (20-30) from June to September. Child care and light housework. Age limits 17-28. Working hours: au pairs 30 hours, Monday to Friday, au pairs plus 40-45 hours weekly, Monday to Friday. Weekly wages £30-£35 for au pairs and £45-£50 au pairs plus. Jobs in France, Spain, Italy, Greece, Austria etc.
Nannies (5-15) in Greece, from June to September. Must be qualified and have 1/2 year's experience and be aged 19-35. £100 plus per week. Long hours, some evenings free and one day off per week.

Applications to the above address.

RICHMOND & TWICKENHAM AU PAIRS: The Old Parsonage, Main Street, Barton Under Needwood, Staffordshire DE13 8AA (☎01283-716611; fax 01283-712299; e-mail vicki@aupairsnationawide.co.uk; www.aupairsnationwide.co.uk). An established agency running since 1992, run by Vicki, who has been a Nanny/Au Pair.
Placements available in Denmark, Spain, Italy and France. Minimum age 18, non-smokers preferred, wages vary from country to country.

Applications to the above address.

WORLDNETUK, Work and Travel Specialists, Emberton House, 26 Shakespeare Road, Bedford MK40 2ED (☎0845 458 1550/1; www.worldnetuk.com).
WorldNetUk is affiliated to The Childcare Solution, which is a leading childcare recruitment agency established for over 20 years. There are four offices in the UK and partner agencies throughout the world.
Ski/Summer Resort Nannies. Destinations include France, Corsica, Spain, Balearics, Turkey, Italy, Sardinia, Greece, Austria and Switzerland. Winter season includes free ski lessons, lift pass and tuition. Summer season includes free water sports and tuition. All applicants must hold a childcare qualification or one years full time experience with children.
Au Pair programme to the UK. Carefully selected families in the United Kingdom. Placements for candidates from all EU countries and Andorra, Bosnia-Herzegovina, Croatia, Cyprus, Czech Republic, the Faroes, Greenland, Hungary, Leichtenstein, Macedonia, Malta, Monaco, San Marino, Slovak Republic, Slovenia, Switzerland, Turkey, Poland, Bulgaria, Lithuania, Estonia and Romania.
Hospitality placements in the UK. Career opportunities in leading hotels

throughout the UK for chefs (all grades), housekeeping and reception staff.

Camp USA. Counsellors and support staff for camps throughout the US; 8-10 week placements. All departures in June, with the opportunity to travel at end of stay. Applicants must be 18 upwards.

Au Pair and Nanny programme to the USA for 18-26 year olds with full driving licence. Placements for qualified NNEB, Btec National Diploma and NVQ level III in childcare to work with young babies. Also placements for unqualified applicants to work with school age children but good babysitting experience would be essential. Applications can be processed from the UK, France, Czech Republic and Turkey.

Au Pair programme to Europe. UK applicants who would like to improve their language skills needed to spend time in France, Spain, Italy or Germany; an excellent way to learn something of another culture and become fluent in another language. Good support always from partner agencies.

For further information *visit* the website www.worldnetuk.com.

Western Europe

Andorra

Only limited opportunities for finding temporary employment exist in Andorra, chiefly because of its small size. Opportunities are best in the tourist industry – particularly in the winter ski season: there is a chapter on Andorra in *Working in Ski Resorts – Europe & North America* (see the *Useful Publications* chapter). Once governed jointly by France and Spain, Andorra has been a sovereign country in its own right since 1993, and while it straddles the borders of France and Spain, Andorra is not itself a member of the European Union. This means that all foreigners, including nationals of EEA countries, need work permits before they can take up employment. These must be obtained by the employer once a job has been pre-arranged.

Hotel Work and Catering

HOTEL ROC BLANC: Placa des Coprinceps, 5, Escaldes, Andorra (☎+376-871400; fax +376-860 244; e-mail hotelrocblanc@gruprocblanc.com).
Receptionist/Restaurant Assistant (1) to work 6 days a week. Required all year. Applicants must have a knowledge of French, English and Spanish. Board and lodging provided.
Applications from April to the above address.

Teaching and Language Schools

CENTRE ANDORRÀ DE LLENGÜES: 15 Carrer del Fener, Andorra la Vella, Andorra (☎+376-804030; fax +376-822472; e-mail centrandorra.lang@andorra.ad; www.call.ad). A small language school established in 1976 in the very centre of Andorra La Vella. Students range from six year old children to professional adult employees.
Teachers (1/2) of English as a foreign language. £750, approximately, per month. To work 27 hours per 5 day week. Board and lodging available from £150 per month. Minimum period of work 9 months between October and June.
TEFL qualifications or two years' experience of teaching English essential. Applicants should be between 22 and 35 and willing to work between 4pm and 9.30pm. Non-smokers preferred: reasonable knowledge of French or Spanish is important.
Applications should be sent with a recent photograph to Claude Benet at the above address in May or June.

Austria

There is also an English language magazine for Austria on the internet - *Austria Today* (www.austriatoday.at). It and the Austrian Embassy's website - www.austria.org.uk are excellent sources of information on jobs the social, cultural and economic conditions of Austria; in particular, look at *Living and Working in Austria* on the website which contains details of immigration, work and residence permits and social security procedures as well as information for the job seeker about Austrian Employment offices.

For many years Austria has offered the seasonal worker jobs in its summer and winter tourist industries. Prospects for finding work are usually good with unemployment below the EU average. However, unemployment is currently around 5.8%. Jobs in the tourist industry can be found both in this chapter. Some knowledge of German will normally be necessary unless you are working for a foreign tour operator with English-speaking clients.

During the summer, fruit is grown along the banks of the Danube, and in the early Autumn chances of finding a job grape-picking are best in the Wachau area around Durnstein west of Vienna, or Burgenland on the Hungarian border around the Neusiedler See.

The public employment service of Austria, the *Arbeitsmarktservice (AMS)*, publishes its vacancies on its website – www.ams.or.at – (or at Arbeitsmarktservice, Vienna, Weihburggasse 30, A-1011 Vienna tel: 0043-1-515 25-0). For hotel and catering vacancies in the South Tyrol try AMS Euro Biz/JobCenter International, Südtiroler Platz 14-16, 6020 Innsbruck (512-58 63 00/fax 512-58 63 00-20). Private employment agencies operate in Austria, but most of these specialise in executive positions or seasonal positions in the tourist industry for German speakers. It is worth checking for leads on the website of Oscar's Agency (Gymnasiumgasse 2, A-6800 Feldkirch; ☎+43-5522 76563; fax +43-5522 82134; e-mail oscars@cable.vol.at; www.oscars.at).

It may be possible to find employment by placing an advertisement in daily newspapers: try *Salzburger Nachrichten* (Karolingerstrasse 40, 5021 Salzburg; ☎+43-662-83730; www.salzburg.com), *Kurier* (Seidengasse 11, A-1070 Vienna; ☎+43-(0)1-52100; fax 01-5210 02263; www.kurier.at) and *Die Presse* (Parkring 12a. 1015 Vienna; ☎0043-(0)1-51414; fax 01-5141 4400; www.diepresse.at). *Die Presse* also organises an annual initiative to get leading Austrian companies to take on students for summer traineeships. These papers advertise job vacancies as well on Fridays, Saturdays and Sundays. See also *Der Standard*, (www.DerStandard.at) one of the biggest newspapers concerning job vacancies.

There are opportunities for voluntary work in Austria arranged by UNA Exchange.

RED TAPE, VISAS & WORK PERMITS

Visa Requirements: visa requirement depends upon the nationality of the visitor. Certain nationals do not require a visa providing their stay in Austria does not exceed 3 months. EU/EEA citizens have the right to live and work in Austria without a work permit or residence permit.

Residence Permits: *EWR Lichtbildausweis* is an ID card which EU/EEA nationals can apply for within 3 months of arrival, though it is not compulsory. For Non-EU/EEA nationals wishing to work or live in Austria must apply for a residence permit *(Aufenthaltsgesetz)*. Once a work permit is granted, it must be presented together with an application for residence permit. The form can be obtained from the Embassy. As a rule, first application for a residence permit must be submitted from abroad either directly to the competent authority or by means of the Austrian Diplomatic Mission (not Honorary Consulates). A residence permit is also required if you intend to take up seasonal work in Austria. It will normally be valid for 6 months.

Work Permits: British and Irish citizens and nationals of other EU/EEA countries (and Liechtenstein) do not need work permits. Non-EU/EEA nationals require work (*Sicherungs bescheinigung*) and residence permits for all types of employment, including au-pair positions. Work permits have to be applied for by the future employer in Austria and must be obtained prior to departure from the country of residence. Work permits are not granted while on a visit to Austria.

Au Pair: au pairs from outside the EU/EEA must obtain work and residence permits as above with the assistance of the mediating agency and/or the au-pair family in Austria who must inform the local employment office (*Arbeitsmarktservice*). A couple of useful organisations in this respect are Au Pair 4You (Hasnerstr. 31/32, 1160 Vienna; ☎+43 1 990 1574; fax +43 1 990 1574 2) and Au Pair-Vermittlung (Johannesgasse 16/1 1010 Vienna; ☎+43 1 512 7941).

Voluntary Work: work permits are also required by non-EEA nationals for work with recognised voluntary organisations.

Agricultural Work

WWOOF AUSTRIA: Einoedhofweg 48, A-8042 Graz, (fax 43-(0)316-464951; mobile +43-(0)676505-1639 e-mail wwoof.welcome@telering.at; www.wwoof.we lcome.at.tf). WWOOF Austria received the Ford Conservation and Environmental Award 2001.

Volunteers required to take part in a form of cultural exchange where you live and help as a farming family, learning about organic farming methods in the process (see WWOOF entry in *Worldwide*). Work is available on more than 140 farms. Movement between farms is possible. Board and accommodation will be provided, however a separate wage will not. Applicants from outside the European Union must secure their own travel insurance and all wwoofers pay for their own travel. In Austria they are covered by an insurance against accidents. A year's membership for WWOOF Austria costs approx. €20 (plus two International Reply Coupons). Membership includes a list of Austrian organic farmers looking for work-for-keep volunteer helpers.

For more information *contact* Hildegard Gottlieb at the above address.

Hotel Work and Catering

HOTEL BRISTOL: Markatplatz 4, A-5020 Salzburg, Austria.
Housemaid: around £450 per month.
Waiting Staff: around £400 per month.
To work 8 hours per day, 6 days per week. Minimum period of work 8 weeks. Please note that no accommodation is available at the hotel. Applicants must speak German.
Applications to the above address.

HOTEL HOCHSFIRST: A-6456 Obergurgl Nr 37, Austria (☎05256-231/232).
Housemaids (2), **Waiters/Waitresses** (2), **Kitchen Assistants** (2). £125-£157 per month. Knowledge of German and experience in the hotel and catering industry required. 10-11 hour days, 6-7 day week. Working shifts between 7am and 10pm. Board and lodging provided free. Minimum work period 2 months.
Applications in January/February to Franz Gstrein at the above address.

HOTEL MARIAHILF: A-8020 Graz, Mariahilfstrasse 9, Austria.
Kitchen Assistants, Bar Staff. Wage by arrangement. Hours 7-10am, 6 days per week. Free board and accommodation. Must have previous experience or some knowledge of

German. Period of work May to October.
Applications to Irmgard Kossar.

PENSION BERGKRISTALL: A-9844 Heiligenbut, Austria.
Assistant to wait at table and clean rooms. £255, approximately per month. To work around 4 hours per day, 7 days per week. In winter it is possible to ski daily from 1pm. Free board and lodging provided. Periods of work from July to September or December to March: minimum period of work two months. Applicants should be able to speak English and German.
Applications to Herr H. Fleissner at the above address in April in the summer season or October for the winter season.

HOTEL POST KG: Fam Hofer, A-5672 Fusch/Glstr, Land Salzburg, Austria.
Waiting Assistant (1) and Receptionist (1). Wages approximately £400 per month. To work 8-10 hours per day, 6 days per week. Minimum period of work is 2 months. Free board and lodging are provided. Knowledge of German and French are required.
Applications to the above address between April and June.

SPORTHOTEL GUNTER SINGER: A-6622 Berwang, Tirol, Austria (tel+43-5674-8181; fax +43-5674-818183). The hotel is a member of Relais & Châteaux hotels and is situated in a small village in the mountains. It caters for international guests.
Assistants (2) to serve and clean in a restaurant.
Housemaid to clean the rooms of guests, the lounge, reception, etc.
Wages from £400 to £500 per month. Around 8 hours per day, 5½ days per week. Free board and accommodation provided. Minimum period of work from 1 July to 10 September. Knowledge of some German required, plus some French if possible. *Applicants must be EU nationals.*
Applications to the above address from January-March.

TRAUM-HOTEL CLUB MONTANARA: Seestrasse 5, A-6673 Haldensee/Gran, Austria (☎+43-5675-6431; fax +43-5675-6436).
Lifeguards, Open Air Swimming Pool Attendants, Buffet Assistants, Wages and period of work by arrangement. To work 9½ hours per day, 47½ hours per week. Board and accommodation provided. Applicants must speak German.
Applications to Frau Sonja Huber at the above address at any time.

TRAVELBOUND: First Choice Holidays, London Road, Crawley, West Sussex RH10 9GX (☎01293-588531; fax 01293-588277; e-mail skijobs@firstchoice.co.uk). Activity/educational tour operator to Austria and France (Alps and Normandy), member of AITO.
Summer Staff (over 250) including resort reps, chalet and hotel staff (Chefs, General Assistants, Kitchen/Night Porters). Full season in Austrian and French Alps lasts May-September and in Normandy February-October. Flexible contract lengths available. Applications are processed in January through to September. Minimum age for hotel positions 18, for Resort Representatives 21. Applicants must have EU passport and National Insurance number. An attractive package which includes food, accommodation, insurance and travel to/from resort. Winter work also available for Ski Season with First Choice Ski.
For more information please send an A4 S.A.E. to Overseas Ski Recruitment at the address above.

Sports, Couriers and Camping

CANVAS HOLIDAYS: East Port House, 12 East Port, Dunfermline, Fife KY12 7JG (☎01383-629018; fax 01383-629071; www.canvasholidays.com). Canvas Holidays are looking for enthusiastic, resourceful people who enjoy a challenge and love the outdoor life. Main positions include:

Campsite Courier. Varied responsibilities. Involves cleaning and preparation of customer accommodation, welcoming and looking after customers during their holiday and ensuring that they have the best holiday ever. As a campsite courier you will have new challenges every day which can lead to one of the most enjoyable summers you will ever have. Variable working hours.

Package includes tented accommodation, medical insurance, full uniform and return coach travel to and from a UK port of entry. Positions are available from March until October.

Applications are invited from individuals and couples. Contact Sandy, Karen or Nina at the above contact details for an application pack.

ESPRIT ALPINE SUN: 185 Fleet Road, Fleet, Hants GU51 3BL (☎01252-618318; fax 01252-618328; e-mail recruitment@esprit-holidays.co.uk; www.esprit-holidays.co.uk) Esprit Alpine Sun run Alpine holidays (France, Italy and Austria) for families in catered chalets and hotels and provide childcare in nurseries and Alpine adventure clubs for children aged 4 months to 12 years old.

Resort Managers. Minimum age 23: should be French , German or Italian speakers, with some management, customer care and accountancy experience.

Chalet Hosts for various grades of responsibilities: minimum age 21, Cordon Bleu/City and Guilds 706/HND/OND or equivalent or experience in cooking professionally required.

Nannies should be aged 18 or over with NNEB, NVQ3, BTECH or RGN qualification.

Nanny Assistants aged 18 or over with NVQ2 or equivalent.

Alpies Rangers with experience as play scheme leaders, children's sports coaches or trained teachers required to run adventure actvity clubs. Minimum age 18. Should have a mature, fun loving personality.

All staff must be EU passport holders available from mid-June to mid-September. Ideal for anyone who has an interest in alpine activities, i.e. mountain walking and biking, white water rafting etc.

All staff assist with chalet cleaning, babysitting and hosting guests. EU holders essential. Weekly wage, with food and accommodation, uniform, swimming pool pass and transport provided.

Applications to the above address.

EUROCAMP: Overseas Recruitment Department (Ref SJ/04) (☎01606-787525). Eurocamp is a leading tour operator in quality self-drive camping and mobile home holidays in Europe. Each year the company seeks to recruit up to 1,500 enthusiastic people for the following positions:

Campsite Courier: job involves cleaning and preparing customer accommodation, providing assistance, acting as an information service and performing some administrative duties. Couriers need to be flexible to meet the needs of the customer to provide them with excellent service. Minimum age 18 years. Applicants should be independent with plenty of initiative and relish a challenging and rewarding position. They should also possess a friendly and helpful personality. Previous customer service experience would be an advantage. Applicants should be available to work from April/May to September.

Children's Courier: work involves organising a wide range of exciting activities for children aged 4-13. Applicants should possess initiative, imagination and enthusiasm along with good safety awareness. Previous childcare experience is essential. Minimum age is 18 years and applicants should be available from April/May to September. Languages are not a requirement but would be an advantage (in particular German). Successful candidates will be asked to apply for an Enhanced Disclosure.

Senior Couriers: required to work alongside a team of Campsite Couriers and organise their daily workload, as well as carrying out the normal day to day duties of a Campsite Courier. Applicants should have good language skills and experience of leading a team.

Site Managers: required to lead a large team of Campsite Couriers, organising their daily workloads and ensuring they provide the very best customer service. Applicants should be 21 or over, have proven managerial experience, excellent communication skills and language ability.

Comprehensive training is provided together with a competitive salary, insurance, return travel and accommodation. Applications are accepted from September/October and *can only be accepted from UK/EU passport holders*. Interviews will be conducted in Hartford, Cheshire between October and April.

Applicants should apply on-line at www.holidaybreakjobs.com or telephone 01606 781525 for an Application Pack.

Teaching and Language Schools

ENGLISH FOR KIDS: A. Postgasse 11/19, 1010 Vienna, Austria (☎+43-(0)1-667 45 79; fax 01-667 51 63; e-mail magik@4kids.co.at; www.e4kids.co.at).

The teaching venue is a beautifully renovated, 17th century, four-square building around a large central yard and it is situated in 40 hectares of meadows and woods.

TEFL Teachers: (6-8) with CELTA or Trinity Certificate (minimum grade B) and some formal teaching experience required for (a) residential summer camps in Upper Austria. Period of work 6-8 weeks in July and August. Pupils' age range is 10-15; (b) day camp in Vienna. Period of work 2-4 weeks in July and August. Pupils range from kindergarten to age 9.

Salary varies depending on qualifications, ranging from €560 - for two weeks plus full board and accommodation and travel expenses within Austria. The teaching style is full immersion with in-house methods following carefully planned syllabus and teachers' manual, supplemented with CD-Roms etc.

Apply to Irena Köstenbauer, Principal at the above address.

Work with Children

AUSLANDS SOZIALDIENST: A-1010 Wien, Johannesgasse 16, Austria (☎1-512-7941; fax 513-9460; e-mail aupair-asd@kath-jugend.at).

Au Pairs placed in Vienna and in other parts of Austria for periods of 8 weeks in the summer or 6 months to 1 year at other times of the year.

The au pair gets free board and lodging, a room of her own and pocket money of £35 per week. The au pair has to work about 25 hours per week, must have one entirely free day per week and has the possibility of attending language classes. A basic knowledge of German, plus some experience with children and domestic work is required.

Applications to the above address 2-3 months before the desired starting date.

ENGLISH FOR CHILDREN-SUMMER CAMP: Weichselweg 4, 1220 Vienna, Austria (☎+43 1958 19 72-0; fax +43 19581972-14; e-mail office@englishforchildren.com; www.englishforchildren.com).
Camp Counsellors: to instruct in sports, arts & crafts, music, Drama/and or English. To work in a total immersion summer camp, motivating children to speak English through different activities: sports, English language classes, arts & crafts, music, and to acquaint children with the different cultures of the English speaking world through games and songs etc.

Applicants must have experience of working with children aged 6-13, and of camps, be versatile, conscientious, oriented towards children and safety and have an outgoing personality. Experience in more than one subject area preferable.

To work during July 8am-4pm over a 4-week period Monday to Friday. Help with finding accommodation is available and lunch is included in the working day.

Applications from English speakers invited from January to English Language Day Camp, at the above address.

YOUNG AUSTRIA GmbH, Alpenstrasse 108a, A-5020 Salzburg, AUSTRIA (tel. +43/662 62 57 58-0, fax: +43/662 62 57 58-2, e-mail: office@youngaustria.at). 'English In Action!' is Young Austria!'s international Summer English language camp for young people, age 9 - 17, in beautiful Alpine settings near Salzburg.
Staff to work in English In Action! Summer English language camps. The English camps are held in two and one-week sessions, throughout the summer (July and August).
Resident Supervisor, English Teaching Positions (Academic Supervisor and Project Coordinators) and in the sports and free-time activities area (**Sports & Activities Supervisor and Coordinators**). Tutors can work on projects of their choice, including drama, grammar and a variety of recreational activities.

More information, including downloading application forms, can be found at www.camps.at, and/or www.youngaustria.at.

Belgium

Unemployment in Belgium is fairly high compared with other Western European countries and is currently reaching 12% but the economy is stable and there are work opportunities.

Although small in area Belgium is densely populated and can seem complicated to the outsider, as three languages are spoken within the country's federal states. These languages are Dutch or Flemish, French and German. In broad terms Dutch is spoken in the north (Flanders) and French in the south (Wallonia), with both being spoken in Brussels in the centre of the country; German is spoken mainly in the Eastern Cantons. With its coastal resorts Belgium has an active hotel and tourism industry in the north which makes seasonal work in Belgium a viable prospect.

EU nationals looking for work can get help from the Belgian employment services, which are organised on a regional basis. They cover three main areas: in the Flemish region the services are known as the *Vlaamse Dienst voor Arbeidsbemiddeling en Beroepsopleiding (VDAB)* - headquarters at Keizerslaan 11, B-1000 Brussels (e-mail info@vdab.be; www.vdab.be); in the French region they are *Office Wallon de la Formation Professionnelle et de l'Emploi (FOREM)* at Boulevard J. Tirou 104, B-6000 Charleroi (☎+32-71-20-61-74; e-mail communic@forem.be; www.hotjob.be/forem.be); and in the Brussels Region they are known as *Office Régional Bruxellois de l'Emploi (ORBEM)/Brusselse Gewestelijke Dienst voor Arbeidsbemiddeling (BGDA)* based at Boulevard Anspach 65, B-1000 Brussels (☎+32-2-505-14-11; e-mail info@orbem.be or info@bgda.be; www.orbem.be or www.bgda.be). There are local employment offices in most towns.

There are also some employment offices specialising in temporary work, known as the T-Interim, which are operated as Dutch and French speaking offices under the aegis of VDAB and FOREM; as may be expected the VDAB T-Interim offices are in Flanders and the French T-Interim offices are found in Wallonia, with ORBEM/BGDA running the T-Interim offices for Brussels. These offices can only help people who visit them in person, and the staff are multilingual in most cases. They can assist in finding secretarial work, especially in Brussels where there are a large number of multinational companies needing bilingual staff. Other opportunities they may have available consist of manual work in supermarkets and warehouses or engineering and computing. They are most likely to be able to help you during the summer, when companies need to replace their permanent staff who are away on holiday. T-Interims can be found on the internet at www.vdab/be/t-interim and www.forem.be/tinterim. Below are addresses of these offices in some of the larger towns:

- *T-Interim:* Sint Jacobsmarkt 66 A1, B-2000 Antwerp (☎03-232-98-60; fax 03-231-27-33).
- *T-Service :* Rue des Faubourg 37, B-6700, Arlon (☎063-22-66-45; fax 063-212-96-48).
- *T-Interim:* 24 Rue Général Molitz, B-6700 Arlon (☎063-22-66-45; fax 063-21-96-48; e-mail mh.pivetta@tinterim.com).
- *T-Interim:* Smedenstraat 4, B-8000 Brugge.
- *T-Interim:* H.Lippensplein 22, B-8000, Brugge (☎050-269-89-50; fax 050-269-89-59).
- *T-Interim:* Keizerslaan 11, B-1000 Brussels (☎02-514-57-00 ; fax 020-511-49-20; e-mail info@vdab.be; www.vdab.be).
- *T-Service Interim:* Anspachlaan 69, 1000 Brussels (☎02 511.23.85).
- *T-Interim:* Boulevard Zoe Drion 25, B-6000, Charleroi (☎071-20-50-40; fax 071-30-93-66).
- *T-Interim:* Neuestrasse 3, B-4700 Eupen (☎087-74-34-75; fax 087/55 22 64; e-mail n.lancel@tinterim.com).
- *T-Interim:* Burgstraat 49, B-9000, Ghent (tel. 09.224.09.20).
- *T-Interim:* Thonissenlaan 18 bi, B-3500 Hasselt (☎011-26-49-90; fax 011-26-49-99).
- *T-Interim:* Reepkaai 3 bus 19, B-8500 Kortrijk (☎056-25-36-90; fax 056-20-29-56).
- *T-Interim:* Boulevard de la Sauveniere 60, B-4000 Liege (☎04-230-30-80; fax 04-232 03 71; e-mail l.dechany@tinterim.com).
- *T-Interim:* Schuttersvest 75, B-2800 Mechelen (☎015-71-94-10; fax 015-71-94-09).
- *T-Interim:* Witherenstraat 19, B-1800 Vilvoorde (☎02-253-98-63; fax 02-252-23-99).
- *T-Interim* can also be found on the internet at www.tinterim.com.

You could also try advertising yourself as being available for work. One of the main newspapers published in Belgium is Le Soir (French) at Rue Royale 120, B-

1000 Brussels (☎02-225-55-00/54-32; e-mail journal@lesoir.be; www.lesoir.be). The daily newspaper De Standaard is published by VUM, Gossetlaan 30a, B-1702 Groot-Bijgaarden (Brussels) (☎032-2-467-22-11; www.standaard.be). There is a weekly English language magazine called The Bulletin; it comes out on Thursdays and is available from newsstands. The Bulletin can be contacted at 1038, Chaussée de Waterloo, B-1180 Brussels (☎02-373-99-09; e-mail info@ackroyd.be;www.belgiumpost.com) and offers of work are listed on their website www.xPATS.com. Twice a year they publish a very useful magazine-type supplement called *Newcomer* aimed at new arrivals in Belgium.

Americans can apply through Interexchange in New York (see entry in Worldwide chapter) to be placed in a summer job, internship or teaching position in Belgium. Applicants over 18 with a working knowledge of French (or Dutch) can be placed in companies or organisations for between one and three months. The programme fee is $700 and the application deadline is late April; full details on the website (www.interexchange.org).

Voluntary work in Belgium can be arranged for UK nationals by Concordia, International Voluntary Service, Youth Action For Peace or UNA Exchange. CIEE in Boston helps to place Americans in short term voluntary positions in this country, as does Service Civil International (see the International Voluntary Service entry). Entries for these organisations can be found in the *Worldwide* chapter at the beginning of the book.

Those looking for work on Belgian farms should be warned that most conventional Belgian farms are highly mechanised and thus offer little scope for casual work.

The *Fédération Infor Jeunes Wallonie-Bruxelles* is a non-profit organisation which co-ordinates 11 youth information offices plus 28 local points of contacts in French-speaking Belgium. These can give advice on work as well as leisure, youth rights, accommodation, etc. A leaflet listing the addresses is available from the *Fédération Infor Jeunes* at Henri Lemaitre 25, B-5000 Namur (☎081/71 15 90; e-mail federation@inforjeunes.be; www.inforjeunes.be). Among Infor Jeune's services, they operate holiday job placement offices (*Service Job Vacances*) between March and September.

For yet further information consult the free booklet *Working in Belgium* published by the Employment Service (see the *Useful Publications* section towards the end of this book) or for jobs abroad you can contact the European Employment Service (EURES; http://europa.eu.int/jobs/eures): EURES VDAB (☎070-345000), EURES BGDA/ORBEM (☎02-505-14-20), or EURES FOREM (☎087-30-71-10). The following three temporary work offices in Brussels are part of the BGDA/ORBEM:

Agence Centrale: Boulevard Anspach 69, 1000 Brussels; ☎02 511 23 85; fax 02 514 09 09; info@serviceinterim.be.

Schaerbeek: Grand Rue au Bois 156, 1030 Schaerbeek; ☎02/733 10 61; 02/733 17 06.

Uccle: Chaussée d'Alsemberg 764, 1180 Uccle; ☎02/333 26 00; fax 02 376 80 77.

RED TAPE, VISAS & WORK PERMITS

Visa Requirements: Visas are not required by EU/EEA citizens, or those of many other countries (including the USA, Canada, Japan, Australia and New Zealand and listed at www.diplobel.org.\uk) provided they have a valid passport and that the visit is for less than three months. Other nationalities will have to obtain an entry permit, which should be applied for at a Belgian Embassy or Consulate in advance of travel in the applicant's country of residence.

Residence Permits: All non-Belgians must register at the local Town Hall within eight days of arrival to obtain a residence permit. EU nationals should take documents proving that they have sufficient funds and a valid passport.

Work Permits: These are not required by EU/EEA nationals; others must first arrange a job, then the prospective employer should apply for a work permit at the regional ministry of employment. There are some exceptions to work permit requirements according to the employment to be taken up; consult embassies and consulates for details.

Au Pair: permitted subject to strict regulation including minimum pay and compulsory language course attendance – contact the embassy.

Voluntary Work: it is not normally necessary to obtain permits for short- term voluntary work with recognised organisations.

Hotel Work and Catering

HOTEL LIDO: Zwaluwenlaan, 18 Albert Plage, B-8300 Knokke-Heist, Belgium (☎050-60 19 25; fax 050-61 04 57; e-mail info@lido-hotel.be or lido.hotel.knokke@vt4.net)

Waiting Staff (2), basic French required,.

Kitchen Assistants (2) to work from 9-12am, 1-3pm and 6-9.30pm. Wages £550 net per month with board and lodging provided free. Minimum period of work one or two months between June and September.

Applications with a CV and recent photograph to A. Simoens at the above address.

HOSTELLERIE 'LE RY D'AVE': Sourd d'Ave 5, B-5580 Ave-ee-Auffe, Rochefort, Belgium (☎+32-(0)84-388820; fax 084-389550; e-mail ry.d.ave@skynet.be; www.rydave.be). A small family run rustic style hotel-restaurant, owned by M & Mme Marot-Champion. M. Marot-Champion runs the kitchen while Mme Marot-Champion is in charge of the restaurant.

Receptionist, Waiter/Waitress required to work a 40 hour week, of 8 hours per day over 5 days, wages around £650 per month. Outgoing friendly personality, with a hotel diploma or relevant experience necessary and preferably knowledge of English, Dutch, French or German. Board and lodging are free. Period of work between mid-May and mid-September.

Applications should be sent between February and May to M. & Mme Marot-Champion.

JULES RICAIL: 5 rue de la Gendarmerie, B-5570 Beauraing, Belgium.

Waiter/Waitress: £500 per month plus tips. To serve, lay tables and wash up. 8 hours work a day, 6 days a week. Applicant should be efficient, good humoured and able to speak French. Board and lodging free. Minimum period of work 2 months between May and July.

Applications to M Jules Ricail at the above address.

HOTEL ROYAL: Avenue de la Mer 180, B-8470 Le Panne, Belgium.

Assistant Cook. £150.34 per month. Must be catering student or qualified.

Waitresses (2). £150.34 per month.

10 hours per day. 6 day week. Free board and accommodation. Knowledge of Dutch and French required. Minimum period of work 2 months between 1st June

and 30th September.
Applications in January to the above address.

Sports, Couriers and Camping

EUROCAMP: Overseas Recruitment Department (Ref SJ/04) (☎01606-787525). Eurocamp is a leading tour operator in quality self-drive camping and mobile home holidays in Europe. Each year the company seeks to recruit up to 1,500 enthusiastic people for the following positions:

Campsite Courier: job involves cleaning and preparing customer accommodation, providing assistance, acting as an information service and performing some administrative duties. Couriers need to be flexible to meet the needs of the customer to provide them with excellent service. Minimum age 18 years. Applicants should be independent with plenty of initiative and relish a challenging and rewarding position. They should also possess a friendly and helpful personality. Previous customer service experience would be an advantage. Applicants should be available to work from April/May to September.

Children's Courier: work involves organising a wide range of exciting activities for children aged 4-13. Applicants should possess initiative, imagination and enthusiasm along with good safety awareness. Previous childcare experience is essential. Minimum age is 18 years and applicants should be available from April/May to September. Languages are not a requirement but would be an advantage (in particular German). Successful candidates will be asked to apply for an Enhanced Disclosure.

Senior Couriers: required to work alongside a team of Campsite Couriers and organise their daily workload, as well as carrying out the normal day to day duties of a Campsite Courier. Applicants should have good language skills and experience of leading a team.

Site Managers: required to lead a large team of Campsite Couriers, organising their daily workloads and ensuring they provide the very best customer service. Applicants should be 21 or over, have proven managerial experience, excellent communication skills and language ability.

Comprehensive training is provided together with a competitive salary, insurance, return travel and accommodation. Applications are accepted from September/October and *can only be accepted from UK/EU passport holders*. Interviews will be conducted in Hartford, Cheshire between October and April.

Applicants should apply on-line at www.holidaybreakjobs.com or telephone 01606 781525 for an Application Pack.

Teaching and Language Schools

VENTURE ABROAD: Rayburn House, Parcel Terrace, Derby, DE1 1LY (☎01332-224-951; 01332-22-49-60; e-mail charlottel@rayburntours.co.uk; www.ventureabroad.co.uk). Venture Abroad organise package holidays for scout and guide groups to the continent. They arrange travel and accommodation and provide representatives in the resort.

Resort Representatives (2-3) to work in Belgium and Switzerland; checking in groups, dealing with accommodation enquiries, organising and accompanying local excursions etc.

Applicants should be practical, resourceful and calm under pressure. Speaking German an advantage. To work six days a week, flexible hours. Five weeks minimum work from June to August.

Applications to the above address.

SKI TEN INTERNATIONAL: Château d'Émines B-5080 Émines, Belgium (☎+32-81-21 30 51; fax 81-20 02 63; e-mail martine@ski-ten.be; www.ski-ten.be) Ski Ten offers a marvellous experience of working a month in an international team at the Château d'Émines which has 14-hectares of grounds with lakes, swimming pool etc.

English Teacher, Tennis Teacher and **Sports Teacher** required to work and live in a summer camp in July and August. The successful candidate will work for six hours a day; duties will include looking after, eating with and arranging games for the children in their care. In return for this, a salary of £600 approx and accommodation will be provided. Some knowledge of French and previous experience working with children would be useful.

Applications should be sent in writing, with a photograph, to the above address.

Denmark

Despite the low level of unemployment (currently around 6%) in Denmark, would-be job seekers there can have a hard time of it, especially if they don't have some notion of the Danish language. Non-EU/EEA citizens will find it hard to obtain a job in Denmark, as work permits are only issued where an employer can prove that there is no EU citizen who can do that job.

Anyone serious about wanting to work in Denmark should obtain a copy of the free booklet *Working in Denmark* published by the Employment Service in Britain (see the *Useful Publications* chapter towards the end of this book). In 2004 there will be a new edition of a useful leaflet called *Working in Denmark* which is available from Use It Tourist Information, part of the Youth Information, at Radhusstraede 13, 1466 Copenhagen K, Denmark (☎+45-33-730620; fax +45 33 73 06 49; e-mail useit@kff.kk.dk; www.useit.dk). Please note that *Use It* is not an employment agency but an information centre for low budget travellers.

Despite the increasing mechanisation of farming there is still a need for fruit pickers during the summer; up to 1,000 people are needed each year for the strawberry harvest. Be warned, however, that the hours can be very long when you are paid by the kilo with picking taking place between 6am and noon. The main harvests are strawberries in June/July, cherries in July/August, apples in September/October and tomatoes throughout the summer. Fruit producing areas are scattered around the country: some of the most important are to be found to the north of Copenhagen, around Arhus, and to the east and west of Odense.

You may be able to obtain a job on a farm or other work by contacting the pan-European agency EURES through your local job centre; vacancies for the fruit harvest and other seasonal work are announced in the spring on the Danish EURES website www.eures.dk where an online application can be made.

Another method is to advertise in the farming magazine LandbrugsAvisen (Vester Farimagsgade 6, 2 sal, DK-1606 Copenhagen V; ☎+45-33-39-4700; fax +45-33-39-4729; www.landbrugsAvisen.dk).

It is also possible to arrange unpaid work on an organic farm. Another possibility is to contact VHH (the Danish WWOOF) to obtain a list of their 25-30 member farmers, most of whom speak English. In return for three or four hours of work per day, you get free food and lodging. Always phone or write before arriving. The list can be obtained only after sending £5/US$10 to Inga Nielsen, Asenvej

35, 9881 Bindslev.

The Danish state employment service is obliged to help Britons and other EU nationals who call at their offices to find a job. The administrative headquarters of the employment service – the National Labour Market Authority (*Arbejdsma rkedsstyrelsen*) – is at Blegdamsvej 56, Postboks 2722, DK-2100 Copenhagen (☎45-3528-8100; e-mail ams@ams.dk; www.ams.dk). When you are actually in Denmark, you can find the address of your nearest employment office under *Arbejdsformidlingen* in the local telephone directory.

There are also opportunities for voluntary work in Denmark, arranged by International Voluntary Service, UNA Exchange, Youth Action for Peace and Concordia for British applicants and CIEE and Service Civil International for Americans. See the *Worldwide* chapter for details. It is also possible to work as a volunteer as the Roskilde Festival (see www.roskilde-festival.dk or go to www.roskilde-festival.dk/object.php?obj=c1000c.

There are a number of private employment agencies in Denmark, but most are looking for trained secretarial staff who speak fluent Danish.

An advertisement in a Danish paper may bring an offer of employment. Crane Media Partners Ltd, 20-28 Dalling Road, Hammersmith, W6 OJB (☎020-8237 8601; fax 020-8735 9941) are advertising agents for *Berlingske Tidende*. *Morgenavisen-Jyllands-Posten*, one of the more important papers for job advertisements, is published at Grondalsvej 3, DK-8260 Viby J, Denmark (☎+45-87-38-38-38).

RED TAPE, VISAS & WORK PERMITS

Visa Requirements: a visa is not required by citizens of EU countries.
Residence Permits: A residence permit (*Opholdsbevis*) should be applied for through Kobenhavns Overpraesidium at Hammerensgade 1, 1267 Copenhagen K, Denmark, (☎33 12 23 80). EU nationals wishing to stay in Denmark for longer than 3 months and all visitors from non-EU countries must gain a residence permit.
Work Permits: The Royal Danish Embassy has indicated that nationals of countries not in the EU or Scandinavia will not be granted work permits except where the employer can prove that the applicant has a unique skill. Further details can be obtained from the Danish Immigration Service website (www.udlst.dk). EU nationals who wish to take up employment in Denmark may stay there for a period not exceeding 3 months from the date of arrival in order to seek employment provided they have sufficient funds to support themselves.
Au Pair: allowed, but subject to the regulations outlined above. Prospective au pairs will need an au pair contract.
Voluntary Work: all work, paid and unpaid, is subject to the above regulations.

Agricultural Work

ALSTRUP FRUGTPLANTAGE: Alstrupvej 1, Alstrup, DK-8305 Samsø, Denmark (☎86591338; fax 86593138, e-mail elicc@samso.com; www.alstrupf rugt.subnet.dk). Samsø is an island with lovely beaches and beautiful scenery. In addition to strawberries the farm has an apple orchard, and around 60 fruitpickers work here each year from across the EU.
Strawberry Pickers. Wages at piece work rates of approximately £0.50 per kilo. To work from 6am to 1pm with one day off a week. The season normally runs from around the 15 June until 20 July, but may be earlier or later. *Applicants must be EU*

nationals aged at least 19. Those accepted will need their own camping equipment.

Applications should be sent before 1 May, and confirmation before 15 May to Carl Christian B. Jensen at the above address.

BIRKHOLM FRUGT & BAER: V/Bjarne Knutsen, Hornelandevej 2 D, DK-5600 Faaborg, Denmark (tel/fax 62602262; e-mail birkholm@strawberrypicking.dk; www.strawberrypicking.dk).
Strawberry Pickers: for the season which lasts for around six weeks from 1st June, approximately. Payment at piece work rates of around £0.50 per kilo. Workers are given space to put up their own tents and have the use of a bathroom and basic cooking facilities. Minimum period of work two weeks. *Applicants must be EEA nationals.*

Contact the above address or check the website for further information.

Sports, Couriers and Camping

EUROCAMP: Overseas Recruitment Department (Ref SJ/04) (☎01606-787525). Eurocamp is a leading tour operator in quality self-drive camping and mobile home holidays in Europe. Each year the company seeks to recruit up to 1,500 enthusiastic people for the following positions:
Campsite Courier: job involves cleaning and preparing customer accommodation, providing assistance, acting as an information service and performing some administrative duties. Couriers need to be flexible to meet the needs of the customer to provide them with excellent service. Minimum age 18 years. Applicants should be independent with plenty of initiative and relish a challenging and rewarding position. They should also possess a friendly and helpful personality. Previous customer service experience would be an advantage. Applicants should be available to work from April/May to September.
Children's Courier: work involves organising a wide range of exciting activities for children aged 4-13. Applicants should possess initiative, imagination and enthusiasm along with good safety awareness. Previous childcare experience is essential. Minimum age is 18 years and applicants should be available from April/ May to September. Languages are not a requirement but would be an advantage (in particular German). Successful candidates will be asked to apply for an Enhanced Disclosure.
Senior Couriers: required to work alongside a team of Campsite Couriers and organise their daily workload, as well as carrying out the normal day to day duties of a Campsite Courier. Applicants should have good language skills and experience of leading a team.
Site Managers: required to lead a large team of Campsite Couriers, organising their daily workloads and ensuring they provide the very best customer service. Applicants should be 21 or over, have proven managerial experience, excellent communication skills and language ability.

Comprehensive training is provided together with a competitive salary, insurance, return travel and accommodation. Applications are accepted from September/ October and *can only be accepted from UK/EU passport holders.* Interviews will be conducted in Hartford, Cheshire between October and April.

Applicants should apply on-line at www.holidaybreakjobs.com or telephone 01606-781525 for an Application Pack.

Voluntary Work and Archaeology

MELLEMFOLKELIGT SAMVIRKE (MS): Stuosgade 20, DK-8000 Arhus C, Denmark (☎8619-7766).
Volunteers to work in international work camps in Denmark and Greenland. The camps normally involve community projects such as **conservation of playgrounds, renovation, conservation, archaeological work, nature protection, reconditioning of used tools to be later sent to Africa,** etc. Board and accommodation are provided but the participants must provide their own travelling expenses.

The camps last from 2 to 3 weeks between July and September. Applicants should be aged over 18. British applicants should apply through IVS, IVS Field Office, Old Hall, East Bergholt, Colchester CO7 6TQ. The work is hard and demands commitment: the traditional IVS slogan is 'Holiday makers need not apply'. IVS welcomes applications from people of all racial, cultural and social backgrounds.

Applications to the above address.

U-LANDSFORENINGEN SVALERNE: Oesterbrogade 49, DK-2100 Copenhagen 0, Denmark (☎+45-35-26-17-47; fax +45-35-38-17-46; svalerne@svalerne.dk; www.svalerne.dk). The Swallows in Denmark is a non-profit grassroots organisation founded in 1963. It is economically and religiously independent and today has 400 members.
Volunteers are needed to help U-lansforeningen Svalerne (Swallows in Denmark) with **rag-picking work for raising funds for grassroot movements among the poor landless people in South India and Bangladesh.** Funds are raised by the sale at second-hand markets of the items collected by volunteers. The camp lasts for four weeks in July. Period of work is two weeks. 6-8 hours work per day. One day (Sunday) and two afternoons off a week. Accommodation and food provided free of charge. Volunteers provide their own travel costs and pocket money. Knowledge of English preferred.

Applications to the above address from January.

Finland

Finland offers short-term paid training opportunities. The Center for International Mobility CIMO (PO Box 343, 00531 Helsinki, Finland; 09-7747 7033/fax 09-7747 7064; cimoinfo@cimo.fi/ www.cimo.fi or http://finland.cimo.fi), coordinates IAESTE (the International Association for the Exchange of Students for Technical Experience) exchange in Finland. IAESTE trainees obtain technical experience abroad relative to their studies. Participation in the IAESTE exchange is normally open to students of universities, institutes of technology and similar institutions of higher education in the fields of engineering, technology and science. British students who are interested in an IAESTE placement in Finland should apply through IAESTE in their home country (www.iaeste.org.uk). The website is in English.

Voluntary work in Finland can be arranged for British applicants by International Voluntary Service, Concordia and UNA Exchange as well as Service Civil International (see the IVS entry) and CIEE for Americans; see the *Worldwide* chapter for details. You may be able to find a job by advertising in a Finnish newspaper. *Helsingin Sanomat* is the largest circulation paper in Finland as well as *Turun Sanomat* and *Aamulehti*.

RED TAPE, VISAS & WORK PERMITS

Visa Requirements: citizens of most countries, including the United Kingdom, the United States of America, Australia and New Zealand and all Western European countries do not normally require a visa for a visit of less than three months unless they are taking up employment.

Residence Permits: EU nationals are allowed to enter and work in Finland for up to three months, if they wish to stay longer then a residence permit must be obtained from the local police station. Non-EU/EEA nationals must obtain work and residence permits.

Work Permits: British and Irish citizens and nationals of other EEA countries do not need work permits in order to work in Finland. If you are from a non-EEA country your application for such permits may be made at a Finnish Embassy and for this you will need a letter and permission to work (obtained by the employer from their local employment office) from your prospective employer in Finland. The application is then taken to your nearest embassy where work and residence permits must be obtained. Anyone intending to work in Finland should not enter the country before all formalities have been completed.

Working Holidays: Australian citizens can now apply to the Finnish Embassy for a working holiday of up to one year. Full details can be found at www.virtual.finland.fi or www.suomi.fi.

Au Pair: in Finland this type of arrangement is popular and can be made for male as well as female students.

Hotel Work and Catering

HOTEL RUOTSINSALMI: Kirkkokatu 14, Kotka 10, Finland

Waiter and **Waitress:** wages by arrangement. Preferably with experience.

Kitchen Assistants/Dish Washers (2). Wages on application.

An 8 hour day, 5 day week is worked. Board and accommodation available at approximately £35 per month. Must have some knowledge of Swedish, and if possible Finnish. Minimum period of work 2/3 months between 1 May and 31 August.

Applications until the end of March to the above address.

France

France has long been one of the most popular destinations for British and Irish people looking for summer work. This is due to its physical proximity: the fact that French is the first (and often only) foreign language learned; and, possibly most important of all, because during the summer France still needs many extra temporary workers for both its vibrant tourist trade and farm work. Theme parks like Disneyland Paris or Parc Asterix need extra staff even though there is currently fairly high unemployment of about 9.0% .

Although Disneyland Paris alone employs many thousands of seasonal workers to supplement their permanent staff, this chapter contains details of many jobs in the tourist industry: you can find others in the *Worldwide* chapter at the beginning of the book and in the weekly hotel trade magazine *L'Hotellerie* published at 5, rue Antoine Bourdelle, 75015 Paris, (☎45 48 64 64; fax 45 48 04 23; www.lhotellerie.fr).

British and Irish citizens, along with other EU nationals, are allowed to use the French national employment service (*Agence Nationale pour l'Emploi*), the headquarters of which is at Le Galilee, 4 rue Galilee, 93198 Noisy-le-Grand (☎149-31-74-00), although the offices in towns throughout France will know more about vacancies in their region. There is also a comprehensive website detailing the services provided by ANPE in both French and English: www.anpe.fr. British citizens can apply for work through the service by visiting any of almost 600 *Agences Nationales pour l'Emploi* (ANPE) around the country. The ANPE for Narbonne (ANPE, BP 802, 29 rue Mazzini, 11008 Narbonne Cedex) has seasonal hotel vacancies from May to September, and others can provide details of when agricultural work is available.

There are also a number of private employment agencies such as *Manpower*, *Kelly*, *Bis*, *Select France*, and *Ecco* in large cities which can help people who speak reasonable French to find temporary jobs in offices, private houses, warehouses, etc. They can be found in the Yellow Pages (*Les Pages Jaunes*) under *Agences de Travail Temporaire*. These can normally only find jobs for people who visit in person.

For further information relevant to British citizens consult the free booklet *Working in France* published by the UK's national Jobcentre Plus (see the *Useful Publications* chapter towards the end of this book).

CIEE in the USA administers a *Work in France Programme* for American citizens, see their entry in the *Worldwide* chapter.

Seasonal farm work can be difficult to obtain from outside France. If you cannot arrange a job in advance using the information in this chapter it is best to be on the spot and approach farmers in person, or ask at the local employment offices, town halls (*mairies*) or youth hostels. A word of warning: if you arrange to go grape picking with an organisation not mentioned in this chapter read the small print carefully: you may be buying just a journey out to France, with no guarantee of a job at the end.

For help in finding temporary work during the grape picking season, you could contact ANPE. ANPE have offices in most large towns in France's main agricultural regions. Each office can offer around 1000 jobs to those who wish to work on farms up to 50km from the town, apple-picking and grape-picking being the most prevalent jobs available and within a the prior month or so, they will be able to inform you of the approximate date of the beginning of the harvest.

The addresses and dates for the ANPE below are provided only as a guide: there is no guarantee either that they will have definite vacancies to offer, and the exact dates of harvests can vary considerably from year to year and from region to region. The work period also varies. The ANPE office in Castelnaudry asked to be removed from this edition as the maize-topping work in their region only lasts 4 days.

For temporary agricultural work (July-September):
   ❍   ANPE, 33 avenue Henri Farbos, F-40000 Mont de Marsan (☎5-58-85-43-40).

For grape picking (by region):
Alsace – 15th October
   ❍   ANPE, 54, Avenue de la Republique, BP 50868021, Colmar (☎3-89-20-80-70; fax 0389-20-80-78).
Beaujolais – 10th September
   ❍   ANPE, 8 Rue du 14 Juillet, 69220 Belleville (☎0-4-74-66-14-10).
Bordeaux – 25th September

KEYCAMP
Holidays

Keycamp is Europe's leading Tour Operator and the leader in self-drive, self-catering holidays on campsites in Europe. Operating in 8 countries throughout Europe on over 100 campsites, we sell family holidays to customers from the UK, Ireland, Holland, and Denmark.

We employ around 1,200 campsite staff every year from many of these countries and can offer a large range of positions to suit all our overseas employees.

We are looking for people for various positions that involve **customer service, working with children, leading a team and administration.** We also employ teams of people at the beginning and end of the season to help us erect and dismantle tents. Successful applicants will be asked to apply for a Standard or Enhanced Disclosure.*

We will provide:
- Competitive Salary
- Accommodation
- Uniform
- Subsidised Insurance
- Training
- Travel To Resort

You will need to be:
- 18+
- An EU passport holder (or have a work permit for any of the countries that we operate in)
- Available to *start* work between April and July

If you think you have the qualities to provide our customers with the 'perfect family holiday' please apply online at **www.holidaybreakjobs.com** or phone **01606 7897525** for an application pack. Please quote **SJ/04**.

* Further information about Disclosures can be found at www.disclosure.gov.uk or by phoning 0870 90 90 811.

○ ANPE, 34, avenue du General Leclerc, F-33210 Langon (☎05-57-98-02-60).
○ ANPE, Chemin du Casse, F-33500 Libourne (☎5-57-55-32-20).
○ ANPE, 19, rue Adrien Chauvet, BP 108, 33250 Pauillac (☎5-56-73-20-50; fax 5-56-59-62-49).

Burgundy – 10th September
○ ANPE, 6 boulevard St. Jacques, B.P. 115, F-21203 Beaune (☎3-80-25-07-06).
○ ANPE, 71 rue Jean-Macé, F-71031 Macon Cedex (☎3-85-21-93-20; fax 03-85-38-46-88).

Languedoc-Roussilon – 15th September
○ ANPE, BP 65, 29 av. Léon Blum, 30205 Bagnols sur Ceze.
○ ANPE, BP 4236, 13 Alphonse Mas, 34544 Beziers Cedex.
○ ANPE, 90 Avenue Pierre Sémard, BP 586 Iéna,11009 Carcassonne Iéna Cedex.
○ ANPE, BP 3054, 60 rue Siegfried, 30002 Nimes Cedex.

Indre et Loire – early September to Mid-October (Apple-picking also available).
○ ANPE Joue Les Tours, Champ Girault, 57 rue Chantepie, B.P. 304, 37303 Joue Les Tours CEDEX (☎2-47-60-58-58).

Workers are also needed to help harvest the following fruits, especially in the valleys of the Loire and the Rhone and the south east and south west of the country. The dates given are only approximate: bear in mind that harvests tend to begin first in the south of the country.

○ *Strawberries:* May to mid-June
○ *Cherries:* mid-May to early July
○ *Peaches:* June to September
○ *Pears:* mid-July to mid-November
○ *Apples:* mid-August (but chiefly from mid-September) to mid-October.

French farmers employ over 100,000 foreigners for seasonal work during the summer. Many of these are skilled 'professional' seasonal workers from Spain, Portugal and Morocco who return to the same regions every year: if there is a choice of applicants for a job, a farmer will prefer an experienced worker to a total beginner. In recent years there has also been an influx of people from Eastern Europe who are desperate for work and prepared to work for less than the minimum wage (*le SMIC*, which is €6.83 per hour) for any farmer who will employ them illegally. Anyone going to France to look for farm work should be prepared to move from area to area in the search for a job: it would also be wise to take enough money to cover the cost of returning home in case of failure. Also be warned that payment is generally by piece work, so there are no wages if picking is suspended because of bad weather.

The publishers Mitchell Beazley produce a series of useful guides to wine regions (Alsace, Bordeaux, Provence, Rhone and Loire) under the title *Touring in Wine Country* which cost £12.99 each. You can remove some of the uncertainty of the job-hunt by visiting farmers to arrange a job before their harvests start: by doing so you should also be given an informed estimate of when the harvest will start. Note that although vineyard owners normally provide accommodation for grape pickers, workers on other harvests will normally need camping equipment.

The increasing sophistication of the ANPE means that grape-picking and fruit picking jobs are advertised on the their website (www.anpe.fr) in English.

France is rich in opportunities for voluntary work, as the entries at the end of this chapter will testify. The CIEE in the US and Service Civil International (see the IVS entry) can assist Americans. International Voluntary Service (IVS), UNA Exchange, Youth Action for Peace and Concordia can help can UK residents to find short term voluntary work; their entries can be found in the *Worldwide* chapter at the beginning of the book.

A great many archaeological digs and building restoration projects are carried out each year. The French Ministry of Culture has two departments dealing with antiquities, one focuses on archaeology and the other on the restoration of monuments (Ministère de la Culture, *Direction de l'Architecture et du Patrimoine, Sous-Direction de l'Archeologie*, 4 rue d'Aboukir, 75002 Paris (☎1-40-15-77-81) and Ministère de la Culture, *Direction du Patrimoine, Sous-Direction des Monuments Historiques* at the same address (☎1-40-15-76-81). Each year the ministry publishes in a brochure and on the internet (www.culture.gouv.fr/fouilles) a list of these archaeological fieldwork projects throughout France requiring up to 5,000 volunteers. Another brochure, *Chantiers de benevoles* published by Rempart (see entry under Voluntary Work), lists projects relating to building restoration. It has pages in English or can be found at www.rempart.com.

Advertising for a job in France can be arranged in the Paris edition of the *International Herald Tribune* contact the London office, 40, Marsh Wall, London E14 9TP (☎020-7836 4802; e-mail ukadv@iht.com), or New York Office, 850 Third Avenue, New York, NY 10022 (☎212-752 3890; e-mail usadv@iht.com), or on the internet www.iht.com.

RED TAPE, VISAS & WORK PERMITS

Visa Requirements: visas are not required for visits to France by EU, American, Canadian, Australian or New Zealand nationals. Others should check with their nearest French Consulate.

Residence Permits: such permits (*cartes de séjour*) are necessary for foreigners staying for more than 3 months in France. Application for this permit should be made on a special form available from the *Prefecture de Police* in Paris, or the local *Prefecture* or *Mairie* (town hall) elsewhere. The following documents are required: passport, birth certificate, proof of accommodation, proof of payment of contributions to the French Social Security, 3 passport photos, a contract of employment, pension receipts or student status documents. Non-EU nationals need to possess a long stay visa before applying for a *carte de séjour*, and a work permit before obtaining either. Application for a long stay visa should be lodged with a French consulate in the applicant's country of residence.

Work Permits: Member of the EU/EEA do not need work permits to work in France. The standard procedure for non-EEA nationals is that the prospective employer in France must apply to the *Office des Migrations Internationales* in Paris (44 Rue Bargue, 75015 Paris; ☎0153-695370; www.omi.social.fr) only after receiving permission from the DDTEFP which oversees the employment of foreign professionals.

Au Pair: the family with which you are to stay should apply to the Direction Departmentale de Travail for the necessary *Accord de Placement au pair d'un stagiaire aide-familial.*

Voluntary Work: a work permit is necessary for non-EEA nationals.

Agricultural Work

BERNARD LACOMBE: Les Crouzets, F-12160 Baraqueuille, France (☎05-65-69-01-46).
Farm Helper to milk cows and feed animals on a farm in the South of France. To work 4 hours a day, 6 days a week. Pocket money and board and lodging provided. Some knowledge of French required. Minimum period of work 1 month at any time of the year. Applicants must be hard-working and like nature and animals. There is also the possibility of some supplementary Bed & Breakfast related work.
Applications to M. Lacombe at the above address.

G. ESPINASSE: Sevignac, Druelle F-12510, Olemps, France.
Farm Helper to carry out all types of work in the field and assist with breeding (mainly sheep), also to study and practise bio-organic farming. No salary but about £30 per month pocket money and the opportunity to learn about herbal medicines and the occult sciences. Board and lodging provided. Some knowledge of French useful. Minimum period of work 2-3 months all year round.
Applications, in French, as soon as possible to the above address.

FERME DES BERTTRANGES: Murlin, 58700 Premery, France (☎386-38-17-58).
General Assistant to work on a 40 hectare farm with goats, pigs, cows etc; duties to consist of general farm work including cheese production, looking after animals, erecting fences etc. Wages of around £115 per month. To work for around ten hours per day, 6 days per week. Period of work by arrangement around the year. Applicants should speak English and French and love animals and nature.
Applications should be sent to Chantal Villain at the above address at any time.

M. MICHEL GARRIC: Cesars, le Pas, F-12510 Druelle, France (☎565-69-33-15).
Student required to assist on a French dairy farm. No salary is paid, but full board and lodging with family, laundry and insurance are provided. It is essential that applicants speak French; they must also be prepared to work hard, face very long hours, improve their spoken French and learn something about agriculture and French family life.
Applications should be sent to M. Garric at the above address.

S.C.A. SOLDIVE: BP 72 - Brie, F-79102 THOUARS Cedex, FRANCE (☎05-49-67-41-61; fax 05-49-67-43-56; e-mail SOLDIVE@wanadoo.fr).
Farm Labourers (1,000) to harvest melons.
Workers (30) to pack the fruit in factories.
Mechanics (30) to repair and maintain farm machinery, must speak French.
Wages are at French SMIC rates. To work 6 days per week and 6 hours per day. Minimum period of work 2 months between August and October. EU nationals, must be in possession of a temporary residence permit, student card.
Applications to the above addres.

Boats

CONTINENTAL WATERWAYS: PO Box 31, Godalming, Surrey GU8 6JH (☎01252-703577; fax: 01252-702860; e-mail crew@continentalwaterways.co.uk; www.continentalwaterways.co.uk (Recruitment); www.continentalwaterways.com

(Marketing)). French Office: Continentale de Croisières SA, 1 Promenade du Rhin, BP 41748, F-21017 Dijon, France (fax +33 380-41-6773). Continental Waterways have operated a fleet of luxury floating hotel barges on the waterways of France for the last 30 years.

Crew Members required to work from March to November in a fleet of 15 luxury hotel barges, including 3 large river boats, crewed by French, British and other EU nationalities. The company require high standards and are looking for highly committed team players to provide excellent service to mainly American passengers. This is an ideal job for those who wish to improve their language skills, appreciate gourmet food, wine and cheese and who wish to immerse themselves in French culture for 7 months. Benefits include three weeks paid holiday, medical insurance, uniform and training. *Applicants must have a valid permanent National Insurance number and hold a British or EU passport.*

Download an *application form* and send it with a CV to Sarah-Jane Borradaile, Crew Recruitment at the above UK address.

CROISIERES TOURISTIQUES FRANCAISES, 2 Route de Semur, F-21150 Venarey-les-Laumes, France (☎3-80-96-17-10; fax 3-80-96-19-18; e-mail ctf.bateau@wanadoo.fr). Croisieres Touristiques Francaises owns and operates five ultra-deluxe hotel barges, offering six-night cruises in five regions of central France The clientele is principally North American.

Chefs. Gross salary from £1.300 per month. Required to plan menus and prepare gourmet cuisine. Professional training and experience in haute cuisine establishments essential. Some knowledge of French useful.

Drivers/Guides. Gross salary from £1,100 per month. Applicants must have a P.S.V. licence, should speak fluent French and have a full knowledge of French heritage and culture.

Pilots. Gross salary from £1,300 per month. Must have French Inland Waterways Permit to drive 38m Hotel Barge and have mechanical experience. Some knowledge of French useful

Stewardesses. Gross salary from £900 per month. Work involves cleaning cabins, general housekeeping, food/bar service and care of passengers. Knowledge of French useful, but not essential.

Deckhands. Gross salary from £900 per month. To assist the Pilot during navigation and mooring and to carry out exterior maintenance of the barge. Some knowledge of French useful.

Crew Members must be EU nationals, or possess appropriate visas permitting work in France and be available for work from April to early November. Salaries quoted are for inexperienced crew members and include accommodation, full board and uniform. Social Security coverage is taken care of by the Company. Gratuities are divided equally amongst crew members. Minimum age 21. For all positions the hours of work are long, over a five to six day week. Applicants must be energetic, personable, and able to provide a consistently high standard of service.

Apply with CV, contact telephone number and recent photo to Mr. Thierry Bresson at the above address.

Holiday Centres

DISNEYLAND PARIS: Casting, BP110, F-77777 Marne La Vallée cedex 4, France. Disneyland Paris will see many exciting developments in 2003.

Permanent or Seasonal Staff to work in the restaurants, on counter service or reception, in sales, for the attractions, sports and leisure attractions of the Disneyland

Paris Resort situated 30 km east of Paris. Both temporary contracts lasting 2-8 months from March (minimum availability July-August) or permanent contracts starting at any time. 35 hour working week; monthly gross wage of €1,103.39 (approx. £775) less social security contributions. Assistance is given in finding accommodation and a contribution towards travel expenses is given to those who complete their contract.

Applicants should be at least 18, have a good working knowledge of French and be customer-service orientated. Experience not essential.

Applications in writing to the above address.

Hotel Work and Catering

HOTEL ABBAYE DE SAINTE CROIX: Val de Cuech, 13300 Salon-de-Provence, France (+33 490 56 98 58; fax +33 490 56 31 12; e-mail cb@abbaye-de-sainte-croix.com; www.relaischateaux/saintecroix). During the high season employs 50 staff for 25 rooms and a restaurant seating 60. Most of the head staff have been at the hotel for 20 years.

Dining Room/Commis Staff (2) in charge of courses between dining room and kitchen and service and cleaning of back office. Restaurant school level.

Kitchen Commis Staff (2) in charge of the basics in kitchen and cold first courses. Restaurant school level and one season minimum training in a guide rated restaurant.

Chamber Staff (3) in charge of the cleaning of hotel rooms. Training given.

Hotel and Restaurant Polyvalents (general assistants) x 3 in charge cleaning kitchen and back ofice after service and silver utensils. Training given.

All salaries of €982 (£687) are given net of all charges (social security, housing, food etc). Minimum period of work is 4 months between March/April and September/October. Basic French necessary or useful according to positions.

Apply from January to Mme Catherine Bossard, Manager at the above address or e-mail.

ALP ACTIVE: Unit 9, Chesterton Mill, Frenchies Road, Cambridge CB4 3NP (☎0845 1209 872; fax 0845 6449385; info@alpactive.com; www.alpactive.com). Alp Active provides activity sports holidays in the French Alps. It is aimed at anyone from keen mountain-bikers to families.

Chefs (3) to work six-day week from 9am-midday and 4.30pm-9pm, catering for maximum 20 people. Wages approximately £500 monthly plus benefits.

Chalet Hosts (4) to work a six-day week same hours as chefs, running a chalet for 12-16 people. Wages approx. £450 plus benefits.

Nannies (6) to work a five-day week from 10am-4pm. Wage approx. £400 plus Must be qualified nanny, nurse or play leader.

All staff get free board and lodging.

Apply immediately to the above address or e-mail.

ALPINE TRACKS: 40 High Street, Menai Bridge, Anglesey LL59 5EF (☎01248-717440; fax 01248-717441; e-mail info@alpinetracks.com; www.alpinetracks.com). Alpine Tracks are a friendly and informal small professional holiday company operating chalets with a high level of personal service in the French Alps for skiers and mountain bikers.

Chef, Cleaners (3), Minibus Driver, Bar person, Mountain Bike and Ski Guides to earn between £350-£500 for dining and bar work, catering for up to 30 people. Applicants should be friendly, outgoing, preferably French speakers and hold relevant qualifications. Hours of work are 7am to 10am and 5pm to 9pm 7 days per week, between 1 July and 30 September; minimum period of work 2 months. Board and lodging are provided at no cost.

Applications are invited from September onwards.

L'ALAMBIC ROCK CAFÉ: 48 Avenue de la Mer, F-85160 St Jean de Monts, France (☎00 33 25158 06 83). A lively and very busy Tex Mex restaurant and Rock Café situated in the main tourist area of St Jean. The friendly French owner employs a staff of 10 for the season.

Barman/Woman, Waiter/Waitress: Dynamic, fun loving and fit young people sought to work in June, July and August. Must speak good French and have previous experience in fast-moving bar/restaurant.Wage £170 per week and free accommodation.

To *apply* send a CV and photo to Bertrand Boissinot at the above address.

HOTEL RESTAURANT ALTAIR: 18 Boulevard Féart, F-35800 Dinard, France (☎02-99 46 13 58; fax 02-99 88 20 49). Pleasant two-star hotel-restaurant with terrace, near St Malo.

Chef, Waiter/Waitress, Chambermaid required to work hours as required by the job over a 5½ day week, minimum of 4 hours work per day. Waiting staff will be serving meals in the restaurant and on the terrace. Wages and period of work by arrangement. Applicants should speak French and English or German, and have some previous experience of hotel work.

Places are available all year round and *applications* should be sent to the above address.

MOTEL ARCADE: 60, Quai de Bosc, F-34200 Sete, France (☎467-74-95-90).
Receptionist: work includes reception duties, setting breakfast and putting away washing up. Wages by arrangement. To work 45 hours per 5½ day week. Free board and lodging provided.

To work either in the Easter holidays or for at least one month between 1 June and 30 October. Applicants must be adaptable, fit in with a team and speak French and some English and German.

Applications to the above address from January.

HOTEL ARVERNE: Ave Antoine Fayets, F-15800 Vic sur Cere, France (☎471-49-60-54; fax 471-49-63-82).
Barman (1), Waitresses (2), Kitchen Porter (1). Wages approx. £180 per month plus tips, food, accommodation and free ski pass. To work 5 days per week during the summer from June to August and in winter from January (or possibly late December) to March. Must have catering experience.

Applications should be sent to Mr Michel at the above address with a curriculum vitae in French and a recent photo, stating when available to work.

L'AUBERGE DU CHOUCAS: F-05220 Monetier le Bains, Serre-Chevalier 1500, Hautes-Alpes, France (☎492-24-42-73; fax 492-24-51-60). The hotel is a converted old farm, and prides itself on its attentive service and its gastronomic food. It is located in a charming and lively village in one of the most important ski resorts in France. The area is a popular tourist destination throughout the year.

Hotel Staff (2); wages and duties by arrangement. To work 5 days per week. Board and accommodation provided. Minimum period of work 12 weeks in the summer or winter, or any other longer period.

There is a family atmosphere, but diligent work is demanded. Applicants should be discreet and well-educated, have a pleasant disposition, speak a minimum of basic French and preferably have previous hotel or restaurant work. The manageress attaches great importance to language ability and sensitivity to the culture. Some knowledge of German would also be an advantage.

Applications should be sent to Nicole Sanchez-Ventura at the above address.

L'AUBERGE SUR LA MONTAGNE: La Thuile, F-73640 Sainte Foy Tarentaise, France (☎4-79 06 95 83; fax 4-79 06 95 96; e-mail sue&andymac@auberge-montagne.co.uk; www.auberge-montagne.co.uk). This private 8-bed hotel is situated in the French alps between Val D'Isère an Bourg Saint Maurice. There are great opportunities for, walking, cycling, watersports and paragliding, as well as glacier skiing in summer.

Waitress/Chambermaid required to clean rooms, public areas (bar, lounge and restaurant), wash up and help serve breakfasts and dinner. Hours of work 7.30-11.30am four days per week, and 7-10pm 7 days per week. Period of work mid-July to end of August. Minimum period of work is six weeks. Wages are €400 (£280) per month with free board and lodging. Applicants should have some previous experience and speak English and French.

To *apply* contact Sue & Andy MacInnes from May onwards.

AUDE HOTEL: aire de Narbonne, Vinasson, Autoroute A9, 11110 Vinasson, France (☎468-45-25-00; fax 468-45-25-20).

Hotel Staff to work in reception, serve in the restaurant, clean, take messages, various other duties as necessary. Wages at the usual national rate. To work 8 hours per day, with one day off per 48 hour week. Period of work by arrangement. Accommodation can be provided at the usual national rate. Applicants should have a good sense of service and a desire to work well; they should also, if possible, speak French, English, German and Italian.

Applications should be sent to the Manager at the above address between March and April.

HOTEL DU BAS-BREAU: 22 Rue Grande, F-77630 Barbizon, France (01-60-66-40-05; fax 01-60-69-22-89; e-mail basbreau@wanadoo.fr; www.bas-breau.com).

Waiting Assistant, Washer up. Wages according to qualifications and experience. To work 5 days per week. Board and accommodation provided. Minimum period of work 2 months. Knowledge of French and English necessary.

Chambermaid to clean rooms and bathroom. 39 hours per week; 2 months minimum. Approx. £375 per month, with board and lodging provided. A little French speaking necessary.

Applications to M Jean Pierre Fava at the above address from the beginning of the year.

HOSTELLERIE LE BEFFROI: BP 85, F-84110 Vaison la Romaine, Provence, France (☎490-36-04-71; fax 490-36-24-78; www.le-beffroi.com).

Reception Assistant, Bar, Kitchen and Restaurant Staff. Duties by arrangement. To work 8 hours per day, 5 days per week. Wages of around €800 (£560) per month, board and accommodation provided. Minimum period of work 3 months between April and the end of September. Applicants should speak French (and German if possible) and must have experience of hotel or restaurant work.

Applications to Yann Christiansen at the above address.

HOTEL LA BELLE ETOILE: Le Bettex, St. Gervais, F-74170 France (☎+33-450 93 11 83; fax; +33-450 93 14 91; e-mail kieron@belleetoile.com; www.belleetoile.com). Small, friendly chalet style hotel run by British family. Clients are mainly British adults on organised walking holidays with some school groups on Field Study Tours.

Chambermaid/Waitress (3) to carry out hotel work including cleaning rooms and public areas, waiting tables and performing a small amount of bar work in Le Bettex, St. Gervais. Guests are normally Britons on walking or skiing holidays. To work split shifts approx.eight hours per day, six days a week. Wages £168 per week plus board and lodging. Minimum period of work 3½ months from early June to mid September. Knowledge of French an advantage but not essential.

Applicants must have common sense, a mature outlook and take pride in their work. The positions would suit people who enjoy an outdoors/mountain environment. Travel from the UK and medical insurance provided and training is given.

Applications from December onwards to the above address.

HOTEL BELLE ISLE SUR RISLE: 112 Route de Rouen, F-27500 Pont-Audemer, France (☎232-56-96-22; fax 232-42-88-96).

Waiter (1); Receptionist (1) to work at reception and switchboard.

Salary according to qualifications and competence. 169 hours work a month. Minimum period of work 1-2 months during the summer vacation: July and August. Accommodation available in the local town at a maximum of £99 per month. Applicants must have excellent presentation. English and/or German languages required.

Applications at any time at the above address.

HOTEL BELLEVUE: F-63790 Chambon-sur-Lac, France (☎473-88-61-06; fax 473-88-63-53; lachotelbellevue@aol.com).

General Assistant. Wages by arrangement. Period of work July-1 September. Applicants must be keen workers, well-educated, and speak French. Knowledge of German and English an advantage.

Applications to Madame Amélie Dabert at the above address from April enclosing an photograph and an International Reply Coupon, or apply by e-mail.

RELAIS DU BOIS SAINT GEORGES: Parc Atlantique, Cours Genet, F-17100 Saintes, France (☎5-46-93-50-99; fax 5-46-93-34-93; e-mail info@relaisdubois.com; www.relaisdubois.com). This charming establishment is featured in *The Good Hotel Guide*.

Bell-boys (1 or 2) to welcome clients and carry their luggage to their rooms.

Kitchen Assistants to help in the kitchens and assist the chambermaids each morning.

Applicants for both positions should be well-presented, motivated and good team workers. The period of work is from July to September; minimum period of work one month, working eight hours per day, five days a week. Board and accommodation is available if needed and is provided free of charge. Applicants should speak English and French.

Applications invited from January.

CAMPING CLUB MAR ESTANG: Mer Méditerranée, 66140 Canet-Plage en Roussillon, France (☎+33 (0)468 80 35 53; fax + 33 (0)468 7332 94; e-mail marestang@wanadoo.fr; www.marestang.com).

Disc Jockey(1), Ice Cream Attendants (2) Swimming Pool Attendants (4 with

or without qualification), **Receptionists(2), Bar Staff(6), Restaurant Staff (2), Beach Boy (1), Ground Staff (3), Night Security Staff (2), Sailing Instructor (1), Restaurant chef (1), Maids (3).** Wages €900 (£630) to €1400 (£980), depending on schedule and abilities.

All contracts are seasonal from 2 to 5 months. Qualifications are needed only for restaurant chef, pool attendants (2) and sailing instructor. French must be spoken for receptionist, bar staff, ice cream, pool and sailing instruction.

Applications: please send I.D. with photo with your application to Mr Laurent Raspaud at the above address.

HOTEL CHATEAU DE MONTREUIL: 62170 Montreuil-sur-Mer, France (☎03 21 81 53 0; fax 03 21 81 36 43; e-mail chateau.de.montreuil@wanadoo.fr). Small, 4-star, family-run hotel in northern France.

General Help (2) to wait at/prepare tables, ironing, cleaning rooms, anything. Previous waiting table experience and basic French. Would suit two friends.

Chamber Staff (2) for breakfast service, room cleaning and preparation. Previous experience helpful but not essential. Basic French. Would suit two friends.

All staff get €450 (£315) per month and work 39 hours per week; five and a half day week. Free food and basic accommodation are provided free. Minimum period of work is three months from 1 June to 31 August.

Apply November to April by e-mail with CV and a passport-type photo to Mme Germain.

HOTEL CHATEAURENARD: F-05350 Saint Veran, France (☎492-45-85-43; fax 492-45-84-20; e-mail chateaurenard@wanadoo.fr; www.chateaurenard-stveran.com). This 20 room chalet style hotel, run by a French speaking Australian with her French chef husband is located at the foot of the ski slopes (2080m). It has spectacular views overlooking the 18th Century village of Saint Veran, the Hautes Alpes, and the border with the Italian Piedmont.

General Assistants (4) to clean rooms, work in the restaurant and the laundry. To work 43 hours a week, 5 days a week. Wages at the usual national rate for hotel work. Board and accommodation provided. To work minimum period of 1 week over Christmas/New Year, 4 weeks in February/March or 4-6 weeks during July to August/September. No special qualifications required except a happy nature and the ability to work with people and to work hard. Knowledge of French is essential.

Applications to the Director at the above address.

HOTEL-RESTAURANT CHEVAL-BLANC: F-67510 Niedersteinbach, France (☎388-09-55-31; fax 388-09-50-24; e-mail contact@hotel-cheval-blanc.fr; www.hotel-cheval-blanc.fr). A 25 room hotel combined with a 120 place restaurant located in a small village in a natural park. Facilities include a tennis court and a swimming pool

Assistant Waitress: €800 (£560) per month plus tips.

Kitchen Assistant: €800 euros per month.

5½ day week. Board and lodging provided free. Must have previous experience and knowledge of French and German. Period of work 3 months minimum from July to November.

Applications to February to M Michel Zinck at the above address.

CLUB CANTABRICA HOLIDAYS LTD: 146/148 London Road, St. Albans, Herts AL1 1PQ (☎01727-866177; fax 01727-843766). A leading coach and camping operator to France and the Mediterranean, they also run three hotels in

France in the Savoix and Chamonix valleys, with the latter being open all year.

Hotel Managers required to run hotels at St Gervais in the French Alps. Approximately 40 hours work per 6 day week, applicants should have French language skills and previous hotel experience. Wages approx. €200 (£140) per week.

Chefs to cook for up to 80 guests. Must have previous experience of working at this level. Wages approx. €200 per week.

General Duty Reps required to help in bar, kitchen cleaning of hotel and reception work, wages approximately £70 per week.

Free accommodation provided. Period of work from April to October.

Applications with curriculum vitae and stamped addressed envelope to the above address from December.

CLUB TELI: 7 rue Blaise Pascal, F-74600 Seynod, France (☎0033-4-5052-2658; fax 4-5052-1016; e-mail clubteli@wanadoo.fr; www.teli.asso.fr). The Club TELI offers an interesting alternative for any person wishing to go abroad whether for a training course, a summer job or a career job. Club TELI is a non-profit organisation.

Secretary: Club TELI seeks interns (rolling – 2 months minimum) who have a good knowledge of French. Age 20-30, good telephone manner. Wages: €150 per month (approx. £105) Seynod is a small town near Annecy (90 km to Chamonix-Mont Blanc, 45 km to Geneva).

Apply by e-mail to Dominique Girerd, Director.

HOTEL-RESTAURANT LA CROIX BLANCHE DE SOLOGNE: Place de l'Eglise R. Mothu, 41600 Chaumont-sur-Tharonne, France; ☎02 54 88 55 12; fax 02 54 88 60 40; e-mail lacroixblanchesologne@wanadoo.fr; www.hotel-sologne.com). Has been an inn since the 15th century (and before that a convent) with a tradition of women chef-owners dating back over 220 years.

Waiting person to work in the dining room. Experience or at least knowledge of how a restaurant dining-room works.

Cooking person with knowledge of *commis*, *aide cuisine* and *plongeur* (dishwasher).

Salary is €900 (£630) including free board and lodging. Hours of work 9am-2pm and 6pm-10pm (35 hours) five and a half days a week. Must speak French. Period of work is 1 July to 31 August.

Applications to Michel-Pierre Goacolou, at the above address any time from 1 January to 31 May.

RESTAURANT CRUAUD: 30 avenue Joffre, 84300 Cavaillonl, France (tel/fax 06 80 26 69 98).

Summer Staff to work in a hotel and restaurant; wages and details of work by arrangement. To work 186 hours per month, 5 days per week. Board and lodging provided. To work from April to October. Applicants must speak French and English.

Monsieur François Cruaud is also a Conseiller Culinaire and Officier du Mérite Agricole and offers cookery courses and Formation for hotel and restaurant trainees.

Applications should be sent to Mr and Mrs Cruaud at the above address from January.

HOTEL DES DEUX ROCHES: 1 Place Font d'Amont, 83440 Seillans, France

(☎04 94 76 87 32; fax 04 94 76 88 68).
Commis de Cuisine (1), **Waiting Assistant** (2), **Housekeeper** (1). Wages €1000/
€1,200 (£700-£840). To work 41 hours per week, five to seven days a week.
Minimum two months between June and September. Board and lodging provided.

Apply from March to the above address.

DOMAINE SAINT CLAIR-LE DONJON: Chemin de Saint Clair, 76790 Etretat,
France (☎+33 235 10 22 80; fax +33 235 1022 89; e-mail direction@hoteletretat.com.
21-room hotel and restaurant for 30 (150 for weddings).
Various dining room and kitchen positions, Receptionist for a two-part
organisation (hotel and restaurant) to work 8 hours per day 5/6 days per week in
reception and room cleaning and in the restaurant (service, bar and kitchen). Wages
from €850/£595 (waiter) to €1500/£1050 (for pastry chef), and €1300 (£910) for
receptionist per month. Board and lodging provided at no extra cost. Period of work
is April to September. Dining room staff should speak French and English, kitchen
positions require experience and the receptionist must be fluent in French and
English and have experience.

Apply to the Director at the above address.

LE DOMAINE DE LA TORTINIERE: F-37250 Montbazon-en-Touraine, France
(☎247-34-35-00; fax 247-65-95-70; e-mail domaine.tortiniere@wanadoo.fr). A
graceful second-empire turreted chateau converted into a hotel in 1954 and managed
by the same family since then; guests are from France and the rest of the world.
Barman/Bellboy (1/2) to serve drinks from 3pm to midnight and to help staff at
front desk, carry suitcases and show guests to their rooms. No wage, but free board
and lodging. Minimum period of work 1 month between 1 March and 25 December.
Applicants should be well presented and speak French and English.

Applications to M.X. Olivereau at the above address.

DOMAINE VALLEE HEUREUSE: Route de Geneve, F-39800 Poligny, France.
Waiter. Hours: 9am-3pm and 7-10.30pm. Cleanliness, cheerfulness and good
appearance essential. Waiting experience preferred. £300 plus tips per month.
Chambermaid. Hours: 8am-noon and 1-5pm. Must be of good appearance. Wages:
£300 per month.

Free board provided. Some knowledge of French is required for both positions.
Minimum age 18 years. Minimum period of work 1st April to 30th September.

Applications during April to the above address.

**EVOLUTION 2/HARRI'S BAR: Le Lavachet, F-73320 Tignes, France
(☎+33 4 79 06 48 11; fax +33 4 79 06 57 13; e-mail info@skibarjobs.com;
www.skibarjobs.com).**
**Bartenders (2) to work in Harri's bar. Shift work, with hours for the summer
season being either from midday to 6pm or 6pm to midnight, with at least one
day off per week. Knowledge of Italian and/or French an advantage.**
**Swimming Pool Supervisor; duties to include pool maintenance and general
supervision. Must hold a lifesaving qualification.**
Chamber/Waiting Staff (4). Knowledge of Italian and/or French helpful.
**To work for a hotel/bar complex that is run by the owners from May to
November and rented to a tour operator for the winter season. Wages approx.
£315 per month plus board and accommodation and fringe benefits including
access to an activity centre and ski hire and passes during the winter season.
Minimum period of work from mid June to mid September, but work is available**

around the year; there will be around 10 vacancies for the winter season from September. Further information is available on the above Website.

Applications to Jeremy Goodall at the above address.

EXODUS TRAVELS: 9 Weir Road, London, SW12 OLT (☎020-8675 5550; fax 020-8673 0779; www.exodus.co.uk).

House Staff (2) required for work in the French Pyrenees. Work is available throughout the year. Job involves cooking, cleaning, shopping, running the bar. 6 days/around 40 hrs work a week. A driving licence, some French and cooking experience are all useful, but not essential. Board, lodging and transport are paid for, and on top of this there is a wage of £120 per week from May-October. From Christmas to April one person is needed and pay is £180.

Applications throughout the year should be sent to the above address, quoting 'Ref: La Feniere.'

HOTEL-RESTAURANT LE FLEURAY: F-37530 Cangey, Amboise, France (☎02-47-56-09-25; fax 02-47-56-93-97; e-mail lefleurayhotel@wanadoo.fr; www.lefleurayhotel.com). This highly acclaimed English-run, country house hotel is situated in a peaceful location in the Loire valley, only 55 minutes from Paris by TGV. It is listed in many *Best Hotel* guidebooks worldwide and has appeared in The Times, the Telegraph and San Fransisco Chronicle newspapers.

Hotel Staff required for all aspects of work in the hotel (including restaurant service, housekeeping, kitchen work and gardening). Male and female staff required. Candidates must be outgoing, friendly, keen to work closely with a sophisticated international clientele and not be afraid of hard work. Knowledge of French is useful but not essential. Applicants will ideally be students, although those taking time off or who have graduated will be considered. To work ten hours per day (split shift – mornings and evenings, with afternoons off) six days per week. Minimum period of work, four months, between March and October. Attractive weekly wage, travel ticket and full board and accommodation provided.

Applications to the Newington Family at the above address.

FOOTSIE BAR RESTAURANT: 10-12 Rue Dannou, 75002 Paris, France (☎ ☎6-8645 4327).

Waiting Staff required to work in a fashionable bar and restaurant; wages, hours, period of work etc. by arrangement.

Applications to the above address.

HOTEL LES FRENES: 645 Avenue Vertes Rives, 84140 Montfavet, France; ☎+33 490 311793; +33 490 239503; contact@lesfren3es.com; www.lesfrenes.com). A Relais Chateaux luxury hotel and restaurant with very high standards.

Waiter (2) to carry plates and trays and other daily tasks. Must have experience of working in high standards restaurants.

Room Staff (2) to clean rooms and other daily tasks.

Chef de Partie (2) daily kitchen duties. Must have experience in a high standard restaurant.

All staff get board and lodging included in the negotiable salary. Staff work 41 hours, 5 days per week. Minimum 3 months between 10 April and 15 November. Must speak fluent French and English and a third language is an asset.

Apply from January to Hervé Blancone at the above address/e-mail.

GARDEN BEACH HOTEL: 15-17 Bd. Baudoin, F-06160 Juan les Pins, France

(☎493-67-25-25).
Chamber Staff (2-4). Wage by arrangement; accommodation available. To work 8 hours per day, 5½ days per week. Period of work from May to October.
Applications should be sent to the Personnel Manager at the above address.

HOTEL IMPERIAL GAROUPE: 770 Chemin de la Garoupe, 06600 Le Cap d'Antibes (☎04 92 93 31 61; fax 04 92 93 31 62; e-mail hotel-imp@webstore.fr; www.imperial-garoupe.com).
Chef de Rang (3), Commis Chef (1) to prepare food in the restaurant.
Chambermaids (3) required to clean and prepare bedrooms for guests.

All staff will work 8 hours a day, 5 days a week for at least 4 months between April and October. Board and accommodation are provided free, along with a wage of approx. £750. Applicants should be able to speak both French and English confidently.
Applications should be sent to Mr Gilbert Irondelle at the above address from January.

L'AUBERGE LIMOUSINE: F-19320 La Roche-Canillac, France (☎05-55-29-12-06).
Waiter, Barman, Chambermaid, Dishwasher required for small hotel. Wages approx. £150 net per month for working a 45 hour week over 5½ days. Period of work April to end of September. Knowledge of English and French essential.
Applications should be made between February and March; contact Michele Coudert at the above address.

HOTEL RESTAURANT 'AU LION BLEU': 176 Rue Koeberlé, Lutzelbourg, Moselle 57820, France (☎0033-387 25 31 88; fax 0033-387 25 42 98; e-mail lion.bleu.ltz@wanadoo.fr; www.hotelaulionbleu.com). Small family business. Lutzelbourg is 45km from Strasbourg. Areas within 2 hours drive or day outings by train include the Black Forest, Baden-baden/Stuttgart, Frankfurt, Basel (Switzerland), Luxembourg, Leige (Belgium).
Kitchen Helps/Housekeepers (2), Waiters/Waitresses (2) required from May until October, candidates can have July to travel around neighbouring countries and resume work in August. Wages are negotiable with full board and lodging plus a share of weekly tips. Hours by arrangement (5½ day week).

Experience is not essential, some training can be given, but spoken German is an advantage as 70 per cent of clients are German/German Swiss.
Applications to Mr & Mrs Jaques Balinski, Owners, at the above address.

LE RELAIS DU LYON D'OR: 4 Rue d'Enfer, 86260 Angles sur L'Anglin, France (☎05494-83253; fax 054984-0228; e-mail thoreau@lyondor.com; www.lyondor.com). The Lyon D'or is a three star hotel and restaurant in Angles sur l'Anglin, near Poitiers. The hotel is listed in all leading guides and is run by Anglo-French owners.
Cleaners/Waiters/Waitresses (3) for general help in the hotel and restaurant. Applicants should have a positive attitude, a sense of humour. English and at least conversational French are essential, and Dutch would be an advantage. To work 10 hours a day, 5½ days per week. Positions available between May and end of October; minumum period two months. The village is very isolated, so own transport is an advantage. Wages of £470 per month, plus bonus, and board and lodging. Applicants must be EU nationals or have the correct permits to work in France.
Applications to Heather Thoreau from December onwards at the above address.

LE LOGIS DU FRESNE: F-16130 Jouillac-le-Coq, France (☎00 33 674 984 675; e-mail tonebutler@aol.com). A three-star hotel run by Norwegian-French owners and situated 10km from Cognac in south-west France.

Cleaners/Waiting Staff to provide general help in the hotel. Wages of approx. £600 per month plus board, lodging and bonus. Minimum period of work one month between May and the end of September. Applicants should have a kindly attitude and speak English and conversational French; they must also either be EU nationals or have the correct permits to work in France.

Applications to Tone Butler at the above address with a photo if possible.

HOTEL MANOIR DE BELLERIVE: F-24480 Le Buisson de Caudouin, France (☎0553-221616; fax 0553-220905; e-mail manoir.Bellerive@wanadoo.fr; www.bellerivehotel.com). A typical French chateau, this hotel is situated near the River Dordogne in the heart of superb and serene grounds.

Dining/Breakfast Assistant, Kitchen Pastry Helper, General Assistant. Wages of approx. £700 per month net (Pastry chef: £725 net per month).

Receptionist: for reception and administrative work. Wages of £700 net per month. Must speak two European languages.

Employees will work split shifts five days per week. Minimum period of work eight weeks between April and October. Board and accommodation provided. Applicants should speak French, and possess the relevant qualifications for hotel work.

Applications from April onwards to the above address.

HOSTELLERIE DE LA MARONNE: Le Theil, F-15140 St Martin-Valmeroux, France (☎+33-(0)4-71-69-20-33; fax 04-71-69-28-22; e-mail maronne@maronne.com; www.maronne.com). A hotel-restaurant in the countryside near Clermont-Ferrand with 21 rooms, heated pool, tennis courts and sauna, attracting customers from all over the world.

Waiting Staff/Reception (2) to serve breakfast and supper. Experience preferred. €1200/£840 per month.

Second Chef (1). Wage of €1400/£980. Serving supper. Must provide a reference. Experience essential.

Experience of working in 3 or 4 star hotels necessary; knowledge of French is preferred but not essential. To work 8 hours a day, 5 day week, for a minimum of two months between 1 May and 15 September. Board and lodging provided free.

Apply from February to Alain Decock at the above address.

HOTEL MAS DE LA FAUGRE: Rate du Petit Rhône, 13460 Sainte Maries de la Mer, France (☎+33 4 90 97 81 02; fax +33 4 90 97 968; e-mail info@masdelafaugre.com; www.masdelafaugre.com). 4-star hotel (grand luxe) with about 20 rooms and suites; about 25 employees.

Server (2) to be assistant to the Maître d'hotel serving in the restaurant gastronomique. €1300 (£910) per month.

Receptionist to assist the head receptionist. €1200 (£840) per month.

Commis de Cuisine to help the head chef and the second chef. €1100 (£770) per month.

All staff are expected to have a reference from a hotel of similar standard. Board and lodging are provided free of charge. 41 hours per week. Minimum period of work is a month during the period from 25 March to 11 November. Knowledge of French and English essential.

Apply to the above address at any time.

HOTEL MIREILLE: 2 Place St. Pierre, F-13200 Arles en Provence, France (☎+33-(0)4-90-70-74; fax 04-90-93-87-28; e-mail contact@hotelmireille.com; www.hotelmireille.com). This hotel is a hideaway nestled in the countryside of the Camargue, not far from the old town of Arles.

Waitress, Chambermaid, Receptionist: wages of £325 per month, with board and lodging included. Receptionists and waitresses must speak very good French and English, preferably with some experience of reception and food service work. Minimum period of work 5 months between March and early October.

Applications to the above address.

CHATEAU DE MONTREUIL: 62170 Montreuil/mer, France, (☎033-321-81-53-04; fax (33)-321-81-36-43; e-mail chateau.de.montreuil@wanadoo.fr; www.chatea udemontreuil.com). A small four star family run hotel with gastronomic restaurant and beautiful gardens, in Northern France.

General Assistant – Service. (2) Waiting at tables, washing glasses, ironing, cleaning rooms etc. Applicants should have basic French and some previous experience.

General Assistant – Maintenance. (2) To work in the garden, run errands, portering and other odd jobs. Should have basic French and an international driving licence.

For both positions: to work a 39 hour week, 5½ days per week. Board and lodging provided. Applicants should have a good sense of humour and be responsable and decorous. Wages of €500 (£350) per month. Minimum period of three months.

Apply now to Mrs Germain at the above address. Applicants should send a CV with a reference and a colour identity photo.

HOTEL MOULIN DES POMMERATS: F-89210 Venisy-St-Lorentin, France (☎86-35-08-04).

Hotel Staff: Wages and duties by arrangement. Board and lodging provided. Minimum period of work 1 month between July and September. Knowledge of languages not required.

Applications to the above address.

HOTEL-RESTAURANT L'OCEAN: 172, rue de St Martin, F-17580 Bois - Plage en Ré (☎05-46-09-23-07; fax 05-46-09-05-40; e-mail ocean@ledeu.com; www.hotel-ocean.com). This hotel and restaurant are in a peaceful location with a unique and pleasant ambience, by a small and picturesque port.

Waiting Staff (2) to work between June and September, and possibly longer. Wages £690 approx in July and August; £660 approx during other months. To work split shifts, with two days free per week. Accommodation costs approx. £200 per month; Board is provided free of charge. Applicants should speak English and French.

Applications to the above address.

HOTEL DE LA POSTE: F-29950 Benodet, France.

Barmaid, Waiting Assistants, Chambermaid, Receptionist. Wages by arrangement. To work around 8 hours per day, 5½ days per week. No accommodation available. Minimum period of work 2 months between April and September. Applicants must speak French and English.

Applications, with photographs, to the above address from March.

RESTAURANT DE LA POSTE & HOTEL LA RECONCE: Le Bourg, 71600 Poisson, France (☎+33 (0)3 85 81 10 72; fax +33 (0)3 85 81 64 34).

Waiter/Waitress. Pay of €1,230 per month (about £200 per week gross). Preparing tables and serving meals in a gastronomic restaurant. Must be well turned out, have good manners, be honest and speak French and English. 15 June to 15 September. To work 43 hours per week. Restaurant is based in a small village in southern Burgundy in the Charolais district and is attached to a small (six-bedroom) hotel.

Applications to Monsieur or Madame Jean Noel Dauvergne at the above address.

HOTEL DU PONT NEUF: F-03320 Le Veurdre, France (☎0033-470-66-40-12; fax 0033-470-66-44-15; e-mail hotel.le.pontneuf@wanadoo.fr; www.hotel-lepontneuf.com). This pleasant 46 room hotel is run by an American and her husband so French is not essential.

Waiter/Waitress to work a five day week, approximately 45 to 50 hours per week. Some experience needed but willing to train in French service. Job includes breakfast, lunch and dinner service, dining room preparations and bar service. There is a break in the afternoons with a rotation for the lunch service. Full room and board included June 15th till October 15th. €500 (£350) per month with a €2000 (£1400) bonus if you stay till the end of the contract.

Kitchen Helper to work a five day week approximately 45 to 50 hours per week. Excellent opportunity for someone who is interested in learning French cuisine. Possibility of a permanent position at the end of the contract. Same pay and conditions as waitress. Only serious applicants need apply. EC residents only. Applicants should be hardworking, pleasant and hoping to improve their French. Board and lodging included.

Applications from EU residents only, to Mrs Denise Ducroix at the above address from January.

RESIDENCE HOTEL LE PONTOT: 89450 Vezelay, France (☎0386-332440; fax 0386-333005).

All-round Hotel Staff (1) for duties which will include reception work, telephoning, portering and gardening in this small hotel. Wages on application and depend on qualifications/experience. Minimum period of work 4 months. To work 9am to 4pm 6 days a week. Positions available from May to October. Free accommodation provided. Applicants should speak good French and English.

Applications should be made to Christian Abadie, Hotel Director, at the above address from 1 December.

HOTEL LE RIVET: F-06450 Lantosque, France.
Chambermaids to serve breakfasts, make beds and do the laundry.
Kitchen Assistants, Waitresses, Handyman, Washer Up.

To work in a small three star hotel. Wages by arrangement: board and lodging provided. To work 8 hours per day, 6 days per week. Minimum period of work 8 weeks between 1 April and 15 October. Applicants should be serious, well behaved and dress in a suitable manner for exclusive hotelwork.

Applications to M Henrik Winther at the above address from 1st March.

CHATEAU DE ROCHECOTTE: 37130 St Patrice, FRANCE (☎0247-961616; fax 0247-696059; e-mail chateau.rochette@wanadoo.fr; www.chateau-de-rochecotte.fr). A chateau hotel in the Val de Loire with 34 rooms and gastronomic cuisine.

Maitre d'Hotel. In charge of the hotel. €1850 (£1295) per month. Minimum of 10 years experience. Speaks English and French.

Chef de Rang. To run the restaurant/dining room. €1300 (£910) per month. Minimum of 5 years experience. Speaks English and French.

Receptionist. €1300 per month. Good presentation. Speaks English and French.
Commis de Salle. €1125.
To work 5 days and 39 hours per week. Minimum period of work 7 months. Positions available from May to October. Accommodation available for €100 a month.

Applications should be made to Mme Brosset at the above address from 1 December 2003.

HOSTELLERIE SAINT CLEMENT: Curebourse, F-15800 Vic-Sur-Cere, France (☎471-47-51-71; fax 471-49-63-02).
Waiter, Bar Person, Chamber Person: Wage £150 per month approximately. 45 hours per week, 5½ days per week. Board and accommodation provided free of charge. Minimum period of work 2 months from July to August. Season runs from 1 June to 15 September. A knowledge of French and English is required.

Applications should be sent to the above address from February/March onwards.

STANFORD SKIING : 16 Sherlock Road, Cambridge, CB3 OHR (☎01223-477644; fax 01223-710318; e-mail info@stanfordskiing.co.uk; www.stanfordskiing.co.uk).
Couple to run chalet/hostel. Friendly, family run company would like to open their alpine chalet/hotel in Megève in summer and are looking for a dynamic couple with lots of ideas to make it work. At present the chalet is closed during summer. Wages would be negotiable (and dependent on profits). Period of work is August. French and English languages essential.

Apply to the above address anytime.

HOTEL DE LA TONNELLERIE: 12 rue des Eaue Bleue, F-45190 Tavers, France (☎+33-2-38 44 68 15; fax +33-2-38 44 10 01; e-mail tonelri@club-internet.fr; www.tonelni.com). A four star, family-run hotel-restaurant with a young staff team, catering to discerning clients; located in a small village between Orleans and Blois.
Room Attendant (1-2) to clean rooms.
Dishwasher (1/2) to clean dishes, pots and pans.
General Help (1-2) to carry luggage, warden duty and pool duty. No experience necessary, healthy, motivated and good-natured.
Breakfast Attendant/Barworker (1) serve breakfast and clean the dishes. Some experience of waiting tables useful.
Hours of work are 41 per 5-day week. Period of work May to September, with a minimum period of work of two months. Wages €950 (£665) per month. Some free board and lodging is available. Ideally candidates should speak French and English.

Applications from 1 March to Marie-Christine Pouey at the above address.

TRAVELBOUND: First Choice Holidays, London Road, Crawley, West Sussex RH10 9GX (☎01293-588531; fax 01293-588277; e-mail skijobs@firstchoice.co.uk). Activity/educational tour operator to Austria and France (Alps and Normandy), member of AITO.
Summer Staff (over 250) including resort reps, chalet and hotel staff (Chefs, General Assistants, Kitchen/Night Porters). Full season in Austria and French Alps lasts May-September and in Normandy February-October. Flexible contract lengths available. Applications are processed in January through to September. Minimum age for hotel positions 18, for Resort Representatives 21. Applicants must have EU passport and National Insurance number. An attractive package which includes food,

accommodation, insurance and travel to/from resort. Winter work also available for Ski Season with First Choice Ski.

For more information please send an A4 S.A.E. to Overseas Ski Recruitment at the address above.

CHATEAU DE TRIGANCE: F-83840, Trigance, France (☎04-94-76-91-18; fax 04-94-85-68-99; e-mail trigance@relaischateau.fr; www.relaischateax.fr/trigance). This beautiful medieval castle-hotel in Provence, has ten rooms, a twenty-five seater gourmet restaurant and a team of 15 staff.

Waiters and Kitchen Helps (2) to wait at tables in the gourmet restaurant and to welcome clients. Also to be in charge of service from midday until evening. Applicants must have relevant experience, be well-presented and have good initiative skills. Applicants should also be organised with a team spirit. Wages £575 (beginning) to £700 approx.

Culinary Staff (2) to set places, change produce and dispatch plates. Applicants should have a good basic knowledge of cooking, and be very organised, motivated and have a team spirit.

All applicants will work 39 hours per five day week. Minimum period of work is two months between beginning April to end October. Board and accommodation is provided. Applicants should speak English and French.

Applications invited from 1st April, to Thomas Guillaume at the above address.

HOTEL-RESTAURANT LES TROIS COLOMBES: 148 avenue des Garrigues, 84210 Saint-Didier-les-Bains, Provence, France (☎04-90-66-07-01; fax 04-90-66-11-54).

A three-star hotel restaurant in the heart of scenic Provence.

Restaurant Staff (2) for waiting service, place-setting, taking orders and washing up, preferably with 2/3 years experience in restaurant work. Hours of work are based around mealtimes over a 5-day week, totalling 177 hours per month, board and lodging are provided for approx. £45 per month. Applicants must be smartly dressed, well-groomed non-smokers, and preferably English speakers.

Applications are invited between April and May, with the working period being between 1 May and 30 September.

UK OVERSEAS HANDLING (UKOH) INTERNATIONAL RECRUITMENT: U.K.O.H., P.O. Box 2791, London, W1A 5JU (☎020-7629 3064; fax 020-7495 0411; e-mail personnel@nbultduk.freeserve.co.uk). UKOH is a London-based recruitment company specialising in providing staff for the hotel and catering industries. UKOH works closely with the French tour operator, Eurogroup, providing hotel and chalet staff.

Restaurant, Night Audit, Reception, Housekeeping, Pool Cleaners, Gardeners and **Maintenance/Handy Staff**: Succesful candidates should be over 18 years of age and EU passport holders with a permanent British National Insurance number. Must be bright, flexible, keen and prepared for hard work. Experience and an excellent standard of French essential for reception and restaurant positions. Some knowledge of French is useful for other posts. Package includes full board and shared accommodation.

Staff required between May and October to work in hotels and tourist residences in the South and South-west coasts of France, and also in the Alps and cities of Paris and Montpellier.

Applications to the above address.

HOTEL RESTAURANT LE VEYMONT: F-26420 St Agnan-en-Vercore, France
(☎475-48-20-19; fax 475-48-10-34).
Chambermaid, Waitress: Wage of £300 per month with accommodation provided.
Period of work by arrangement; staff needed around the year. Applicants should
speak some French.
  Applications should be sent to the Manager at the above address.

Industrial and Office Work

THE AUTOMOBILE ASSOCIATION: European Operations, 13th Floor, Fanum
House, Basing View, Basingstoke RG21 4EA (☎01256-492398; e-mail elaine.bad
ham@theaa.com).
Call Handlers (up to 70) to assist the AA's multilingual European Call Centre in
Limonest, north of Lyon: the Centre provides 24-hour assistance to AA customers
who have broken down or become involved in a road traffic accident in Europe.
Wages by arrangement. To work 35 hours per week on shifts. Minimum period
of work 8 weeks between May and September (July and August essential). Local
accommodation can be arranged. Applicants must speak English (mother-tongue),
be fluent in French and preferably one other European language; you will need to be
efficient, responsible, compassionate and able to work under pressure.
  Please *e-mail* your CV to Elaine Badham by e-mail or write to the above address.

A·C·T·A

THE AUTOMOBILE ASSOCIATION

The AA is part shareholder of a 24-hour multi-lingual European Call Centre situated in
Limonest, just north of Lyon. Each year we employ up to 70 individuals to assist with our
ever-increasing summer workload. Minimum age for applicants is 18 years so if you want to
gain unique work experience with us, we are seeking English mother-tongue speakers with
fluency in French, plus ideally another European language, to be available to work from
May through to September 2004 (minimum work duration 8 weeks, July and August
essential.) Longer contracts are also available. Full training induction courses will be
phased in at intervals.

The job involves working to a shift pattern, 35 hrs per week, as a Call Handler providing a
high standard of customer care and incident management for AA customers who have
broken-down or have been involved in a road traffic accident in Europe. Your language
skills are essential for liaising with garages and other suppliers.

You will need to be efficient, responsible, and compassionate when dealing with customers
in what can sometimes be stressful circumstances. The ability to work professionally in a
high-pressure environment is essential.

Subsidised accommodation can be arranged locally.

For more information please contact me at elaine.badham@theaa.com or telephone me at
AA European Operations on 01256 492398.

The AA is part of Centrica PLC

HORIZON HPL: Signet House, 49/51 Farringdon road, London EC1M 3JB
(☎020-7404-9192/93; fax 020-7404-9194; e-mail horizonhpl.london@btinternet.
com). Horizon HPL is a training centre established in 1991 which organises paid

work placements in hotels, shops and companies in the UK and in France for EU citizens. This includes English and French tuition and preparation to sit British and French examinations.

Hotel Work/Company and Shop Staff: placements are available all year round (in a variety of fields) from three months up to one year. Staff receive a trainee wage and free accommodation if working in a hotel. Applicants accepted between 17-50 years old.

Other contacts: Paris (☎0033-1-40-01-07-07; e-mail horizon1@club-internet.fr), Aix-en-Provence (☎0033-4-42-26-50-85; e-mail hplaix@clubinternet.fr) and Dublin (☎00353-1874-5002; e-mail horizonhpl@eircom.net).

Applicants should contact the agency two months in advance of intended work date, as an interview is necessary.

SOLTOURS: 46 rue de Rivoli, F-75004 Paris, France.
Sales Assistant to work for a travel agent. Wages of approximately £700 per month. To work 8 hours per day, 5 days per week. No board or accommodation available. Minimum period of work 3 months between March and June. Applicants should be efficient, responsible and speak English.

Applications to the above address from February.

Sports, Couriers and Camping

BALLOON FLIGHTS – FRANCE MONTGOLFIERES: La Picoulière, 41120 Valaire (☎02-5444-1641; fax 02-5444-1918; jane@franceballoons.com; www.franceballoons.com).
Balloon Crew required April-November to work for passenger-carrying operation with bases in the Burgundy and Loire Valley regions. Duties include maintaining and cleaning of vehicles and balloon equipment, driving and navigation of balloon chase vans, helping out in a balloon repair workshop, passenger liaison, etc. Farm work is also available. Knowledge of French preferred. *Applicants should be EU nationals or possess correct working papers.* Minimum age 21, with clean driving licence. No fixed days off; hours can be very long. Wages £500-£600 per month.

Please *send* a cv, a photo, and a copy of your driving licence.

BELLE FRANCE: 45 High Street, Tunbridge Wells, Kent, TN1 1XL; (☎01892-559595; fax 01892-517478; e-mail enquiries@bellefrance.co.uk).
Belle France is part of the Mark Hammerton Group Ltd., specialist in tour operating and publishing. A small, dynamic and friendly organisation.
Bike Representatives (10) to work for a tour operator offering cycling holidays in France. The job includes maintaining bikes, transporting luggage, collecting customers from station, etc. Wage from about £125 per week. To work 30 hours per week. Period of work from May to October. Applicants should be well organised, capable of working on their own and speak some French.

Applications to the above address around Christmas.

BENTS BICYCLE & WALKING TOURS: The Blue Cross, Orleton, Ludlow, Shropshire SY8 4HN (☎01568-780800; fax 01568-780801; e-mail info@bentstours.com; www.bentstours.com).
Company Representatives (4-5) for a tour operator offering cycling and walking holidays in France, Germany and Austria. Duties to include meeting clients at the airport, maintaining bicycles, transporting luggage between hotels and generally taking care of the needs of clients. Wages of around £600 per month with board

and accommodation provided. To work varied hours as needs of work dictate, but generally around 40 hours per up to 7-day week.

Minimum period of work 8 weeks between the end of May and end of September. Applicants should speak fluent French (German for Germany and Austria) and English and possess a full clean driving licence.

Applications should be sent, with a photograph, to Stephen Bent at the above address from January.

BOOTS & BIKES: Hunter Kingston Holidays Ltd, 15 Husseywell Crescent, Bromley BR2 7LN (☎020-8462-6522; e-mail julia-kingston@bootsandbikes.co.u k; www.bootsandbikes.co.uk). Boots & Bikes organises independent walking and cycling holidays in France. They offer tours lasting 6-10 days, between small hotels and guest houses in rural France.

Holiday Representatives (5) to meet clients on arrival, give tour briefings, move bags between hotels, carry out cycle maintenance, deal with hoteliers, keep accounts and carry out other duties as necessary. Representatives should be fit, active young people, with an interest in outdoor activities, especially cycling and walking.

Boots & Bikes require adaptable, resourceful people who can think on their feet in a variety of situations. Minimum age 21 years. English and French language skills and a full, clean driving licence a must. Hours/days of work are flexible but the minimum period of work is two months between April and October. Wages £480 per month, with accommodation provided.

Applications invited from January 2004, interviews will be held in London in early 2004.

CAMPING CLUB MAR ESTANG: Mer Méditerranée, 66140 Canet-Plage en Roussillon, FRANCE (☎+33 (0)468 80 35 53; fax + 33 (0)468 7332 94; e-mail marestang@wanadoo.fr; www.marestang.com).

Disc Jockey(1), Ice Cream Attendants (2) Swimming Pool Attendants (4 with or without qualification), Receptionists(2), Bar Staff(6), Restaurant Staff (2), Beach Boy (1), Ground Staff (3), Night Security Staff (2), Sailing Instructor (1), Restaurant chef (1), Maids (3). Wages €900 to €1400, depending on schedule and abilities.

All contracts are seasonal from 2 to 5 months. Qualifications are needed only for restaurant chef, pool attendants (2) and sailing instructor. French must be spoken for receptionist, bar staff, ice cream, pool and sailing instruction.

Applications: please send I.D. with photo with your application to Mr Laurent Raspaud at the above address.

CANVAS HOLIDAYS: East Port House, 12 East Port, Dunfermline, Fife KY12 7JG (☎01383-629018; fax 01383-629071; www.canvasholidays.com). Canvas Holidays are looking for enthusiastic, resourceful people who enjoy a challenge and love the outdoor life. Main positions include:

Campsite Courier. Varied responsibilities. Involves cleaning and preparation of customer accommodation, welcoming and looking after customers during their holiday and ensuring that they have the best holiday ever. As a campsite courier you will have new challenges every day which can lead to one of the most enjoyable summers you will ever have. Variable working hours.

Children's Courier. As a Canvas Holidays Children's Courier you will have had formal experience of working with children. You will organise and carry out a six day programme which involves five hours a day of Children's Club for children between the ages of 4 and 11. You will be expected to help out with courier duties

WHY NOT WORK UNDER CANVAS THIS SUMMER?

Canvas Holidays, the originators of self-drive camping holidays over 38 years ago, are looking for hardworking, enthusiastic, flexible, level-headed individuals and couples to join their European team for the summer season!

We have positions for around 300 people on over 100 luxury campsites across 8 European countries - mainly **France** but also **Spain, Italy, Germany, Austria, Luxembourg, Switzerland and Holland.**

Positions include:

Campsite Couriers, Children's Couriers, Activity Couriers, Senior Couriers, Site Supervisors, Site Managers and Wildlife Couriers.

Positions are available from end March to end October (some high season positions are also available June – end of September) and minimum age is 19 for France, 18 for all other countries. Although not essential, it is certainly useful to have a working knowledge of a major European language (French, Spanish, Italian, German or Dutch).

For an application pack please contact our Overseas Personnel Department on

01383 629018

or visit www.canvasholidays.com

GO ON –
IT REALLY IS THE BEST FUN HARD WORK CAN BE!!

as and when requried. For many customers, the Children's Club is one of the main parts of the holiday. You will need to have the energy of a seven-year-old and the imagination of an eleven year old to succeed!

Package includes tented accommodation, medical insurance, full uniform and return travel to and from a UK port of entry. Positions are available from March until October.

Applications are invited from individuals and couples: contact Sandy, Karen or Nina at the above contact details for an application pack.

CARISMA HOLIDAYS: Bethel House, Heronsgate Road, Chorleywood WD3 5BB (☎01923-284235; e-mail personnel@carisma.co.uk). Carisma specialises in self-drive, family holidays in mobile homes on private sandy beaches in the sunny south-west of France. All Carisma's campsites are family-run and located on beaches.

Site Managers. £100 per week plus tips and accommodation. To work from 1 May to 24 September. French speakers preferred.

Full Season Couriers: £95 per week plus tips and accommodation. To work from May 12th to September 24th. French speakers preferred.

High Season Couriers: £90 per week plus tips and accommodatin. To work from 1 July to 13 September. French speakers preferred.

To work on beach sites in France. To be responsible for client families, with duties involving welcoming families, providing information and advice, cleaning and maintaining mobile homes and babysitting. Self-catering accommodation is provided in tents.

Applicants should have a helpful and friendly disposition and experience of dealing with people. Travel costs are paid and full training is given on site. *Applicants should be EU nationals.*

Applications to C. Simpson at the above address.

CENTRE D'ECHANGES INTERNATIONAUX: 1 rue Gozlin, F-75006 Paris, France.

Youth Leaders to teach one of the following activities; sports, dancing, music, crafts. Around £200 per month. To work in international holiday centres. Hours can be long; one day off per week. Free board and lodging provided.

Period of work covers July and August. Applicants must speak French: some knowledge of German an advantage. Applicants must have previous experience as an instructor in holiday camps.

Apply to the Director at the above address between March and May.

CENTRE DE VOILE L'ABER-WRAC'H: 4, Port de l'Aber-Wrach, F-29870 Landeda, France (☎298-04-90-64; fax 298-04-97-22).

Sailing Instructors (2), **Sailing Camp Leaders** (2) to work in Brittany. Period of work is July and August. Pay is around £110 weekly plus free board and lodging. Instructors work six and a half hours a day, six days a week and leaders six days a week all day and evenings. The minimum age is 18 and sailing instructors should be qualified.

Applications to the address above.

CHATEAU DE L'EPERVIERE: F-71240 Gigny sur Saone, Bourgogne Sud, France (☎0033-385-941-690; fax 0033-385-94-1697; e-mail domaine-de-leperviere@wanadoo.fr; www.domaine-eperviere.com). A four star castle/campsite situated in the heart of Burgundy with indoor and outdoor pool, a jaccuzi and sauna.

The campsite's key-words are conviviality and family atmosphere.

Staff, ideally students, to work on a campsite. Wages by arrangement. Minimum period of work two months between April and September; those available from early in April or until late September would be at an advantage. Applicants should have some qualifications or experience in waitressing, bartending or reception work.

Applicants must speak French, be aged 20-30, hard working, and be flexible, prepared to work long hours and friendly with clients; to *apply* send a CV and picture to Gert-Jan Engel at the above address.

CITY CRUISER HOLIDAYS LTD: c/o Harry Shaw, Mill House, Mill Lane, Binley, Coventry (☎024-7645-5544; fax 04-7645-0774; e-mail robertshaw@har ryshaw.co.uk; www.harryshaw.co.uk). Have been in business for nearly 50 years. Arrange coach, camping and mobile home holidays in a variety of sites in France and Spain. Also arrange coach and air travel to European and worldwide destinations.

Campsite Representatives (5) to clean accommodation, show clients accommodation, undertake small repairs.

French and Spanish would be an advantage. To work 9am-12 pm and 2pm-7pm five or six days per week Minimum of four months between April and October.

Apply from January onwards to the above address.

DISCOVER ADVENTURE LTD: Throope Down House, Blandford Road, Coombe Bissett, Salisbury SP5 4LN; ☎01722-718444; fax 01722-718445; www.d iscoveradventure.com; e-mail darren@discoveradventure.com. Discover Ltd. need staff for the 2004 season (March to October) based in their field studies centre in the Cevennes National Park in the mountains of southern central France. They provide a relaxed and friendly service for school and university groups from the UK and Europe.

General Assistants/Housekeepers (4) Cleaning and kitchen duties, bar and shop work. £80 per week plus board and lodgings.

Cooks (2) to cook for up to 100 people. Good wholesome food required. Wage approx. £80-100 per week, depending on experience and qualifications.

To work from approx 7am-noon and 5.30-9.00pm, 6 days per week, with some paid leave as possible during season. Vital skills include the ability to live and work as part of a small team, flexibility and a willingness to muck-in and be supportive of one another.

Applications to the above address.

EUROCAMP: Overseas Recruitment Department (Ref SJ/04) (☎01606-787525). Eurocamp is a leading tour operator in quality self-drive camping and mobile home holidays in Europe. Each year the company seeks to recruit up to 1,500 enthusiastic people for the following positions:

Campsite Courier: job involves cleaning and preparing customer accommodation, providing assistance, acting as an information service and performing some administrative duties. Couriers need to be flexible to meet the needs of the customer to provide them with excellent service. Minimum age 18 years. Applicants should be independent with plenty of initiative and relish a challenging and rewarding position. They should also possess a friendly and helpful personality. Previous customer service experience would be an advantage. Applicants should be available to work from April/May to September.

Children's Courier: work involves organising a wide range of exciting activities for children aged 4-13. Applicants should possess initiative, imagination and enthusiasm along with good safety awareness. Previous childcare experience is

Eurocamp

Eurocamp is Europe's leading Tour Operator and the leader in self-drive, self-catering holidays on holiday parcs and campsites. Operating in 9 countries throughout Europe on over 150 parcs and sites, we sell family holidays to customers from the UK, Ireland, Holland, Germany, Switzerland, Austria, Denmark, Sweden and Poland.

We employ 1,500 campsite staff every year from many of these countries and can offer a large range of positions to suit all our overseas employees.

We are looking for people for various positions that involve **customer service, working with children, leading a team and administration.** We also employ teams of people at the beginning and end of the season to help us erect and dismantle tents. Successful applicants will be asked to apply for a Standard or Enhanced Disclosure.*

We will provide:	**You will need to be:**
• Competitive Salary	• 18+
• Accommodation	• An EU passport holder (or have a
• Uniform	work permit for any of the
• Subsidised Insurance	countries that we operate in)
• Training	• Available to *start* work between
• Travel To Resort	April and July

If you think you have the qualities to provide our customers with the 'perfect family holiday' please apply online at **www.holidaybreakjobs.com** or phone **01606 7897525** for an application pack. Please quote **SJ/04.**

* Further information about Disclosures can be found at www.disclosure.gov.uk or by phoning 0870 90 90 811.

essential. Minimum age is 18 years and applicants should be available from April/ May to September. Languages are not a requirement but would be an advantage (in particular German). Successful candidates will be asked to apply for an Enhanced Disclosure.

Senior Couriers: required to work alongside a team of Campsite Couriers and organise their daily workload, as well as carrying out the normal day to day duties of a Campsite Courier. Applicants should have good language skills and experience of leading a team.

Site Managers: required to lead a large team of Campsite Couriers, organising their daily workloads and ensuring they provide the very best customer service. Applicants should be 21 or over, have proven managerial experience, excellent communication skills and language ability.

Comprehensive training is provided together with a competitive salary, insurance, return travel and accommodation. Applications are accepted from September/ October and *can only be accepted from UK/EU passport holders*. Interviews will be conducted in Hartford, Cheshire between October and April.

Applicants should *apply on-line* at www.holidaybreakjobs.com or *telephone* 01606 781525 for an Application Pack.

FLEUR HOLIDAYS: 4 All Hallows Road, Bispham, Blackpool, Lancs FY2 0AS (☎01253-593333; fax 01253-595151; e-mail employment@fleur-holidays.com; www.fleur-holidays.com). A company which offers mobile home and tent holidays on quality sites in France, chosen for the ambience.

Area Controllers required to cover groups of campsites to ensure couriers are performing to the required standards. Previous courier experience is essential. Wages in the region of £630 per month, plus £14 per week bonus paid on completion of contract; dependent on service. Vehicle provided or mileage allowance given. Accommodation provided. Period of employment may cover: start season – Easter to July, and/or High season – July to September. Basic French required.

Representatives/Couriers required to meet clients at reception, prepare mobile homes and tents, organise social events and children's clubs. Wages in the region of £430 per month plus £14 per week bonus paid on completion of contract. Each vacancy is an all round position with responsibility for the clients together with Fleur's representation at the campsite. Period of employment may cover any or all of: Start season – Easter to July; Mid season – May to July; High season – July to September. Basic French an advantage.

Montage/Demontage: required to assist in the preparation of mobile homes and the erecting of tents at the start of the season and /or the closing of mobile homes and taking down of tents at the end of the season. Period of employment: 6 to 8 weeks from March to May and/or 6-8 weeks in September and October.

Applicants should be 18+, and be physically fit and motivated. For Area Controllers and Couriers experience of working within the service industry would be an advantage.

For all positions, please *send a full CV* and covering letter with head and shoulders photograph, stating the exact dates that you are available to the above address: alternatively, request an application form from the Personnel Manager.

FRENCH LIFE HOLIDAYS: Kerry House, Kerry Street, Horsforth, Leeds LS18 4AW (☎0113-205 292; fax 0113-258 4211; e-mail overseasemployment@frenchli fe.co.uk; www.frenchlife.co.uk). French Life holidays are specialists in France and Spain and offer first class accommodation at over 30 campsites.

Couriers and **Children's Couriers** (100) to work as campsite representatives and children's clubs representatives. Pay from £400 monthly; board and lodging included. 35 hours per week, 6 days per week. Minimum period of work is 8 weeks between March/April and September/October. Knowledge of French not essential. High season positions available as well.

Apply to Jo Hayes from November at the above address/e-mail.

FANTASTIC OPPORTUNITIES IN EUROPE

Are you available between March and September?
Are you looking for a challenge?

We are a leading UK Tour Operator and we currently have vacancies for the following staff on our 4 star campsites throughout France, Spain and Italy.

CAMPSITE COURIERS

CHILDRENS COURIERS   **SENIOR COURIERS**

- **COMPETITIVE SALARY PLUS COMMISSION!**
- **FREE ACCOMMODATION!**
- **Interested? Call 0113 2050237 for information pack**

www.frenchlife.co.uk   overseasemployment@frenchlife.co.uk

MARK HAMMERTON TRAVEL: 96 High St, Tunbridge Wells, Kent, TN1 1YF (☎01892-525456; fax 01892-510055; e-mail enquiries@markhammerton.co.uk). Mark Hammerton Travel is a young, dynamic tour operator based in Kent and offering top quality tent and mobile home holidays throughout France and Italy.

Operations Team Members (10) required to prepare and/or dismantle campsite accommodation in France. Staff are needed for the first twenty days of May and September. Irregular hours according to weather. Applicants should be at least 18 years old and must be prepared for heavy, physical work. A driving licence is advantageous. Full board and accommodation, insurance and travel expenses are provided. A wage of £95 per week will also be paid.

Applications for the above positions or for team leader/driver positions should be made to the above address.

HAVEN EUROPE: HR Department, 1 Park Lane, Hemel Hempstead, Herts. HP2 4YL (☎01442-203970; fax: 01442-241473; www.haveneurope.com). Haven Europe is a market leader with over 25 years experience in providing family holidays. They are the owner and lead operator of eight parks in France, as well as providing holidays on many selected parks throughout France, Spain & Italy. Haven Europe offer the following varied roles in an Anglo-French working environment.
Park/Assistant Park Representatives, Children's Club Representatives,

Reception Team Members (must be fluent in French), **Accommodation and Facility Team Members, Lifeguards** (must be NPLQ qualified), **Bar Servers** (must have conversational French), **Entertainers, Maintenance/Grounds Team Members.** Team Members will receive a competitive salary, accommodation on site, a free uniform, medical insurance and travel to site. Working as part of a team, your main aim will be to provide excellent customer service. Applicants must be over 18 and preferably available from March to September (some high season positions are available).

Those interested should *ring or write* to the above address.

Work Hard, Play Hard

Haven Europe is part of Bourne Leisure, the UK's largest holiday provider. We are looking for enthusiastic, lively and hard working individuals to fill the following seasonal positions OVERSEAS:

NPLQ qualified lifeguards

Childrens representatives

Park representatives

Accommodation and Facility team members

Bar team members
(must be conversational in French)

Reception team members
(must be fluent in French)

Grounds/Maintenance team members

We offer a competitive salary, accommodation on park, a free uniform and travel to park. If you are over 18 and interested in applying, please call us on 01442 203970 for an information pack, quoting ref. No. SJ01.

Visit our website – www.haveneurope.com

HEADWATER HOLIDAYS: The Old School House, Chester Road, Castle, Northwich, Cheshire, CW8 1LE (☎01606-720033; fax 01606-720001; e-mail info@headwater.com; www.headwater-holidays.co.uk). Headwater offers relaxed discovery and adventure holidays; their hallmarks are personal service, warm friendly hotels and good regional cuisine. Headwater guides and information packs help clients make their own discoveries off the beaten track.

Overseas Representatives to work for an activity holiday company in France. Duties include meeting clients at airports and stations, supervising local transportation for them and their luggage, hotel and client liaison, bike maintenance and on the spot problem solving. Good, working French, and full, clean driving licence required. Organisational skills, resourcefulness and cheerfulness essential. Minimum age 21 years.

Canoeing Instructors: duties etc. as for Overseas Representatives but also include giving canoe instruction.

Wages from £115-150 per week; accommodation provided. To work hours as required. Staff required for full season from April to October.

Further information and an on-line *application* form can be found on their website, or an application form can be requested from the above address.

IAN MEARNS HOLIDAYS: Tannery Yard, Witney Street, Burford, Oxon OX18 4DP (☎01993-822655; fax 01993 822650; e-mail enquiries@ianmearnsholidays.co.uk; www .ianmearnsholidays.co.uk). Ian Mearns Holidays has 18 years' experience of operating family self-drive camping holidays in France.

Campsite Courier to be responsible for the day-to-day running of campsite, ensuring that clients get the highest level of customer service. Duties include preparing customers' accommodation for their arrival, welcoming them to the campsite and being on hand to help during their stay. Must be fit and hardworking. Minimum age 18.

Area Supervisors to be responsible for overseeing operations on up to nine campsites. Duties include montage/demontage team leader, visiting campsites to offer couriers support and supervision. Applicant should be over 21. Must have proven managerial experience, language skills and knowledge of the camping industry.

Montage/demontage Assistants to work with a small team of people setting up or closing down the company campsite operations in France for 6-8 weeks before and after the season. Minimum age 18.

All staff receive wages, accommodation, insurance, uniform, training and transport provided. Season dates are Easter/May-September, although some half-season positions are available.

Application forms and job descriptions can be requested from Karen at the above address.

Ian Mearns Holidays has 18 years experience of taking families on self-drive camping holidays in France. We are looking for hard-working, enthusiastic people with customer service experience. We have positions on 14 luxury campsites throughout France in the following roles: Campsite Couriers, Area Managers and Montage or Demontage Assistants.

IAN MEARNS
Holidays

You need to be available from March or May and be able to work until September or October. We have a limited number of half-season vacancies from May-July or July-September.

For an application form please telephone:
or e-mail enquiries@ianmearnsholidays.co.uk   **01993 822655**

INTERNATIONAL LIFE LEISURE: Kerry House, Kerry Street, Leeds, LS18 4AW (☎0113-2050292; fax 0113 2584211; e-mail overseasemployment@frenc hlife.co.uk; www.frenchlife.co.uk). International Life Leisure run campsites and holidays throughout France. A branch of their organisation is French Life Holidays, who have tents and mobile homes about 30 campsites in France.

Couriers to greet clients on arrival, prepare accommodation and carry out general duties whilst clients are on the campsite. Wage £105 per week. Good customer relations skills are important and experience is an advantage.

Children's Couriers required to organise kid's club, entertain children and carry out general cleaning duties. Wage £95 per week. Experience of working with children is preferable.

No qualifications are required, but knowledge of French would be beneficial and a hard-working, flexible attitude is required. Period of work at least 3 months between early March and September, 6 days, 37 hours per week. Free accommodation is available.

Applications to the above address from December.

KEYCAMP HOLIDAYS: Overseas Recruitment Department (Ref: SJ/04), Hartford Manor, Greenbank Lane, Northwich CW8 1H (☎01606-787525; www.ho lidaybreakjobs.com).

Campsite Couriers: to look after British, Dutch and Scandinavian customers on campsites in France. Duties include welcoming customers, providing local information, organising social activities on site and ensuring that all accommodation is prepared prior to arrival.

Chidren's Courier: to organise and provide up to 24 hours of activities per week for children aged 4-13 years, to advertise the club activities and visit families on arrival.

Senior Courier: incorporating the role of campsite courier with the additional responsibility of organising and managing the team and ensuring the smooth running of the Keycamp operation on site.

Montage/Demontage: for a period of approximately 6-8 weeks at the beginning/ end of season to erect/dismantle equipment.

Minimum age 18 years. Accommodation, uniform, competitive salary and return travel and training provided. A working knowledge of French would be an advantage. Period of employment between March and July/October.

Applicants should apply on-line at www.holidaybreakjobs.com or telephone 01606-787525 for an Application Pack.

MARK WARNER: telephone 020-7761-7300 (24 hour) or 020-7761 7340 for childcare recruitment.

Managers, Accountants, Receptionists, Watersports Instructors, Tennis and Aerobics Instructors, Chefs, Kitchen Porters, Waiting and Bar Staff, Nannies, Handymen, Nightwatchmen and more are required to work in hotels in Corsica during the summer from April to October. Wages from £50 per week plus full board, medical insurance, travel expenses and free use of watersport and activity facilities. Some reserve staff also needed throughout the season. Requirements for languages, age, experience, qualifications etc. vary according to the job applied for.

For further details, please call the Resorts Recruitment Department on the above number.

MATTHEWS HOLIDAYS: 8 Bishopsmead Parade, East Horsley, Surrey KT24 6RP.

Couriers/Campsite Representatives to receive clients and maintain and clean mobile homes in western France. £120 per week. 35 hour, 6 day week. Accommodation provided. Knowledge of French essential. Applicants should be at least 20 years of age and available to commence work during April or May and work until mid/late September. A few vacancies available for the period July-September.

Applications to the above address enclosing an s.a.e. and giving details of age, present occupation and other relevant experience, and date available to commence work.

NSS RIVIERA HOLIDAYS: 288, Chemin du Caladou, F-06560 Valbonne, France. (tel/fax +33-4 93 12 95 81; e-mail nss@wanadoo.fr). NSS has a number of agents working in several European countries. Customers come from the UK, Holland, Belgium, Germany, Switzerland and Denmark. Working language is English.

Active Couples aged 45 or older needed to offer short-term help to a small British, privately-owned holiday operation in the South of France; to work in a complex of 27 chalets, cottages and mobile homes on a 4 star holiday village complex at Frejus, between St. Tropez and Cannes. Maintenance duties require people with some of the following DIY skills to a good standard: joinery, plumbing, electrics, building, painting & decorating, gardening and cleaning. In exchange for 3 days' work per week couples will receive free self-contained, furnished accommodation with own patio and private parking plus free electricity, gas, water, local rates, local taxes and site fees.

Maintenance Helpers are needed for periods ranging from 3-6 weeks in the Spring and Autumn. In addition we have one couple working full-time as our **Representatives** on site from March to October. Applicants should be enthusiastic, self-motivated, self-taught and disciplined adults, preferably non-smokers, who own a reliable car.

Applications should be sent to Don Nimmo at the above address and provide information on each person, a recent photograph, a summary of the relevant skills for each person and stating preferred dates.

NST TRAVEL GROUP: Recruitment, Chiltern House, Bristol Avenue, Blackpool, Lancashire FY2 OFA (☎01253-503011; fax 01253-356955; e-mail info@nstjobs.co.uk; www.nstjobs.co.uk). NST Travel have two residential centres in France. Le Chateau, offering educational and French language courses for secondary school groups and Lou Valagran which offers adventurous activity holidays for secondary school groups.

Group Co-ordinators (7) for Le Chateau to accompany guests on excursions around the French countryside. Excellent working knowledge of French required.

Activity Instructors (20) for Lou Valagran to instruct a range of outdoor activities and to assist with the evening entertainment programme. Qualifications in canoeing, kayaking, caving, or climbing advantageous.

Catering Assistants (5) for Lou Valagran to assist the Catering Manager and be involved in all aspects of kitchen work. No previous experience required.

Support Staff (6, for both centres), including positions for drivers, boat loaders, bar, shop, support, cleaning and maintenance staff. No experience required though a full driving licence is needed for driving positions.

Staff required from January through to November. All positions are residential. Minimum period of work 2 months: average working week 42 hours over 6 days.

For more information and an application form please *contact* the above address.

PGL TRAVEL: 874 Alton Court, Penyard Lane, Ross-on-Wye, Herefordshire HR9 5GL (☎01989-767833; e-mail pglpeople@pgl.co.uk; www.pgl.co.uk/people). With 25 activity centres located in France and Spain, PGL Travel provides adventure holidays and courses for children. Each year 2,500 people are needed to help run these adventure centres.

Children's Group Leaders required to take responsibility for groups of children, helping them to get the most out of their holiday. Minimum age 18. Previous experience of working with children is essential.

General positions available in catering, administration, driving (car or PCV), stores, site cleaning and nurses (RGN or SEN) etc.

Experienced Children's Activity Instructors in canoeing, sailing, windsurfing, pony trekking, multi-activities and drama.

From £60-£90 per week plus full B & L. Vacancies available for short or long periods between March and September. Overseas applicants eligible to work in the

UK welcome.

Applications can be made online or a form obtained from the above address.

ROCKLEY WATERSPORTS: Poole, Dorset BH15 4RW (☎01202-677272; fax 01202-668268; e-mail info@rockleywatersports.com). Based in beautiful Poole harbour and South-West France, Rockley teach watersports to all abilities and ages; and are one of Europe's most highly regarded watersports centres.

Watersports Instructors (50); experienced instructors, senior instructors and sailing managers are required to work in South West France at two of the largest RYA recognised watersports centres in Europe.

Couriers (10) for duties including assisting in the kitchens, cleaning and general site duties. The jobs offer the opportunity to gain watersports experience and use all the facilities of the centres.

The above are needed to work for flexible periods during the summer season which runs from March until October.

Those interested should *contact Richard Percy* for an application form.

SANDPIPER HOLIDAYS LTD: Walnut Cottage, Kenley, Shrewsbury, SY5 6NS (☎01746-785123; fax 01746-785100; e-mail sandpiperhols@bigfoot.com). Small friendly holiday tour operator specialising in self-drive camping holidays to France. Reps are chosen for their enthusiasm; they work hard, have a lot of fun and definitely improve their French.

Representatives (8) to look after clients, clean and maintain tents, mobile homes and organise children's activities on camp sites in France. Wages by arrangement (c.£400 per month). Period of work from mid May to mid September: applicants must be prepared to work for at least half the season.

Applicants must be over 19, prepared to work hard, and have a sense of humour. Accommodation is provided in tents.

Telephone the above number for an application form before the end of January.

SELECT FRANCE: Murcott, Kidlington, Oxford OX5 2RE (☎01865-331350; e-mail jobs@selectfrance.co.uk; www.selectfrance.co.uk). Select France is a family company with a reputation for personal service. They use campsites in Brittany, Vendée, Charente and the Western Mediterranean.

Campsite Representative: Successful applicants will be responsible for ensuring that the accommodation provided for clients is kept clean and well maintained. They will also be expected to keep up to date with a small amount of paperwork and organise some activities for children and adults. Some sites require couples.

Applicants, preferably over 21, must be cheerful, pragmatic, responsible, self-reliant and above all, honest. Knowledge of French and a clean driving licence is an advantage. Free accommodation and casual uniform provided. Period of work is from mid-May to end of September. Wages of around £400 per month, with the opportunity to earn more.

Applications to the above address.

SIMPLY CORSICA: Simply Travel, King's Place, 12-42 Wood Street, Kingston-upon-Thames, Surrey, KT1 1SG (☎0870 888 0028; e-mail www.shgjobs.co.uk). Simply Travel is part of the Specialist Holidays Group, providing holidays for the discerning traveller. Offering a selection of top Mediterranean destinations as well as a winter ski programme in the top ski destinations.

Resort Representatives: seasonal and year-round. Working to very high company expectations, applicants should be hard working, self-motivated and have initiative.

Simply Travel look for staff with excellent customer service and problem solving skills. A second European language and full clean driving licence are essential for all customer-facing positions. The representative's job is to ensure that customers have an enjoyable holiday exceeding their expectations.

A competitive package including salary, accommodation, transport to and from resort and insurance is offered. Other roles positions available for: **Chamber Persons, Drivers, Chefs, Watersports Instructors**.

Contact the Overseas Recruitment Department on 0870-888 0028.

SKI FANATICS: Route de la Telecabine, 74300 Les Carroz d'Araches, France (☎0870 068 9882; fax 0870 068 9880; e-mail snowbeds@btclick.com; www.snowbeds.com). Chalet operator and agency for supplying good value ski accommodation to a wide range of clients with an emphasis on service and professionalism. Has just started offering summer holidays.

Sales staff (2) to deal with sales enquiries, database input, and admin. Computer skills (MS Office and Access advantageous). Good customer manner. French an advantage, also Italian and German.

Representative (1) for collecting clients and hosting new summer holiday. French an advantage and clean driving licence required.

Chef (1) to provide breakfast and evening meal and ordering. Food hygiene and budgeting. Should have NVQ or equivalent or equivalent experience. Should be versatile and numerate. Attitude and ability more important than qualification.

Pay is negotiable and board and lodging is included. Work is six days a week for a minimum of one month during July to September.

Apply to the above address anytime.

SODISTOUR: Mme Roussel, 126 Rue de la Fayette, 75010 Paris. Operates three family entertainment centres.

General Assistants and Tour Guides needed: details on application.

Applications to the above address.

SOLAIRE HOLIDAYS: 1158 Stratford Road, Hall Green, Birmingham, B28 8AF (☎0121-778 5061; fax 0121-778 5065; e-mail holiday@solaire.co.uk; www.solaire.co.uk). Solaire Holidays provides self-drive self-catering holidays to France and Spain. They also have their own holiday park in Southern Brittany.

Site Couriers (20) to look after clients and prepare accommodation. Knowledge of French/Spanish desirable. Wage £280-£400 per month.

Children's Couriers (4) to run a children's club. Previous experience of working with children is required. Wage £280-£400 per month.

Applicants can apply for work between April and October, May and September or July and August. Hours of work vary according to demand, but applicants can expect to work for six days a week, on a rota system. Accommodation is provided as part of contract. Food is not provided.

Applications are invited from October onwards to the above address.

SUSI MADRON'S CYCLING FOR SOFTIES: 2-4 Birch Polygon, Rusholme, Manchester M14 5HX (☎0161-248 8282).

Company Assistants to work for a company offering cycling holidays in France. Fixed wage plus bonus. Minimum period of work 2 months between May and September. Full training in bicycle maintenance is given. Must be a keen cyclist, non-smoker, aged over 20 and speak French.

Application forms can be obtained by telephoning the above number.

TJM TRAVEL: Penhalveor East, Redruth, TR16 6NL (☎01209-860000; fax 01209-860998; e-mail jobs@tjm-travel.co.uk). TJM run hotels and activity centres in France, Spain and the UK in the summer months, and they operate ski holidays from French Alpine hotels in the winter.

Qualified Sailing, Canoe, Windsurfing, Snorkelling, Climbing, Mountain Biking Instructors, Hotel Staff; Manager, Chef, Bar, Waiting, Chamber, Kitchen Staff, Handymen. All required for hotel or activity centre work in France, Spain or the UK, all staff must have appropriate qualifications, experience and skills. Wages vary between £300 and £700 per month according to job and experience. Board and lodging provided. Staff work 7 hours a day per 6 day week, with the minimum period of work being 3-4 weeks. Working period is May to August and December to April.

Applicants can *apply* any time of year by letter, must include *passport photos*, full photo, current cv and copies of any relevant certificates: apply by post or e-mail.

VENDEE LOISIRS VACANCES: 30 Parc des Demoiselles F-85160 St Jean de Monts, France (☎0033 251-58-04-02; e-mail vlv@wanadoo.fr; www.vlv.fr). Linda and Mark run a small friendly business offering mobile home holidays on a campsite, with direct access to the beach in St Jean de Monts. They live locally and are on hand for help and advice.

Representative/Children's Entertainment (2) The job of the rep is to welcome, check out, and provide information for the client and to clean the mobiles. The children's entertainer runs a Children's club and shares other duties. Both organise activities like boules, quizzes, canoeing etc.

Period of work mid-May to beginning of September. Wages £100 a week plus free accommodation in caravan on site, day off, and most afternoons free. Must be French speaker, experienced with children and enjoy meeting people. Ideal for 2 friends, or a couple.

Write to Linda Aplin at the above address enclosing a cv and photo.

VILLAGE CAMPS INC: Personnel Office Dept. 815, 14 Rue de la Morâche, 1260 Nyon, Switzerland. (☎+41 22 990 9405; fax +41 22 990 9494; e-mail personnel@villagecamps.ch; www.villagecamp.com). Village Camps has been organising educational and activity camps for children from all over the globe for over 25 years with a serious commitment to client and staff alike.

Specialists and General Counsellors required for outdoor education, orienteering, leadership training, nature/environmental studies, swimming, archery, tennis, outdoor education, soccer, arts and crafts, mountain biking, gymnastics and drama etc.

Qualified Instructors in rock climbing, canoeing, mountain leading, watersports.

Language Teachers for English, French and German classes.

Nurses/Medical Staff: must be qualified RSN or equivalent.

Kitchen and **Domestic Staff** (EU passport holders only for these domestic positions)

Drivers

Junior Staff: for the Day Camp only (No accommodation included).

The Outdoor Education Programme occurs from May to June in Switzerland and France and in the autumn, August to October in Switzerland. The Summer Residential and Day Camps occur from June to August in Switzerland, UK, Holland, France and Austria. Room and board, accident & liability insurance and a generous allowance are provided. All staff must be over 21. Much is expected of staff but the rewards are generous. Experience working with children is essential and knowledge of a second language is an advantage. Motivated staff are required for short seasonal positions.

Applications: visit the above website for more information or contact the Personnel Department at the address above for an application pack.

Teaching and Language Schools

MRS JULIE LEGREE: Syndicat Mixte Montaigu-Rocheserviere, 35 avenue Villebois Mareuil, F-85607 Montaigu cedex, France (☎02-51 46 45 45; fax 02-51 46 45 40; e-mail julie-legree@yahoo.co.uk; www.explomr.com/english). This is a local government scheme which has been running for twelve years. They are looking for Francophiles who wish to develop their social and professional skills.

TEFL Teachers (4) to teach English to 9-11 year old pupils in 29 different primary schools in the Vendée. Applicants should be outgoing, independent, organised and mature enough to act on their own initiative, as well as having a love of France and children.

TEFL Teacher to teach 14-21 year olds in a college and lycée as an *assistante*. Candidates will need the maturity and self-confidence to deal with teenagers, and be able to relate to a large teaching staff.

All posts require 20 hours a week teaching, per 4 day week, with no work on Wednesdays, weekends or school holidays. Full training is given and contracts run from October until May. Included in the remuneration package is free board and lodging with local families and an allowance of approx. €185.35 per month, after national insurance contributions.

Applications by post to Mrs Julie Legree at the above address.

Winter Jobs

HARRI'S BAR: Evolution 2, Hotel le Lavachet, F-73320 Tignes, France (☎+33 4 79 06 48 11; fax +33 4 79 06 57 13; e-mail info@skibarjobs.com; www.skibarjobs.com). Evolution 2 is a French company based in the ski resort of Tignes running Harri's Bar, on of the biggest and liveliest bars in the resort with a mainly English speaking clientele.

Bar Staff with enthusiastic, presentable, outgoing and fun-loving personalities needed. Although previous experience is not necessary, applicants must be hard-working and able to fit into a team quickly.

Chef: should have experience of ordering for and setting up three course menus for up to 100 hotel guests for the pre-season period. During the main season the chef will run a pub-food menu, prepare local speciality meals for up to 100 people several times a week and provide staff meals each evening.

Kitchen Hands for cleaning and washing-up duties, also to fill in for chef with the pub-food menu on days off.

Staff should be willing to work as a team and infuse the bar with a positive and enthusiastic spirit. Main season (December-April) hours of work are 3.30pm-1.30am with a meal break, and there are two full days off per week. Wages start at £300 net per month not including tips and there is a discretionary end of season bonus. Good quality shared accommodation is provided as well as a daily evening meal, ski pass and ski hire. There is also the chance to take part in ski lessons and generally to ski every day. Positions are open to male and female candidates and start around the 7th of October. Further details can be found on www.skibarjobs.com.

Application forms can be obtained from the above address.

Voluntary Work

Archaeology

CONSERVATEUR DU PATRIMOINE: 3 rue Gregoire de Tours, F-63000 Clermont-Ferrand, France (☎473-91-61-97/473-41-27-23; fax 473-41-27-69).
Volunteers (5) for archaeological **field work in the volcanic Cantal Massif**, France. To **assist a dig of a mesolithic hunters settlement dated 10,000** years BC. To work 7 hours a day, 5 days a week. Volunteers required from July to August; minimum period of work 2 weeks. Accommodation provided at a cost of £120. Experience not essential but would be an advantage. Knowledge of French not necessary but useful.
Applications from March to Frédéric Surmely at the above address.

INSTITUT D'HISTOIRE: Universite du Mans, Avenue O. Messiaen, Le Mans, F-72017 France (☎243-83-31-64; fax 243-83-31-44).
Volunteers (20) to assist on archaeological digs. 8 hour day, 5½ day week. Board and lodging provided free. Applicants should be in good health and enjoy working as a team. Knowledge of French or English required. Minimum period of work 3 weeks in July.
Applications from April to Annie Renoux at the above address.

PROFESSOR HENRY DE LUMLEY: Lab. de Préhistoire, IPH, 1 rue René Panhard, F-75013 Paris, France.
Volunteers to take part in archaeological digs in France. To work 8½ hours per day, 6 days per week. Minimum period of work 15 days between April and June or 30 days between July and August. Minimum age 16. Applicants should be students or researchers in prehistory, archaeology or the natural sciences.
Applications to Professor de Lumley at the above address.

LOUIS ROUSSEL: 28 Rue du Bourg, F-21000 Dijon, France (e-mail malaingam@hotmail.com).
Volunteers (20) to work on an archaeological dig involving the **restoration of a medieval château and a Gallo-Roman site** near Dijon in July: in addition to **digging,** the jobs to be done include **reassembling and drawing the finds.** Accommodation is provided in exchange for around 8 hours work per day, 5 days per week and a weekly contribution of around €15. Applicants must be at least 18 years old: experience in any of the above fields would be an advantage.
Applications to M. Roussel at the above address.

SERVICE ARCHEOLOGIQUE DE DOUAI: 191 rue St. Albin, F-59500 Douai, France. This is a local association for archaeology and the preservation of local cultural heritage.
Supervisors (2) to manage part of an archaeological excavation. 7-hour day, 5 day week. £500 per month. Board and lodging provided free. Period of work 2 months from July 9 to beginning of September. Applicants should have experience in field archaeology and, if possible, a knowledge of French.
Volunteers also required to assist with the **excavation and drawing of maps**. About 70 adults are engaged annually.
Applicants must have tetanus vaccination and valid passport. Volunteers should bring a sleeping bag and high boots. Minimum stay 2 weeks. Accommodation is provided Monday to Friday. Application fee of €22,87.

Applications to P. Demolon at the above address from April.

SERVICE REGIONAL DE L'ARCHEOLOGIE: 6, rue de la Manufacture, F-45000 Orleans, France (tel: 238-78-85-41).
Diggers and Draughtsmen (50). To work on an archaeological dig in Orleans or in one of the other digs in Central France. Should have relevant experience: some knowledge of French is desirable. 8-hour day, 5-day week. No salary, but board and lodging are provided free. Minimum period of work 2 weeks between June and September.
Applications in April to the above address.

SERVICE REGIONAL DE L'ARCHEOLOGIE DE BRETAGNE: Hotel de Blossac, 6 rue du Chapitre, F-35044 Rennes Cedex, France (☎299-84-59-00; fax 02-99-84-59-19).
Volunteers (10-30 per site) to take part in **various archaeological digs in Brittany** between April and September. To work 7 hours per day, 5-5½ days per week. Board and accommodation, usually on a campsite, is in most cases provided free of charge, but on some sites there is a charge of £5 to cover insurance etc. Minimum period of work 2 weeks. No previous experience is necessary, but a basic knowledge of French is required. Applicants must be at least 18 years old.
The new programme will be available in April; *applications* should be sent to the above address from March.

Heritage

BARDOU: Klaus & Jeane Erhardt, Mons La Trivalle, F-34390 Olargues, France (☎+33-4-67-97-72-43). The hamlet of Bardou is situated at the heart of a Natural Regional Park in southern France. It attracts artists, classical musicians and nature lovers, with accommodation for volunteers and paying guests.
Volunteers to help **restore and maintain 16th century stone houses and to assist with a flock of pedigree sheep** in a remote mountain hamlet. Free lodging is provided in a self-catering house in exchange for 20 hours of help per week. Minimum stay 1 month between 1st March and 1st July and 1st September and 1st December.
Please *send* a CV and an International Reply Coupon for details to Klaus and Jean Erhardt at the above address.
Applications to Genest Jacques, President of the Association, at the above address.

CLUB DU VIEUX MANOIR: Abbaye du Moncel à Pontpoint, F-60700 Pont Ste Maxence, France. Founded in 1953, this is a volunteer association for young people who wish to spend some of their spare time doing rescue and restoration work on historic monuments and ancient sites. The volunteers share in the day to day organisation of the camp and site. The centres are at the Château Fort de Guise (Aisne), the Abbey Royale du Moncel à Pontpoint (Oise) and the Château d'Argy (Indre).
Volunteers required for work on the **restoration of ancient monuments and similar tasks**. Minimum age for volunteers is 15 years. There are no set hours to work but everyone is expected to lend a hand when the group decides to work on a project. Work is, of course, unpaid and volunteers are expected to contribute around £8 per day towards the cost of their keep. Accommodation is usually in tents. Training organised for participants of 16 years and over.

Long-term stays are a possibility for volunteers at the Château Fort de Guise. After a trial period of 15 days board and lodging will be offered by the association, minimum stay two months.

Applications to the address shown above.

LA SABRANENQUE: Centre International, rue de la Tour de L'Oume, F-30290 Saint Victor la Coste, France (☎466-50-05-05; e-mail info@sabranenque.com). La Sabranenque is a non-profit organisation that has been working for 30 years for the preservation of rural habitat and traditional architecture.

Volunteers (10 per session) to help with the **restoration of villages, sites and simple monuments in France, using traditional building methods.** Work includes restoration of roofs, terraces, walls, paths or the reconstruction of small houses. Minimum period of work 2 weeks between 1st June and 30th August; at least one day each 2-week period is spent visiting the region. Board and accommodation are provided at a cost of £160 approx. per 2-week period. Applicants must be at least 18 years old and in good health.

Applications to the above address at any time.

REMPART : 1 rue des Guillemites, F-75004 Paris, France (☎1-42-71-96-55; fax 1-42-71-73-00; e-mail contact@rempart.com; www.rempart.com pages available in English)

Volunteer restorers and preservers for various **castles, fortresses, churches, chapels, abbeys, monasteries, farms, ancient villages, Gallo-Roman sites**, etc. on the 150 sites organised by REMPART every year, during holidays. Board and accommodation are provided at a cost of £4-£5 per day. Most stays are for two weeks. Volunteers pay their own travel expenses and should bring their own sleeping bags and working clothes. Work includes **masonry, woodwork, carpentry, coating, restoration and clearance work**. Opportunities for swimming, tennis, riding, watersports, cycling, exploring the region, taking part in local festivities. Minimum age is 13, but preferably 18 for non-French residents, with no upper age limit. Some knowledge of French is needed. Previous experience is not necessary.

Contact the above address for this year's programme.

Physically & Mentally Disabled

ASSOCIATIONS DES PARALYSES DE FRANCE: 17 Boulevard Auguste-Blanqui, F-75013 Paris, France.

Assistants required for **work in holiday centres for physically handicapped adults**. Pocket money given. Board and accommodation and expenses provided. Minimum age 18 years. Period of work 15-21 days during the summer vacation. Applicants should be able to speak a little French.

Applications to APF Evasion at the above address.

Workcamps

LES AMIS DE CHEVREAUX – CHATEL: Rue du Chateau, F-39190 Chevreaux, France (tel/fax +33-3-84-85-95-77; e-mail accjura@free.fr; http://accjura.free.fr). The chateau of Chevreaux is situated in a hilltop village above the Bresse Plains. Les Amis de Chevreaux is a place where young people of different nationalities can meet and spend time together. The work site in the Jura requires willing volunteers to help with the **restoration of the 13th century castle of Chevreaux**. Volunteers are needed for the last three weeks in July and the first three weeks in August and will be lodged on site (at the castle) in tents with a campbed; all sanitary and kitchen facilities are provided. Duties involve **cleaning, reconstruction of the ruins, stone working, carpentry, masonry, archaeology or topography.**

The work lasts 6 hours per day, 5 days a week. After work activities include swimming, horse riding and volleyball. At the weekends there is the opportunity to discover the rich patrimony and landscapes of the Jura. Age limits: 18-25. No special qualifications needed apart from good motivation, enthusiasm and willingness to plan your part in keeping the camp running smoothly.

Applications to the above address.

APARE: 41, Cours Jean Jaurès, F-84000 Avignon, France (☎33-(0)4-90-85-51-15; fax 33-(0)4-90-86-82-19; e-mail apare@apare-gec.org; www.apare-gec.org) APARE is a voluntary organisation which aims to promote participation (especially among young people) through volunteering in local development projects. APARE, set up in 1979, by a group of people who shared a passion for Provençal dry stone architecture. It has organised more than 300 voluntary workcamps in over 100 communes.

International Voluntary Work Camps in Provence and the Mediterranean Region-see also GEC/APARE entry in *Vacancies Across Europe* section.

Applications to the above address.

ASSOCIATION CHANTIERS HISTOIRE & ARCHITECTURE MÉDIÉVALES: 5 et 7 rue Guilleminot, 75014 Paris, France (☎33-1 43 35 +15 51; fax 33-1 43 20 46 82 e-mail cham@cham.asso.fr).

Volunteers required for **conservation workcamps** at various locations in France. The work includes **restoration and repair of historic monuments, chateaux and churches.** Volunteers must be at least 16 years old and in good health. Board and lodging provided at 10 euros per day. Placements are available from April to the end of August with some camps active at other times of the year, with a minimum stay of ten days recommended. Volunteers receive on the job training under qualified supervisors and work about 6 hours per day, 6 days a week. Registration 30 euros.

For full details of the workcamps *write* to C.H.A.M. at the above address.

CHANTIERS DE JEUNES PROVENCE COTE D'AZUR: 7 Avenue Pierre de Coubertin F-06150 Cannes, La Bocca, France (☎0493-47-89-69; fax 0493-48-12-01; e-mail cjpca@club.internet.fr; www.club.internet.fr/perso/cjpca/).

Volunteers aged 13-17 to take part in the **restoration of historic monuments and in environmental protection projects:** projects consist of 5 hours work in the morning and organised activities such as sailing, climbing and diving in the afternoons/evenings. Accommodation provided. Camps take place in the country near Cannes or the island of Sainte Marguerite, and run for one or two weeks during the summer, Christmas or Easter holidays. Applicants must be sociable and speak French.

For further details *send* two international reply coupons to the above address with a letter written in French.

CONCORDIA: Heversham House, 20-22 Boundary Road, Hove, East Sussex BN3 4ET (☎01273-422218; fax 01273 421182; e-mail info@concordia-iye.org.uk; www.concordia-iye.org.uk).

Concordia offers young people aged 16-30 the opportunity to take part in international volunteer projects lasting 2-3 weeks, from June to September. The work is community based and ranges from **nature conservation, renovation,**

construction and social work including children's play schemes and teaching. Volunteers pay a registration fee of approx. £85 and fund their own travel. Board and accommodation are free of charge.

For further information *write* enclosing s.a.e. to: International Volunteer Co-ordinator at the above address.

ETUDES ET CHANTIERS (UNAREC): Délégation Internationale, 3 rue des Petits-Gras, F-63000 Clermont-Ferrand, France (☎473-31-98-04; fax 473-31 98 09).
Organise voluntary workcamps for the upkeep, development and preservation of the environment. Work camps lasting for two or three weeks are held over the summer. Tasks vary and include such activities as **river cleaning, the preservation of old buildings and districts in small towns, organising local cultural festivals, etc.** Minimum age 18 years; camps are also held for younger teenagers aged 14-17. Application fees approx. £65 (including membership and insurance). An annual programme is produced in March.

For further details contact by e-mail workcamps.unarec@wanadoo.fr.

JEUNESSE ET RECONSTRUCTION: 10 rue de Trevise, Paris 9, France.
Volunteers needed for workcamps throughout France. Type of work varies from camp to camp, ranging from the **construction of community centres to digging drains in wet areas.** Work is unpaid, but free board and accommodation are provided. About 7 hours work per day, 5 days per week. Volunteers are likely to come from all over the world.

Applicants should normally be at least 18 years old, though there are some vacancies for 17-year-olds. Most camps last for 3 weeks. There are also possibilities for voluntary work lasting for three months, which provides pocket money.

Applications to the above address.

LES DEUX MOULINS: Gontard, Dauphin, F-04300 Forcalquier, France.
Volunteers to construct new buildings and improve existing amenities at this holiday centre built by and for young people of all nationalities. Minimum age of entry is 18 years and the centre is open throughout the summer. Volunteers pay part of the cost of board and accommodation. The organisation would like to stress that volunteers are unpaid but the work is by no means rigid or exacting.

For further details *contact* the address above.

NEIGE ET MERVEILLES: F-06430 St. Dalmas de Tende, France (☎493-04-62-40; fax 493-04-88-58; e-mail Neige.merveilles@wanadoo.fr; www.neige&merveill es.com).
Volunteers (4) to take part in **international workcamps,** which take place between April and October. Food and accommodation provided. To work 6 hours per day, 5 days per week. Volunteers must pay their own insurance costs of approximately £50. Minimum age 18. This organisation also organises international workcamps for young people aged 15-17.

For *further details* contact the Recruitment Department at the above address.

Other Volunteer Work in France

CENTRE INTERNATIONAL D'ANTIBES/INSTITUT PREVERT: 38 Bd d'Aguillon 06600 Antibes (☎4-92 90 71 70/92 90 71 71). The Centre is situated on the French Riviera, and teaches French to more than 3,000 foreign students a year.

Assistants for numerous work exchange places available including help with administration, helping in kitchens, chambermaid duties or general maintenance duties in a French language school for foreigners. No wages are paid but French courses and/or accommodation are provided. Places are available all year round for varying periods of one to six months.

For more information on their various work exchange programmes, or *to apply*, contact 'Work Exchange' at the above address, or e-mail karine@cia-france.com.

MADAME DE MONTESQUIEU: La Bassie, Bloux, 03320 Lurcy-Levis .(☎04 70 67 96 13; fax 04 70 67 84 52; e-mail malaure2@wanadoo.fr).
Voluntary Assistants (1 or 2) to offer general help in and around a very pretty house with a garden, swimming pool and tennis court. No wages are paid, but board and lodging is provided. Period of work (minimum one and a half months) by arrangement with work available *all year*. Applicants must love cats and dogs (five and two of them respectively) and nature. The positions would be ideal for those who wish to perfect their French. A **housekeeper** is also required.

For more details *contact* Mme Marie Laure de Montesquieu at the above address.

MEINRAD BETSCHART: Rue du Presbytére, F-21140 Montigny sur Armançon, France (☎0033-(0)3-80-97-18-85).
Helpers (4) to assist with the renovation of an old house belonging to a sculptor and his German speaking family. Work includes tasks from wall-building to laying carpets, and working in the garden and in the kitchen. To work 6 hours a day, 6 days a week. Pocket money of £82 per month plus board and accommodation. Minimum period of work 2 weeks. Applicants must be willing to perform practical work and have an interest in art.

Applications to the above address one month before date on which you wish to start work.

PAX CHRISTI: 58 avenue de Breteuil, F-75007 Paris, France (☎01-44-49-06-36; fax 01-44-49-02-15; e-mail pax.christi@wanadoo.fr).
Volunteers to **run a temporary youth hostel** operated over the summer by Pax Christi, the International Catholic Movement for Peace. During the summer months of each year it organises a centre at Lourdes for international encounters. This meeting place, offering bed and breakfast at modest prices, tries to encourage dialogue between different nations, races and religions.

The centre is run by teams of young volunteers who take **care of the practical running of the house.** In addition to this, however they invite visitors to join them in reflection, dialogue and prayer and in exploring Lourdes. The purpose of the centre is to give a living witness that peace is possible. Volunteers are usually between 18-30 years old and must speak French fluently. Each team runs the centre for 15 days. Their work demonstrates a very real commitment to peace.

Applications to the above address.

SOURIRE ET NATURE: chez André Risetti, rue de la Fontaine St. Marc, F-21140 Montigny sur Armançon, France (☎03-80-97-32-46).
Volunteers required for the renovation of a hostel 70km west of Dijon, including **construction of stone walls, painting, gardening, and domestic work.** Instruction offered in methods and use of tools. Work can be tailored to applicants' particular skills. Work is available for volunteers aged 21-40 during July and August and for volunteers aged 19-40 for the rest of the year, to work 5½ days per week, minimum

period of work two weeks. Board and lodging are included. Knowledge of French (preferably), or English required.

Option 1: 33 hours work per week with approx. £10 pocket money provided. Option 2: 15 hours work per week, with the applicant paying approx. £21 per week towards project costs.

Applications, in writing, all year round to the above address enclosing a CV and references.

Au Pairs, Nannies, Family Helps and Exchanges

L'ACCUEIL FAMILIAL DES JEUNES ETRANGERS: 23 rue du Cherche-Midi, F-75006 Paris, France (☎1-42-22-50-34; fax 1-45-44-60-48; e-mail accueil@afje-paris.org).

Au Pairs: (boys and girls) to assist families with housework and look after children for about 30 hours a week. Summer placements from 1 to 3 months possible all over France; applications for these must be received by 15 May. Also placements for the school year, preferably from the beginning of September or January to the end of June.

Paying Guest: stays for a usual minimum of 2 weeks in Paris and the suburbs (but in the provinces only during the holidays) also arranged for boys or girls aged over 18.

For further details *contact* the above address.

'BUTTERFLY ET PAPILLON' SCHOOL OF INTERNATIONAL LANGUAGES & AU PAIR AGENCY: 8, Av de Genève, F-74000 Annecy, France (☎+3 450-67-01-33; fax +33 450-67-03-51; e-mail aupair.france@wanadoo.fr; www.butterfly-papillon.com).

Au Pair: Butterfly et Papillon welcome foreign 18-26 year old students for summer and year long au-pair placements and French courses in the French Alps (Annecy is close to the Swiss border and Geneva). Pocket money at least £170 per month. Board and French lessons available. 30 hours a week plus two evenings babysitting. Age limits: 18-25. Basic French required. Driving licence and experience with children preferred.

Butterfly et Papillon also run a **work exchange programme**. Under the auspices of the EU's Leonardo scheme, this programme offers foreign students the unique opportunity to live and work in France for up to 13 weeks.

Applications to Fleur Martin, Main Secretary, at the above address.

CENTRE DE VACANCES D'AULON: F-65440 Guchen, France.

Assistant Group Leaders to work with children 6-12 years and 13-17 years. Approximately £105 to £115 per month according to ability. Free board and lodging. Minimum age 19 years.

Applications to the above address.

INTERNATIONAL CATHOLIC SOCIETY FOR GIRLS (ACISJF) ADVISORY SERVICE: 55 Nightingale Road, Rickmansworth, Herts, WD3 7BU (☎01923-778449 Office Hours Mon-Fri 10.30am-12.30pm).

Advice on au pair placements abroad, mainly in France, for English applicants. Minimum age 18 years: minimum stay 3 months approx.

Any *enquiries* should be made enclosing a stamped addressed envelope, to the above address.

INSTITUT EURO PROVENCE: 69 rue de Rome, F-13001 Marseille, France (☎+33-4-91 33 90 60; fax 4-91 33 77 36; e-mail euro.provence@wanadoo.fr; http:

//perso.wanadoo.fr/euro.provence).

Au Pairs needed to look after children and carry out light housework required to work 30 hours per week plus two evenings baby-sitting. Au Pairs are required all year round, with the minimum period of work being two months in the summer and six months the rest of the year. Board and lodging are provided free and au pairs are paid by the family. Applicants will need basic French, but the institute provides low cost French classes.

For more details contact Mrs Patricia Guedj-Gandolfo.

THE NORFOLK CARE SEARCH AGENCY: 19 London Road, Downham Market, Norfolk PE3 9BJ (☎01366-384448; fax 01366-385226).

Au Pair positions arranged in the South of France. All year-round for stays of three months to one year. Summer placements for 6-12 weeks in the Nice/Corsica area. Especially suitable for University students wishing to practice the French language during the summer holidays; ideal GAP year placements. Pocket money of £200 per month, plus board and accommodation. Applicants should be aged between 18 and 27 and have EU citizenship. A charge is made for this service.

For *application* forms phone, e-mail or write to the agency at the above address. S.a.e. preferred.

SOAMES INTERNATIONAL SERVICES/PARIS NANNIES: 6 Route de Marlotte, F-77690 Montieny s/Loing, France (☎01-64 78 37 98; fax 01-64 45 91 75; e-mail soames.parisnannies@wanadoo.fr).

Au Pairs: wage approximately £45 per week.

Nannies: wage min. £160 per week.

Mothers' Helps: wage around £120 per week.

Minimum period of work 2 months; minimum age 18. Previous childcare experience desirable.

For further details *contact* the above address.

Other Employment in France

CENTRE D'INFORMATION ET DE DOCUMENTATION JEUNESSE: 101 quai Branly, F-75740 Paris Cedex 15, France (☎01-44 49 12 00; e-mail cidj@cidj.com; www.cidj.com).

Advertises temporary jobs on a daily basis, mainly in Paris and the surrounding area, available to young people. It also gives information on cheap places to stay, on French university courses for foreigners and practical advice on the regulations as part of its general information serviced for young people. CIDJ also publishes booklets on a range of subjects for young people.

Please note: to get details of the jobs you must visit the centre personally; the CIDJ does not not send out information on this subject; opening hours are 10am-6pm, Monday, Wednesday and Thursday; 9.30am to 1pm, Saturday: 10am to 7pm, Tuesday and Friday (nearest metro: Bir-Hakeim).

SEJOURS INTERNATIONAUX LINGUISTIQUES ET CULTURELS: 32 Rempart de l'Est, F-16022 Angoulême Cedex, France (☎+33-5-45 97 41 90; fax 5-45 94 20 63; e-mail france@silc.fr; www.silc-france.com).

Work Experience placements throughout France, as well as a variety of language **Study Courses, International Summer Centres, Individual Homestays and Private Tuition.**

For details *contact the above address.*

Germany

Germany is a very good prospect for seasonal work, most opportunities being in the western and southern regions. The benefits of membership of the European Union are that British and Irish jobseekers and those of the other EU states must be given the same treatment as a German when applying for a job. However, unemployment rose to a level of 11% in February 2003 and economists predicted no improvement for 5 years.

Many of the seasonal jobs available are in hotels, especially in tourist areas such as the Bavarian Alps, the Black Forest and resorts on the North Sea Coast. People going to work in a German hotel should note that managers may demand extra hours of work from their employees, and some will not always give extra time off or pay overtime as compensation. They may also ask workers to do jobs that are not specified in their contract by asking them to fill in for other members of staff. Anyone who feels that their contract is being breached and who cannot come to any agreement with their employer should appeal to the local *Arbeitsamt* (see below) for arbitration. Jobs in other sectors in the tourist industry can be found in this chapter and in the *Worldwide* chapter at the beginning of this book.

There are also fruit-picking jobs available, although not nearly as many as in France. During the summer the best region to try is the *Altes Land* which stretches between Stade and Hamburg in north Germany and includes the towns of Steinkirchen, Jork and Horneburg. The work there consists of picking cherries in July and August, and apples in September. Try also the Bergstrasse south of Frankfurt where apples and many other fruits are grown. Germany's vineyards also provide a source of work, particularly because in recent years, German winemakers have found it increasingly difficult to find workers to help with the grape harvest. The harvest begins in October and continues into November: the vineyards are concentrated in the south west of the country, especially along the valleys of the Rhine to the south of Bonn and Moselle.

The Happy Hands programme (Anne von Gleichen, Roemerberg 8, 60311, Frankfurt/Main, Tel: 069-293733 Fax: 069-295564 E-Mail: Anne.Gleichen@t-online.de; www.workingholiday.de) arranges working holidays on farms or in family-run country hotels for British and European students who know some German. Participants are given monthly pocket money and full board and lodging with families on farms or in country hotels. In return they help in the kitchen, serving German guests, look after children and/or horses, farm animals for 3-6 months though a six-week commitment is also allowed; some vacancies for female students in the autumn available. There is usually a higher proportion of female than males participants recruited. There is a registration fee. Contact first with an e-mail before booking. Early requests are appreciated.

It may also be possible to arrange voluntary work on an organic farm: see the entry on WWOOF in the *Worldwide* chapter for details. Volunteers would receive free board, lodging and training in return for their work. For more details contact WWOOF-Deutschland, Postfach 210259, 01263 Dresden, Germany (e-mail info@wwoof.de; www.wwoof.de). Membership of the German branch of WWOOF costs about £10, and gives access to about 160 farm addresses.

On arrival in Germany, EU nationals may go the *Arbeitsamt* (employment office) in the area in which they wish to work and obtain information on job opportunities: its address will be in the local telephone directory. It is, however, simpler to arrange a job in advance through the EURES contact in your local employment office or through the Zentralstelle fur Arbeitsvermittlung (ZAV, Villemombler Str. 76, 53123 Bonn; 0228-713-0; fax 0228-713 1111; www.arbeitsamt.de) which is the official government office dealing with job applications from abroad. Alternatively, your nearest Department of Employment which has contacts with German employment offices. The Zentralstelle may be able to help find work in hotels, on farms, or in factories: it has a special department to help students find summer jobs, applications for which must be received before the end of February. For further information about the official German employment service and other aspects of work there consult the free fact sheet *Working in Germany* published by Jobcentre Plus. This is available from the European and International Jobsearch Advice Team, Jobcentre Plus, Yorkshire & The Humber Regional Office, 33-41 Park Place, Leeds, LS1 2RD; 0113-285-8660, and Jobcentre Plus offices throughout the UK. CIEE in the US administers a *Work in Germany Programme* for American citizens, see their entry in the *Worldwide* chapter.

In addition to those listed in this chapter there are opportunities for voluntary work in Germany; British applicants can apply through International Voluntary Service, UNA Exchange, Youth Action for Peace and Concordia; CIEE and Service Civil International (see the IVS entry) can help US residents; their entries can be found in the *Worldwide* chapter.

An advertisement in a German newspaper may bring an offer of a job; *Rheinische Post* is published at Zulpicher Strasse 10, 40196 Dusseldorf, Germany (☎+49-211-505 2880). The following weekly newspapers might also be of interest: The *Süddeutsche Zeitung*, Sendlicher Str. 80331 München; ☎+49 89 21830; fax +49 89 2183 787; www.sueddeutsch.de; the *Bayernkurier* Nymphenburger Str. 64, D-80005 München, Germany (☎089-120040; fax 089-1293050; e-mail redaktio n@bayernkurier.de), *Die Welt* at Axel-Springer Strasse 65, GKP 20350, Brieffach 2410/10888 Berlin (fax 030-3591 71606), or the *Frankfurter Allgemeine Zeitung*, which can be found at Hellerhofstr. 2-4 60327 Frankfurt/Main (☎069-75910; fax 069-7591 1743), can also sell you an advertisement promoting your availability to work.

RED TAPE, VISAS & WORK PERMITS

Visa Requirements: a visa is not required by citizens of EU/EEA nations or Iceland or Norway. British citizens should hold a 'European Community' passport. Members of other countries who wish to go to Germany to do paid work need a Visa/Residence Permit before entering Germany.

Residence Permits: this permit is required for any visit of more than three months or where employment is intended. Applications should be made to the Visa Section of the nearest Embassy or Consulate General of the Federal Republic of Germany. Or in the case of EU Nationals already in Germany, to the Foreign Nationals Authority *(Auslanderamt)* in the town or district *(Kreis)* of intended residence. Nationals of Switzerland, the USA, Australia, New Zealand, Japan, Canada and Israel can apply for a residence permit after arriving in Germany unless they have secured a job before arriving.

Work Permits: To find work in Germany it is essential to speak some German. The regulations for work permits are the same as for visas. EEA Nationals intending to look for work for more than 3 months might have to show the local authority that they are self-supporting while conducting a job hunt.

Au Pair: Agencies in Germany no longer have to be licensed so there are now lots of private agencies. Agencies in Germany include IN VIA Germany (Ludwigstr. 36, Postfach 420, 79004 Freiburg; 0761-200208; invia@caritas.de) with 43

branches, and Verein für Internationale Jugendarbeit, Goetheallee 10, 53225 Bonn (0228-698952/fax 0228-694166; au-pair.vij@netcologne.de/ www.vij-Deutschland.de). The German YWCA (VIJ) has more than 20 offices in Germany and places both male and female au pairs for a preferred minimum stay of one year. Pocket money is paid.
Voluntary Work: there are no restrictions on work of this nature.

Hotel Work and Catering

HOTEL BAYERISCHER HOF/HOTEL REUTEMANN/HOTEL SEEGARTEN: Seepromenade, D-88131 Lindau, Germany (☎08382-9150; fax 08382-91 55 91; e-mail hotel@bayerischerhof-lindau.de; www.bayerischerhof-lindau.de).
Waiting Staff (9). Must speak reasonable German.
Kitchen Assistants (8). Knowledge of German not essential.
Chambermaids (8). Knowledge of German not essential

Wage approx. £510 (€ 845) net per month for 8 hours work per day, 5 days per week. Board and accommodation available at a small charge. Minimum period of work 3 months. Applicants must be students.

Applications to the above address.

BERGHOTEL JOHANNESHOHE: Wallhausenstr. 1, D-57072 Siegen 1, Germany.
Buffet Assistants (2). Wage approximately £460 per month plus free board and lodging. To work a 40 hour week. To work for at least 12 weeks; period of work by arrangement. Applicants must speak German.

Applications should be sent to the above address from April 6th.

HOTEL BRUDERMUHLE BAMBERG: Schranne 1, D-96049 Bamberg, Germany (☎09-51 955 220; fax 09-51 955 2255; e-mail info@brudermuehle.de; www.brudermuehle.de).
Hotel Managers, Waitresses (2) with knowledge of German and relevant professional training to work 5 days a week, 8-10 hours a day at varying times during the day. Those working in the restaurant will serve food, drinks and wine. Applicants should be prepared to work for a minimum of 3 months. Wage of about £775 per month provided.
Cook (1) with cooking qualifications and knowledge of German is required to help prepare food with the French cook. Wage of about £840 a month provided.

Subsidised board and accommodation is available at around £100 per month.

Applications are invited at any time to the above address.

BLOOMSBURY BUREAU: 37 Store Street, London WC1E 7PN (☎020-7430 2280; fax 020-7813 4038; e-mail bloomsburo@aol.com). Specialists in au pair and hotel/catering placements for thirty years the Bureau promises an individual service and personal commitment, efficient introductions and a caring, responsible attitude towards applicants.
Hotel Staff (30-40) to work as general assistants, mixed duties of chamber staff, kitchen help, general cleaning or waitressing. Also a few posts for male helpers washing up and kitchen duties. Work available in family owned hotels in Bavaria from beginning of May to mid/end October. Accommodation and free board and net wages of approx. £360 per month, for up to 45 hours work per week. Applicants should preferably be students or school leavers, over 18 and speak some German.

Only EU nationals can be considered for work in Germany.
Applications to Marianne Dix, Principal, at the above address.

HOTEL BOLD, RINGHOTEL OBERAMMERGAU: Konig-Ludwig Strasse 10, D-82487 Oberammergau, Germany.
Commis de Rang (1/2). £350 per month. Must be experienced.
Chambermaid (1/2). Salary as above. Must be neat and clean.
Dishwasher (1/2). As above.
To work 8-9 hours per day, 5 days per week. Board and accommodation provided free. Minimum period of work from 30 May to 30 September.
Applications before May to the above address.

HOTEL-RESTAURANT BURGFRIEDEN: J. M. Muhlental 62, D-56814 Beilstein/Mosel, Germany.
Restaurant Staff to work in a buffet, serving food and drink and cleaning. Approx. £320 per month. To work a 48 hour week from 8am-6pm or 2-9pm. Free board and lodging provided. Minimum period of work 2 months. Knowledge of German necessary.
Applications to Frau Sprenger-Herzer at the above address before the end of April.

BURGHOTEL AUF SCHONBURG: D-55430 Oberwesel/Rhein, Germany (☎+49-6744 93930; fax 06744-1613; e-mail huettl@hotel-schoenburg.com; www.hotel-schoenburg.com). Schönburg Castle is a beautiful medieval castle in the romantic Rhine Valley with a superior hotel-restaurant and interntational guests. This is a small and friendly hotel with a young and enthusiastic staff.
Chambermaid (1) to work part time in the morning, or full time from 8am-4.30pm. Duties include cleaning rooms.
To work 5 days per week: full time staff work 8 hours per day (salary €500, and part timers work 4-5 hours per day (salary €300. Board and accommodation provided free. Minimum period of work two months. Applicants should speak good German.
Applications should be sent to the Familie Hüttl at the above address in March.

CITYHOTEL-METROPOL: D-56068 Koblenz am Rhein, Germany (☎0261-350-69).
Musicians (1-3) to perform folk and popular music for evening entertainment: must already have a wide repertoire of songs. Wages by arrangement. To work around 8 hours per day, 5 or 6 days per week. Board and accommodation available. Period of work by arrangement.
Applications to the above address at any time.

HOTEL DEUTSCHES HAUS: D-91550 Dinkelsbuhl, Weinmarket 3, Germany.
Kitchen Assistants (2). Pay negotiable. Hours: 09.00-14.00, 18.00-21.00, 6 days per week. Free board and accommodation. Minimum period of work 2 months.
Applications until April to the address above.

EUROTOQUES: Winnender Str 12, D-73667 Ebnisee/Schwäbischer Wald, Germany (☎+49-7184-91055; fax 07184-91053; e-mail office@eurotoques.de; www.Eurotoques.de).
Kitchen Assistants, Waiting Staff for placements in the restaurants of some of Germany's top cooks all over Germany. No wage, but free board and lodging is provided. To work 9 hours per day, 5 days per week. Minimum period of work three months at any time of year. Applicants should speak German.
Applications to the above address.

FAMILIEN UND SPORTHOTEL ALLGAEUER BERGHOF: D-87544 Blaichach, Southern Bavaria, Germany (☎08321-8060; fax 08321-806219; e-mail m.neusch@allgaeuer-berghof.de; www.allgaeuer.berghof.de). A 180 bed hotel with 50 staff situated in a hill-top ski resort, with access to world-cup races, hiking, tennis and mountain biking.
Chambermaids: knowledge of German not necessary.
Buffet, Kitchen Assistants and **Restaurant Assistants:** knowledge of German required.
Wages €613 (£380) approx. net per month by arrangement for 40 hours work per week. Free board and lodging. No previous hotel experience required. Minimum age 18.
Enquiries to Mrs Neusch at the above address.

REST. FRIEDRICHSHOF: D-76596 Forbach/Murgtal, Landstrasse 1, Germany.
Kitchen Assistant (female). £335 approx. per month. Hours: 9am-2pm and 6-9pm, 5½ days per week. Free board and accommodation. Minimum period of work 2½ months between June and the end of September. Those with allergies should note that there are cats in the hotel.
Applications should be sent with a photo to the above address.

GASTHOF UND PENSION ADLER: Ehlenbogen 1, D-72275 Alpirsbach Schwarzwald, Kreis Freudenstadt, Germany (☎+49-7444-2215; fax 07444-4588). Family run hotel restaurant and farm in the black forest between Stuttgart and France.
Chambermaid. Around £400 per month plus board and lodging. Work includes helping with the laundry.
Waiter/Waitress. Approximately £400 per month including tips plus board and lodging. Must have a knowledge of German and the ability to get on with people.
Kitchen Assistant to prepare vegetables and wash up (using machine). Around £400 per month plus board and lodging.
Farmhand/Groom to work around the farm and/or help with the horses. Wage c. £340 plus board and lodging.
To work eight to ten hours a day, 5½ days per week, shiftwork. Time off by arrangement. Salaries quoted are net, deductions having been made for board and accommodation. Staff should be prepared to help in other departments. Minimum period of work 2 months.
Applications throughout the year to Georg Dietel at the above address.

HOTEL GASTSTATTE HOHN: D-65385 Rudesheim am Rhein, Postfach 1206, Germany.
Chambermaids (4). Salary by arrangement. 8 hours per day, 6 day week. Minimum age 18 years. Reasonable knowledge of German desirable. Minimum period of work 4 months July to October.
Applications in March to the above address.

HOTEL GOGGL: H.V. Herkomer Strasse 19/20, D-86899 Landsberg-Lech, Germany (☎08191 3240; fax 08191 324-100).
Chambermaid, Waitress, Receptionist to work five days per week, eight hours per day. Waitress to serve breakfast. Knowledge of German essential for Receptionist position.
Applications to the above address.

HOTEL GROSSFELD: Schlosstrasse 4-6, D-48455 Bad Bentheim, Germany (tel: 05922-828; fax 05922-4349). A 120 bed hotel with spa, sauna, Turkish bath and restaurant/café.

General Assistants (4) to work in a hotel and cafe. Wage approximately £115 per month net with free board and lodging. To work 8 hours per day, 5 days per week between 9am and 5pm. Minimum period of work 2 months. Some knowledge of the Dutch language would be an advantage.

Applications with a passport photo should be sent to Herr Johannes Grossfeld from the beginning of the year until 1 April.

HOTEL HAMM: D-56068 Koblenz, St. Josef Strasse 32-34, Germany (☎0261-34546; fax 0261-160972).

Chambermaids (2). 5 day week, 5 hours per day.

Waitress to serve breakfast and dinner and do some reception work. 5 day week, 8 hours per day.

Night Porter to man the reception desk between 7.30pm and 3am, 6 nights a week. Knowledge of German essential.

Wages on application. Free board and accommodation provided. Applicants must be available for at least 3 months (5 or more preferred) between May and September.

Applications to the above address.

HOLIDAY INN FRANKFURT AIRPORT-NORTH: Isenburger Schneise 40, D-60528 Frankfurt, Germany (☎069-67840; fax 069-678 4190). Set in Germany's largest stretch of urban woodland near the old city, the Queen's Hotel is one of Frankfurt's premier hotels.

Serving Staff required for the hotel's restaurant, bar and beer-garden. To work seven and three-quarter hour shift work per day not including a 30 minute break, over a 5 day week. The hours worked will vary according to the shifts. Board and lodging are available at a cost of c.£28 per month for board. Wages by negotiation. Staff should speak English and German.

Applications to Frau Sonia Thierer at the above address.

INTERNATIONALES HAUS SONNENBERG: Clausthalerstr. 11, D-37444 St Andreasberg, Germany (☎+49-05882-944118; fax +49-05582-944100; e-mail sonnenberg@tu-clausthal.de).

Domestic Assistants (6) needed from 1st August for at least 3 months. The work is in the Housekeeping department and involves working in the dining hall, washing up, and cleaning in the kitchens, accommodation and conference rooms. The hours of work are 7.30am-1.45pm and 4.45-7.30pm, up to a total of 381/2 hours per week. Within each four-week period there are eight days off which will not necessarily fall on weekends. Overtime is available and can be accumulated and taken as time off. Wages are £430 approx. per month and accommodation is provided at a cost of around £54 per month.

Applicants should be over 18, no previous experience is necessary but a basic knowledge of German and any requisite work permits are required. Staff may also take part in a conference towards the end of their stay.

For further details *contact* Reception at the centre.

HOTEL JAKOB: Schwarzeweg 6, D-87629 Fussen-Bad Faulenbach, Germany (fax 08362-913270)

General Assistants: around £300 per month, hours by arrangement. Free board and lodging provided. Period of work from mid May to mid October. A basic knowledge of German is necessary.

Applications to Frau G. Jakob at the above address.

KLOSTER HORNBACH: Loesch GmbH Im Klosterbezirk, D-66500 Hornbach, Germany (☎0049-6338 91010-0; fax 0049-6338 91010-99; e-mail c.loesch@kloster-hornbach.de). Kloster Hornbach used to be a monastery founded in 742, and was rebuilt over the last 5 years into a 4-star hotel with 34 rooms, 2 restaurants, a large garden restaurant and several banqueting rooms.

Hotel and Restaurant Staff required.

Applications by e-mail to Christiane und Edelbert Loesch at the above address.

HOTEL KONIGSSEE-BETRIEBE: Seestrasse 29, D-83471 Konigssee-Berchtesgaden, Upper Bavaria, Germany. This hotel company is one of the largest in Bavaria. Konigssee is in the Alps, in a region famous for its beautiful landscape, mountains, forests, lakes and castles. It is thirty minutes from Salzburg Airport.

Ice-Cream Sellers (3). £285 per month net. Moderate knowledge of German required.

Chambermaids (3-4) to clean rooms and make beds. £285 per month net. Moderate knowledge of German required.

Assistant Waiters/Waitresses (2) to serve meals. £285 per month net. Moderate knowledge of German required.

Kitchen Assistant to wash vegetables, prepare food and assist cooks. £285 per month net. Moderate knowledge of German required.

To work 8½ hours per day, 5 days per week. Minimum period of work 2½ months. Free board and lodging provided.

Applications to the above address at any time.

ROMANTIK PARKHOTEL WEHRLE: KG, Gartenstrasse 24, D-78098 Triberg/Black Forest, Germany (☎07722-86020; fax 07722-860290; e-mail info@parkhotel-wehrle.de; www.parkhotel-wehrle.de). Romantic Black Forest hotel with 100 guest rooms and a 140 seat restaurant.

Chambermaids to clean rooms, foyer area, restaurant and toilets. Language skills and a hospitable nature required as the job involves some contact with guests.

Kitchen Assistants to clean plates and dishes, and help prepare vegetables and salads. Previous experience and a German kitchen hygiene certificate required.

Porters to help arriving and departing guest with their luggage, driving for transport and transfers, and moving furniture within the hotel. Should have a hospitable friendly outlook for dealing with guests, and a full driving licence.

All staff work 8 hours per day over a 5 day week, for £490 approx. (€700) per month. Board and accommodation are provided at a cost of £145 approx. (€208) per month. Minimum period of work is 3 months and candidates should speak German and English.

Applications accepted from February to Gerald Henningsen at the above address.

POSTHOTEL: Obermarkt 9, D-82481 Mittenwald/Karwendel, Germany.

Chambermaids (2) to clean guest rooms, corridors, toilets, swimming pool etc. To work from 6.30am-4pm, with one hour break.

Kitchen Assistants/Washers Up (2) to wash tableware and cooking utensils, peel potatoes, clean vegetables, etc. To work from 7am-2pm and 5.30-9pm with 1½ hour break.

£650 per month, approximately. To work 8-9 hours per day, 5 days per week. Board and lodging available for around £100 per month. Minimum period of work 2½ months between July and October and between 20 December and 31 March.

Some knowledge of German an advantage: other languages are not essential. *Applicants only accepted from students holding EU passports or those studying in Germany who have the relevant work permit from the employment office.*

Applications, enclosing proof of student status from school, college or university stating that you are a full time student there (International Student Identity Cards will not suffice) to the above address.

HOTEL PRINZ-LUITPOLD-BAD: D-87541 Hindelang/Allgäuer Alpen, Germany (☎08324-8900; fax 08324-890379; e-mail luitpoldbad@t-online.de; website www.luitpoldbad.de). A 110 bedroom spa hotel built in 1864 in a quiet mountain location with glorious views of the Allgäu in the Bavarian Alps. Features include their private mud baths and their sulfur spring, which is the highest in Germany. The hotel is 70km from Lake Constance and 45km from the king's castle Neuschwanstein/Füssen.
General Assistants (2). Should speak fluent German.
Chambermaids (3), **Kitchen Helps** (3). £400 net per month, approx., plus around £50 net bonus per month. To work 5 days a week. Free board and accommodation provided. Minimum period of work 3 months all year round. Raise of £30 per month from the fourth month onwards.
Applications from EU passport holders only to the above address.

MONCH'S POSTHOTEL: Doblersk.2, 76328, , Bad Herrenalb, Germany (☎070-837440; fax 070-8374-4122)
Waiting Assistant, Room Attendant, General Assistant. Wages approx. £240 per month. To work 9 hours per day, 5 days per week. Board and accommodation provided free. Knowledge of low German or English or French needed.
Applications to the above address in spring.

RHEINHOTEL LORELEY: Rheinallee 12, D-53639 Königswinter 1, Germany (☎02223-9250; fax 02223-925100). A tourist and conference hotel open all year, set beside the Rhine. Family-run with employees of various nationality.
Chambermaids (1-2) to tidy rooms and change the beds. Approx. €500 per month. Must have previous relevant experience and knowledge of German.
Waiters (1-2) to serve food. Around €500 per month. Previous experience of waiting desirable. Must have knowledge of German.
To work 9 hours per day, 5 days per week. Working days variable. Applicants must be friendly people who are willing to work for at least three months. Food and lodgings free.
Applications to Manfred Maderer at the above address between 1 March and 15 March only.

ROMANTIK HOTEL FASANERIE: Fasanerie 1, D-66482 Zweibrücken/ Rheinland-Pfalz, Germany (☎+49-6332-9730; fax 06332-973111; e-mail D.Heiden@zadra-hotellerie.de; ; www.landschlossfasanerie.de).
Two hotels in Zweibrücken require **Waiting Staff** to work in a restaurant and buffet. Wages around £246 per month, with accommodation and meals included. To work 8-10 hours per day between 6.30am and midnight, 6 days per week. Period of work by arrangement between April and October.
Applicants should speak German and be flexible and adaptable; additional

knowledge of French and English would be helpful.

Applications should be sent to Doris Heiden at the above address 2-3 months before the desired start of work.

HOTEL SCHASSBERGER EBNISEE: Winnenderstr. 10, D-73667 Ebnisee, Germany (☎07184-292-0; fax 07184-292-204; e-mail iris.schassberger@schassb erger.de; www.schassberger.de). The hotel is one of the most attractive resorts in Germany, in the heart of the Swabian forest northeast of Stuttgart.

Kitchen Assistants, Waiting Staff, Housekeeping Staff to work for a spa and health resort hotel situated in the Swabian forest nature park, 40 km from Stuttgart specialising in short sporting/relaxation breaks.

Ages 18-30. Knowledge of German required. Some previous experience desirable. Minimum period of work 2 months. Board and accommodation provided. Initially no salary, but wage will be paid from the 4th month depending on performance. To work 9 hours per 5 day week. On days off there are a variety of activities available to staff both in and outside the hotel, including a Finnish sauna, tennis, swimming, hiking, fishing, horse riding and continuing education classes.

Applications should be sent to Iris Schassberger at the above address at any time of year.

HOTEL SCHLOSS HUGENPOET GmbH: August-Thyssen-Strasse 51, D-45219, Essen (☎02054-120436; fax 02054-12045; e-mail personal@hugenpoet.de; www.hugenpoet.de). The Hotel Schloss Hugenpoet is a beautiful building, not far from Düsseldorf. It belongs to the Relais and Chateaux Hotel Group.

Gardeners, General Assistants, Chambermaids, Laundery Assistants needed. Applicants should be flexible, friendly and polite, and should have a little German and/or English. Wages €600 approx. gross, monthly. Staff work eight hours per day over a five day working week during the summer months. Accommodation is provided at €105-€120 (per room) per month and cost of food is €75 per person, per month.

Applications are invited from six months prior to starting date if possible.

HOTEL SCHLOSS PETERSHAGEN: Schlosstrasse 5-7, D-32469 Petershagen, Germany. (☎++49-05707-9313-0; fax 05707-2372; schloss-petershagen@t-online.de; www.romantikhotels.com/petershagen).

Kitchen Assistant, Waiter/Barman, Housekeeping Assistant: To work 5 hours per day over a 5 day week. Wages £63 approx. (€103) per week plus free board and lodging. Basic knowledge of spoken German required. Applications to the above address 3 months before desired period of starting work.

E-mail *applications* preferred.

SCHLOSSHOTEL LISL & JAGERHAUS: Neuschwansteinstr. 1-3, D-87645 Hohenschwangau, Germany (☎08362-8870; fax 08362-887102; e-mail: info@hohenschwangau.de).

Seasonal Staff for jobs including chambermaids, dishwashers, buffet assistants, restaurant assistants and waiting staff. Minimum wage £350 per month, approximately. To work 8 hours per day, 5 days per week: no night work required. Free board and lodging provided.

Some knowledge of German required. Minimum period of work 3-4 months from April to November.

Applications to G. Meyer, Manager, at the above address until 31 March: replies will only be sent if a job is offered.

SCHLOSS REINHARTSHAUSEN: Hauptstrasse 41, Erbach m Rheingau, D-65346 Eltville, (☎06123-676355; fax 06123-676490; e-mail ines.larsen-schmidt @reinhartshausen.com; www.schloss-hotel.de) Small, leading 5-star hotel with 54 rooms, 11 conference rooms, 3 restaurants, a beautiful terrace and a winery. Run by a young team.

Waiting Staff (3) required to prepare or serve food, clear tables, etc. To work for about 5 hours a day, 5 days a week. Salary approx £550 per month Must be open minded, guest-orientated, friendly and enjoy serving.

Banqueting Set-Ups (3) required to prepare meeting rooms, serve food etc. To work 5 days a week. Salary £460 per month approx.

Kitchen Helpers (2) required to prepare food, especially for breakfasts and buffets. Cooking ability an advantage. 5 days work a week. Salary around £550 per month.

Working time ranges from 5-10 hours a day for banqueting set-ups and kitchen helpers. Applicants must be prepared to work for at least 3 months, and must speak German and English. Accommodation and board may be available, depending on the number of requests, for approx £150 per month.

Applications to the above address from December.

SCHWARZWALD HOTEL: Rothaustr. 7, D-79848 Bonndorf, Germany (fax 07703-442).

Chambermaid, Kitchen Assistant, Buffet Assistant. Wage £200 per month. To work 8 hours per day, 5 days per week. Board and accommodation provided free. Minimum period of work 2 months. Applicants must be able to speak German or English.

Applications to the Family Mohringer at the above address.

HOTEL SCHWEIZ: Goethe Str. 26, D-80336 München, Germany (☎+49-89-5436 960; fax +49-89-5436 9696; e-mail info@hotel-schweiz.de; www.hotel-schweiz.de).

Receptionists, Restaurant Staff (20-30) required to work in reception and to serve breakfast in a new hotel in Munich. Applicants should speak good English, be computer literate, friendly, open-minded and in good health. Minimum period of work 6 months. Wage to be confirmed. The hotel will help to find accommodation for the successful candidates.

Applications should be made to the above address.

HOTEL SIEBENGEBIRGE: D-53639 Konigswinter, Haupstrasse 342, Germany (☎0 22 23-2-13-59; fax 0 22 23-2-18-03).

Chambermaid/Kitchen Assistant for general help in the kitchen and around hotel. £350 per month. Free board and accommodation provided. Period of work from May to October.

Applications before end of April to Herr Theo Münchrath at the above address.

HOTEL SONNE-POST: Klosterreichenbach, Murgtalstrasse 167, D-72270 Baiersbronn 6, Germany (☎0744-2277).

Waiter/Waitress to serve in an a la carte restaurant. Should possess a knowledge of wines, beer etc. and possess dark clothing and a white apron/jacket.

General Assistant to clean rooms and help with the washing up.

Wages are from £320-£400 per month depending on experience, with opportunities for earning overtime. 8/9 hour day, 6 day week. Free board and accommodation. Minimum period of work 3 months, at any time of the year. Some knowledge of German is necessary.

Applications to the Manager at the above address at any time of the year.

URBASCHEK'S GASTRONOMISCHE BETRIEBE: Haupstrasse 6, 92436 Bruck, Germany (☎0049-9434 1206; fax 0049-9434 902923).
Waitresses/Barmaids. Wages by arrangement, accommodation provided. Experience not necessary, but applicants should be young and friendly.
Applications with photograph to the above address.

GASTHOF & HOTEL VIKTORIA: D-87561 Rubi bei Oberstdorf, Allgäu, Germany (☎8322-977840; fax 8322-9778486).
General Assistant for buffet and housework. Wage over £320 per month. Free board and accommodation. Minimum period of work 3 months between beginning of June and mid October.
Applications not later than mid April to Frau Julia Ess.

HOTEL RESTAURANT ZUM WAGNERSTUBLE: Wilderbaderstrasse 45, D-75335 Dobel/Schwarzall, Germany.
Assistant. Wages by arrangement. To work 8-9 hours per day, 6 days per week (10am-3.30pm and 7-10.30pm). Free board and lodging, minimum period of work 2 months.
For further details *contact* the Familie Kieferle at the above address.

WARNER BROS. MOVIE WORLD GmbH & Co KG: Warner Allee 1, D-46244 Bottrop-Kirchellen, Germany (☎02045-899540; fax 02045-899505; e-mail info@freizeitsparks.de). Hollywood movie styled theme and entertainment park in the west of Germany.
Caterers (420) for food and concession stands in the theme park. Previous experience would be useful, as staff will be serving in restaurants, bakeries, and at hamburger and ice-cream stalls. To work 20-40 hours per week according to post, from around 9am to 7pm or sometimes to 9pm and later. Applicants should be able to speak Dutch, German and English. Wages are approx £4 per hour net. Accommodation is not available but a staff canteen is provided where meals cost around £2.
Applications should be sent to the above address.

HOTEL-WEINHAUS-OSTER: Moselweinstrasse 61, D-56814 Ediger-Eller 2, bei Cochem/Mosel, Germany (☎02675-232; fax 02675-1570; e-mail hoteloster@t-online.de). A family hotel facing the magnificent river Mosel, with many attractions including the local wine festivals and wine-tastings arranged by the owner's brother.
Waiting Assistant, General Assistant. Wages approximately £320 per month plus tips and free board and accommodation. To work 7 hours per day, six days per week. Minimum period of work 3 months between May and October. Applicants must speak German.
Applications to Mrs M.L. Meyer-Schenk at the above address from January.

WALDHOTEL FORELLENHOF: D-76534 Baden-Baden, Gaisbach 91, Germany (☎07221-974-299).
House Assistants/Chambermaids/Waitresses (2). Salary by arrangement. Hours from 6.30am-5.30pm (with 1½ hours free for meals) 5 days per week. Free board and accommodation. Knowledge of German required. Minimum period of work 5 months between 1 May and 30 September.
Applications to Georg Huber at the above address in January.

HOTEL WITTELSBACHER HOF: Prinzenstrasse 24, D-87561 Oberstdorf, Germany (☎08322-605-0; fax 08322-605-300; e-mail info@wittelsbacherhof.de; www.wittelsbacherhof.de)

Chambermaids, Dishwashers, Kitchen Assistants, Restaurant Assistants (males and females) to work in a 140 bed hotel. Wages €500 net approx. per month plus help with travelling expenses. 8 hours per day, 5 day week. Knowledge of German preferred. Board and lodging provided free of charge. Minimum period of work 2 months from May to July, July to October or December to March. Positions also available from 20 December to 10 January, or for both the summer and winter seasons.

Applications from *EU citizens only* to the above address enclosing a photograph, CV and proof of student status.

HOTEL WOLF: Dorfstr. I, D-82487 Oberammergau, Germany (☎08822-9233-0; fax 08822-9233-33; e-mail info@hotel-wolf.de; www.hotel-wolf.de).

Waiter/Waitress/Chambermaid/Kitchen Assistant. £400 to £600 per month, 5 days per week. Free board and lodging. Period of work May-October.

Applications to the above address before May.

HOTEL SCHASSBERGER: Wimenash 10, D-73667, Florisce, Germany (☎0049-7184-2970; fax 0049-7184-797204; e-mail kurriere@schassberger.de; www.shassberger.de). This luxury hotel is near Stuttgart. For more information see the website.

Assistants (1-2) to help serve food, in kitchen and with maintenance.

Should speak basic German. €50, free board and lodging. €100 after three months, or upon performance.

Apply to the above e-mail address.

Sports, Couriers and Camping

BENTS BICYCLE & WALKING TOURS: The Blue Cross, Orleton, Ludlow, Shropshire SY8 4HN (☎01568-780800; fax 01568-780801; e-mail info@bentstours.com; www.bentstours.com).

Company Representatives (4-5) for a tour operator offering cycling and walking holidays in Germany, Austria and France. Duties to include meeting clients at the airport, maintaining bicycles, transporting luggage between hotels and generally taking care of the needs of clients. Wages of around £600 per month with board and accommodation provided. To work varied hours as needs of work dictate, but generally around 40 hours per up to 7-day week.

Minimum period of work 8 weeks between the end of May and end of September. Applicants should speak fluent German (French for France) and English and possess a full clean driving licence.

Applications should be sent, with a photograph, to Stephen Bent at the above address from January.

CANVAS HOLIDAYS: East Port House, 12 East Port, Dunfermline, Fife KY12 7JG (☎01383-629018; fax 01383-629071; www.canvasholidays.com). Canvas Holidays are looking for enthusiastic, resourceful people who enjoy a challenge and love the outdoor life. Main positions include:

Campsite Courier. Varied responsibilities. Involves cleaning and preparation of customer accommodation, welcoming and looking after customers during their holiday and ensuring that they have the best holiday ever. As a campsite courier you will have new challenges every day which can lead to one of the most enjoyable summers you will ever have. Variable working hours.

Package includes tented accommodation, medical insurance, full uniform and return road travel to and from a UK port of entry. Positions are available from March until October.

Applications are invited from individuals and couples; contact Sandy, Karen or Nina at the above contact details for an application pack.

EUROCAMP: Overseas Recruitment Department (Ref SJ/04) (☎01606-787525). Eurocamp is a leading tour operator in quality self-drive camping and mobile home holidays in Europe. Each year the company seeks to recruit up to 1,500 enthusiastic people for the following positions:

Campsite Courier: job involves cleaning and preparing customer accommodation, providing assistance, acting as an information service and performing some administrative duties. Couriers need to be flexible to meet the needs of the customer to provide them with excellent service. Minimum age 18 years. Applicants should be independent with plenty of initiative and relish a challenging and rewarding position. They should also possess a friendly and helpful personality. Previous customer service experience would be an advantage. Applicants should be available to work from April/May to September.

Children's Courier: work involves organising a wide range of exciting activities for children aged 4-13. Applicants should possess initiative, imagination and enthusiasm along with good safety awareness. Previous childcare experience is essential. Minimum age is 18 years and applicants should be available from April/May to September. Languages are not a requirement but would be an advantage (in particular German). Successful candidates will be asked to apply for an Enhanced Disclosure.

Senior Couriers: required to work alongside a team of Campsite Couriers and organise their daily workload, as well as carrying out the normal day to day duties of a Campsite Courier. Applicants should have good language skills and experience of leading a team.

Site Managers: required to lead a large team of Campsite Couriers, organising their daily workloads and ensuring they provide the very best customer service. Applicants should be 21 or over, have proven managerial experience, excellent communication skills and language ability.

Comprehensive training is provided together with a competitive salary, insurance, return travel and accommodation. Applications are accepted from September/ October and *can only be accepted from UK/EU passport holders*. Interviews will be conducted in Hartford, Cheshire between October and April.

Applicants should apply on-line at www.holidaybreakjobs.com or telephone 01606 781525 for an Application Pack.

KEYCAMP HOLIDAYS: Overseas Recruitment Department (Ref: SJ/04), Hartford Manor, Greenbank Lane, Northwich CW8 1H (☎01606-787525; www.ho lidaybreakjobs.com).

Campsite Couriers: to look after British, Dutch and Scandinavian customers on campsites in Germany. Duties include welcoming customers, providing local information, organising social activities on site and ensuring that all accommodation is prepared prior to arrival.

Chidren's Courier: to organise and provide up to 24 hours of activities per week for children aged 4-13 years, to advertise the club activities and visit families on arrival.

Senior Courier: incorporating the role of campsite courier with the additional responsibility of organising and managing the team and ensuring the smooth running of the Keycamp operation on site.

Montage/Demontage: for a period of approximately 6-8 weeks at the beginning/end of season to erect/dismantle equipment.

Minimum age 18 years. Accommodation, uniform, competitive salary and return travel and training provided. A working knowledge of German would be an advantage. Period of employment between March and July/October.

Applicants should apply on-line at www.holidaybreakjobs.com or telephone 01606-787525 for an Application Pack.

RIECHEY FREIZEITANLAGEN GMBH: D-23769 Wulfen-Fehmarn, Germany (☎04371-86280; fax 04371-3723).

Kitchen Helpers (2). Duties include washing dishes, salad preparation and serving food. Must speak German.

Sales Assistants (2) to unpack goods, and see to sales and bike/tv hire. Knowledge of German and competence with German currency essential.

Children's Representatives (2) to look after and entertain children, which may include drawing and arts and crafts. Must speak German and be creative.

Catering Staff (2) to order and sell fast food. Knowledge of German and competence with German currency essential.

All staff to work 8 hours per day, 5-6 days per week. Wages approximately £420 net per month plus free board and lodging or approximately £900 gross, with self-catering accommodation available at a cost of £70 per month. Minimum period of work 8 weeks.

Applications from 15 January to the above address.

Voluntary Work and Archaeology

ARBEITSKREIS DENKMALPFLEGE e.V: Goetheplatz 9B, D-99423 Weimar, Germany (☎+49-3643 502390; fax +49-3643 851117; e-mail info@ak-denkmalpflege.de; www.ak-denkmalpflege.de).

Building Assistants (25), Carpenters (7), Joiners (4), Bricklayers (5), Students of Architecture (6-12), Civil Engineers (3), Office Assistants (4), Unskilled Staff (25) for voluntary work with an organisation conducting **restoration work on historic monuments** in eastern regions of Germany. This project involves mainly young people, mainly from abroad. No payment, but accommodation is provided; for students the work may be recognised by their place of study as practical work experience. 4-8 hours of work a day will be expected for 3-6 days per week; the normal minimum period of work is one week. Most of the projects take place between May and October, but help is needed in the office around the year. A basic knowledge of German is desirable, but English, French, Russian or Czech may be acceptable.

Applications should be sent to Bert Ludwig at the above address.

AKTION SUHNEZEICHEN FRIEDENSDIENSTE (ASF, ACTION RECONCILIATION SERVICE FOR PEACE): Auguststr. 80, 10117 Berlin, Germany (☎+49-30-28395-135; fax +49-30-28395-135; e-mail asf@asf-ev.de; www.asf-ev-de). ASF works for reconciliation and peace through long-term and short-term volunteer service.

Volunteers for the 'Sommerlager' programme in Belarus, Belgium, Czech Republic, France, Germany, Great Britain, Israel, the Netherlands, Norway,

Poland, Russia and the United States. For volunteers from West Europe, USA and Israel, the cost is €100. Volunteers must pay travel expenses. To **help with the maintenance of Jewish cemeteries and memorial centres, work in social facilities and involve themselves in projects that support intercultural experiences.** In addition there is much discussion concerning historical and current issues. To work on the Summer camps (two weeks long) between 1st March and 1st September. All nationalities are welcome: Short term volunteers do no need a visa or work permit.

Applications to the above address.

CAMPHILL SCHULGEMEINSCHAFT BRACHENREUTHE: d-88662, Uberlingen, Germany (☎00-49-7551-80070; fax 00-49-7551-800750; e-mail brachenreuthe@t-online.de; www.brachenreuthe.de).

Brachenreuthe is a therapeutic community/boarding school for children and adolescents (5-17 years) with special needs in which staff not only work with the children but also live with them in a family-like way, i.e. in 9 different houses.

Volunteers to help with the **care of the children, and with recreational activities and housework.** Volunteers are invited to participate in any cultural and religious festivals.

Applicants must be over 18, healthy, with a basic knowledge of German. Longer stays are preferred although the organisation is flexible in this respect. Volunteers are paid approx. £125 per month, and provided with free board and lodging. Volunteers are covered against accidents.

Apply by e-mail, post or fax to the address above.

CONCORDIA: 20-22 Boundary Road, Hove, East Sussex BN3 4ET (☎01273-422218; fax 01273 421182; e-mail info@concordia-iye.org.uk; www.concordia-iye.org.uk).

Concordia offers young people aged 16-30 the opportunity to take part in international volunteer projects lasting 2-3 weeks, from June to September. The work is community based and ranges from **nature conservation, renovation, construction, to social work including children's playschemes and youth work.** Volunteers pay a registration fee of approx. £85 and fund their own travel. Board and accommodation are free of charge.

For further information *write* enclosing an s.a.e. to the International Volunteer Co-ordinator at the above address.

HEIMSONDERSCHULE BRACHENREUTHE: D-88662 Uberlingen, Germany (☎07551-80070; fax 07551-800750; e-mail brachenreuthe@t-online.de).

Volunteers to work as **helpers in a residential community for mentally handicapped children.** Pocket money of £140, approximately, per month plus board and lodging in shared room and insurance. Most vacancies exist for a period of 6 months or longer around the year; the school is closed for July and much of August. The ideal candidates for the school would work from the end of August to the end of the following July. Minimum age 19. A knowledge of German is essential.

For further details *contact* the above address.

INTERNATIONALE BEGEGNUNG IN GEMEINSCHAFTSDIENSTEN eV: Schlosserstrasse 28, D-70180 Stuttgart 1, Germany (☎0711-6491128; fax 711-6409867; e-mail ibg-workcamps@t-online.de; www.ibg-workcamps.org).

Volunteers to attend international youth workcamps in Germany. Projects include

restoring an old castle, environmental protection, children's playschemes and media projects. Each workcamp consists of a group of about 15 people aged 18-30 from all over the world living and working together for the public benefit.

There is a registration fee of approximately £55; food and accommodation are provided free on the camps. IBG's new programme is published in March.

Applications to the above address.

IJGD INTERNATIONALE JUGENDGEMEINSCHAFTSDIENSTE eV: Kaiserstrasse 43, D-53113 Bonn, Germany (☎228-2280011; fax 228-2280024).
Volunteers (300) to work on summer projects such as **environmental protection, the restoration of educational centres, and to assist with city fringe recreational activities.** 30 hours per week of work for periods of 3 weeks at Easter or between June and September. Free board and accommodation provided. Applicants should be aged between 16-26. Knowledge of German required on social projects.

Applications should be made to the above address as early as possible.

NIG E.V.: ☎0049-381 4922914; fax 0049-381 4900930; e-mail NIGeV@aol.com.
Volunteers to work for a non-profit organisation, which organises 20 workcamps, for people aged 18-30, in Germany and various countries. The camps focus on **environmental protection, nature conservation, archaeology and cultural projects.** Some projects are aimed at conserving the remains of concentration camps and developing museum projects there to educate people about the Jewish holocaust.

Accommodation and food are provided free, but volunteers will need to pay a registration fee of approximately £60.

Further details can be obtained from the address above.

NOTHELFERGEMEINSCHAFT DER FREUNDE eV: Fuggerstr. 3, D-52351 Düren, Germany (☎02421-76569; e-mail ndf-dn@t-online.de; www.nothelfer.org).
Volunteers for spring and summer work camps arranged by the organisation. The work may involve **building, gardening or social work.** 35 hours per week approximately. Special workcamp with German language courses normally held mid July-mid August. Work is unpaid but free board and accommodation and insurance against sickness, accident and liability are provided.

Applicants should be aged 16-20 years. Camps normally last for 1 month. Volunteers are responsible for their own travel costs.

Applications in April or May at the latest to the above address.

PRO INTERNATIONAL: Bahnhofstrasse 26 A, D-35037 Marburg, Germany (☎06421-65277; fax 06421-64407; e-mail: pro-international@lahn.net; www.pro-international.de).
Following the concept of 'Peace through Friendship' Pro International organises international vacation work camps during the Easter and summer vacations. On these camps, which last for up to 3 weeks, 10 to 15 people aged between 16 and 26 years old from different countries participate. The participants work about 5 hours a day on **public or social projects** and spend their time together. Accommodation and food supply are free; the participants pay only their tickets and €65 (approx. £40) to cover administration.

Applications have to be sent to the above address.

Other Employment in Germany

FAMILIENWEINGUT OSTER & FRANZEN: Calmonstrasse 96, D-56814 Bremm/Mosel am Calmont, Germany (e-mail oster-franzen@re-online.de. A small family business set in the beautiful surroundings of the Mosel Valley. A wonderful opportunity to learn about wine and vine.

Two people (preferably a couple) to work in vineyards, home and cellars, 8 hours per day, 6 days per week. Minimum age normally 24, although younger but mature applicants may be considered. The ability to speak English or German is essential. A driving licence would be an advantage. Full board and lodging provided in the family home, with a family atmosphere. Periods of work: two months between May and July and September to November. For further details contact the above address enclosing an international reply coupon.

Applications to the above address will be considered from February onwards. *EC passport holders preferred.*

WEINGUT FREIHERR VON LANDENBERG 'SCHLOSKELLEREI': Moselweinstr. 60, D-56814 Ediger-Eller (Mosel), Germany (☎02675-277; fax 02675-207). 500 year old vineyard and cellars in the heart of the Mosel wine region. Many connoisseurs of wine, young and old, buy direct from the estate because of its quality.

Sales Woman to sell wines and gifts in this award winning vineyard and castle's shop. To work 8 hours per day over a 6 day week for approx. £270, with free board and lodging. Applicants must speak German. Dates of work are variable between May and October.

Applications in writing to Frau H. Trimborn von Landenberg at the above address.

ZENTRALSTELLE FUR ARBEITSVERMITTLUNG: ZAV, Studentenvermittlung 21-22, Villemombler Strasse 76, D-53123 Bonn, Germany. This is the official government labour agency which places German-speaking students in summer jobs throughout Germany. Applicants must be at least 18 years old, have a good command of German, (how good it must be depends on the individual job) and agree to work for at least two months. Work is available in hotels and restaurants, as chambermaids or kitchen helpers, or in agriculture. Contact the ZAV at the above address for application forms and further information; there is no fee for this service.

Apply before March.

Au Pairs, Nannies, Family Helps and Exchanges

IN VIA: Katholische Mädchensozialarbeit, Deutscher Verband eV, Karlstrasse 40, Postfach 420, D-79004 Freiburg, Germany (☎761-200206; fax 761-200638; e-mail au-pair-invia@caritas.de).

Au Pair positions in Germany; with regional offices in 42 cities there IN VIA can arrange to place au pairs between 18 and 25 years with German families. Minimum length of stay 6 months, but stays of 1 year preferred.

For further information please contact the above address.

VEREIN FÜR INTERNATIONALE JUGENDARBEIT: Goetheallee 10, 53225 Bonn, Germany (☎+49-228 698952; fax 0228-694166; e-mail au-pair.vij@netcologne.de; www.vij-deutschland.org; www.au-pair-vij.de).

Au Pairs: girls and boys between 18 and 24 years can be placed as au pairs with families in Germany. Preferred length of stay is 1 year, with an absolute minimum of 6 months. Pocket money of around £130 per month; season ticket for local transport also provided. Applicants must have a reasonable command of German.

Those interested should *contact* the above address.

Great Britain

There are so many opportunities for summer work in Great Britain that the opportunities are collected together in the separate title *Summer Jobs in Britain*; for details see the *Useful Publications* chapter at the end of this book. However, a number of the employers and voluntary organisations listed in the *Worldwide* chapter can place people in the UK.

US students seeking temporary work in the UK can benefit from the *Work in Britain Program*. This allows full-time college students and recent graduates over the age of 18 to look for work in Britain, finding jobs through programme listings or through personal contacts. Jobs may be pre-arranged, though most participants wait until arrival in Britain to job hunt. They must first obtain a 'British Universities North America Club (BUNAC) Card', which is recognised by the British Home Office as a valid substitute for a work permit; this BUNAC Card must be obtained before leaving the US for Britain, as it acts as an entry document. It allows the holder to work for a maximum of six months at any time of year: extensions are never granted. The BUNAC card is available for a fee of approx. $250 (2002) from BUNAC (toll free ☎1-888-GO BUNAC) or by applying online after reading their brochure – full details at www.bunac.org/usa/.

A similar programme, called the Student Work Abroad Programme (SWAP), is organised for Canadian students, graduates and young people, with varying age restrictions applying. It is administered by the Canadian Universities Travel Service, which has over 40 offices in Canada. For details see www.swap.ca where you can apply online or see a listing of the numerous Travel Cut offices, including Granville Island, 1516 Duranleau St, Vancouver, BC V6H 3S4, (604) 659-2820 where applications can be made in person.

Greece

Every year Greece receives around ten million foreign tourists, and it is the tourist trade with employers such as those listed in this chapter that offers the best chances of finding temporary work to the foreigner. One reason for this is that in the tourist industry having a native language other than Greek is an asset rather than a liability. Such work is best found by making opportunistic enquiries once at the main tourist destinations.

Other opportunities for foreigners involve domestic work with Greek families, helping with the housework and perhaps improving the family's English. Wages in Greece are generally low, but are enough to permit an extended stay. In recent years wage levels for unskilled work have been depressed in some areas because of the large number of immigrants – legal and otherwise – from Albania and other countries in Eastern Europe who are willing to work for low rates.

British, Irish and other EU nationals are permitted to use the Greek national employment service: local branches are called offices of the *Organisimos Apasholisseos Ergatikou Dynamikou,* or OAED (the Manpower Employment Organisation: Ethnikis Antistasis 8 str., GR-17456 Alimos, Greece; ☎+30-1-9989000; www.oaed.gr). For further information consult the free booklet *Working in Greece* published by the UK Employment Service. Jobs are also advertised in the local major newspapers such as *Ta Nea, Eleftheros Typos, Eleftherotypia* and *Apogevmatini.*

Although many people have succeeded in finding casual farm work, such as picking oranges and olives, it is almost impossible to arrange this from outside Greece. Oranges are picked between Christmas and March, especially south of Corinth. Grapes are grown all over the mainland and islands, and growers often need casual help during the September harvest. Those who are prepared to take a chance on finding casual work in Greece will find further information on harvests in the book *Work Your Way Around the World* (see the *Useful Publications* chapter).

There are opportunities for voluntary work in Greece arranged by International Voluntary Service, Youth Action for Peace, Concordia and UNA Exchange for British applicants and Service Civil International and CIEE for Americans: see the *Worldwide* chapter for details.

It may be possible to obtain a job by means of an advertisement in one of the English language newspapers in Athens. The *Athens News* is a weekly newspaper published every Friday whose classified department is at 9 Christou Lada str, 102 37 Athens, Greece (☎ 010 3333404; fax 010 3223746; e-mail: an-classified@dolnet.gr). The minimum charge for an advertisement is €8 for 15 words. You can check the classified advertisements in the Athens News on the internet on www.athensnews.gr

RED TAPE, VISAS &WORK PERMITS

Visa Requirements: citizens of the UK and other EEA countries and Australia, Canada, New Zealand and the USA do not require a visa to travel to Greece.
Residence Permits: those wishing to stay in Greece for longer than three months require permission to do so from the Aliens Department *(Grafeio Tmimatos Allodapon)* or Tourist Police in the area. You must present your passport, a letter of intent of employment and a Medical Certificate.
Work Permits: a permit must be obtained by a prospective employer on behalf of a non-EEA national prior to arrival in Greece. Failure to follow this procedure may result in refusal of entry to the country. EEA nationals do not require a work permit to work in Greece.
Au Pair: allowed; a work permit must be obtained for non-EEA citizens.

Hotel Work and Catering

HOTEL AGIOS GORDIS: Thyris Kerkyras, Corfu, Greece.
Cooks (3) to prepare food for around 400 people daily. From £400 per month. Should have previous experience of professional cooking of international specialities, with an emphasis on Italian cooking. 8 hour day, 6 day week. No accommodation provided, but rooms are available locally for around £100-£120 per month. Minimum period of work 4 months between 10 April and 1 October.
Applications to Paul Rizos, Manager, at the above address.

ARISTOTELES HOTEL: 15 Acharnon Street, GR-104 38 Athens, Greece (☎30-1-522 8126; fax +30-1-523 1138).
Cleaners, Bar Staff, Couriers are needed for a three star hotel. Wage £250 per month (plus commission for courier) with free accommodation and breakfast provided. Most vacancies are for the Summer, but some exist all year round. Minimum age 24.
Applications to Mr Vakis Ovvadias at the above address.

HOTEL ASTIR: 16 Agiou Andrew Street, Patras, Greece.
Catering Manager (1), **Chef Cook** (1). To work eight hours a day, six days a week. No accommodation is provided. Previous employment and knowledge of English is required. Minimum period of work eight months from 15 October to 15 June.
Applications to the above address.

HOTEL CAPRI: 6, Psaromilingou Street, Athens, Greece (☎01-3252091/3252085; fax 01-3252091).
Cleaners, Bar Staff, Couriers and **Nannies** are needed for a three star hotel. Wage £250 per month (plus commission for couriers), free accommodation and breakfast. Most vacancies are for the summer but some exist around the year. Minimum age 24.
Applications to Mr Vakis Oadias.

COLOSSOS BEACH HOTEL: PO Box 105, 85100 Faliraki, Rhodes, Greece (☎0241-85502; fax 0241-85679; www.colossosbeach.gr).
The hotel has vacancies for work and training in the kitchens, restaurants and bars. These vacancies are only open to students who can prove their student status. Period of work is May to October; staff staying the whole period will receive a refund to cover their normal fare ticket.
In return for working 8 hours a day per 6 day week, staff will receive approximately £140 a month, full board and accommodation, training and free medical/hospital insurance. Applicants should preferably speak English and German and have previous experience or qualifications in hotel/restaurant work.
Applications with a recent photograph to Mr D. Rozalis at the above address befor the end of February.

CORINA'S PLACE-IL GIARDINO: Logaras, Paros, Greece (☎30-284-41049; fax 30-284-41492).
Kitchen Porter (1), **Commis Chefs** (2), **Chef de Partie** (1), **Waitresses** (2). Salary at Greek rates with eventual possibility of free accommodation. Period of work 1 April to 15 October. Split and straight shifts; 5 day week during low season, 6 day week during high season.
Applicants for kitchen work should be male, while applicants for waitressing should be female. *All applicants should be EU nationals*, hard-working, of neat appearance and have at least 2-3 years previous experience.
Applications: *send* curriculum vitae and references, enclosing a recent photo, to Miss Corina Harcourt at the following address between November and March: 10 rue Carnot, Versailles 78000, France; at the above address after April or telephone the above number after 9pm.

DISCO BAR STROVILLI: Kardamylla 82300, Chios, Greece (☎+30 (0) 272 22560).
Bar Staff required for both winter and summer seasons. To work from 10pm to 3am daily; no overtime. Applicants must be aged between 18 and 25.

Applications to Mattae Manonhs at the above address.

DORETA BEACH HOTEL: Tholos, Rhodes, Greece (☎82540/1/2/3/4/5; fax 82446).
Barman, Barmaid, Waitresses. Around £450 per month. Knowledge of German required.
Applications to Michalis A. Yiasiranis, Manager, at the above address.

HOTEL ERI: Parikia Paros, Greece (☎winter 01-5228126; fax 01-5231138;).
Bar Staff, Couriers needed to work in this hotel in the Cyciades, on the Island of Paros.
Applications to the above address.

RESTAURANT KAMARES: 80100 Kapsali, Kythira, Greece (tel/fax +30-736-31-064; mobile 0944-363732).
Kitchen Helps (2-4). Some knowledge of Greek would be an advantage.
Waiters/Waitresses (4). Some knowledge of Greek is essential, and applicants should have some restaurant experience.
Wages starting at £290 per month approx. with food and accommodation provided; to work shifts of 9-10 hours per day. Period of work from 1 July to 15 September.
Applications with a full length photo should be sent to Antonis Magiros at the above address.

KIVOTOS CLUB HOTEL: Ornos Bay, GR-84600 Mykonos, Greece (☎+30-289 24094, 25795/6; fax 289 22844) H/O: 10 Thetidos St., GR 11528 Athens (☎1-7246766/7; fax 1-7249203; e-mail Kivotos-1@hol.gr; www.agn.hol.gr/hotls/Kivotos/Kivotos/.htm). Kivotos Club Hotel is a member of the Small Luxury Hotels Group.
Receptionists (2). Must have a relevant qualification in the hospitality industry. Wage approx. £330-£360 per month. Will work 7 days a week either from 7am to 3pm or from 3 to 11pm.
Waiters/Waitresses (3) required to serve breakfast, lunch and dinner at the main restaurant or serve at the restaurant by the pool. Must have a relevant qualification in the hospitality industry. Wage approx. £330 to £360 per month in return for 9 hrs work a day, 7 days a week.
Maitre'D (1) to be responsible for running the food and beverage departments of the hotel. To work 11-12 hours a day, 7 days a week. Wage approx. £450 a month. Must have graduated with a qualification relating to the hospitality industry.
Board and accommodation is available for all positions. Applicants should be prepared to work for a minimum of 3 months (6 months for the Maitre'd). Knowledge of English, German, Italian or French is useful.
Applications are invited from November to the address given above for the head office for work in the following summer.

HOTEL PORTO LOUTRO: Loutro, Sfakia, Crete, Greece 73011 (☎0030-821043941 / 0030-825091433/44; fax 0030-8250 91091; e-mail portolou@otenet.gr; www.hotelportoloutro.com). The hotel is in a village on the South coast of Crete with no cars or roads and is only accessible by foot or ferry.
Breakfast/Bar Staff for duties including evening bar work and serving breakfasts in a small English/Greek family beach hotel. Wage around €500 per month plus shared tips and accommodation. To work shift work 9 hours per day, i.e. 7.30am-3.30pm

or 3.30pm-midnight. Staff should only apply if they can work from April 1st until mid-October. Experience required.

Applicants should be aged 24-28; no experience is necessary but should be enthusistic, honest, reliable and outgoing. *Applications* enclosing a photo and telephone number from November to February, the earlier the better, to Alison Androulakakis at the following address: 21 Papanastasiou, Hania 73100, Crete (tel/fax 0821-43941).

Applications from November for the next season, to Captain Stavros Androulakis, 21 Papanastasiou, Hania 73100, Crete (0030-821043941/0030-825091433/44), enclosing a photo and telephone number and e-mail address.

SANI RESORT: Kassandra 63077 Chalkidiki, Greece (☎+30 23740 99447; fax +30 23740 99441; e-mail hrdtrain@saniresort.gr; www.saniresort.gr). This long established ecological resort, on the Haldiki peninsula, guarantees its guests' enjoyment by focusing on the training and motivation of its staff.

Training placements available for 18-20 year-old Hotel, Catering and Tourism trainees in this popular Greek resort, the training programme includes financial, social and cultural elements, so that this is as much a cultural exchange as a working environment. **Front of Office Staff** (10), **Sales and Marketing Staff** (2), **Bar Staff** (20), **Guest Relations Staff** (5), **Restaurant** (30), **Animators** (10) **Control Staff** (5), **Maintenance** (2). A basic training wage is paid plus full board and lodging, for a basic 8 hour day, overtime being paid extra. Staff work 5-6 days per week according to requirements.

Places are available form April to October, minimum period of work is 5 months. Applicants should speak English or German.

For more details *contact* Dimitrios E. Koupis at the above address.

VILLAGE INN: 300 Laganas St., Mouzaki, Zakynthos 29092, Greece (☎+30-695-51033; fax +30-695-52387; e-mail village@mail.otenet.gr). A medium size resort on the Greek island of Zakynthos, catering to a mostly British clientele.

Entertainers/Bar Staff (2) to plan, organise and perform entertaining events such as music quizzes, karaoke nights etc, and to work as bar staff in the resort's pool bar. Wages approx. £400 per month according to qualifications.

Mini-Market Staff (2) to work in the resort's mini-market. Wages c.£400 per month.

Staff work 8 hour days in 6 day weeks. Work is available between 1 May and 30 October. Board and lodging is available, and candidates should speak English.

Applications to the above address are invited from 15 March.

Sports, Couriers and Camping

GOLDEN SUN HOLIDAYS: Masons House, 1-3 Valley Drive, Kingsbury, London NW9 9NG (☎020-8206 4733; fax 020-8206 4769; e-mail irena@goldensun.co.uk; www.goldensun.co.uk). A rapidly expanding Cypriot owned tour operator with 26 years of experience.

Overseas Representatives (75) to work in Greece or Cyprus for at least three months between 14 April and 31 October assisting guests at a holiday resort. Applicants should be at least 21 years old and have some customer service experience. Representatives will work 8 hours per day on a shift basis, 6 days a week in return for free accommodation (no food) and a salary of €510 (£360) a month plus commission. Applicants should be fluent English speakers.

Applications should be made to the above address from November.

HILLWOOD HOLIDAYS: Lavender Lodge, Dunny Lane, Chipperfield, WD4 9DD (☎01923-290-700; fax 01923-290-340; e-mail sales@hillwood-holidays.co.uk; www.hillwood-holidays.co.uk) This family tour operator have a child care club and creche and sailing boats.

Children's Representatives (4) to work six hours a day, six days a week. Should have NNEB or equivalent. Wages of £340 plus accommodation (food is extra).

RYA Sailing Instructors (2) to work six hours a day, six days a week. Should be an RYA Instructor. Wages of £340 plus accommodation (food is extra).

Positions are in the Crete resort of Bali. Minimum period of work is six weeks between 1st June and September.

Apply from February to the above address.

MARK WARNER: telephone 020-7761-7300 (24 hour) or 020-7761 7340 for childcare recruitment.

Managers, Accountants, Receptionists, Watersports, Instructors, Tennis and Aerobics Instructors, Chefs, Bar Staff, Nannies, Handymen Nightwatchmen and more are required to work in hotels in Greece during the summer from April to November. Wages from £50 per week plus full board, medical insurance, travel expenses and free use of watersport and activity facilities. Some reserve staff also needed throughout the season. Requirements for languages, age, experience, qualifications etc. vary according to the job applied for. *For further details*, please call the Resorts Recruitment Department on the above number.

OLYMPIC HOLIDAYS 1 Torrington Park, Finchley, London N12 9SU (☎0208-492-6742; fax 0870-429 4142; e-mail julian@olympichoildays.co.uk; www.olympicholidays.co.uk). Olympic Holidays was one of the first tour operators in Greece over 36 years ago and they also have a large complex in Ayia Napa. They are one of the top specialist tour operators to Greece and Cyprus. They cover most resorts from young and lively to upmarket, and ethnic.

Overseas Resort Representatives: (180) to act as ambassadors of the comany, so applicants must be prepared to have a PR role. Duties involve airport transfers, hotel visits, guiding excursions, administration, health and safety checks, complaint handling, welcome meetings. Applicants should have customer service experience, and sales experience is preferable. Maturity, a calm manner and good organisation are all necessary skills. Wages are approx. £100 per week, plus generous commission, flights, insurance and accommodation (meals not included). Representatives work six days per week with variable hours and may be on call 24 hours a day, seven days a week.

Overseas Administrators: (25) For office based administration work, arranging flights and transfers, accommodation allocation and guest related reports along with accompanying guests on transfers. Applicants should be able to use Word, Excel, and possess advanced PC skills along with good organisational skills. Applicants should have good organisational skills. Wages are approx. £600 per month and flights, insurance and accommodation (but not food) are provided. Employees work six days a week. Hours are variable. The season begins in March/April until October, but high season positions (June to September) are also available.

For both positions, Greek language skills are an advantage, but not essential.

Applications should be sent to Julian Pearl at the above address, or via fax or e-mail; enclose a CV and covering letter explaining why you would be suitable for the role.

PAVILION TOURS: Lynnem House, 1 Victoria Way, Burgess Hill, West Sussex, RH14 9NF (☎0870-241 0425/7; fax 0870-241 0426; e-mail: info@paviliontours.com). An expanding, specialist activity tour operator for students, with bases in Greece and Spain. Watersports include: windsurfing, dinghy sailing, water skiing and canoeing. Keen to recruit highly motivated staff.

Watersports Instructors required to instruct sailing/windsurfing etc. and to assist with evening entertainments. Hours of work variable, 7 days a week. Wages approx. £400 per month. Minimum period of work 1 week between May and August. Board and lodging provided.

Applications from January to the above address, please include current instructor qualifications.

SKYROS: 92 Prince of Wales Road, London NW5 3NE (☎020-7267 4424/020-7284 3065; fax 020-7284 3063; e-mail connect@skyros.com; www.skyros.com). Skyros offer holistic holidays: They combine a holiday in a Greek island with the chance to participate in over 200 courses from yoga to sailing and cooking.

Work Scholars to assist in the smooth running of Atsitsa, a holistic holiday centre on Skyros island. Duties include **Cleaning, Bar Work, Laundry, Gardening and General Maintenance.** Allowance of around £40 per week plus full board and accommodation. Variable working hours, but normally between 6 and 8 per day, 6 days per week.

Period of work three months; either April to July or July to October. Work scholars live as part of the community; in exchange for their hard work they may participate in the courses (such as yoga, dance and windsurfing) where their duties allow. Applicants must be aged over 18: qualified nurses, chefs and Greek speakers preferred.

Applications should be sent to the above address between January and February.

Teaching and Language Schools

ENGLISH LANGUAGE SCHOOL: 66 Tepeleniou Street, New Liossia, 13123 Athens, Greece (☎Athens 5014000; e-mail jackyschool@ath.forthnet.gr; jackysch ool.homestead.com/init.html)

English Teachers to teach English to Greek students (mainly teenagers) in a school with easy access to the city centre and beach. Wages according to qualifications, with national insurance covered and holidays paid. To work Monday-Friday; hours by arrangement. Period of work from mid September to May. Applicants should have a BA in English literature (an EFL qualification would be an advantage), be aged 22-30 and be happy, outgoing people genuinely interested in living in Greece. Full and extensive training is given to inexperienced teachers.

Applications to to Jacky Wilson-Vamvaka at the above address.

ESAC: Cosmos Center, 125-127 L. Kifisias, 11524 Athens, Greece (tel/fax +6995824). English courses for children and newly established courses for adults, professionals and students preparing for British universities. Other languages are taught in small groups of 2-3 students.

EFL Teachers for schools around Greece. Wages by arrangement: accommodation provided. To teach 25-30 hours per week. Period of work either from June to 30 September or from 1 September to 31 May. Minimum qualification necessary a BA in languages or related subject.

For further details *contact* the above address enclosing an International Reply Coupon.

Work at Sea

SETSAIL HOLIDAYS: The Business Centre, 140 Station Road, Redhill, Surrey, RH1 1ET: (☎01737-764443; fax 01737-765985; e-mail boats@setsail.co.uk; www.setsail.co.uk). Setsail Holidays are a specialist tour operator providing flotilla sailing and bareboat charter holidays to Greece, Turkey and Croatia.

Skippers, Hostesses and Engineers organising, operating and running flotilla sailing holidays. The skipper, hostess and engineer work together to co-ordinate and run the flotilla, which can consist of up to twelve yachts. Should have sailing experience and qualifications and the ability to work well with people. First Aid qualifications would be useful. Accommodation is provided on the 'lead yacht'. Minimum period of work, seven months.

Applications to John Hortop at the above address.

UNIQUE EXCURSIONS: Steve and Jo Clarke-Lens, P.O. Box 6710, Nidri, Lefkas Island, 31084 Greece: (☎+30 26450 93116; e-mail unique excursions@aias.gr; www.uniqueexcurs.com). Small family business with ten years' experience running tourist boat excursions in the Lefkas area of Greece.

Marine Guides (2) for 'Marine Adventure' boat excursions. Should be experienced snorkeller, possess a life saving certificate and have a knowledge of marine life ; marine-qualified in marine biology or marine ecology an advantage. To work in a small boat (maximum 40 passengers) and give information on marine life and teach snorkelling skills. Wages €600 (approx £400) per month plus free board and lodging. To work 8am-5pm and 6pm-11pm evenings, 6 days and 2 evenings per week. Period of work from May to September. Minimum July/August.

Applications to Steve and Jo Clarke-Lens at the above address.

Voluntary Work and Archaeology

ARCHELON SEA TURTLE PROTECTION SOCIETY OF GREECE: Solomou 57, GR-104 32, Athens, Greece (tel/fax +30-210 523 1342; e-mail stps@archelon.gr).

Archelon is a non-profit-making NGO founded in 1983 to study and protect sea turtles and their habitats as well as raising public awareness. Each year over 300 volunteers participate in STPS projects.

Volunteers are required for summer fieldwork on the the islands of Zakynthos, Crete and Peloponnesus, where the Mediterranean's most important loggerhead nesting beaches are to be found. Volunteers will participate in all aspects of the projects including **tagging turtles and public relations,** and receive on-site training. The work can involve long nights in the cold or long days in the heat, so a resilient, positive and friendly attitude is essential, especially as the Society's work requires constructive co-existence with local communities.

The projects run from mid-May to mid-October, with free accommodation provided at basic campsites. Volunteers will need to provide their own tents and sleeping bags; warm clothing will be required for night work as the temperature can get quite cold and smart clothes are needed when working in hotels and information stations. The minimum period of participation is 4 weeks, and there are greater needs for volunteers at each end of the project (May, June, September, October).

Volunteers are also required to **work at the Sea Turtle Rescue Centre near Athens.** This is a new centre set up on the coast 20km from Athens to help treat and rehabilitate turtles caught in fishing nets or injured by speedboats. Volunteers will **help in the treatment of injured turtles, assisting the ongoing construction**

of the site and carry out public relations work with visitors. A basic knowledge of animal care is helpful but not essential. Free accommodation is provided in converted railway carriages.

Would-be volunteers for either project need to be over 18 and willing to work in teams with people from other nationalities and backgrounds. Volunteers will have to provide a participation fee of around £50 which goes towards supporting the project and includes a one year membership of the Archelon, including 3 issues of 'Turtle Tracks', their newsletter. Archelon cannot provide any financial assistance but estimates that volunteers will need to allow about £6 per day to cover food costs. Volunteers should be able to communicate in English and have their own health insurance. Successful applicants will be informed within one month of application.

Application forms can be obtained by contacting the above address including an International Reply Coupon.

CONSERVATION KORONI: Poste Restante, Koroni 240 04, Messinias, Greece. Unique opportunity of helping to protect the pre-historic turtles in their natural environment, in addition to experiencing the cultural and aesthetic attractions of Greece.
Conservation volunteers needed for five phases over the summer; from 16 May to 15 June (15), 16 June to 15 July (15), 16 August to 15 September (15), and 16 September to 15 October (15); 25 volunteers are needed from 16 July to 15 August, to **clean up the local beach and surrounding habitats of the loggerhead turtle** near Koroni in the Peloponnese in southern Greece. Duties also include some **monitoring of their behaviour, data recording and material preparation.**

Volunteers pay for their own transport costs etc. and an accommodation charge of approx. £90 for the month. To work 1-3 hours per day, 5 days per week; some leisure activities organised in time off. No special qualifications are necessary; applicants under 18 must have adult supervision.

For further details *contact* Claire Johnston and Darren Dorsett at the above address until late May enclosing an International Reply Coupon.

CONSERVATION VOLUNTEERS GREECE: Omirou 15, GR-14562, Kifissia, Greece (☎+30-1-623 1120; fax +30-1-801 1489; e-mail cvgpeep@otenet.gr; www.cvgpeep.org).
Volunteers required for projects in Greece between June and the end of August. Volunteers will be **working on projects that have a strong emphasis on Greek culture** and take place in remote areas of Greece. Volunteers will work a 6-7 hour day over a 6-day week, minimum period of work two weeks. CVG provides food, shared accommodation, and accident insurance.

Applications can be sent to the above address from 1 June; prospective volunteers from the UK can also apply through UNA Exchanges and Concordia (see *Worldwide* chapter).

GREEK DANCES 'DORA STRATOU' THEATRE: 8 Scholiou Street, GR-10558 Athens Plaka, Greece (☎0103244395 fax 30 210 324 6921; e-mail mail@grdance.org; www.grdance.org). The official government-sponsored organisation for Greek folk dance, music & costume. The theatre provides: daily performances, courses, workshops, field research programmes, books, CDs, CD-roms, tapes, videos costumes and more, related to Greek dance and folk culture.
Voluntary trainee assistants (2) **to learn theatre management, costume maintenance** or **computer production of cultural CD-Rom** between May and October. No accommodation provided, but help may be given in finding it: the cost

will be around £20 per day. No previous experience is necessary.

Also trainees (2) to learn dance research.

For further information *contact* Dr A. Raftis, President, at the above address.

SEA TURTLE PROJECT RHODES ISLAND: CHELON, Viale val Padana 134B, I-00141 Rome, Italy (☎+39-6-812 5301; e-mail chelon@tin.it). CHELON is a research group working to protect and obtain in-depth knowledge of marine turtles.

Volunteers (12) to help protect rare loggerhead turtle nest sites on Rhodes; until recently it was assumed that the beaches of southern Rhodes were no longer suitable for turtles to nest on. Volunteers take part in **nest censuses, the protection and observation of nesting behaviour, as well as helping researchers tag turtles for ongoing observation studies.** The work also involves beach vegetation studies and conservation awareness raising among local people and tourists. English, Italian and Greek language skills will therefore prove useful, but no previous experience or skills are required.

Volunteers provide their own tents for accommodation, as well as meeting travel and insurance costs. The registration fee of approx £380 covers the cost of meals. The project runs between June and September and the minimum stay is two weeks, but volunteers can stay longer subject to approval. CHELON also runs projects in Italy and Thailand.

Contact CHELON at the above address for further information and an *application form*.

Au Pairs, Nannies, Family Helps and Exchanges

AU PAIR ACTIVITIES-KALLIOPY RAEKOU: P.O. Box 76080, 17110 Nea Smyrni, Athens, Greece (☎30-1-93-26-016; fax 30-1-93-26-016; www.ninemuses.gr).

Au Pairs/Summer Companions/Mothers' Helps/Nannies. Main periods of work June to August, July to August, May to September. Wages from £40 per week for 6-7 active hours a day, for six days a week up to £134 depending on the hours worked, duties and qualifications. Accommodation with the family room shared with the children or own room provided. Applicants must be aged between 18 and 29; should be fun-loving, active, adaptable and open to Greek culture and mentality.

Applications to the above address.

Ireland

The rapid growth of the Irish economy in recent years is resulting in shortages of skilled employees in some sectors such as information and computing technologies, construction and nursing. Ireland offers a number of opportunities for seasonal work. The greatest demand for summer staff is in the tourist industry which is concentrated around Dublin and in the West, South West and around the coast. Dublin is a boom town at present for the tourist industry.

There is a fair chance of finding paid work on farms and also scope for organising voluntary work. Two organisations can help those wishing to work voluntarily on Irish farms or who are interested in learning organic farming techniques; Willing Workers on Organic Farms and the Irish Organic Farmers and Growers Association. To obtain details of World Wide Opportunities on

Organic Farms write to c/o Rose O'Brien, WWOOF, Harpoonstown, Drinagh, Co. Wexford, Ireland. For information enclose a stamped addressed envelope or an International Reply Coupon. For membership, enclose a subscription fee of US$15. For information on the Irish Organic Farmers and Growers Association, contact them at Organic Farm Centre, Harbour Road, Kilbeggan, Co. Westmeath, Ireland (☎(+353) 0506-32563 fax (+353) 0506-32063 e-mail: info@irishorganic.ie; www.irishorganic.ie).

FAS is Ireland's Training & Employment Agency. In addition to accessing details of Irish vacancies on their website www.fas.ie, job seekers can also register their CV and state what type of job they would like to do. Job seekers with a work permit in Ireland can call to the local FAS office for details of vacancies (Dublin office is at 27-33 Upper Baggot Street, Dublin 4, ☎+353-1-6070500; www.fasjobs-ireland.com). Jobseekers from outside Ireland can also gain access to vacancies by using the European Commission's EURES placement system – http://europa.eu.int/jobs/eures. Forfas (www.askireland.com), is another state body, which promotes industrial and technological development, may have information of vacancies available.

Those seeking temporary work in Ireland's hospitality and leisure industry can leave their details with www.irishjobsearch.com. Potential employers can then access the website's database and contact you to invite you to apply for jobs they are offering. Those using the service must be available to work in any job offered for a minimum of 2 months. Registering for this service is free, but jobseekers must e-mail the website each month to confirm they are still seeking employment.

Foreign students are under certain employment restrictions in Ireland with the exception of students from the USA, Canada, Australia and New Zealand, which have reciprocal agreements with Ireland. Recent changes mean that students from other nations studying in Ireland may work up to 20 hours per week in term and full-time in vacations until their permission to stay expires. As their primary cause for being in Ireland is study, work permits are not required but working beyond the above limits will be construed as a breach of the students' study visa. This change in the availability of casual work for students does not remove the financial support requirements for student visas.

In addition to the opportunities listed in this chapter voluntary work can be arranged by International Voluntary Service for British applicants and Service Civil International for Americans: see the *Worldwide* chapter for details.

Placing an advertisement in an Irish newspaper may lead to a job. The *Irish Times* can be contacted at 10-16 D'Olier Street, Dublin 2; the *Irish Independent* and *Evening Herald* are based at 90 Middle Abbey Street, Dublin. Several newspaper websites carry information on job vacancies. You might also try the websites for job listings; these include the *Irish Examiner* (www.examiner.ie), the *Irish Independent* (www.loadza.com), the *Irish Times* (www.ireland.com), the *Sunday Business Post* (www.sbpost.ie) or the *Sunday Tribune* (www.tribune.ie).

RED TAPE, VISAS & WORK PERMITS

Visa Requirements: a visa is not required by citizens of most European countries, Australia, Canada, New Zealand, the United States and most other countries in the Americas or the South Pacific if they are entering Ireland for a visit as tourists.
Residence Permits: those planning a stay of over three months must register with the police or the Department of Justice, Equality and Law Reform and be able to provide evidence of how they are supporting themselves.
Work Permits: are not needed by nationals of the United Kingdom or any other

EEA country. Non-EEA nationals taking up paid employment in Ireland must have a valid work permit before they enter the country. This must be obtained by the prospective employer from the Department of Enterprise, Trade and Employment, Davitt House, 65a Adelaide Road, Dublin 8. (☎+353 1 6313079; fax +353 1 6313268).

Working Visas/ Work Authorisations: The Irish Government introduced a new visa system in 2000 for certain categories of employees from non-EEA countries, mainly in IT, construction and in the nursing profession. The new system replaces the Work Permit system for professional employees in the designated categories. A working visa or work authorisation is usually valid for two years. Holders are allowed to change their employers after arrival in Ireland as long as they continue to have authorisation to work and reside in the country. Applications must be accompanied by a completed application form, a job offer from an employer in Ireland, a passport valid for two years, a photograph and an application fee (approx £50) Further information is available from the Department of Foreign Affairs, 80 St. Stephen's Green, Dublin 2 (☎+353-1-4780822) or from the Visa Office in the Embassy of Ireland, 106 Brompton Road, London SW 1JJ (☎020-7235 7700 between 2:30pm and 4:30pm).

Working Holiday Permit: is available for one year to Australians only. Applications should be made to the Department of Enterprise, Trace and Employment in Canberra, Embassy of Ireland, 20 Arkana St, Yarralumla, Canberra, ACT2600 (☎00612-62733022; fax 00612-62733741) preferably before departure. Allow six weeks processing time. Further information may be available from Treasa Woods, Dept of Foreign Affairs, Visa Section, Hainault House, 69-71 St Stephen's Green, Dublin2 (☎00-353-1-408 2763; e-mail treasa .woods@iveagh.irlgov.ie)

Au Pair: only nationals of EEA countries, Iceland and Switzerland can be accepted as au pairs in Ireland.

Voluntary Work: a foreigner does not need a work permit in order to take part in an organised voluntary work project in Ireland providing (a) the scheme lasts for less than three months and (b) the work is unpaid.

Hotel Work and Catering

ARDAGH HOTEL: Clifden, Co. Galway, Ireland (☎095-21384; fax 21314; e-mail: ardaghhotel@eircom.net).
Chambermaids, Waiting/Bar Staff, Chefs, Kitchen Porters, Reception/Bar Staff. Wages according to experience: accommodation provided. Period of work from April to October. Applicants must speak English, have experience in the hotel trade and be flexible and have an interest in catering.
Applications to Mr and Mrs Bauvet at the above address.

ATLANTIC BAR: The Square, Kenmare, Co. Kerry, Ireland (064-41094).
Bar/Catering Staff to work in a busy pub for the summer season May-September. Work includes bar service and general duties. Outgoing personality and willingness to learn essential. Accommodation provided.
Applications should be sent in writing to the above address.

BLUE HAVEN HOTEL: 3 Pearse Street, Kinsale, Co. Cork, Ireland (☎00-353-21; fax 00353-21; e-mail bluehaven@iol.ie; www.bluehavenkinsale.com). The Blue Haven is a small family owned and run, 18-bedroom hotel. They pride themselves on friendliness and efficiency.

Bar/ Restaurant Staff (5-6). Responsible for service and hygiene. €7.50 per hour. Relevant experience desirable.

Kitchen Junior Chef's (2-3). Preparation, presentation and service of food. Cleanliness in the kitchen. Experience preferred. €7.50 per hour.

Receptionist (1-2). Greeting, administration, hospitality. Computer skills required. Wages of €8 per hour.

Accommodation Assistants (1-2). Cleaning of all bedrooms and public areas. Wages of €7.50 per hour. Computer skills required.

To work 39 hours per week, five days a week. Minimum period of work is three months between 1st May and 31st October. Accommodation is not provided (about €80 per week locally).

Apply to the above address with CVs and a recent photograph.

CARAGH LODGE: Caragh Lake, Co. Kerry, Ireland (☎+353-66-976 9115; fax +353-66-976 9316; e-mail caraghl@iol.ie; www.caragh lodge.com). An award winning small country house hotel with 15 bedrooms and a 40 seat restaurant.

Waitresses for morning and evening shifts 8am-1pm and 7pm-11pm, and to help with room cleaning.

Kitchen Staff for evening shifts only 7pm-11pm.

Housekeeping Staff for morning and evening shifts as above.

Staff are required from mid-April to mid-October and work a maximum of 45 hours per week over a 5-6 day week: the minimum period of work is 5 months. Wages are by negotiation based on previous hotel experience. Free accommodation is provided for suitable employees in a staff cottage, situated 1.5 km from the premises.

Applications are accepted from November onwards.

CASTLE LESLIE: Glaslough, Co Monaghan, Ireland (☎+353-47-88109; fax +353-47-88256; e-mail ultan@castle-leslie.ie; www.castleleslie.com). Irish country castle with specialist accommodation catering to local and international clientele.

Commis Chef to work in the restaurant kitchens under the supervision of a senior chef, preparing meals for guests. Wages £150 per week.

Restaurant Staff (3) to wait on tables under the supervision of the restaurant manager. Previous experience required but further training will be given. Wages £120-£160 per week, depending on experience.

Front of House Staff to process check-in and check-out of guests and generally look after guests' needs. Should be computer literate, with some telephone skills, further training provided. Wages £160 per week.

Restaurant and front of house staff should be fluent English speakers. Staff work a 40 hour, 5 day week, and work is available any time of year. The minimum period of work varies according to position, between 3 months (kitchen) and 6 months (restaurant/front of house). Board and lodging is available.

Applications are invited at any time to Samantha Leslie at the above address.

DELPHI LODGE: Leenane, Co. Galway, Ireland (☎+353-954 2222; fax +353-954 2296; e-mail delfish@iol.ie; www.delphilodge.com). A country house hotel and fishing lodge in a stunning but remote valley in Connemara, on the west coast of Ireland.

Housekeeper (4), Waitress (4), Kitchen Help (2), Chef/Cook required to work as part of a team running this remote fishing lodge/country house hotel. Wages £150 per week. Board and lodging is included.

Staff work 8 hours per day, five days per week. Work is available from February to October, and the minimum period of work is two months. Applicants should have a good grasp of English.

Applications for these posts will be accepted from February.

EVISTON HOUSE HOTEL: Killarney, Co. Kerry, Ireland. The Eviston House is a family run hotel in the centre of beautiful Killarney. It comprises 75 rooms, the 'Colleen Bawn' restaurant, the famous 'Danny Mann' Pub and 'Scoundrels' nightclub. Staff are admitted free to pub and nightclub when off duty.
Bar Staff. Minimum age 18 years. Wages on application.
Chefs all grades of chef required.
Receptionists experience preferred.
Waiter/Waitress. Wages on application. Preferably with experience. Minimum age 18 years.
Minimum period of work 4 months between May and September.
Applications during March/April to the above address.

GOLF LINKS HOTEL: Glengariff, Co. Cork, Ireland.
Waitresses (3). Wages on application. Average 55 hours per week. Minimum age 17 years.
Barmaid. Wages and hours as above. Minimum age 19 years.
Hall Porter. Wages and hours as above. Minimum age 18 years.
Laundry Maid. Wages as above. Average 40 hours per week. Minimum age 18 years.
Housemaids (2). Wages and hours as above. Minimum age 17 years.
Chef/Cook. Wages and hours as above. Must have some experience of commercial catering. Free board and accommodation. Minimum period of work 5 weeks between mid-May and September.
Applications from April to the above address.

HODSON BAY HOTEL: Hodson Bay, Athcone, Co. Westheath, Ireland (☎0-902-80500; fax 0-902-80520; e-mail info@hodsonbayhotel.com; www.hodsonbayhotel.com). This 133 bedroom hotel has two restaurants, two bars, a leisure centre and nine conference rooms.
Waiter/Waitress (2-3) To serve at breakfast, lunch and dinner.
Catering Assistant(1-2) General duties include serving tea/coffee and pastries in the café, clearing tables and ensuring general health and safety standards are being met.
For both positions: £212 per week, plus meals when on duty, taxi service and free use of leisure club. Must have good spoken English; some previous experience desirable. Season is end of May to beginning of September. Applicants must be eligible to work in Ireland or have a valid work permit for Ireland.
Applications from March to the above address.

THE OLDE RAILWAY HOTEL: The Mall, Westport, County Mayo, Ireland (☎+353-98-25166; fax 353-98-25090; e-mail railway@anu.ie; www.theolderailwa yhotel.com). Charming 18th Century coaching inn, situated alongside the Carrowbeg river in the centre of the pretty town of Westport on the West Coast of Ireland. Plenty to do in time off; new town leisure centre, beaches, walks, fishing etc.
Cooks, Chefs, Waiting Staff and **Pianist** (4) to work 40 hours per five-day week. Pay from €250 per week plus free board and lodging (provided if available). Must have relevant experience/qualifications. Minimum period of work 2 months; staff required all year round. Full knowledge of English essential.

Applications to Karl Rosenkranz at the above address.

PARK LODGE HOTEL: Park, Spiddal, County Galway, Ireland (☎091-553159; fax 091-553494).
Chef to cook 30-40 mainly *table d'hôte* dinners per day. Duties to include planning and providing full meals of starters, soups, main courses and desserts in straightforward Irish/English cuisine. Wage of approx. £700 per month. Normal working hours from 1-9pm, 5 days per week. Board and accommodation provided free of charge in basic/spartan accommodation shared with other staff; meals on a 'help yourself' basis. Minimum period of work by arrangement between early June and late September.
Applications to Geraldine Foyle at the above address as soon as possible.

SINNOTT HOTELS: Furbo, Co. Galway, Ireland 9 (☎091-592108). This is quality employer hotel is a leading four star property in the west of Ireland, and is part of a progressive group. There is a strong emphasis on professional customer service.
Chefs/Commis Waiting Staff, House Assistants, Bar Staff, Porters. Wages by arrangement, depending on experience. For shift work, five days per week. Minimum period of work three months between April and October. Applicants should be able to speak English; previous experience is desirable but not essential.
Applications to the above address from January.

ZETLAND COUNTRY HOUSE HOTEL: Cashel Bay, Connemara, Co Galway, Ireland (☎095-31111; fax 095-31117; e-mail zetland@iol.ie; www.connemara.net/zetland/). A 4-star country house hotel on Ireland's west coast.
Receptionist for reception desk work, welcoming guests etc.
Commis Chef (2) for breakfast and dinner catering.
Waiter/Waitress (4) to serve guests at breakfast and dinner.
Housekeeper to oversee upkeep of house and guest rooms.
Chambermaid (4) to clean and tidy guest rooms.
Kitchen Porter (2) for general kitchen duties.
Apart from the kitchen porter and chambermaid positions, some previous hotel/catering experience is necessary. Staff wages are £480 (except for Housekeeper £600) per month live in. Hours of work are 8-10 hours per day within a 5½ day week. Period of work 1 April-31 October, with a minimum period of work of one month. All staff should speak English.
Applications from 1st March to the above address.

Sports, Couriers and Camping

ERRISLANNAN MANOR: Clifden, West Galway, Ireland (☎353-95-21134). The manor is situated on Ireland's western seaboard, where the Gulf Stream allows palm trees and fuschias to grow. The local habitat of sandy beaches and rockpools is home to wonderful seabirds, sea shells and wildflowers.
Au Pair, Receptionist and Coffee Shop Assistant. €50 per week. To work between July and August. Flat provided.
Junior Trek Leaders (2) and **Instructors** €100 per week. Flat provided. Knowledge of languages essential.
To work with 30 Connemara ponies on a trekking and riding centre mainly for children, the manor also breeds and schools ponies. Hours from 8.30am-5.30pm daily. Minimum period of work 3 months between early April and the end of September. Saturdays and Sundays free. Knowledge of French or German an

advantage.

Applications to Mrs S. Brooks at the above address during January and February.

Voluntary Work and Archaeology

THE BARRETSTOWN GANG CAMP FUND: Barretstown Castle, Ballymore Eustace, Co. Kildare, Ireland (☎+353-45-864115; fax +353-45-864711; e-mail ann-marie.brown@barretstowngc.ie; www.barretstowngc.ie). The Barretstown Gang Camp offers an international activity-based programme of therapeutic recreation. The camp serves children (7-16) and their families from 20 European countries, suffering from or affected by various forms of childhood cancer and other serious blood diseases.

Carer (18) to be responsible for the day and night time needs of children. The carers live in shared accommodation with the children in their care. Carers must be at least 19 years of age. Fluent English is required and a second European language is desirable.

Activity Specialists (14) responsible for designing, planning and directing one of fourteen activity programmes including: photography, canoeing, creative writing, arts and crafts, horse-riding archery and others. A formal qualification is required to instruct in some activities. Experience in that activity and a creative and flexible approach are important while skills in a second language are desirable

Barretstown runs seven ten-day sessions each summer. There is no typical working day with contact hours varying, but staff can expect to work quite long days. Staff are given 3/4 days off between sessions with some time off every day during sessions including one 24 hour block.

Summer staff work from the beginning of June to mid-September and applicants must be available for the full period of the contract. Full shared accommodation is provided as well as payment of approximately £119 per week for the duration of the contract. All applicants must be fluent English speakers.

Application forms can be downloaded from the website or had by request from The Barretstown Gang Camp; closing date for *applications* for the Summer programme is 19 February.

CONSERVATION VOLUNTEERS IRELAND: The Steward's House, Rathfarnham Castle, Dublin 14; ☎495 2878; fax 495 2879; e-mail info@cvi.ie).
Conservation Volunteers Ireland is an agency that co-ordinates, organises and promotes **environmental working holidays**. Volunteers are required to work on the conservation of Ireland's natural and cultural heritage: no previous experience is required as full training is provided on site, but a knowledge of English is essential. Volunteers work 8 hours per day. Please note that this work is unpaid; board and lodging are provided at a reasonable cost. Work ranges from 3 days to 2 weeks all year round.

Applications to the above address for further information and a booking form.

PILGRIM ADVENTURE: 27 Oldbury Court, Fishponds, Bristol, BS16 2HH (☎0117-9655-454). Pilgrim Adventure groups travel light, sharing fellowship and food while exploring Ireland and also the remoter Celtic parts of Great Britain. They specialise in journeys on foot and by boat. Pilgrim Adventure is an ecumenical Christian organisation founded in 1987.

Volunteer team members to **help lead groups of all ages** 10-25 people and **assist with worship** and general chores in Ireland and Great Britain. Volunteers receive full board accommodation and travel. Volunteers must be able to co-lead for at least seven consecutive days and help plan journeys as part of a team, throughout the year. Team members should have a Christian commitment and an interest in outdoor activities, especially hillwalking.

Applications to David Gleed, Chair, at the above address.

SIMON COMMUNITIES OF IRELAND: St Andrews House, 28-30 Exchequer Street, Dublin 2, Ireland (☎+353-1 671 1606; fax +353-1 671 1098; e-mail noel een.ocallaghan@simoncommunity.com; www.simoncommunity.com). The Simon Community of Ireland has Communities in Cork, Dundalk Dublin and Galway. They aim to provide accommodation and services for the homeless and long term to eliminate homelessness.

Volunteers required for **work alongside homeless men and women** in Ireland. The main duties of the volunteer include **befriending residents and general housekeeping.**

Volunteers work shifts and receive full board and lodging. In addition they receive £50.00 per week allowance and regular holidays. A minimum commitment of 6 months is required. Applicants must be 18 years of age.

For more information *contact* Noeleen O'Callaghan at the above address.

VOLUNTARY SERVICE INTERNATIONAL: 30 Mountjoy Square, Dublin 1, Ireland (☎855-1011; fax 855-1012; e-mail vsi@iol.ie; www.vsiireland.org).

Volunteers to work with VSI (the Irish branch of Service Civil International). The aim of the organisation is to promote peace and understanding through voluntary service in Ireland and throughout the world. VSI organise 30 short-term voluntary **workcamps** in Ireland each summer and welcome the participation of volunteers from other countries.

Enquiries must go through your local SCI Branch or workcamp organisation.

Other Employment in Ireland

AILLWEE CAVE CO. LTD.: Ballyvaughan, Co. Clare, via Galway, Ireland (☎+353-65-7077036; fax 065-7077107; e-mail info@aillweecave.ie.; www.aillweecave.ie). Ireland's premier show cave, Aillwee Cave is situated in a remote rural area of the famous region the 'Burren'. It is a place of wonder, beauty and discovery. From the terrace there are breathtaking views of Galway Bay and the Connemara Mountains.

Cave Tour Guides (5) to lead a maximum of 35 persons on a 45 minute tour through the caves. Wages are (€1100) £650 approx. per month gross, plus tips. Training will be given. Knowledge of geology a help but not essential.

Catering Staff (6) to work as counter hands for the salad bar, fast food outlet and potato bar. From (€1100) £650 gross per month. Experience necessary.

Sales Staff (2) to work in the gift shop. From €1000 per month. Previous experience an advantage.

Sales Staff (2) to work in a farm shop in which cheese is made daily on the premises. Wage as above.

For all positions, hours of work are 40 hours over 5 days a week. Minimum period of work 2 months; work commences March, majority of staff needed by the end of April. Board and shared accommodation are available at the staff hostel at a cost to be arranged. Proficiency in English essential and a genuine wish to work in tourism.

Applicants from outside the EU must be in possession of a current work permit

and health insurance.
Applications to Polly Perkins at the above address.

Italy

The rate of unemployment in Italy has fallen to around 9%. The best chances of obtaining paid employment in Italy are probably with the tour operators in this and the *Worldwide* chapter at the beginning of the book. Other possibilities involve teaching English as a foreign language, though most who get jobs have a TEFL qualification and are prepared to stay longer than a few months of the summer. If you want to try and find this sort of job once you are in Italy look up *Scuole di Lingua* in the *Yellow Pages*. Those with special skills are most likely to find work: for example an experienced secretary with a good knowledge of English, Italian and German would be useful in a hotel catering for large numbers of German, British and American tourists. Otherwise it is surprisingly difficult to find work in hotels and catering. People looking for hotel work while in Italy should do best if they try small hotels first: some large hotel chains in northern resorts take on staff from southern Italy, where unemployment is especially high, for the summer season and then move them on to their mountain ski resorts for the winter season.

Although Italy is the world's largest producer of wine, a similar problem exists with the grape harvest (*vendemmia*): vineyard owners traditionally employ migrant workers from North Africa and other Arab countries to help the local work force. Opportunities are best in the north west of the country, for example in the vineyards lying south east of Turin in Piemonte, and in the north east in Alto Adige and to the east and west of Verona. The harvest generally takes place from September to October. For details of the locations of vineyards consult the *World Atlas of Wine* by Hugh Johnson and Jancis Robinson (£24.50 from Amazon) in a public library; the same publishers also produce the useful *Touring in Wine Country: Tuscany* (£12.99).

There are other possibilities for fruit picking earlier in the year, but again there will be competition for work. Strawberries are picked in the region of Emilia Romagna in June, and apples are picked from late August in the region of Alto Adige and in the Valtellina, which lies between the north of Lake Como and Tirano. More information about finding casual farm work is given in *Work Your Way Around the World* (see the *Useful Publications* chapter). When in Italy you should be able to get information on local harvest work from *Centri Informazione Giovani* (Youth Information Offices) which exist throughout the country for the benefit of local young people: consult telephone directories for their addresses.

EU nationals are allowed to use the Italian state employment service when looking for a job in Italy; its head office is the *Ministero del Lavoro* at Via Flavia 6 in Rome. To find the addresses of local employment offices in Italy either write to the above Italian address or look for the *Ufficio del Lavoro* in the telephone directory of the area where you are staying. Note that these offices will only deal with personal callers. For further information consult the free booklet *Working in Italy* published by the UK Employment Service.

International Voluntary Service (IVS), Youth Action for Peace, UNA Exchange and Concordia can assist British applicants to find voluntary work in Italy, and Service Civil International and CIEE can aid Americans; see the *Worldwide* chapter for details.

An advertisement in an Italian newspaper may produce an offer of employment. Smyth International, 1 Torrington Park, London N12 9GG deal with *La Stampa* (Turin daily), and other provincial papers. The Milan paper *Il Giornale* is published at Via Gaetano Negri 4, I-20123 Milan.

RED TAPE, VISAS & WORK PERMITS

Visa Requirements: full citizens of the United Kingdom, of the United States, Australia, New Zealand and most western European countries do not require a visa for visits of up to 3 months.

Residence Permits: visitors staying in a hotel will be registered with the police automatically. Those intending to stay for more than 3 months should apply to the local police at the *Questura* (local police headquarters) for a *permesso di soggiorno* which is valid for 90 days. If you arrive with the intention of working, EEA nationals must first apply to the police *(questura)* for a *Ricevuta di Segnalazione di Soggiorno* which allows them to stay for up to three months looking for work. Upon production of this document and a letter from an employer, you must go back to the police to obtain a residence permit – *Permesso di Soggiorno*. Then in some cases you will be asked to apply for a *Libretto di Lavoro* (work registration card) from the town hall or *Municipio* (although, in theory, this should not be necessary for EU nationals).

Work Permits: a work permit is issued by the local authorities to the prospective employer, who will then forward it to the worker concerned. Non-EU citizens must obtain the permit before entering Italy.

Au Pair: no problem for EEA citizens but very difficult for others. Some Italian au pair agencies encourage their non-European au pairs to tell the authorities that they are in Italy as house guests or on a cultural exchange rather than face the bureaucracy. Other agencies simply do not accept non-Europeans onto their books.

Hotel Work and Catering

THREE HOTELS ON ITALY'S LAGO D'ORTA: Hotel L'Approdo, Villa Crespi, Hotel Giardinetto: for address see below. The Lake D'Orta is a popular tourist destination, full of marvellous gardens and green meadows in a Mediterranean haven. Attractions on offer include watersports, horse-riding, golf and tennis.

Assistant Receptionists (2-3) required for hotel reception tasks, language skills helpful.

Chambermaids (2-3) to clean hotel rooms.

Waiting Staff (2-3) to serve meals and beverages.

Kitchen Staff (2-3) to help prepare food for meals and desserts.

Staff required for all posts from May until September, minimum period of work 3 months. Staff work 8-9 hours per day over a 5 1/2 day week. All posts come with board and accommodation in addition to wages varying between £130-£190 approx. according to position. Applicants should speak at least English and Italian.

To apply *contact* Caterina Primatesta at the Hotel Giardinetto, Via Provinciale 1, Pettenasco, Italy (☎+39-323-89118; fax +39-323-89219; e-mail hotelgiardinetto@tin.it; www.lagodortahotels.com).

RELAI CA' MASIERI: I-36070 Trissino, Italy (☎445-490122; fax 445-490455; e-mailinfo@camasieri.com; www.camasieri.com).

Waiters/Waitresses, Kitchen Staff. Wages around £80 per week. To work 8-12 hours a day, 5-6 days a week. Free board and accommodation provided. Period of work 3-6 months between end of March and end of October. Knowledge of German, Italian or French required.

Applications as soon as possible to Mr Vassena Angelo.

ALBERGO RISTORANTE COLIBRI: Via Cristoforo Colombo 57, I-17024 Finale Ligure (Savona), Italy.

Commis Waiters to set and clear tables and clean dining room. Some hotel experience an advantage.

Chambermaids for general cleaning duties and room service. Experience and some knowledge of languages an advantage.

Dishwashers to operate dish washing machine, assist cooks and clean the kitchens.

Salaries for all positions approximately £530 per month. To work 9 hours per day, 6 days per week. Free board and accommodation provided. Applicants must be available for at least 4 months between March and October and be at least 18 years of age.

Applications as soon as possible to the above address.

RELAIS IL CANALICCHIO: Via della Piazza 4, 06050 Canalicchio, Italy (☎+39 075 870 7325; fax +39 075 870 296; e-mail relais@relaisilcanalicchio.it; www.re laisilcanalicchio.it). Elegant relais just south of Perugia with 50 rooms. Friendly, international environment, vacation clients, multi-lingual.

Restaurant and **Bar Staff** (2) for table service. €720 (£505) plus tips and free board and lodging. To work 8 hours per day, 6 days a week for a minimum of 2 months from 1 May to 30 Sept. Staff should speak basic Italian, good English, good French and basic German.

Apply anytime from March onwards to Diane Kunst, Manager.

HOTEL CANNERO: I-28821 Cannero Riviera, Lake Maggiore, Italy (☎+39-323-788046; fax +39-323-788048; e-mail info@hotelcannero.com).

Receptionist. To work 10 hours per day, 6 days per week. Free board and accommodation. Knowledge of English, basic German and Italian required. Period of work 5 months between April and September.

Chambermaid. To help in the bar and the garden. Working hours and period of work approximately as for receptionist.

Applications at the above address.

HOTEL CAPO SUD: I-57037 Lacona, Isola d'Elba, Italy.

Waiter. Knowledge of Italian and German required.

Receptionist. Knowledge of Italian and German required. Applicants must be of good appearance.

Applications from January to the above address.

HOTEL CAVALLINO D'ORO: I-39040 Castelrotto (BZ), Sudtirol, Dolomites, Italy (☎0-471-706337; fax 0-471-707172; e-mail cavallino@cavallino.it; www.cavallino.it). This carefully renovated hotel in the old village square of Kastelruth, dates from 1393, thus it has a history of hospitality spanning 600 years.

Assistant Manager (1), **Waiters**(2), **Kitchen Helps**(2), **Dish Washers** (2), **Chambermaids** (2). Wage depends upon experience and qualifications. To work 8 hours per day, 6 days per week. Minimum period of work 10 weeks. Free board and lodging provided. Knowledge of German and/or Italian would be an advantage, and is essential for the managerial position.

Applications to the above address from January.

GRAND HOTEL CESENATICO: Forli, Italy.
Secretary. Duties include bookkeeping and reception work. Knowledge of several languages required.
Waiters: duties by arrangement.
8 hours per day. Wages by arrangement, with free board and accommodation provided. Must have knowledge of French and German. Minimum period of work 3 months between 1st June and 20th September.
Applications in February to the address above.

HOTEL CONTINENTAL: I-44024 Lido di Spina/FE, Italy.
Kitchen Staff (2 females). £200-£220 per month. To do general kitchen work.
Waitresses (5). Salary as above.
Room Maids (5). Salary as above. To clear rooms.
Staff work an average of 8 hours per day, 6 days a week. Board and accommodation free. Minimum period of work 4 months between May and October.
Applications for both to Ennio E. Casacci at the Hotel Continental.

HOTEL EDEN GIGLI: Viale Morelli 11, I-60026 Numana (AN), Riviera del Conero, Italy (☎071-9330652; fax 071-9330930); www.giglihotel.com. This 35 bed, family-run hotel is situated by a sheer drop overlooking the sea, near Mount Conero. The hotel places emphasis on peace and restfulness, and the owners aim to meet the needs of their employees as well as their customers.
Bar Staff. Male or female applicants must have a good knowledge of Italian and experience in mixing cocktails (at least two years). To work 12.30pm-9pm/9.30pm-. Wages €930-1035 depending on experience.
Receptionist. To work 8pm-2am/3am with a good knowledge of Italian. Wages €930-1000.
The company also has a restaurant-pizzeria (self-service, American bar) called La Rotonda Gigli which needs **bar staff** to work 4pm-1am/3am (wages c. €1500 and **waiting staff** (wages €930-1500). La Rotonda staff get accommodation included.
Employees for all positions will work eight to nine hours per day, seven days a week. Minimum period of work is three months between 10th June and 10th September. Board and accommodation is provided free of charge.
Applications accepted from March onwards.

COUNTRY HOTEL FATTORIA DI VIBIO: Doglio, I-06057 Montecastelo di Vibio (PG), Italy (☎075-8749607; fax 075-8780014; e-mail info@fattoriadivibio.c om; www.fattoriadivibio.com). A family-run country house.
Barman/Waiter required to serve at tables in the restaurant/bar.
Chambermaid required to clean rooms and carry out other general cleaning jobs.
Salary approximately £265 per month, board and accommodation provided. Applicants should have relevant experience, be 20 to 35 years of age and have a basic knowledge of spoken Italian and English. Minimum 2 month stay required between 15 June and 15 September, working 8 hours a day, 6 days a week.
Applications are invited to the above address from February 2004.

HOTEL FRANCESCO: Via Santa Maria 129, 56126 Pisa, Italy (tel/fax +39 050 830780; www.hotelpisa.com).
Receptionist (also waits tables) needed from 2 June to 1 August and 1 August to 31 September. Wages approximately €100 per week.

Apply to Giovanni Bragna.

HOTEL DES GENEYS SPLENDID: Via Luigi Einaudi 21, 10052 Bardonecchia, Casella Postale 45, Italy (fax +39-122-999295; e-mail geneys@libero.it). A hotel with a youthful and family atmosphere. An ideal place to learn Italian, to study and to rest in a beauty spot.
Chambermaids (2) for general duties. Wages by arrangement. 6 day week of 48 hours. Free board and accommodation. Minimum period of work July and August.
Applications from May to the above address.

HOTEL PENSIONE LA LANTERNA: Via Osteria, I-53030 Livigno (50) Italy.
Kitchen Staff: £160-£180 per month to do general kitchen work.
Waitresses (5). Salary as above.
Room Maids (2). Salary as above. To clear rooms.
Staff work an average of 9 hours per day, 6 days a week. Free board and accommodation. Minimum period of work 2 months between May and October.
Applications to Ennio E. Casacci at the above address.

HOTEL MORANDI ALLE CROCHETTA: Via Laura 50, 50121 Firenze, Italy (☎+39 055 2344747; fax +39 055 2480954; e-mail welcome@hotelmorandi.it; www.hotelmorandi.it). Small, three-star hotel in the centre of Florence.
Reception/Breakfast Clerk to take care of the reception in the hotel cafeteria. Must be well-groomed, have fluent Italian and English and knowledge of French and/or German. €6 (£4.20) per hour. Board and lodging not provided. to work seven and a half hours a day 3/4 days per week for a minimum of 2 months.
Apply to Paolo Antuono at the above address.

IL PARETAIO: Strada delle Ginestra 12, Barberino Velsa-Firenze, Italy (☎+39 (0) 55 8059218; fax +39 (0)55 8059; il paretaio@tin.it; www.ilparetaio.it). Country house accommodation and horse riding school half an hour from Florence and Siena.
Groom (2) to look after horses. Salary negotiable from €300 (£210) per month plus lodging and food. Must be experienced with horses.
Chambermaid (1) to clean 10 rooms. Salary negotiable.
Waiter/kitchen help (1) to be in charge of breakfast and serving dinner for 20 people. No cooking, just serving and cleaning. Salary negotiable from €800 (£560) per month plus board and lodging.
Staff work 8 hours a day, six days a week (Mon-Sat).
Applications at any time to Giovanni de Marchi at the above address or e-mail.

POSTA HOTEL POST: I-39043 Chiusa-Klausen, Sudtirol, Italy (☎0472-847514; fax 0472-846210).
Chambermaid. Wage approximately £500 per month. To work 6 days per week. A knowledge of German and Italian would be an advantage, but is not essential.
Applications to Johannes Reiserer at the above address.

ROMANTIK HOTEL TENUTA DI RICAVO: Ricavo, 53011 Castellina in Chianti, Italy (☎0577-740221; fax 0577-741014; e-mail ricavo@ricavo.com; www.ricavo.com). A four-star hotel amidst typical Chianti landscape half an hour from both Siena and Florence.
Dishwasher (1) to work morning or night shifts. Pay is €1000 (£700).
Waiter (1) to work at breakfast, lunch, dinner as service, filling up stock, stocking

minibar, cleaning restaurant. €1000.

Staff work 40 hours a week, six-day week. Work period is from July to September/October and minimum period is a month.

Apply May/June to the above address or e-mail.

PARKHOTEL VILLA GRAZIOLI: Via Umberto Pavoni 19, I-0046 Grottaferrata, Rome (☎0039-06-9454001; fax 0039-06-9413506; e-mail info@villagrazioli.com; www.villagrazioli.com). This historic sixteenth century hotel, sited 20km from Rome, belongs to the international association, 'Relais and Chateaux'.

Waiting Staff (2). To work in restaurant and bar. Some English and French required. Wages c. €500 (£310) per month.

Reception Clerk. Must speak English and French. Wages c.€ 500 (£310) per month.

Chambermaid. Wages c. €400 (£245) per month.

All employees to work eight hours per day, five days a week between mid July and the end of August. Board and accommodation is provided.

Applications should be sent to the above address from March.

HOTEL ZIRMERHOF: Oberradein 59, 39040 Radein, South Tyrol, Italy (☎+39 0471 887215; fax +39 0471 887335; info@zirmerhof.com; www.zirmerhof.com).

Waiting Staff (2) and **Room Maid** to work from 9am to 6pm, 6 days a week. Board and accommodation are free. Period of work is mid-May to 9 November. Minimum period of work is six months. Knowledge of German and Italian are required.

Apply in January to Sepp Perwanger at the above address.

Industrial, Sales and Office Work

TRENKWALDER SRL: Via Santi G/6, 4100 Modena, Italy (☎+39 059 82 22 09; fax +39 059 82 13 04; e-mail p.bergamini@trenkwalder.com; www.trenkwalder.it). Trenkwalder is an employment bureau supplying temporary workers to companies. It has 25 branches in Italy.

IT Manager to work on maintenance of Net, PC, printers and server. Wages are €400 monthly plus accommodation. To work 8 hours a day, five days a week. Minimum period of work is one month. Must speak Italian and English or German.

Apply from 1 May to the above address.

WELCOME HOTELS & RESORTS: Via Bologna 1043, I-44100, Ferrara, Italy (☎0039-532-713604; fax 0039-532-713609; e-mail welcotel@tin.it).

Translator and Computer Application Person and **Telephone Marketing Person** to translate text from Italian to English and put text on computer for a readership of tourists, writing English messages and news for an English newspaper. Bed and breakfast accommodation provided plus £25 weekly. To work 4 hours, 5 days a week. Minimum period of work 2 weeks between June and 10 August. Applicants must be Italian and English speaking, and provide a reference and personal assurance. This position is not centrally located and requires people who like to live a simple life.

Applications from 1 May at the above address; e-mail communication will be preferred.

Sports, Couriers and Camping

ASSOCIAZIONE NAZIONALE ANIMATORI: Via Sicilia 166/B, 00187 Rome, Italy (☎+39 06 6781647; fax +39 330 636836; e-mail associazionenazionaleanima

tori@hotmail.com; www.ilportaltedegliartisti.it/ana.htm).
Thousands of **Animateur, Sports Animateurs** and **Baby & Mini Club Animateurs** to work in a professional association organising all types of free time activities (social, cultural, ecological, touristic, events etc) for all ages and abilities and disabilities, all over Italy. Salaries: from €300/£210 (baby and Mini Club) to €800/£560 maximum (general animateurs). No experience needed for animateurs and baby/mini club, but sports diploma needed to lead sports. Hours are 8/10 daily for 6/7 days per week for a minimum of one month between 1 May and 31 October. Board and lodging is provided free. Italian-speaking essential.

Applications to the above address or e-mail accepted all year.

BOLERO INTERNATIONAL HOLIDAYS: The Old Airfield, Master Road, Thornaby Teesside, TS17 OBE (☎01642-767222; fax 01642-767677; e-mail info@ boleroholidays.co.uk; www.boleroholidays.co.uk). Bolero Holidays was established in 1984 and is a small family business specialisting in family holidays to Spain and Italy.
Campsite Courier (6) to carry out cleaning and maintenance and entertainment. £120 per week.
Children's Campsite Courier (4) for running Kids Club for ages 4-14 and cleaning duties. £120 per week. Children and craft skills preferable.
Coach Courier (4) to travel on coaches to and from Spain and Italy and loading bike trailer, and on board entertainment, quizzes, videos etc..

Hours of work are 9am-1pm and 3pm-6pm, 6 days per week for a minimum of 3 months between April and October. Lodging provided but not board. Knowledge of Italian required.

Apply from January.

CANVAS HOLIDAYS: East Port House, 12 East Port, Dunfermline, Fife KY12 7JG (☎01383-629018; fax 01383-629071; www.canvasholidays.com). Canvas Holidays are looking for enthusiastic, resourceful people who enjoy a challenge and love the outdoor life. Main positions include:
Campsite Courier. Varied responsibilities. Involves cleaning and preparation of customer accommodation, welcoming and looking after customers during their holiday and ensuring that they have the best holiday ever. As a campsite courier you will have new challenges every day which can lead to one of the most enjoyable summers you will ever have. Variable working hours.
Children's Courier. As a Canvas Holidays Children's Courier you will have had formal experience of working with children. You will organise and carry out a six-day programme which involves five hours a day of Children's Club for children between the ages of 4 and 11. You will be expected to help out with courier duties as and when requried. For many customers, the Children's Club is one of the main parts of the holiday. You will need to have the energy of a seven-year-old and the imagination of an eleven year old to succeed.

Package includes tented accommodation, medical insurance, full uniform and return road travel to and from a UK port of entry. Positions are available from March until October.

Applications are invited from individuals and couples; contact Sandy, Karen or Nina at the above contact details for an application pack.

ESPRIT ALPINE SUN: 185 Fleet Road, Fleet, Hants GU51 3BL (☎01252-618318; fax 01252-618328; e-mail recruitment@esprit-holidays.co.uk; www.esprit-holidays.co.uk) Esprit Alpine Sun run Alpine holidays (France, Italy and Austria) for families in catered chalets and hotels and provide childcare in nurseries and Alpine adventure clubs for children aged 4 months to 12 years old.

Resort Managers. Minimum age 23: should be French , German or Italian speakers, with some management, customer care and accountancy experience.

Chalet Hosts and Hostesses for various grades of responsibilities: minimum age 21, Cordon Bleu/City and Guilds 706/HND/OND or equivalent or experience in cooking professionally required.

Nannies should be aged 18 or over with NNEB, NVQ3, BTECH or RGN qualification.

Nanny Assistants aged 18 or over with NVQ2 or equivalent.

Alpies Rangers with experience as play scheme leaders, children's sports coaches or trained teachers required to run adventure activity clubs. Minimum age 18. Should have a mature, fun loving personality.

All staff must be EU passport holders available from mid-June to mid-September. Ideal for anyone who has an interest in alpine activities, i.e. mountain walking and biking, white water rafting etc. All staff assist with chalet cleaning, babysitting and hosting guests. EU holders essential. Weekly wage, with food and accommodation, uniform, swimming pool pass and transport provided.

Applications to the above address.

EUROCAMP: Overseas Recruitment Department (Ref SJ/04) (☎01606-787525). Eurocamp is a leading tour operator in quality self-drive camping and mobile home holidays in Europe. Each year the company seeks to recruit up to 1,500 enthusiastic people for the following positions:

Campsite Courier: job involves cleaning and preparing customer accommodation, providing assistance, acting as an information service and performing some administrative duties. Couriers need to be flexible to meet the needs of the customer to provide them with excellent service. Minimum age 18 years. Applicants should be independent with plenty of initiative and relish a challenging and rewarding position. They should also possess a friendly and helpful personality. Previous customer service experience would be an advantage. Applicants should be available to work from April/May to September.

Children's Courier: work involves organising a wide range of exciting activities for children aged 4-13. Applicants should possess initiative, imagination and enthusiasm along with good safety awareness. Previous childcare experience is essential. Minimum age is 18 years and applicants should be available from April/May to September. Languages are not a requirement but would be an advantage (in particular German). Successful candidates will be asked to apply for an Enhanced Disclosure.

Senior Couriers: required to work alongside a team of Campsite Couriers and organise their daily workload, as well as carrying out the normal day to day duties of a Campsite Courier. Applicants should have good language skills and experience of leading a team.

Site Managers: required to lead a large team of Campsite Couriers, organising their daily workloads and ensuring they provide the very best customer service. Applicants should be 21 or over, have proven managerial experience, excellent communication skills and language ability.

Comprehensive training is provided together with a competitive salary, insurance, return travel and accommodation. Applications are accepted from September/October and *can only be accepted from UK/EU passport holders*. Interviews will be conducted in Hartford, Cheshire between October and April.

Applicants should apply on-line at www.holidaybreakjobs.com or telephone

01606-781525 for an Application Pack.

G & D GRUPPO VACANZE: Via del Portonaccio 1, 47100 Forlì, Italy (☎+39 0543 26199; fax +39 0543 379784; e-mail info@gedgruppovacanze.com.
Camp Activity Organiser (20) to organise activities including sports, mini club, lifeguard, choreography, dancing, music and theatre activities. Pay starts at €430 (about £300) per month; more for experienced applicants. Free board and lodging. To work 8 hours, six days a week. Minimum period of work 3 months. Knowledge of Italian, German or French required.
Apply to Giuliano de Astis at the above address.

HAVEN EUROPE: HR Department, 1 Park Lane, Hemel Hempstead, Herts. HP2 4YL (☎01442-203970; fax: 01442-241473; www.haveneurope.com). Haven Europe is a market leader with over 25 years experience in providing family holidays. They are the owner and lead operator of eight parks in France, as well as providing holidays on many selected parks throughout France, Spain & Italy. Haven Europe offer the following varied roles in an Anglo-French working environment.
Park/Assistant Park Representatives, Children's Club Representatives, Reception Team Members (must be fluent in French), **Accommodation and Facility Team Members, Lifeguards** (must be NPLQ qualified), **Bar Servers** (must have conversational French), **Entertainers, Maintenance/Grounds Team Members.** Team Members will receive a competitive salary, accommodation on site, a free uniform, medical insurance and travel to site. Working as part of a team, your main aim will be to provide excellent customer service. Applicants must be over 18 and preferably available from March to September (some high season positions are available).
Those interested should *ring or write* to the above address.

HEADWATER HOLIDAYS: The Old School House, Chester Road, Castle, Northwich, Cheshire, CW8 1LE; (☎01606-720033; fax 01606-720001; e-mail info@head-water.com; www.head-water-holidays.co.uk). Holidays travelling at the customers pace, on foot by bike or in a canoe through beautiful unspoilt regions.
Overseas Representatives to work for an activity holiday company in Italy. Duties include meeting clients at airports and stations, supervising local transportation for them and their luggage, hotel and client liaison, bike maintenance and on the spot problem solving. Good working Italian, and full clean driving licence required. Organisational skills, resourcefulness and cheerfulness essential. Minimum age 21 years.
Wages from £115-150 per week; accommodation is provided. To work hours as required. Staff required full season from April to October.
Further information and on-line *application* forms are to be found on their website, or a form can be requested from the above address.

KEYCAMP HOLIDAYS: Overseas Recruitment Department (Ref: SJ/04), Hartford Manor, Greenbank Lane, Northwich CW8 1H (☎01606-787525; www.ho lidaybreakjobs.com).
Campsite Couriers: to look after British, Dutch and Scandinavian customers on campsites in Italy. Duties include welcoming customers, providing local information, organising social activities on site and ensuring that all accommodation is prepared prior to arrival.
Children's Courier: to organise and provide up to 24 hours of activities per week for children aged 4-13 years, to advertise the club activities and visit families on arrival.

Senior Courier: incorporating the role of campsite courier with the additional responsibility of organising and managing the team and ensuring the smooth running of the Keycamp operation on site.

Montage/Demontage: for a period of approximately 6-8 weeks at the beginning/end of season to erect/dismantle equipment.

Minimum age 18 years. Accommodation, uniform, competitive salary and return travel and training provided. A working knowledge of Italian would be an advantage. Period of employment between March and July/October.

Applicants should apply on-line at www.holidaybreakjobs.com or telephone 01606-787525 for an Application Pack.

MARK HAMMERTON TRAVEL: 96 High St, Tunbridge Wells, Kent, TN1 1YF (☎01892-525456; fax 01892-510055; e-mail enquiries@markhammerton.co.uk). Mark Hammerton Travel is a young, dynamic tour operator based in Kent and offering top quality tent and mobile home holidays throughout France and Italy.

Operations Team Members (10) required to prepare and/or dismantle campsite accommodation in France. Staff are needed for the first twenty days of May and September. Irregular hours according to weather. Applicants should be at least 18 years old and must be prepared for heavy, physical work. A driving licence is advantageous. Full board and accommodation, insurance and travel expenses are provided. A wage of £105 per week will also be paid.

Applications for the above positions or for team leader/driver positions should be made to the above address.

MARK WARNER: telephone 020-7761 7300 (24 hour) or 020-7761 7340 for childcare positions.

Managers, Accountants, Receptionists, Watersports Instructors, Tennis and Aerobics Instructors, Chefs, Waiting and Bar Staff, Nannies, Handymen, Nightwatchmen and more are required to work in hotels in Italy and Sardinia during the summer from May to October. Wages from £50 per week plus full board, medical insurance, travel expenses and free use of watersport and activity facilities. Some reserve staff also needed throughout the season. Requirements for languages, age, experience, qualifications etc. vary according to the job applied for. *For further details*, please call the Resorts Recruitment Department on the above number.

Teaching & Language Schools

SMILE: v.Vignolese 454, I-41100 Modena, Italy (☎+39-059-363868; fax 059-363868).

Tutors required to take **Classes in English and Supervise Games** and sporting activities involving groups of 10-12 children. Applicants should be between 20 and 25 years old, well-behaved and cheery with an interest in culture, be keen and able sportsmen and should play a musical instrument. Experience of working with children and any relevant special abilities would be an advantage. Applicants will work from 9am to 5pm from Monday to Friday and for two hours on Saturday morning. There will be a day of training in Modena before the placement begins.

Applicants should be prepared to work between either 12 June and 15 July or 25 Aug and 14 Sept. Free accommodation and food will be provided, as will a wage of between £130 and £150 per week. There will also be the opportunity to travel in Italy; SMILE may be able to pay for a part of the cost of a flight to Italy.

Applications to the above address.

SUMMER CAMPS: Via Roma 54, 18038 San Remo, Italy (tel/fax +39-0184-506070; e-mail: info@acle.org; www.acle.org). Summer Camps is a non-profit association which was the first in Italy to teach English through Theatre in Education and organise drama courses recognised by the Italian Ministry of Education.

Summer Camp Counsellors/Tutors required in camps throughout Italy. Working in association with the Italian Ministry for Education, ACLE provides full immersion English camps for Italian children. Staff would be expected to work eight to ten hours a day, at residential and non-residential camps, providing fun and exciting programmes in English for children between 5 and 16. Applicants must be over 18, native English speakers and have the ability to create English lessons involving songs, games, sport, art and drama. Successful applicants will be invited to San Remo for full training and introductory TEFL course prior to working between 2 and 10 weeks. Applicants must love working with children and have energy and enthusiasm.

Application forms and details on the web site; *applications* accepted between January and April.

THEATRINO: Via Roma 54, 18038 San Remo, Italy (tel/fax +39-0184-506070; e-mail camps@acle.it; www.acle.org). Theatrino is part of ACLE, a non-profit organisation, which was the first to teach English to children and teenagers through Theatre in Education (TIE), and to organise drama courses recognised by the Italian Ministry of Education for Teachers. This small touring English language theatre company and the small routing French language theatre company both recruit from January to April, April to June and September to December (auditions one month prior to tour start).

Native English Speaking TIE Actors required. Also **French-speaking TIE Actors**. Should be young, enthusiastic actors with plenty of energy to work in Italy on a 'Theatre in Education' tour.

Actors tour Italian schools in groups of three and present graded interactive English Language shows. These are followed by workshops consisting of sketches adapted for a particular age group focusing on a particular theme and grammatical point. The overall emphasis is on promoting spoken English in a fun way.

Applicants must be flexible, able to work in a team, be able to handle being 'on the road' and love working with children.ACLE provides accommodation, transport, your flight to Italy ex-London, and a weekly wage. It's a great opportunity.

Applicants must visit the website for details and an application form. Auditions are held in London throughout the year.

Voluntary Work

ABRUZZO NATIONAL PARK: Viale Tito Livio 12, 00136 Rome - Italy (☎06-35403331; fax 06-35403253; e-mail post@pna.it).

Volunteers to spend 15 days working with other young people who are interested in protecting flora and fauna in an outpost of the Abruzzo National Park. Participants **collaborate with the operators, researchers, technicians and guards of the Park in activities such as assisting and educating visitors, maintenance and research.** Volunteers should have experience in the field of nature and be able to spend time in the mountains even in tough living conditions. Minimum age 18. Accommodation and a contribution towards food expenses are provided.

For more information *contact* the above address, or better still, both their

International Centre in Villetta Barrea (☎++39-086489102; fax ++39-086489132; e-mail pna.international:flashnet.it) and the International Parks Centre in Rome (above).

AGAPE: Centro Ecumenico, I-10060 Prali (Torino), Italy (☎+39-0121-807514; fax +39-0121-807690; e-mail campolavoro@agapecentroecumenico.org). AGAPE is situated in the village of Prali in the Germanasca valleys, about eighty miles from Turin. The centre organises national and international meetings during the holiday period. Its isolated position provides the oportunity to experience life away from modern stresses, although this means that the volunteers should be good at entertaining themselves.

AGAPE is an 'ecumenical centre', where believers of different faiths and denominational backgrounds can meet with non-believers in an open and relaxed atmosphere.

Volunteers for manual work alongside the permanent staff. Job **includes helping with cooking, cleaning, laundering etc.** Board and lodging provided. To work for from 20 days to five weeks between the middle of June and September. Shorter workcamps are also held at Christmas and Easter. Applicants must be aged at least 18; knowledge of Italian an advantage.

Applications should be sent to the above address.

CHELON MARINE TURTLE CONSERVATION & RESEARCH PROGRAMME: Viale val Padana 134B, I-00141 Rome, Italy (☎+39-06-8125301; e-mail chelon@tin.it). Founded in 1992 CHELON is a research group within the Tethys Institute; its researchers work to obtain in-depth knowledge of the biology of marine turtles and aid their conservation.

Volunteers to help researchers studying loggerhead turtles in the Mediterranean (Greece, Italy) between June and September. Volunteers will assist in **gathering data on nesting behaviour, tagging turtles for observation and taking part in conservation awareness raising among local people and tourists.** English and Italian language skills in particular will prove useful.

Volunteers contibute about £380 per two weeks, this covers food and accommodation. Travel and insurance costs are not included. The minimum stay is two weeks, but volunteers can stay longer subject to approval. CHELON also runs projects in Thailand.

Contact CHELON at the above address for further information and an application form.

LA SABRANENQUE: Centre International, rue de la Tour de l'Oume, F-30290 Saint Victor la Coste, France (☎466-50-05-05; e-mail info@sabranenque.com). La Sabranenque is a non-profit organisation working with volunteers toward the preservation of traditional Mediterranean architecture. Participants learn skills, share experiences within a diverse group and live in these beautiful villages.

Volunteers (10) to help with the restoration of villages, sites and simple monuments, using traditional building methods, in Altamura, Southern Italy and the hamlet of Gnallo, Northern Italy. Work includes **restoration of walls, paths or the reconstruction of small houses.** Period of work 2-3 weeks between early July and August.

Board and accommodation is included in the project cost, which is equivalent to £180 per 3 week project. At least one day during each 2-3 week session is spent visiting the region. Applicants must be at least 18 years old and in good health.

Applications to the above address at any time.

Au Pairs, Nannies, Family Helps and Exchanges

A.C. LINK: via F. Ugoni 7/B, I-25100 Brescia, Italy (30-375 4471).
Au Pairs and **Mothers' Helps:** placed all over Italy. 6-12 month placements and summer placements of 2-3 months available. Minimum age 18 years. Applicants must be well educated and mature with proven child-care experience. Knowledge of Italian not usually essential.

For further information *contact* the above address.

A.R.C.E.: Attività Relazioni Culturali con l'Estero, Via XX Settembre, 20/124, 16121 Genova, Italy (☎010-583020; fax 010-583092; e-mail arceita@tin.it; http://space.tin.it/associazioni/chiorl). Their Italian families are well selected and applicants can choose placements between large and small towns, as well as being able to rely on A.R.C.E. for support.
Au Pairs (100)/**Mothers' Helps** (50) for placements in Italy; to babysit and perform a little light housework. Au pairs work 6 hours a day, mothers' helps work 8 hours a day, 6 days a week. Wages approx. £150-£240 per month. Board and accommodation provided. Applicants should be aged between 18 and 30. Minimum period of work 1 month from June/July to end of August/September. Childcare experience essential. Knowledge of English and possibly Italian required.

Applications (male or female) from April to the above address.

Luxembourg

The official language in Luxembourg is Luxembourgish but German and French are spoken and understood by almost everyone, and casual workers will normally need a reasonable knowledge of at least one of these. EU citizens can use the State Employment Service when they are looking for work. Its headquarters can also give general information on the current work situation: write to the *Administration de l'Emploi*, 10 rue Bender, L-1229 Luxembourg (☎+352-478 5300; www.etat.lu/ADEM/adem.htm). There is also useful information in the free booklet *Working in Luxembourg* published by the UK Employment Service (see the *Useful Publications* chapter towards the end of this book).

In recent years Luxembourg has consistently had one of the lowest unemployment rates in the EU and currently has one of the lowest level of all at less than 3% and so prospects of finding temporary work there are good. Employment agencies specialising in temporary work include *Manpower-Aide Temporaire*, 42 rue Glesener, L-1630 Luxembourg (☎+352-48 23 23; fax +352-40 35 52; e-mail cmathenot@manpower.lu). Employment agencies are listed in the yellow pages under *Agences de Travail*.

For information about holiday jobs, students are advised to contact the *Administration de l'Emploi* at the above address where a special service run by EURES counsellors – the *Service Vacances* – exists: this must be visited in person by those interested.

In March or April of each year, a special forum for summer jobs is organised by the Youth Information Centre in Luxembourg City, where students can meet employees and firms offering summer jobs and be informed about their rights.

The centre also runs a special service for summer jobs from April to August. The Youth Information Centre can be found at *Centre Information Jeunes*, 26 place de la Gare, L-1616 Luxembourg (☎+352-26 29 32 00; fax +352-26 29 32 03; e-mail cij@info.jeunes.lu; website www.cij.lu).

The Luxembourg Embassy in London can also be of use by supplying a list of the main British firms based there, and another of hotels, some of which may be willing to take on temporary workers (please send a s.a.e. or IRC when asking for these lists).

People are sometimes needed to help with the grape harvest, which normally begins around the 20th September and continues for four or five weeks.

To advertise in newspapers contact *Tageblatt* at 44 rue du Canal, L-4050 Esch-Alzette (☎+352-54 71 31; fax +352-54 71 30; www.tageblatt.lu) who also publish a French weekly called *Le Jeudi* aimed at foreigners living in Luxembourg. There is a weekly English language newspaper, the *Luxembourg News* at 25 Rue Philippe II, L-2340 Luxembourg (☎+352-46 11 221; fax 461122-500); the same publisher also produces *Luxembourg Business*, a monthly business magazine.

RED TAPE, VISAS & WORK PERMITS

Visa Requirements: no visa is necessary for entry into Luxembourg by members of an EEA country or citizens of the USA, Canada, Australia or New Zealand.

Residence Permits: if you wish to stay in Luxembourg for longer than three months, you must obtain permission in advance from the Administration Communale of the Municipality of Residence unless you are an EU national. Non-EU nationals must produce a medical certificate and radiographic certificate issued by a doctor established in Luxembourg as well as the other documents required by all applicants: proof of identity and proof of sufficient means of support or a *Déclaration Patronale*.

Work Permits: are necessary for any non-EEA national wanting to work in Luxembourg. Permits are issued by the *Administration de l'Emploi* to the prospective employer. Non-EEA nationals must obtain a job and a work permit before entering Luxembourg.

Au Pair: permitted in Luxembourg. However the prospective employer must obtain an *Accord Placement Au Pair*. This agreement describes in detail the conditions governing the au pair's stay, as well as their and their employer's obligations. The host family is responsible for filling in this agreement and forwarding it to the au pair for signature. The agreement is then submitted for approval to the *Administration de l'Emploi*. This contract must be concluded before the au pair leaves her country of residence.

Voluntary Work: foreigners are free to carry out voluntary work for recognised international bodies.

Hotel Work and Catering

HOTEL DE L'ABBAYE: 80 Grand'rue, L-9711 Clervaux, Luxembourg.

Waiting staff (1/2). £440-£550 per month, plus tips and share of service charge. A little cleaning work. Knowledge of French or German required. Minimum period of work 3 months under contract.

General Assistants (1/2). £470-£530 per month plus tips. To help in the kitchen and with cleaning.

8-12 hours per day, 6/7 days per week. Free board and accommodation. The order of the house must be accepted by those wishing to live in. A married couple would be acceptable. Minimum period of work 3 months between 15 March and 15 October. Training may be given.

Applications to Mr Paul Wagner, Director.

HOTEL LE ROYAL: 12 Boulevard Le Royal, L-2449 Luxembourg, Luxembourg (☎+352-241 6161; fax +00352-24-16-16-782; e-mail humanresources@hotelroyal.lu; www.hotelroyal.lu). Located in the heart of Luxembourg City, this 5 star hotel has 210 rooms and suites, and prides itself on the attentive but discreet service of its staff.

Stagiares (2) required to take up six month placements in this leading hotel. Successful candidates may be employed as restaurant and banquet waiting staff or assistant receipt controllers and auditors. Staff will earn around £170 per month for working 40 hour weeks, with board and lodging available. Applicants should ideally speak French. As a trainee, staff will earn: 1-2 months, €150; 2-4 months, €200; 4-6 months, €300; 6-12 months, €450.

Applications are invited immediately and should be sent to Albanse Millot-Royer, Human Resources Manager at the above address.

SHERATON AEROGOLF HOTEL LUXEMBOURG: Executive Hotels Sarl, BP 1973, L-1019 Luxembourg.

Driver/Bellboy to operate a bus shuttle, take care of the luggage of clients, welcome clients and perform other tasks in the hotel. Wage approximately £500 per month net. To work 8 hours per day, 5 days per week. Free accommodation provided in a staff house. Period of work from 1 August to 30 September. Applicants must hold a driving licence and speak English, French and basic German.

Applications should be sent to Beatrice Bockholtz, Personnel Manager, at the above address.

Sports, Couriers and Camping

CANVAS HOLIDAYS: East Port House, 12 East Port, Dunfermline, Fife KY12 7JG (☎01383-629018; fax 01383-629071; www.canvasholidays.com). Canvas Holidays are looking for enthusiastic, resourceful people who enjoy a challenge and love the outdoor life. Main positions include:

Campsite Courier. Varied responsibilities. Involves cleaning and preparation of customer accommodation, welcoming and looking after customers during their holiday and ensuring that they have the best holiday ever. As a campsite courier you will have new challenges every day which can lead to one of the most enjoyable summers you will ever have. Variable working hours.

Children's Courier. As a Canvas Holidays Children's Courier you will have had formal experience of working with children. You will organise and carry out a six day programme which involves five hours a day of Children's Club for children between the ages of 4 and 11. You will be expected to help out with courier duties as and when requried. For many customers, the Children's Club is one of the main parts of the holiday. You will need to have the energy of a seven year old and the imagination of an eleven year old to succeed.

Package includes tented accommodation, medical insurance, full uniform and return coach travel to and from a UK port of entry. Positions are available from March until October.

Applications are invited from individuals and couples; contact Sandy, Karen or Nina at the above contact details for an application pack.

EUROCAMP: Overseas Recruitment Department (Ref SJ/04) (☎01606-787525). Eurocamp is a leading tour operator in quality self-drive camping and mobile home holidays in Europe. Each year the company seeks to recruit up to 1,500 enthusiastic people for the following positions:

Campsite Courier: job involves cleaning and preparing customer accommodation, providing assistance, acting as an information service and performing some administrative duties. Couriers need to be flexible to meet the needs of the customer to provide them with excellent service. Minimum age 18 years. Applicants should be independent with plenty of initiative and relish a challenging and rewarding position. They should also possess a friendly and helpful personality. Previous customer service experience would be an advantage. Applicants should be available to work from April/May to September.

Children's Courier: work involves organising a wide range of exciting activities for children aged 4-13. Applicants should possess initiative, imagination and enthusiasm along with good safety awareness. Previous childcare experience is essential. Minimum age is 18 years and applicants should be available from April/May to September. Languages are not a requirement but would be an advantage (in particular German). Successful candidates will be asked to apply for an Enhanced Disclosure.

Senior Couriers: required to work alongside a team of Campsite Couriers and organise their daily workload, as well as carrying out the normal day to day duties of a Campsite Courier. Applicants should have good language skills and experience of leading a team.

Site Managers: required to lead a large team of Campsite Couriers, organising their daily workloads and ensuring they provide the very best customer service. Applicants should be 21 or over, have proven managerial experience, excellent communication skills and language ability.

Comprehensive training is provided together with a competitive salary, insurance, return travel and accommodation. Applications are accepted from September/October and *can only be accepted from UK/EU passport holders.* Interviews will be conducted in Hartford, Cheshire between October and April.

Applicants should apply on-line at www.holidaybreakjobs.com or telephone 01606-781525 for an Application Pack.

Malta

It may be possible to arrange a holiday job in Malta with the following organisation:

MALTA YOUTH HOSTELS ASSOCIATION (MYHA): 17 Triq Tal-Borg, Pawla PLA O6, Malta (☎+356-693957; e-mail myha@keyworld.net). The MYHA offers temporary, free accommodation to persons needing social assistance. It also receives young travellers and workcamp volunteers to assist in the achievement of this aim. The MYHA operates workcamps all round the year, whereby volunteers are accommodated in return for a minimum of 3 hours per day of unpaid work as directed by the MYHA.

Volunteers to work on a Short-term Workcamp. Volunteers, (aged 16-30) from all countries may stay for between two weeks and three months. Accomodation is in the youth hostels.

Apply sending three International Reply Coupons. Where IRCs are unavailable, two US dollars will suffice; application forms should be received six months before the camp is due to start.

The Netherlands

The Netherlands has one of the lowest unemployment rates in the EU. Most Dutch people speak excellent English, and so a knowledge of Dutch is not essential for those looking for unskilled seasonal jobs. The tourist industry employs large numbers of extra workers over the summer: it is worth noting that the bulb fields attract tourists from spring onwards, and so the tourist season begins comparatively early for Europe. Early application is therefore important. A good overview of the job market can be found on the website http://europa.eu.int/scadplus/citizens/en/nl/01069.htm.

Although this chapter lists only details of paid employment in the Netherlands, there are in fact a number of opportunities for voluntary work. International Voluntary Service, Youth Action for Peace, Concordia and UNA Exchange recruit Britons and CIEE and Service Civil International (see the IVS entry) in the USA recruits Americans for camps there; see the *Worldwide* chapter for details.

Eurocamp (see opposite page) offers jobs in the Netherlands.

Holland has many private employment agencies (*uitzendbureaus*) which are accustomed to finding short term jobs for British and Irish workers. These jobs normally involve unskilled manual work, such as stocking shelves in supermarkets, working on factory production lines, or washing up in canteens. Most of the agencies will only help people who visit them in person. To discover nearby addresses look up *uitzendbureaus* in the *Gouden Gids* (Yellow Pages); Randstad, ASB, Unique and Manpower are among the best known names.

Some agencies handle vacancies for work in flower bulb factories, which need large numbers of casual workers from mid-April to October to pick asparagus, strawberries, gherkins, apples and pears: the peak period is between the middle of June and the beginning of August. At the same time of year there are jobs in greenhouses and holiday parks. These jobs are popular with locals and usually can be filled with local jobseekers. From the end of September/beginning of October until January of the following year, jobs might be available in the bulb industry (bulb picking and in factories). Although bulbs are grown elsewhere in Holland, the industry is concentrated in the area between Haarlem and Lisse, especially around the town of Hillegom. There are also a limited number of jobs every year in the fruit and vegetable producing greenhouses of the 'Westland' in the province of Zuid-Holland.

EU (EEA) nationals can make use of the service of the European Employment Services (EURES) represented in their own Public Employment Service and in the Netherlands. EURES provides jobseekers with information and advice about living and working in another country of the EEA. The Euroadvisers also have an overview of temporary and permanent vacancies available in the Netherlands. Contact the nearby local employment office for more information. In the Netherlands addresses of local Dutch Euroadvisers can be obtained through the *Landelijk Bureau Arbeidsvoorziening*; look up *Arbeidsbureau* in a telephone directory. For further information consult the free booklet *Working in The Netherlands* published by the UK Employment Service (Jobcentre Plus).

Those wishing to place advertisements in Dutch newspapers may contact De Telegraaf, a major Dutch newspaper, at Basisweg 30, 1043 AP Amsterdam, The Netherlands (☎010-20-5852208; e-mail com.bin@telegraaf.nl; www.telegraaf.nl).

RED TAPE, VISAS & WORK PERMITS

Visa Requirements: citizens of the United Kingdom, United States, EEA countries, Canada, Australia, New Zealand, Switzerland and Japan do not need a visa. Members of countries needing a visa, will have to apply for one at the Netherlands embassy. The application will need to be accompanied by a full details of means of support, accommodation and prospective employment.

Entry may be refused to all travellers who are unable to show that they have the means to support themselves whilst in the Netherlands and to buy a return onward ticket.

Residence Permits: Members of those countries not requiring a visa who intend to stay for more than three months must acquire a sticker in their passport from the local aliens police (*Vreemdelingenpolitie*) or Town Hall, normally over-the-counter, within 8 days of arrival. Non-EEA members may be required to undergo a medical check for tuberculosis, take out comprehensive medical insurance, submit evidence of suitable accommodation and means of support, and sign a statement that they do not have a criminal record.

Work Permits: Subjects of the EU or EEA do not need work or employment permits. North Americans, Antipodeans and others who require no visa to travel to the Netherlands are allowed to work for less than three months, provided they report to the Aliens Police within three days of arrival and they and their employer have obtained a *tewerkstellingsvergunning* (employment permit) (the employer may do this for them). In practice, the *tewerkstellingsvergunning* is unlikely to be issued for casual work. Non-EU nationals wishing to work for longer than three months must obtain a work permit before arrival in the Netherlands from the local labour exchange in the Netherlands.

Working Holiday Scheme. The scheme is open to Australians, New Zealanders and Canadians who are aged between 18 and 30. They may obtain temporary work for up to a year to finance their holiday in the Netherlands. Applications must be made in person for a provisional residence permit (MVV) to the Dutch Embassy from which further details of personal requirements are available.

Au Pair: such arrangements are allowed, subject to the conditions outlined above.

Voluntary Work: permission to take work of this type may be obtained on your behalf by the sponsoring agency in the Netherlands.

Hotel Work and Catering

HOTEL MALIE: Malienstraat 2, N-3581 SL Utrecht, The Netherlands (☎+31-30-2316424; fax 030-2340661; e-mail info@maliehotel.nl)

Chambermaids wanted for June, July, August to work 8 hours per day per 5 day week. Wages by arrangement, with board and lodging available according to space. Staff should speak a foreign language: English, French, German, Italian or Spanish and if possible Dutch. The minimum period of work is three months.

Applications are invited from January marked for the attention of Mr E.R. van Driel at the above address.

GRAND HOTEL & RESTAURANT OPDUIN-TEXEL: Ruyslaan 22, 1796 AD De Koog, Texel, The Netherlands (☎0031-222-317445; fax 0031-222-317777; e-mail info@opduin.nl; www.opduin.nl). A luxurious 4 star hotel with 100 rooms, 50 employees, gourmet restaurant, and swimming pool. It is just 200 metres from the beach on a beautiful island in 'the top of Holland'

Kitchen Porters (2) for general kitchen work including dishwashing and cleaning. No previous experience necessary.

Assistant Waiters (2) for general work in their service department during breakfast, lunch and dinner. Previous experience is recommended but not necessary. Good appearance essential.

Chambermaids (2) for general cleaning work in the hotel. Good health essential.

Applicants for these positions must be available for at least 3-4 months during the period March to November.

Applications with photograph from January to Mr C den Ouden Esq. at the above address .

HOTEL WILHEMINA/HOTEL KING: Koninginne Weg 167-169, NL-1075 CN Amsterdam, The Netherlands.

Receptionists (2), Chambermaids (3). Approximately £700 gross per month. To work 4-8 hours per day, 5 days per week. No accommodation available. Applicants must speak English.

Applications, enclosing a processing fee of £10, to the above address as soon as possible.

Work with Children

ACTIVITY INTERNATIONAL: PO Box 7097, NL-9701 JB Groningen, the Netherlands (☎050-3-130-666; fax 050-3-131-633; e-mail info@activity.aupair.nl;/ www.activityinternational.nl).

Au Pairs (500) for placements in the Netherlands. Pocket money of approx. €315 per month in exchange for around 30 hours childcare and light household duties per week, with medical insurance covered. A tuition fee (for language courses) of up to €227 is also paid for by the host family. Placements are for between 6 and 12 months. Applicants should have an interest in Dutch culture and learning the Dutch language. Once in the Netherlands au pairs can join the agency's *Go Dutch* club and join activities such as city tours and weekend trips. *Applicants should be from EEA countries*, speak English, be aged 18-25, have experience of childcare and be able to provide references. Activity International work with a number of partner agencies throughout Europe. For Dutch citizens only, Activity International also offers several work and volunteer opportunities worldwide including work on farms, national parks etc.

Applicants should contact the above address for details of the nearest agency to them.

Norway

Norway voted not to join the European Union a few years ago, but it is a member of the European Economic Area (EEA) which means that EU nationals can enter and look for work for up to 6 months. They can seek work through local offices of the Norwegian employment service and work without needing work permits.

Try a telephone job line *Grønn Linje* 800-33166, which provides information on vacancies registered with the Employment Service and is free within Norway.

The rate of unemployment in Norway is currently less than half the EU average, which makes the country a good prospect for the job-hunter although a slight worsening of its oil-fuelled economy has made it a little harder to find jobs in the last year. There are a number of well-paid jobs available in Norwegian hotels over the summer. English is widely spoken and so knowledge of Norwegian is advantageous but not essential. As elsewhere in Europe, the tourist industry appreciates people who can speak more than one language. People who are in Norway may also be able to find unpleasant but lucrative work in fish processing factories in such towns as Trondheim, Bergen or Vardo, but over-fishing has reduced the possibilities of finding such work. When looking for work it is worth bearing in mind that Norwegian students are on vacation between 15 June and 15 August (approximately), and so there will be more opportunities before and after these dates. Those aged 18-30 can take advantage of a 'Working Guest' programme whereby visitors can stay with a Norwegian family in a working environment such as a farm or in tourism or as an au pair; details can be found on their www.atlantis-u.no/index2-eng.html or under the Atlantis Youth Exchange Entry under *Agricultural Work*: an application form and further details can be obtained from Concordia in the UK or Interexchange in the US (see the *Worldwide* chapter for details) see and at other outlets in other countries.

The Norwegian employment service (*Arbeidsdirektoratet*) is unable to help people looking for summer jobs. British citizens may be able to find voluntary work in Norway through Concordia or International Voluntary Service and Americans through Service Civil International (see the *Worldwide* chapter for details). A booklet entitled *Norway-A Guide to Living and Working in Norway* is published by Aetat (the public employment service). Apply for a copy to: Directorate of Labour, PO Box 8127 Dep, N-0032, Oslo, NORWAY (www.aetat.no) or to your nearest Norwegian Embassy.

Oslo has a Use It office (Ungdomsinformasjonen), one of whose aims is to find work and accommodation for young visitors while offering a range of services, as in Copenhagen. Use It is located at Møllergata 3, 0179 Oslo (22 41 51 32/fax 22 42 63 71; e-mail Post@unginfo.oslo.no) and is open year round from 11am to 5pm with longer opening hours during the summer. Their website www.unginfo.oslo.no/streetwise in English carries tips for living and working in Oslo.

Those wishing to advertise in Norwegian newspapers may contact Crane Media Partners Ltd, 20-28 Dalling Road, Hammersmith, London W6 OJB (020-8237 8601; fax 020-8735 9941), who handle the national daily *Dagbladet* (www.dagbladet.no). *Aftenposten* (www.aftenposten.no/english) has a job section and is published at Biskop Gunnerus'g 14A, 0185 Oslo.

RED TAPE, VISAS & WORK PERMITS

Visa Requirements: a visa is not required by citizens of most EEA for a visit of less than three months, provided that employment is not intended.

Residence Permits: this permit may be obtained before entering Norway through a Norwegian foreign service or in Norway at the local police station for any stay of more than three months – your passport, two photographs and proof that you are financially self-supporting are required. Even if obtained before entering the country, you must report to the local police with a 'Confirmation of Employment' within 3 months of arrival. EEA nationals, with the firm intention of taking up employment, may enter and stay in Norway for up to 3 months while seeking work, but before the expiry of this period they too must obtain a residence permit and report to the local police where they must prove that they have sufficient funds to support themselves. They may be asked to return to their country.

Work Permits: British, Irish and nationals of other EU/EEA/EFTA countries do not need work permits in Norway. Non-EEA citizens must obtain a work and residence permit before entering Norway. Permits should be applied for at least 3 months before you intend to arrive in Norway. Having been offered a job and a place to live, you should obtain application forms for a work permit from the nearest Norwegian Embassy or Consulate General, which will send the completed applications to the Directorate of Immigration in Oslo for processing. Applicants may not enter Norway during the period in which the application for a work-and-residence permit is under consideration.

Permits for Skilled and Seasonal Workers. Skilled workers with higher level training whose position cannot be filled by Norwegian nationals or EEA members may be provided with a work permit for at least one year. Non-EEA nationals looking for seasonally-determined work may be granted a work permit for a period of usually no greater than 3 months. Applications for such permits should be made to the Norwegian Embassy.

Working Holiday Visas. A working holiday visa scheme exists between Norway and Australia; applicants must be Australian nationals, intend primarily to holiday in Norway for up to a year, be aged between 18 and 30 years at time of application, possess reasonable funds and travel insurance. Applications can be made through the consular offices of the Royal Norwegian Embassies in Australia or London.

Au Pair. Atlantis runs a programme for 100-150 incoming au pairs who must be aged 18-30, able to speak English and willing to stay at least six months but preferably 8-12 months. Details are available on their website www.atlantis-u.no and also see their entry under *Agricultural Work*. Atlantis charges a registration fee, non-refundable if the placement doesn't go ahead. See entry for Atlantis under farming. Au pairs from an EEA country can obtain the residence permit after arrival whereas citizens of non-EU countries must arrange the paperwork before arrival.

Voluntary Work: this is permitted, but is subject to the regulations outlined above.

Agricultural Work

ATLANTIS YOUTH EXCHANGE: Kirkegata 32, 0153 Oslo, Norway (tel/fax +47-22 47 71 79; e-mail post@atlantis-u.no; www.atlantis-u.no).

Atlantis, the Norwegian Foundation for Youth Exchange, arranges stays on Norwegian farms for people of any nationality who are aged 18-30 and speak English. Participants share every aspect of a farmer's family life, both the work and the leisure; free board and lodging are provided. The work may include haymaking, weeding, milking, picking berries, fruit and vegetables, caring for animals etc.: pocket money of approx. £56 per week is paid for a maximum of 35 hours work a week.

Stays are for between eight and twelve weeks all round the year. EU applicants can apply for up to twenty-four weeks though. *Applications* must be received 3-4 months before desired date of starting work for non-EU applicants: EU applicants may be accepted closer to the arrival date. The registration fee is approx. £100 (£200 for a placement of 12-24 weeks); if not placed all but approximately £20 is returned.

Prospective applicants should contact the above organisation direct for details of partner organisations in their own country. British applicants can apply through Concordia.

Hotel Work and Catering

FRETHEIM HOTEL: Post Box 63, 5742 Flåm, Norway (☎57636300; fax 57636400; e-mail mail@fretheim-hotel.no; www.fretheim-hotel.no.

Waiting Staff (15) for silver service, buffet and à la carte. Wages NOK 17,445+ per month. Must be qualified with good knowledge of wine an advantage.

Bar Staff (2) for hotel bar seating 80 persons. Wages: same as waiting staff. Must have good knowledge of drinks, familiar with micros system and speak Scandinavian language.

Chefs (10) all grades for buffet, à la carte, lunches and breakfast. NOK 18,500 per month. Must have NVQ level and 2 or C&G 7061 and 2.

Chamberstaff (12) for cleaning rooms and other parts of the hotel. NOK 17,000 per month.

Café Personnel (4) to make salads/sandwiches/speciality coffee and to work in bar two nights per week. Wages NOK 17,445 per month.

All staff get board and accommodation (cost NOK 650 for room and NOK 1878 for food per month), work 35.5. hours per week, 5 days per week. Period of work is from May/June to August/September. Minimum period of work is 2 months.

Applications in Jan/Feb/Mar to the above address or e-mail.

HOVRINGEN HOGFJELLSHOTEL: N-2673 Hovringen, Norway.

Waitresses (2). Wages according to experience.

Chambermaids (2). Wages according to experience.

Kitchen Assistants (2). Wages according to experience.

A 7 hour day, 6 day week is worked. Board and accommodation provided at NKr. 2000 per month. Minimum period of work 6 weeks between 1 July and 30 September. This is a small family hotel in the mountains.

Applications from mid-April to the above address.

KVIKNE'S HOTEL: Box 24, 6898 Balestrand, Norway (☎+47 57 69 42 00; fax +47 57 69 42 01; www.booking@kviknes.no; www.kviknes.no). One of Norway's largest tourist hotels with 210 rooms, 400 guests, conference facilities.

Chamber staff (10), **Waiting staff** (15), **Bartender** (5), **Chef** (10), **Kitchen Help** (8), **Luggage Porters** (3), **Night Porters** (2).

Staff work 152 hours per month, 5/6 days a week. Accommodation and board are provided for NOK 1190 per month. Minimum period of work 1 June to 31 August. Previous experience is an advantage as are languages (German, French, Scandinavian).

Apply to the above address from 1 February.

LINDSTROM HOTEL: N-6886 Lardal, Norway. ☎057666900.

Hotel Staff (20) to work in the kitchen, dining room and cafeteria and to clean rooms. Payment on an hourly basis at £8.50 per hour. Board and lodging available at a charge. To work 8 hours per day, 5 days per week. Minimum period of work 6 weeks between 1 May and 30 September. Applicants should be aged at least 18 and speak English.

Applications to Knut Lindstrom at the above address from January.

STALHEIM HOTEL: N-5715 Stalheim, Norway. This busy first class, family run hotel is beautifully situated in the Fjord country of western Norway, 140km from Bergen. It has an International clientele and is open from May to October.

Chefs (8). Wages approx. £1,300 per month, must be fully trained, experienced, and hold appropriate certficates.

Chambermaids (8), Waiters/Waitresses (10), Pantry Boys/Girls (8), Cooks (5). All paid approximately £1,200 per month. Previous experience a plus.

Sales Girls (5) for the gift shop. £1,200 per month. Must be sales minded.

All staff work 7½ hours per day, 5 days a week, occasional overtime required. Salaries taxed at approximately 25%. Board and accommodation provided at approximately £184 per month. Uniforms available. Minimum period of work 3 months between 10 May and 25 September.

Applications giving date of birth and details of education, experience, references and dates available and enclosing a recent photograph should be sent to Ingrid Tonneberg, Managing Director, at the above address.

HOTEL ULLENSVANG: N-5774 Lofthus, Hardanger, Norway.

Waiters, Waitresses, Chambermaids, Kitchen Assistants, Cooks. Wages by arrangement according to qualifications. 38 hours per 5 day week. Board and accommodation available at £60 per month. Period of work 1 May to 1 November.

Applications as soon as possible to the above address.

HOTEL VORINGFOSS: N-5783 Eidfjord, Hardanger, Norway.

Waiters/Waitresses and **Chambermaids**. Board and accommodation available. Experience preferred but not essential. Minimum period of work 3 months between April and October.

Applications in March-April to the above address; so not send International Reply Coupons: reply not guaranteed.

Portugal

Although unemployment in Portugal is currently lower than the European Union average, the best chances of finding paid employment are with tour operators (see below and the organisations in the *Worldwide* chapter), or teaching English as a foreign language, or in hotels in tourist areas such as the Costa do Sol and the Algarve. Private employment agencies such as Manpower may however be able to provide casual jobs for which a knowledge of Portuguese is necessary.

American and British citizens can arrange some voluntary work places through International Voluntary Service/Service Civil International, see their entry in *Worldwide* for details.

British and Irish citizens and other EU nationals are permitted to use the Portuguese national employment service: look under *Centro do Emprego* in a telephone directory. There are also a number of private employment agencies, principally in Lisbon and Oporto: for agencies specialising in temporary work look under *Pessoal Temporàrio* in the yellow pages (*Pàginas Amarelas*). For further information consult the free booklet *Working in Portugal* published by the Employment Service.

Short-term voluntary work can be arranged for British travellers by UNA Exchange and Youth Action for Peace. Their entries in the *Worldwide* chapter give more details about their organisations.

An advertisement in the English language *Anglo Portuguese News (APN)* may lead to an offer of a job; its address is Apartado 113, P-2766-902 Estoril, Portugal (☎+351-21-466 1551; fax 21-466 0358; e-mail apn@mail.telepac.pt). *Expresso* is published at Rua Duque de Palmera 37-2, P-1296 Lisbon (☎21-526141; fax 21-543858).

RED TAPE, VISAS & WORK PERMITS

Visa Requirements: for holiday visits of up to three months a visa is not required by full citizens of EEA countries. The maximum period is two months for US citizens. Australians will need a visa even for holiday visits.

Residence Permits: for stays longer than three months a residence permit should be obtained from the nearest immigration office (*Serviço de Estrangeiros e Fronteiras*). The address of the headquarters of the *Serviço de Estrangeiros* is Rua Conselheiro José Silvestre Ribeiro 4, 1600-007 Lisbon (☎21-711 5000), while the regional Lisbon office is at Avenida Antònio Augusto Aguiar 20 (☎21-315 9681). To obtain a residence permit, you must be able to provide a letter from your employer in Portugal confirming your employment.

Work Permits: EU/EEA nationals do not require work permits to work in Portugal, only a residence permit as above. Non-EU nationals must provide an array of documents before they can be granted a work visa, including a residence visa obtained from the Portuguese Consulate in their home country, a document showing that the Ministry of Labour *(Ministerio do Trabhalho)* has approved the job and a medical certificate in Portuguese. The final stage is to take a letter of good conduct provided by the applicant's own embassy to the police for the work and residence permit.

Au Pair: permitted but not customary; a work permit is required.

Voluntary Work: there are no restrictions applied to work of this nature.

Hotel Work and Catering

HOTEL ESTALAGEM VALE DA URSA: Cernache do Bonjardim, P-6100 Serta, Portugal (☎274-90981; fax 274-90982).

Waitresses/Restaurant Assistants (1/2), Kitchen Porters (1/2) to help in the dining room, bar and kitchen. Some experience in the catering industry would be an advantage.

Applications should be sent to the Manager at the above address in April and May.

LAWRENCES HOTEL: Rua Consiglieri, Pedroso, 38-40, Vila de Sintra,Sintra, Portugal (☎21-910-5500; fax 21-910-5505; e-mail lawrences-hotel@hotmail.com; www.portugalvrtual.pt/lawrences). A five star hotel and restaurant situated in the beautiful heritage town of Sintra.

Kitchen Staff (3), Restaurant Staff (3), Receptionists (3) required to work 5 days a week for a minimum of three months between 1 May and 15 October. Salary £150 per month approx. Knowledge of English is required. Some knowledge of French, Portuguese or German would be advantageous.

Applications are invited from February to the above address.

MAYER APARTMENTS: Praia Da luz, 8600-157 Luz Lagos, Algarve, Portugal (☎00351-282-789313; fax 00351-282-788809).

Bar Person. Outgoing, hardworking, independent individual to serve drinks and snacks at a busy poolside bar. Wages are £100 per month plus commission. No experience necessary since full training is given. To work 10am to 7pm from 1st May to 31st October. Accommodation is included. Applicants must speak English

To apply send CV and photo to Mr Adrian Mayer at the above address from February onwards.

QUINTA DO BARRANCO DA ESTRADA: 7665-880 Santa Clara A Velha, Portugal (☎+351 283-933065; fax +351-283-933066; e-mail paradiseinportugal @mail.telepac.pt; www.paradise-in-portugal.com; www.birding-in-portugal.com). This small, family-run hotel is in some of the most remote and unspoilt countryside in Europe. On the shore of a vast freshwater lake, the hotel is ideal for nature lovers and those interested in watersports.

Bar Staff, Gardeners, Entertainers, Waiters/Waitresses, Cooks. All staff are required to work eight hour per day, five days per week. Minimum period of work is three months between March and October. Wages vary according to experience; board and accommodation are provided. A knowledge of Portuguese, English, French and German would be useful. Driving licence, and knowledge of ornithology or nature are also useful.

Apply early in the year to Frank and Lulu McClintock

Sports, Couriers and Camping

OPEN HOLIDAYS: The Guildbourne Centre, Chapel Road, Worthing, BN11 1LZ (☎01903-201864; fax 01903-201225; e-mail recruitment@openholidays.co.uk; www.openholidays.co.uk). Open Holidays offers villa and apartment holidays in the Algarve and various locations in Spain.

Overseas Representatives required between March/April and October. Staff look after holidaymakers staying with the company, hosting welcome meetings, checking properties. The working week is 43 hours over 6 days. Wages vary according to age and experience, but start at £750 (gross) per month, with a net accommodation allowance of £150 per month.Applicants must have a full driving licence and be over 21.

To apply contact the Personnel Manager at the above address, or email recruitment@openholidays.co.uk.

Voluntary Work and Archaeology

ATEJ/TURISMO ESTUDANTIL: Apartado 4586, P-4009 Porto Codex, Portugal.

Volunteers to work on farms, archaeological digs, with the handicapped, etc. To work 5-8 hours per day. Free board and lodging provided. Period of work from 1 July to 30 September. Knowledge of Spanish and English or French required.**Au Pairs** can also be placed in Portugal by this organisation: for further information, write to the above address in February or March.

Applications, enclosing a curriculum vitae, to the above address in April, or March at the latest.

Spain

Unemployment has dogged the Spanish economy in recent years mainly due to regulations restricting fluidity in the job market. However, annual growth rates in GDP of 3.1% for 2001 and 2.3% for mid-2003 indicate a stable economy and there remain opportunities for finding temporary work. Opportunities for foreigners are best in the tourist industry or teaching English, both areas where the knowledge of another language is an asset.

Many jobs in the tourist industry are described both in this chapter and the chapter at the beginning of the book. Some of the best opportunities for work in Spain are in hotels so that applications to hotels in tourist areas could result in the offer of a job. Since many of these hotels cater for tourists from Northern Europe, a good knowledge of languages such as German, Dutch, French and English will be a great advantage to foreign workers. The website www.gapwork.com has information about working in Ibiza and provides the web addresses for clubs and other potential employers. It is estimated that about 6,000 Britons try to find work on Ibiza each year so it is important to offer a relevant skill.

It should be remembered that hotel workers in Spain work very long hours during the summer months and foreign workers will be required to do likewise. In many cases at the peak of the tourist season hotel and restaurant staff work a minimum of 10 hours per day and bar staff may work even longer hours. A 7-day week is regarded as perfectly normal during the summer. Despite these long hours, salaries are generally somewhat lower than elsewhere in Western Europe.

A knowledge of English and Spanish may help an experienced secretary to get bilingual office work with companies in large cities. There are also a number of jobs for teachers of English: the definitive guide to this type of work is *Teaching English Abroad* (see the *Useful Publications* chapter).

British and Irish citizens and other EU nationals who are in Spain and confident of their knowledge of Spanish may use the Spanish national employment service: look under *Oficina de Empleo* in a telephone directory. Private employment agencies are known as *Empresas de Trabajo Temporal:* for addresses consult the Yellow Pages (*Pàginas Amarillas*). For further information consult the free booklet *Working in Spain* published by the UK Jobcentre Plus (see the *Useful Publications* chapter towards the end of this book). Alternatively you can contact your nearest embassy: the Spanish Embassy in London produces information leaflets, one of which is entitled *Working in Spain* which gives a general guide to the travelling employee. Others are aimed at students and voluntary workers.

It is always worth checking the English language press for the sits vac columns which sometimes carry adverts for cleaners, live-in babysitters, chefs, bar staff, etc. Look for SUR in English (www.surinenglish.com) which has a large employment section and is used by foreign and local residents throughout southern Spain. It is published free on Fridays and distributed through supermarkets, bars, travel agencies, etc. If you want to place your own ad, contact the publisher Prensa Malaguena, Avda. de Maranon 48, 29009 Malaga or this can be done through the website. Advertisements can be placed in Spanish newspapers including El Mundo, a national daily, which is handled by Smyth International, Archgate Business Centre, 825 High Road, London N12 8UB (☎020-8446 6400; fax 020-8446 6402; e-mail alastair@smyth-international.com; www. smyth-international.com). El Pais, the leading national daily, is published at Prisa, Miguel Yuste 40, E-28037 Madrid.

There are also opportunities for voluntary work in Spain arranged by Concordia, UNA Exchange, Youth Action for Peace and International Voluntary Service for British citizens, and CIEE and Service Civil International for US nationals; see the *Worldwide* chapter for details.

RED TAPE, VISAS & WORK PERMITS

Visa Requirements: a visa is not required by citizens of the United Kingdom, United States and of EEA countries for non-working visits to Spain. Since March 2003, it has not been necessary for British and other EU/EEA citizens to apply for a residence card to reside in Spain. Residence cards can however be applied for on a voluntary basis (apply direct to the local *Comisaria de Policia* or *Oficina de Extranjeros*. Further details on the Ministry of the Interior's website (www.mir.es).

Non-EEA nationals taking up a paid job must obtain a visa from the Spanish Consulate before travelling to Spain: this can take 3 months to process. To avoid delay, anyone requesting information or visa forms should write stating their nationality and the purpose of their intended stay, enclosing a stamped addressed envelope.

Residence Permits: Non EEA citizens who intend to stay more than three months must apply for a residence card *(Tarjeta de Residencia)* within 30 days of arrival. Application should be made to the local police headquarters *(Comisarìa de Policia)* or to a Foreigners' Registration Office *(Oficina de Extranjerìa)*. The documents necessary for the *residencia* are a contract of employment, three photos, a passport and (sometimes) a medical certificate. This information can be confirmed with the Spanish General Consulates your own country or at www.mtas.es/consejerias/reinounido. You may also wish to register your stay in Spain with your country's consulate in Spain.

Further information on residing in Spain can also be obtained from the Spanish Consulates General in London, Manchester and Edinburgh and with the British Consulate-General in Spain (c/ Marqués de la Ensenada 16-2°, 28004 Madrid; 91-308 5201). Their notes *Settling in Spain* include detailed advice on sorting out red tape as well as the addresses of all 14 British Consulates in Spain.

Work Permits: are not required by EEA nationals. The immigration situation for non-EU citizens has become increasingly difficult forcing employers of non-Europeans to embark on an expensive, complex and lengthy process. Non-EU nationals must first obtain a *visado especial* from the Spanish Embassy in their country of residence after submitting a copy of their contract, medical certificate in duplicate and authenticated copies of qualifications. In some cases a further document is needed, an *antecedente penale* (certificate proving that they have no criminal record). The employer must obtain a work permit on your behalf from the Spanish Ministry of Labour through the relevant *Delegacion Provincial de Trabajo y Seguridad Social*.

Au Pair: The status of an au pair is between that of a worker and a student. If from a non-EEA country au pairs should apply for a student visa before leaving their country of residence. Once in Spain, they should report to the local police authorities and show a letter from the family and another one from the school where they are studying Spanish.

Voluntary Work: there are no restrictions applied to work of this nature.

Hotel Work and Catering

HOTEL ANCORA: Lloret de Mar, Costa Brava, Spain.
Receptionist. Wages on application. Hours approximately 9am-1pm and 4-8pm, shift work. Board and accommodation provided free of charge. Knowledge of Spanish and English essential, German useful. Must be able to work minimum of 3 months, between May and end of September.
Applications from February to the Director.

6 PLACEMENTS AGENCY: 9 Wish Road, Hove, East Sussex, BA3 4LL (☎01273-776660; fax 01273-776634; e-mail sharon@anglocontinental.fsnet.co.uk; www.anglocontinentalplacement.co.uk). Established 1985.
Chefs, Receptionists, Waiters, Waitresses, Chambermaids, Kitchen Porters for hotel work UK and Spain. Applicants must be EU nationals, or must have a Visa for the appropriate country.
Applications enclosing 4 International Reply Coupons to Mrs Sharon Wolfe at the above address.

BAR FORBIDDEN PLANET JEREMY GRAY NIF:X2285668-C: C/Deveses 23-25, l'Estartit, E-17258 Girona, Costa Brava, Spain (☎972-75 15 77 ; e-mail kategray@coronet.com). Professionally run family entertainment bar, providing good quality amateur productions of popular family shows such as Rocky Horror, Blues Brothers, Grease and comedy sketches (e.g. Almost Full Monty) and much more.
Kitchen Staff (5) to cook basic pub food either alone or as part of a team. To work 10 hours per day, 6 days per week. Applicants should be aged 18-30 and fast, competent workers with basic experience of food/cooking; training will be given. Wages from €200 (£140) per week plus tips.
Bar/Entertainment Staff (12) to work for a very busy theatre bar; duties to include serving drinks and food, stock control plus involvement in amateur shows. Applicants must be aged 18-30 with experience of bar work, hardworking and honest, with bubbly personalities; training will be given. The ability to sing or dance would be advantageous. Wages from €180 (£125) plus tips.
Accommodation provided in a shared house with food, drink and medical cover included (but water and electricity costs to be paid by staff). Contracts will be issued. Period of work April-October. The bar is looking for staff who are good all-rounders and who work well as part of a team.
Applications to Kate Gray, Personnel Manager, at the above address.

HOTEL BONSOL: Paeso de Illetas 30, 07181 Illetas, Mallorca (☎971-4021-11; fax 971-40-25-59; e-mail barnsol@fehm.es; www.la-chateau.com/bon-sol). This family run hotel has 92 rooms and three restaurants.
Nanny (2) to care for and entertain children. Must be kind and be able to care for babies. Wages £525 (€760) per month.
Beach Boys (2) to look after the pools, beach and garden. Applicants must be qualified pool attendants, and should be friendly, professional and kind. Wages £545 (€790) per month.
Waiters (2) to serve meals and drinks. Must be friendly, kind and professional. Wages £545 per month.
Commis Waiter (2). To assist the waiter. Wages £525 per month.
Dish Washer (2) should be clean and professional. Wages £525 per month.
Trained Cook: (2) To organise the working of the kitchen. Should be professional

with good experience of working in a kitchen. Wages c. £930 (€1,350) per month.
Buffet and Snack Kitchen Helper (2) to prepare food and assist with buffet. Should be clean, with a knowledge of cooking. Wages £545 per month.For all positons, employees will work 40 hours over a five day week. Minimum of two months work betwen June and October. Accommodation is shared and costs £100 (€145) per month. For all positions except kitchen staff, a knowledge of German, English and Spanish is necessary.

Applications from March onwards.

HOTEL BON REPOS: Calella (Barcelona), Spain.
Receptionist. Wages on application. Must be able to type. Average 10 hours work per day. Board and accommodation provided free of charge. Knowledge of Spanish and English essential, of German or French helpful. Minimum period of work 3 months between beginning of May and end of September.

Applications from February to the above address.

HOTEL-RESTAURANT CAN BOIX DE PERAMOLA: Can Boix, S/N, E-25790, Peramola, Spain (☎+34-973 470266; fax +34-973 470281; e-mail hotel@canboix.com; www.canboix.com). A small hotel situated in the low Catalan pyrenees run by the Pallarès family for many generations. Well-known restaurant.
Waiter(s) (1/2) to work in the restaurant or in the bar. Wage depending upon skills.
Cook (1). Wage depending upon ability.
Chambermaids (1/2) required to clean and prepare the rooms, public areas and laundry service. Wage depending upon ability.

To work for a minimum of six months between April and October. 6 days a week, 9 to 10 hours a day. Board and accommodation are available free of charge. A good knowledge of both English and Spanish is required.

Applications are invited at any time to Mr. Joan Pallares at the above address.

HOTEL CAP ROIG: 17250 Playa de AroCtr, Spain (☎+34-972 652000; fax 972-650850). The hotel is situated directly over the sea. It is frequented by international clients and is open all year round.
Waitresses (2), Waiters (3), Bar Assistants, Bar and Pool Assistants (2), Chambermaids (3) with relevant experience required. Salary approx. £500 per month.
Cook (Assistant) (1) with relevant experience required. Salary approx. £575.

6-8 hours work a day, 6 days a week, either between 8am and 4pm or between 2pm and 10pm. All applicants must be prepared to work for a minimum of 6 to 8 weeks between June and September. Board and accommodation is included. Those who can speak relevant languages such as Spanish are preferred. All applicants must have a valid EU passport.

Applications are invited as early as possible to Peter Siebauer at the above address.

HOTEL CASTILLO DE MONZON S.L.: Carretera Santander, Monzon de Campos 34410, Palencia, Spain.
General Assistants (2) to work in a hotel as cleaners and waitresses. Approximately £165 per month. Board and accommodation provided. Period of work from 2 to 6 months. Applicants should have an experience of hotel work and be able to speak Spanish and French.

Applications to Jose Diez Sedano at the above address in June.

HOTEL CUEVA DEL FRAILE: Hoz del Huecar, E-16001 Cuenca, Spain (☎34-966-21-15-71; fax 34-966-25-60-47).
Waiters (5), Cooks (2) to work in a restaurant and at an outside barbecue. Wages depend upon qualifications, experience etc.; free board and lodging provided. To work 8 hours per day, 5-6 days per week. Minimum period of work 2 months between 1 June and the end of September. Knowledge of Spanish, English and French would be advantageous.

Applications should be sent to Mr Borja Garcia at the above address from March.

HOTEL CASTILLO EL COLLADO: Paseo el Collado, 1, E-01300 Laguardia, Alava, Spain (☎+34 945 62 12 00; fax +34 945 62 12 56; e-ail: hcastilloedlado@e uskalnet.net).
Waiting Staff (3) to help the head waiter, lay tables, clean cutlery, and serve and help in the bar/coffee shop. Should have experience of restaurant and bar service.
Cook Assistant (2) to help the chef, and clean his/her job area. Must have basic knowledge of kitchen work.

All staff get wages €600 (£420) per month. Minimum period of work 3 months during the season June to October. 4-6 hours per day, 6 days per week. Must speak Spanish. Board and lodging available for about €300 (£210) in village hostel.

Applications to Javier Arcillona Santa Maria at the above address.

HOTEL DURAN RESTAURANT: Lasauca 5, E-17600 Figueres, Spain.
Waiters (2), Cook (1), to carry out usual catering duties: the cook will be expected to prepare easy meals. Approximately £380 per month. 8 hours work a day, 5½ days a week. Board and accommodation are provided free of charge. Minimum period of work one month between 1st June and 30th September. Applicants must be able to speak French and English, and must be of smart appearance.

Applications should be sent to the above address one or two months before the desired period of work.

EASY WAY ASSOCIATION: Calle Gran Via 80 Of. 1017, E-88013 Madrid, Spain (☎+34-9154 88679; fax +34-9154 88919; e-mail info@easywayspain.com; www.easywayspain.com).
Restaurant Staff to work in Madrid and Barcelona as fast-food staff, waiters and commis waiters. Full and part-time work available. Accommodation is available in shared flats. Minimum period of work is two months at any time of year. Applicants can be with or without relevant qualifications but should be aged 18-28.

Applications to the above address.

EMILIO'S BAR: Paseo Maritimo, Puerto Sherry, Puerto Santa Maria, Cadiz, Spain (☎956 540112; fax 01643-702134; e-mail mail@emiliosbar.com; www.emiliosbar.com). Busy beach bar.
Cook and Waiting Staff. Accommodation in own room in the Marina development for a minimum of 5 hours work a day plus one day off (more if wanted) plus a wage and tips . Spanish speaker is essential or student wishing to improve Spanish language skills.

Please e-mail or telephone us for *further information*.

HOTEL FESTA BRAVA: Lloret de Mar (Costa Brava), Spain.
Receptionist. Wages on application plus commission and tips. Knowledge of Spanish and English essential, German useful.

Chambermaids. Wages as above.

Board and accommodation provided free of charge. Minimum period of work 3 months between May and end of September.

Applications from February to Sr Angel Panes Rius, Director, at the above address.

HOTEL FLAMINGO: Lloret de Mar (Costa Brava), Spain.
Assistant Receptionist. Salary on application. Average 9-10 hours daily, shift work. Free board and accommodation. Knowledge of Spanish, English and German essential. Minimum period of work beginning of May to beginning of October.

Applications from February to the above address.

HOTEL LA RESIDENCIA: 07179 Deia, Mallorca, Spain (☎+34 971 639011; fax +34 971 63 83 70; e-mail rrhh@hotel-laresidencia; www.hotel-la residencia). Part of Orient-Express Hotels, 'Small leading hotels of the world'; 160 staff to 110 guests maximum.
Waiter/Assistant Waiter (2 of each) to work in beverages and restaurant. €1001 (£702).
Chef de Rang, Cook, Assistant Cook and **Chef de Partie (2 of each).** Must be experienced and have good CVs. Minimum salaries from €931 (£650) to €1074 (£750), but are negotiable depending on CVs and experience.

There is a charge for accommodation. Staff work 40 hours; five-day week for a minimum period of six months from April to October. Knowledge of Spanish and English required.

Apply all year round to Jacinta Escalas, Human Resources Manager at the above address.

HOTEL LAS VEGAS: Carretera de Francia, Calella (Barcelona), Spain.
Receptionists (2). £300 per month. 8 hours per day, 6 day week. Free board and accommodation. Good knowledge of German and Spanish essential. Period of work 1 July to 30 August.

Applications from January to the above address.

HOTEL MONTE CARLO: Lloret de Mar (Costa Brava), Spain.
Waiters (2). Wages on application plus tips. Hours: 8-10am, 1-3pm and 8-10pm. Board and accommodation provided free of charge. Knowledge of Spanish and English essential. Must be able to work for a minimum of 5 months, from April to October.

Applications from March to the address above.

HOTEL MONTEMAR: Calle Puntaires 20, Pineda de Mar (Barcelona), Spain (☎+93-767 00 02; fax +93-767 15 79).
Assistant Animateur. Must be Dutch.
Receptionist. £550 per month. Must be Dutch.

To work 7 hours per day, 6 days per week. Board and accommodation provided free of charge. The ability to speak Dutch, Spanish and German is essential and some knowledge of French is required. Applicants must be Dutch and available for at least 4 months from May to October.

Applications from February to the above address.

HOTEL-RESTAURANT MONT SANT: Xativa, Valencia, Spain (+34 96 2275031; fax +34 96 2281905). Small (7 bedrooms) purpose-built on the site of an ancient farmstead and situated in its own landscaped gardens with Michelin recognised restaurant, gymnasium and swimming pool.

Chefs (2) for cold starters, desserts, hot meals, sauces etc. €800-1200 (£560-840) per month to work 8 hours a day, 5-day week .

Waiting staff (2) serving food in a good restaurant, banquet work. €750-1000 (£525-700) per month.

There is a charge of about £30 approx per month for board and lodging. Staff work 8 hours a day, five days per week. The work period is from three to six months. Should speak English, French or German.

Apply to Javier Andrés Cifre, Director from February 2004.

NICO-HOTEL: CN-II km 150, 42240 Medinaceli (Soria) Spain (☎975-326111; fax 975-326474; e-mail jacinto.3017@cajazural.com). This hotel is in an historic village 150km from Madrid, with a high class Spanish clientele. There is a staff of fifty, aged between 20 and 40. Customers are mainly Spanish, although other nationalities often visit in summer.

Kitchen Staff needed all year round. Wages on application. To work 7 hours per day, 6 days per week.

Waitresses (5). Wages on application. To work 8 hours per day, 6 days per week. Previous experience preferred. Some knowledge of Spanish required. Minimum period of work 3 months.

Chambermaids (4). Wages and conditions as above, although slightly shorter hours are worked.

Secretary. Wages on application. To work 6 hours per day, 6/7 days per week. Some knowledge of Spanish required. Minimum period of work 2 months.

Free board and accommodation provided. All applicants must be at least 18 years of age. The work period is April to October. The Manager of this hotel wishes to stress that Medinaceli is not situated on the coast. There are also vacancies at the Hotel Duque de Medinaceli, CN-II 150, Medinaceli (Soria), Spain.

Applications from February to the Manager at the above address, enclosing a full-length photograph.

HOTEL PICASSO: Torroaella de Monteri, Girona, Spain.
Waiters, Maids. . £400 per month.

To work at least 5 hours per day, 7 days per week. Board and accommodation available. Minimum period of work between July and August. Experience required.

Applications to J.M. Ferrer at the above address in spring.

HOTEL RIGAT: Playa de Fanals, Lloret de Mar, Costa Brava, Spain. (e-mail direccion@rigat.com; www.rigat.com) A 5 star Mediterranean hotel located on the sea, 68km from Barcelona. Those with or without hotel work experience are welcome to apply.

Waiter/Assistant/Receptionist/Barmaid: must be able to type. Wages by arrangement according to type of job and qualifications. 8 hours per day, 6 day week. Free board and accommodation. Age 19-28. A knowledge of French and German is required. Applicants must be considerate, polite and in good health. Girls should take a blue knee-length skirt and white blouses. Minimum period of work July and August but there are vacancies from June to September.

Applications from February to Mr Sebastian Gispert, Cadena Hotelera Rigat, c/o Ave de America No.1, Lloret de Mar (17), Spain (Cost Brava).

HOSTAL DEL SENGLAR: Plaga Montserrat Canals, 73440- L'Estluga De

Francoli, Spain (☎0034-977-870-121; fax 0034-977-870-127; e-mail reception@ hostaldelsenglar.com; www.hostaldelsenglar.com). This two star hotel has a well-known restaurant and is situated in an attractive location.

Receptionist (1). Administration and client check-in. Wages €750 (£525) net. Should be a PC user. To work eight hours per five day week for a minimum of two months between June and October. Board and lodging is provided.

Must speak Spanish. *Applications* to the Manager at the above address.

Sports, Couriers and Camping

BOLERO INTERNATIONAL HOLIDAYS: The Old Airfield, Master Road, Thornaby Teesside, TS17 OBE (☎01642-767222; fax 01642-767677; e-mail info@ boleroholidays.co.uk; www.boleroholidays.co.uk). Bolero Holidays was established in 1984 and is a small family business specialisting in family holidays to Spain and Italy.

Campsite Courier (6) to carry out cleaning and maintenance and entertainment. £120 per week.

Children's Campsite Courier (4) for running Kids Club for ages 4-14 and cleaning duties. £120 per week. Children and craft skills preferable.

Coach Courier (4) to travel on coaches to and from Spain and Italy and loading bike trailer, and on board entertainment, quizzes, videos etc.

Hours of work are 9am-1pm and 3pm-6pm, 6 days per week for a minimum of 3 months between April and October. Lodging provided but not board. Knowledge of Spanish required.

Apply from January.

CAMPING GIOBO ROJO: Barangé-Brun C.B., Carretera Nacional II, km 660'9 08360 Canet de Mar (Barcelona), Spain (tel/fax 93-794 1143; e-mail cgrojo@teleline.es; www.globo-rojo.com).

Receptionist, Waiter/Waitress, Qualified Swimming Pool Guard required for this campsite near Barcelona (40km). All staff should be polite, with relevant experience. The wages are c. £375 per month for 8-9 hour days over a 7 day week, with free board and lodging. Ideally applicants should speak English, German, and some Spanish, while the job provides an excellent chance to improve Spanish.

The work is available between 1 July and 30 August; *applications* are invited from April onwards.

CANVAS HOLIDAYS: East Port House, 12 East Port, Dunfermline, Fife KY12 7JG (☎01383-629018; fax 01383-629071; www.canvasholidays.com). Canvas Holidays are looking for enthusiastic, resourceful people who enjoy a challenge and love the outdoor life. Main positions include:

Campsite Courier. Varied responsibilities. Involves cleaning and preparation of customer accommodation, welcoming and looking after customers during their holiday and ensuring that they have the best holiday ever. As a campsite courier you will have new challenges every day which can lead to one of the most enjoyable summers you will ever have. Variable working hours.

Children's Courier. As a Canvas Holidays Children's Courier you will have had formal experience of working with children. You will organise and carry out a six day programme which involves five hours a day of Children's Club for children between the ages of 4 and 11. You will be expected to help out with courier duties as and when requried. For many customers, the Children's Club is one of the main parts of the holiday. You will need to have the energy of a seven year old and the imagination of an eleven year old to succeed.

Package includes tented accommodation, medical insurance, full uniform and return coach travel to and from a UK port of entry. Positions are available from March until October.

Applications are invited from individuals and couples; contact Sandy, Karen or Nina at the above contact details for an application pack.

CITY CRUISER HOLIDAYS LTD: c/o Harry Shaw, Mill House, Mill Lane, Binley, Coventry (☎024-7645-5544; fax 04-7645-0774; e-mail robertshaw@har ryshaw.co.uk; www.harryshaw.co.uk). Have been in business for nearly 50 years. Arrange coach, camping and mobile home holidays in a variety of sites in France and Spain. Also arrange coach and air travel to European and worldwide destinations.
Campsite Representatives (5) to clean accommodation, show clients accommodation, undertake small repairs.

French and Spanish would be an advantage. To work 9am-12 pm and 2pm-7pm five or six days per week Minimum of four months between April and October.

Apply from January onwards to the above address.

CLUB PUNTA ARABI: Apartado Correos 73, Es Cana/Santa Eulalia del Rio, Ibiza, Balearic Islands, Spain (☎971-33 06 50/51).
Staff for a wide range of jobs in one of 2 holiday centres in Ibiza. Work includes sports instruction, including sailing, windsurfing and tennis, disc jockeys, theatre work where experience in make up, costumes and lighting is needed, etc. German essential and Spanish useful.
Amateur Entertainers for club shows-sketches, mime etc.
Guitarists/Folk Singers/Buskers for parties, excursions etc.
Managers with experience of running bars, restaurants etc.

Wages by arrangement. Applicants should have a reasonable knowledge of German: Spanish also useful. Period of work 1 May to 15 October.

Application forms available from Miss Sarah Steiner, Director, Club Punta Arabi.

EUROCAMP: Overseas Recruitment Department (Ref SJ/04) (☎01606-787525). Eurocamp is a leading tour operator in quality self-drive camping and mobile home holidays in Europe. Each year the company seeks to recruit up to 1,500 enthusiastic people for the following positions:
Campsite Courier: job involves cleaning and preparing customer accommodation, providing assistance, acting as an information service and performing some administrative duties. Couriers need to be flexible to meet the needs of the customer to provide them with excellent service. Minimum age 18 years. Applicants should be independent with plenty of initiative and relish a challenging and rewarding position. They should also possess a friendly and helpful personality. Previous customer service experience would be an advantage. Applicants should be available to work from April/May to September.
Children's Courier: work involves organising a wide range of exciting activities for children aged 4-13. Applicants should possess initiative, imagination and enthusiasm along with good safety awareness. Previous childcare experience is essential. Minimum age is 18 years and applicants should be available from April/ May to September. Languages are not a requirement but would be an advantage (in particular German). Successful candidates will be asked to apply for an Enhanced Disclosure.
Senior Couriers: required to work alongside a team of Campsite Couriers and

organise their daily workload, as well as carrying out the normal day to day duties of a Campsite Courier. Applicants should have good language skills and experience of leading a team.

Site Managers: required to lead a large team of Campsite Couriers, organising their daily workloads and ensuring they provide the very best customer service. Applicants should be 21 or over, have proven managerial experience, excellent communication skills and language ability.

Comprehensive training is provided together with a competitive salary, insurance, return travel and accommodation. Applications are accepted from September/October and *can only be accepted from UK/EU passport holders*. Interviews will be conducted in Hartford, Cheshire between October and April.

Applicants should apply on-line at www.holidaybreakjobs.com or telephone 01606 781525 for an Application Pack.

FRENCH LIFE HOLIDAYS: Kerry House, Kerry Street, Horsforth, Leeds LS18 4AW (☎0113-205 0292; fax 0113-258 4211; e-mail overseasemployment@frenchlife.co.uk; www.frenchlife.co.uk). French Life holidays are specialists in France and Spain and offer first class accommodation at over 30 campsites.

Couriers and **Children's Couriers** (100) to work as campsite representatives and children's clubs representatives. Pay from £400 monthly; board and lodging included. 35 hours per week, 6 days per week. Minimum period of work is 8 weeks between March/April and September/October. Knowledge of Spanish not essential. High season positions available as well.

Apply to Jo Hayes from November at the above address/e-mail.

HAVEN EUROPE: HR Department, 1 Park Lane, Hemel Hempstead, Herts. HP2 4YL (tel: 01442-203970; fax: 01442-241473; www.haveneurope.com). Haven Europe is one of Europe's market leaders in self-drive camping and mobile home holidays. They are the owner and lead operator of eight parks in France, as well as providing holidays on many franchised campsites throughout France, Spain and Italy. In Spain Haven Europe offer the following positions:

Park Representatives: duties include greeting new arrivals to site, cleaning and maintaining accommodation, administration and organising team rotas. Applicants must be over 21 years old (mature couples welcome).

Campsite Representatives: duties include preparation of guest accommodation, reception work and problem solving.

Children's Representatives: duties include creating and running an entertainment programme for children ranging between 5 and 12 years old. Experience of working with children is an advantage.

Staff will receive a competitive salary, accommodation on site, a free uniform, medical insurance and travel to site. Working as part of a team, your main aim will be to provide excellent customer service. Applicants must be over 18 and preferably available from March to September/October (some high season positions are available).

Those interested should *ring or write* to the above address.

KEYCAMP HOLIDAYS: Overseas Recruitment Department (Ref: SJ/04), Hartford Manor, Greenbank Lane, Northwich CW8 1H (☎01606-787525; www.holidaybreakjobs.com).

Campsite Couriers: to look after British, Dutch and Scandinavian customers on campsites in Spain. Duties include welcoming customers, providing local information, organising social activities on site and ensuring that all accommodation is prepared prior to arrival.

Chidren's Courier: to organise and provide up to 24 hours of activities per week for children aged 4-13 years, to advertise the club activities and visit families on arrival.

Senior Courier: incorporating the role of campsite courier with the additional responsibility of organising and managing the team and ensuring the smooth running of the Keycamp operation on site.

Montage/Demontage: for a period of approximately 6-8 weeks at the beginning/end of season to erect/dismantle equipment.

Minimum age 18 years. Accommodation, uniform, competitive salary and return travel and training provided. A working knowledge of Spanish would be an advantage. Period of employment between March and July/October.

Applicants should apply on-line at www.holidaybreakjobs.com or telephone 01606-787525 for an Application Pack.

OPEN HOLIDAYS: 29 Guildbourne Centre, Worthing, West Sussex BN11 1LZ (☎01903-201864; fax 01903-201225; e-mail: recruitment@openholidays.co.uk; www.openholidays.co.uk). Upmarket tailor-made villa, apartment and hotel holidays, specialising currently in Andalucia, Costa Blanca, Majorca and Menorca in Spain and the Algarve in Portugal.

Resort Representatives to assist clients and work 8 hours per day, 6 days per week. Salary £500-£700 per month. Board and accommodation negotiable. Minimum period of work 6 months from April to October. Minimum age 21. Knowledge of Spanish preferred. Must hold a full UK driving licence, car provided.

Applications from September-December to the Personnel Manager at the above address or email recruitment@open holidays.co.uk; successful applicants must attend a training course in the UK during February.

PAVILION TOURS/CLUB PAVILION: Lynnem House, 1 Victoria Way, Burgess Hill, West Sussex, RH14 9NF (☎0870-241 0425/7; fax 0870-241 0426; e-mail: sales@paviliontours.com). An expanding, specialist activity tour operator for students, adults and families with bases in Greece and Spain. Watersports include: windsurfing, dinghy sailing, water skiing. Keen to recruit highly motivated staff.

Watersports Instructors required to instruct sailing/windsurfing etc. and to assist with evening entertainments. Hours of work variable, 7 days a week. Wages approx. £400 per month. Minimum period of work 1 week between May and August. Board and lodging provided.

Applications from January to the above address, please include current instructor qualifications.

PGL TRAVEL: Alton Court, Penyard Lane (874), Ross-on-Wye, Herefordshire HR9 5GL (☎01989-767833; e-mail pglpeople@pgl.co.uk; www.pgl.co.uk/people). With 25 activity centres located in France and Spain, PGL Travel provides adventure holidays and courses for children. Each year 2,500 people are needed to help run these adventure centres.

Children's Group Leaders required to take responsibility for groups of children, helping them to get the most out of their holiday. Minimum age 18. Previous experience of working with children is essential.

General Positions Available in catering, administration, driving (car or PCV), stores, site cleaning and nurses (RGN or SEN) etc.

Experienced Children's Activity Instructors in canoeing, sailing, windsurfing, pony trekking and multi-activities.

From £60-£90+ per week plus full B & L. Vacancies available for short or long periods between February and October. Overseas applicants eligible to work in the UK welcome.

Applications can be made online or a form obtained from the above address.

SOLAIRE HOLIDAYS: 1158 Stratford Road, Hall Green, Birmingham, B28 8AF (☎0121-778-5061; fax 0121-778-5065; e-mail jobs@solaire.co.uk; www.solaire.co.uk). Solaire Holidays provides self-drive, self-catering holidays to Spain and France.

Site Couriers (20) to look after clients and prepare accommodation. Knowledge of French desirable. Wage £280-£400 per month.

Children's Couriers (4) to run a children's club. Previous experience of working with children is required. Wage £280-£400 per month.

Applicants can apply for work between April and October, May and September or July and August. Hours of work vary according to demand, but applicants can expect to work for six days a week, on a rota system. Accommodation is provided as part of contract. Food is not provided.

Applications are invited from October onwards to the above address.

TJM TRAVEL: Penhalveor East, Redruth, TR16 6NL (☎01209-860000; fax 01209-860998; e-mail jobs@tjm-travel.co.uk). TJM run hotels and activity centres in France, Spain and the UK in the summer months, and they operate ski holidays from Alpine hotels in the winter.

Qualified Sailing, Canoe, Windsurfing, Snorkelling, Climbing, Mountain Biking Instructors, Hotel Staff; Manager, Chef, Bar, Waiting, Chamber, Kitchen Staff, Handymen. All required for hotel or activity centre work in France, Spain or the UK, all staff must have appropriate qualifications, experience and skills. Wages vary between £300 and £700 per month according to job and experience. Board and lodging provided. Staff work 7 hours a day per 6 day week, with the minimum period of work being 3-4 weeks. Working period is May to August and December to April.

Applicants can apply any time of year by letter, must include *passport photos*, full photo, current CV and copies of any relevant certificates; apply by post or e-mail.

Teaching and Language Schools

ABC ENGLISH: Calle Sol de Abajo 3, Antoñana, 01128 Alava, Spain. ABC English organise summer English language camps in the Basque country. They are not a language academy.

English Teachers (6) required in July to organise activities for Spanish children aged between 8-14. Applicants must be at least 18 years old and should have outdoor skills, a creative nature and complete proficiency in English.

Applications, from *EU citizens* only, should be sent to Tulio Browning at the above address no later than 30 March.

ENGLISH EDUCATIONAL SERVICES: C/ ALCALA 20-29, 28084 Madrid (☎34-91-531-4783; fax 34-91-531-5298; e-mail movingparts@wanadoo.es).

English Teachers (80-110) with recognised EFL qualfication such as CELTA or TESOL Trinity College required by recruitment specialists for EFL in Spain. Positions available in various parts of the country including Madrid. Standard length of contact is 9 months; teaching mainly in the evenings from 5pm onwards. Salary depends on the client school the teacher is employed by, as does provision for accommodation. Most client schools will help their teachers find a place to live.

There is also an English-speaking theatre company operating October-June. which has opportunties for candidates with a native speaker's standard of English.EU Citizens are preferred. Interviews may be carried out in the UK and Ireland at peak times.

Applications should be made to the above address.

ITC INTERNATIONAL TEFL CERTIFICATE, BARCELONA: Rocafort, 104, 08015 Barcelona, Spain (US Voice mail 1-800-915-5540; US Fax (815) 550-0086; ☎(Barcelona) (34) 93 423 9482; e-mail info@itc-training.com; www.itc-training.com).

ITC International TEFL Certificate 110 hour intensive training courses in Prague or Barcelona give you practical experience living, working, and interacting abroad before you even begin teaching. Caring support staff, lifetime job assistance worldwide. ITC offers in Spain the internationally recognised 4-week TEFL Certificate Course that qualifies graduates to teach English worldwide. Sessions are held year-round and on a monthly basis. Upon completion of the course ITC can guarantee a job in Eastern Europe, provides lifetime job guidance worldwide and has employment contacts throughout the globe. Over 1,500 teachers have graduated from ITC and are now working throughout the globe.

Trainees receive extensive supervised teaching practice with foreign students during the course and housing is available during the course. ITC is registered by the Ministry of Education in Spain. ITC also maintains a list of summer teaching opportunities in Spain and nearby countries. See the *Czech Republic* chapter for information on ITC's Prague programme.

Applications to the above address.

THE MANGOLD INSTITUTE: Marques de Sotelo 5, Pasaje Rex, Valencia E-46002, Spain (☎96-352-77-14 or 351-45-56; fax 96-351-45-56; e-mail: mangold@mangold-valencia.com; www.mangold-valencia.com).

Teachers. To teach general English including the technical aspects of the language. 30-34 hours work per week for wages of £550-£750 per month. No accommodation available. Applicants must be university graduates and hold an E.F.L. certificate or similar. They should be dynamic and outgoing. Minimum period of work 9 months, October to June.

Applications in May to the above address or come in person.

RELACIONES CULTURALES INTERNACIONALES: Callez Ferraz no. 82, Madrid E-28008, Spain (☎91-541-71 03; fax 91-559-11-81).

Supervisors, Language Assistants. Approx. £100 per month. 5-8 hours per day. 5 to 6 days per wk. Should like children and have studied at higher education establishment. Teaching and/or sport orientated applicants preferred. Minimum period of work 1 to 2 months around the year.

English Language Teachers for private Spanish colleges and kindergartens. Wages from £130 per month. To teach English and look after children aged from 4 years onwards. Should be qualified teachers, preferably with EFL experience. Minimum period 1 month all year round.

Au Pairs to live and help with light household chores in a Spanish family, or take care of children and help teach English. Ages 18-28 years. Placements all over Spain and over the whole year. Full social assistance during the stay is provided by RCI. Summer stays from one to three months, or around the year for 6 to 12 months. No special requirements are necessary. Paying stays are also arranged.

Counsellors (80) to supervise and teach English sports on 3 summer camps.

Applications to the above address as soon as possible.

CASTRUM LENGUAS CULTURAS Y TURISMO: Carretera de Rueda 33, bajo, 47008 Valladolid, Spain (☎+34 983 457563 or +34 983 222213; e-mail: info@castrum.org). A youth organisation operating four programmes in Spain:
Language and culture exchange programme: participants teach their own mother tongue to a host Spanish family for three hours a day in return for board and lodging. The rest of the day when they are not teaching is free time for the participant.
Language and culture exchange programme with young Spanish students: Similar to the above but with emphasis also on the participant learning Spanish and about the customs of Spain.
Cooperation programme (au pair).
Summer camps in Spain with Spanish students.
   Further *details* of these programmes from Elena Garcia Perez, Director of Castrum at the above address or see the website www.castrum.org.

C.P.N. AZTERLARIAK: Apartado nùmero 3191, 01002 Vitoria-Gasteiz, Spain (☎945-281794; e-mail azterlaria@euskalnet.net). C.P.N. Azterlariak, run nature camps in sessions of two weeks during the summer to provide a balanced programme of leisure activities for children and teenagers aged 8-18. The camps take place near Urbion's beautiful mountains.
Volunteers are required to work for two weeks 15th-30th July.
Monitors (2) to be responsible for the children 24 hours a day; overseeing activities, looking after their personal belongings, planning their outdoor activities. Monitors should be energetic, imaginative patient and sensitive. Being an extrovert is not necessary. Monitors will also be involved in general cleaning/camp maintenance duties. Some knowledge of Spanish is essential and Monitors are required to attend a short training course preceding the camp.
Cooks (1-2) Experience of cooking for large numbers is useful, and applicants will preferably hold a relevant qualification. Cooks must be prepared for outdoor cooking.
   For all positions, employees receive full board, accommodation in tents and liability insurance. Monitors are unpaid volunteers: Cooks receive £130-£185 depending on numbers attending.
   Apply by e-mail, or to the address above.

VIGVATTEN NATUR KLUB: Apartado 3253, E-01002 Vitoria-Gasteiz, Spain (☎945-28-17-94; fax 945-28-17-94). Staff needed to live and work with children in the outdoors in the most beautiful places in Spain; the Klub offers a unique and unforgettable international experience.
Monitors (15) to be responsible for children 24 hours a day, with duties including planning, organising and directing outdoor activities. Wage of approx. £290 per month. Previous experience of working with children is essential,
Support Staff (12) to see to the maintenance and cleaning of the camps and food preparation, serving and clearing away after meals. Wage of approx. £290 per month. Possession of a certificate of competence in food hygiene would be helpful.
Cooks (3) to be responsible for the daily cooking. Wage of approximately £290 per month. Must have experience of cooking for large numbers of people and should preferably hold a relevant qualification.
Camp Nurses (3) to be responsible for the health and welfare of the children and staff. Wage of approx. £290 per month; must hold nursing qualifications.
   Full board and accommodation provided. Minimum period of work two

weeks over the summer. Applicants should speak English; knowledge of Spanish is also desirable. Applicants are required to make and pay for their own travel arrangements.

Applications to Laureano Varela, Director, at the above address in February or March.

Voluntary Work and Archaeology

CANARY NATURE and ATLANTIC WHALE FOUNDATION: St Martins House, 59 St Martins Lane, Covent Garden, London WC2N 4JS (e-mail edb@huron.ac.uk; www.canarynature.com and www.whalefoundation.org.uk).

Volunteers required to **assist in whale and dolphin research** with researchers from the Atlantic Whale Foundation. Two projects: (a). Bottlenose dolphin research in Los Gigantes – small teams, dedicated zodiac, super accommodation – relaxed, informative, informal, stimulating and great fun. (b) Sailing the Canaries in autumn and spring to **track migrating species** (28 cetacean species are either resident to or migrate through Canary waters). Possibility of similar sailings in the Caribbean and in the Mediterranean. To live on board with researchers, small groups, visit places off the beaten track. Proceeds help fund the education, research and conservation work of the Atlantic Whale Foundation – see below.

Volunteers required for **work on whale watching boats as researchers/ guides and as children's animators (for Atlantic Whale Foundation)**. £100pw (£500 for 8 weeks) covers half board accommodation, full training and funds the project. Volunteers also help with children's workshops, cetacean public art works (murals), organising and running the European Festival of the Whale.

Further details available on application or on websites.

THE SUNSEED TRUST: Apdo. 9, E-04270 Sorbas, Almeria, Spain or PO Box 2000 Cambridge, CB4 3UJ (☎+34-950 552 770; e-mail sunseedspain@arrakis.es; www.sunseed.org.uk). The Sunseed Trust is a British and Spanish registered charity looking for ways to contain or reclaim deserts and also practises organic gardening and act as a field trial site for low-tech research into tree nurseries and soil regeneration.

Short and longer-term volunteers are required year round. Work includes **gardening, dryland regeneration, solar technology construction, cooking including solar cooking, publicity and more**. Longer-term volunteers can carry out their own projects in this field which may be suitable as dissertation projects.

Year round sunshine, beautiful rural location, friendly community and delicious vegetarian food. Volunteers make a weekly contribution of between £49 and £98 (depending on length of stay and hours worked).

Applicants see website or contact the Centre directly for further details.

Au Pairs, Nannies, Family Helps and Exchanges

ABB AU-PAIR FAMILY SERVICE: Via Alemania 2, 5°A, E-07003 Palma de Mallorca Spain (?+34-971-752027; fax +34-971-298001; abbaupair@telefonica.n et). Friendly au pair agency with high quality services and carefully chosen host families.

Au Pairs required to help families look after children and carry out general housekeeping work. Applicants should have a mature outlook, be responsible and have a love of children. Au-pairs normally work 25-30 hours over a 5-6 day week. Placements are available all year, with a minimum stay of 3 months in the summer.

Applicants should speak either English or Spanish, English and French or English and German.

Applications accepted all year, and should be sent to Clara Managin at the above address and please remember to mention your telephone number.

CENTROS EUROPEOS PRINCIPE, S.L.: C/Principe 12, 6A-28012 Madrid, Spain (☎+34-91 532 72 30; fax +34-91 521 60 76; e-mail ceprincipe@inicia.es). This is a small agency with many years' experience, dealing with all types of linguistic programmes. There is supervision in all centres.

Au Pairs to work 30-35 hours per week; pocket money of around €60 (approx. £42) per week. Placements of 2/3 months are possible over the summer, but it is easier to arrange placements of 9/10 months for the whole school year, or for 6 months from January or April.

Paying Guests for stays in Madrid, Alicante, Segovia, Salamanca, Valencia, Toledo, Barcelona, Cordoba, Granada, Seville or Santander.

Exchanges also arranged between Spanish and British students aged 12-25 for 2-4 weeks.

In addition there are Spanish courses all year round and accommodation for independent or work placement students.

Applications to the above address.

Sweden

As Sweden is a member of the European Union, nationals of EU and EEA countries are free to enter to look for and take up work. Although the rate of unemployment is considerably lower than it has been (4.8% in July 2003), there are strict limits on the number of foreigners allowed to work in Sweden.

The Swedish labour service cannot help jobseekers from non-EEA countries to find work in Sweden. General information and addresses of local employment offices may be obtained from *Arbetsmarknadsstyrelsen* at Kungstensgatan 45, S-113 99 Stockholm, Sweden (☎46-8-5860 6000; e-mail arbetsmarknadsstyrel sen@ams.amv.se; www.ams.se which is in English). It is up to the individual to get in touch with employers. Long-term vacancies and summer jobs can now be sought by those with a knowledge of the Swedish language on the internet: http://jobb.amv.se.

There are also opportunities for voluntary work in Sweden arranged by International Voluntary Service for British people and Service Civil International for Americans: see the *Worldwide* chapter for details.

Advertisements in Swedish newspapers may be placed through Crane Media Partners Ltd, 20-28 Dalling Road, Hammersmith, London W6 OJB (☎020-8237 8601; fax 020-8735 9941), who handle *Dagens Nyheter, Goteborgs Posten* and *Sydsvenska Dagbladet*.

RED TAPE, VISAS & WORK PERMITS

Visa Requirements: EU citizens excepted, a visa is required by many nationalities for a tourist visit to Sweden.

Residence Permits: EU citizens can apply for residence permits from within Sweden by contacting the Swedish Migration Board (Migrationsvertet), 60170 Norrköping; ☎011-156000; e-mail migrationsverket@migrationsverket.se) and completing the application forms. Applicants should note that the procedure of obtaining a Residence Permit can take between 2 and 5 months.

Non-Europeans must submit to their local Swedish Embassy a written offer of work on form AMS PF 101704, at least two months before their proposed arrival. The procedure involves an interview at the Embassy. Immigration queries should be addressed to Migrationsverket, the Swedish Migration Board (601 70 Norrköping; 11-15 60 00; www.migrationsverket.se). Full details are posted in English on their web pages or you can request printed leaflets.

Work Permits: Citizens of EU countries do not need work permits in order to work in Sweden. For others a work permit requires an offer of employment to have been obtained, application forms for the necessary permit should then be obtained from your nearest Swedish Embassy. The application will be processed by the Swedish Migration Board and the procedure can take 1-3 months. Applications for work permits are not accepted from foreign visitors who are already in Sweden.

Au Pairs: Au pairs are subject to the same regulations as all other foreign employees so non-EU nationals must obtain a work permit before leaving their home country. The Scandinavian Institute in Malmö (Box 3085; 040-93 94 40/fax 040-93 93 07; info@scandinavianinst.com) makes au pair placements in Swedish families and throughout Scandinavia.

Agricultural Work

CARL-HENRIK NIBBING: Skillinggrand, 9, S-11120 Stockholm, Sweden.
Farm Assistant. Wages by arrangement: free travel. Board and lodging provided; helper lives as member of the family. General duties around summer residence/farm in southern Sweden. Age 14-19 years. Applicants should be competent and good natured. Period of work June to August.

Applications to C.H. Nibbing.

Hotel Work and Catering

PENSIONAT HOLMHALLAR: S-62010 Burgsvik, Sweden (☎0498-4980-30; fax 0498-498056).
Hotel Workers (2) to clean rooms and work in the kitchen and restaurant. Wages £860 approx. per month. To work 40 hours per week of hotel work.

Applications to Carl Hansen at the above address in February/March.

Switzerland

Switzerland has managed to keep one of the lowest unemployment rates in the world , and to preserve that state it imposes strict work permit requirements on all foreigners who want to work there. Although Switzerland is not yet a member of the European Union, it is moving in the direction of integration. Since the Bilateral Agreement between Switzerland and the European Union on the free movement of persons came into effect in June 2002, Switzerland has been undergoing a huge shift in its immigration and employment policy. The category of seasonal worker has been abolished and from 2004 employers will no longer be entitled to give priority to indigenous workers. The system is now more in line with the rest of Europe so that EU job-seekers can enter Switzerland for up to three months (extendable) to look for work. If they succeed they must show a contract of employment to the authorities and are then eligible for a short-term residence permit, valid for up to one year and renewable. The idea is that the free movement of labour will be introduced step by step. Until June 2004, quotas of foreign workers in each canton will remain in place. The aim is that from 2007, the unfettered movement of workers into Switzerland will be permitted.

Switzerland has always needed extra seasonal workers at certain times of the year, and traditionally issues a quota of short-term work permits. The tourist industry in particular needs staff for both the summer and winter seasons (July to September and December to April).

Jobs in the tourist industry are described both in this chapter and the Worldwide chapter at the beginning of the book (for example see entry for Village Camps). Students looking for hotel work should note the entry below for the *Schweizer Hotelier Verein* (Swiss Hotels' Association). Hotel work can be hard: in the past some workers have found they have been expected to work longer hours than originally promised without any compensation in the form of overtime payments or extra time off, or be asked to do jobs other than those specified in their contracts. In return, however, wages should be higher than average for hotel work in the rest of Europe.

Farmers also need extra help at certain times of the year: see the entry below for the Landdienst-Zentralstelle, which can arrange working stays on Swiss farms. Opportunities in the short but lucrative grape harvest in October (particularly in the Lausanne area) would be greater were it not for the difficulty of getting work permits. Some knowledge of German or French is normally needed, even for grape-picking. Italian is also spoken, particularly in the canton of Ticino.

Placing an advertisement in a Swiss paper may lead to the offer of a job. Tribune de Geneve is published at 11 rue des Rois, CH-1211 Geneva (www.tdg.ch – go through Google to translate the site into English).

There are opportunities for voluntary work in Switzerland with the organisations named at the end of this chapter and British applicants can also apply through Concordia and International Voluntary Service, and Americans through Service Civil International; see the *Worldwide* chapter for details.

RED TAPE, VISAS & WORK PERMITS

Visa Requirements: citizens of the United Kingdom, the United States, Canada, Australia, New Zealand and most other European countries do not normally require visas for tourism. Nationals of most other countries need a visa.

Residence/Work Permits: the Swiss Residence Permit (Aufenthaltsbewilligung or autorisation de séjour) covers both the right of abode and employment. These are required for all persons entering to take up employment and entitle the holder to live in a specific canton and work for a specified employer. They can be applied for inside Switzerland and processing of the application takes 6-8 weeks. Hence if you wish to work in Switzerland, you can secure a job before or after entering the country.

The permits come in several types: for temporary work, the relevant one is a permit for seasonal employment up to a maximum of 12 months (usually 4-5 months) for jobs in the tourist and building industry. Long-term permits are valid for up to five years. Once you have obtained a job your employer in Switzerland must then apply to the Cantonal Aliens Police for a permit for you. Nationals who require an entry visa should apply to their local Embassy/Consulate for their visa at the same time as the employer applies for the work permit. After granting a Work Permit an authorisation to issue the entry-visa is sent to the appropriate Swiss Embassy/Consulate where the foreign national has to collect the said visa. After arrival foreigners should register with the Aliens Police within 8 days and before starting work.

Au Pairs also require a permit as above.

Voluntary Work: a permit is required as above.

Agricultural Work

LANDDIENST-ZENTRALSTELLE: Postfach 728, CH-8025 Zurich, Switzerland (☎1-261-44-88; fax 1-261-44-32; e-mail admin@landdienst.ch; www.landdienst.ch). Landdienst is a non-profit making, publicly subsidised organisation which each year places around 3,000 Swiss and 500 foreign farmers assistants.

Farmers' Assistants to work on family farms. Wages £200 per month plus free board and lodging. To work 8 hours per day, 6 days per week. Minimum period of work 3 weeks between the spring and autumn; maximum period is two months. Knowledge of German and/or French essential. Individual applicants should be aged 18-25.

British applicants can obtain more information by sending a s.a.e. to Concordia, Heversham House, 20/22 Boundary Road, Hove, East Sussex BN3 4ET; Danish applicants should contact EXIS, Postboks 291, DK-6400 Sonderborg; Dutch applicants through Travel Active Programmes, Postbus 107, NL-5800 AC Venray; Portuguese applicants through International Friendship League, R. Ruy de Sausa Vinagre 2, P-2890 Alcochete. A six-week group stay for applicants from Eastern Europe will also be arranged from mid-August to late September: contact the above address for contact addresses in Poland, the Czech Republic, Slovakia and the Baltic States.

Applications are invited at least 4 weeks prior to desired starting date. Individual applicants must be nationals of a country in western Europe and pay a registration fee.

Hotel Work and Catering

CHALET-HOTEL ADLER: Fam.A & E Fetzer, CH-3718 Kandersteg, Switzerland (☎033-675 8010; fax 033-675 8011; www.chalethotel.ch). This hotel is set in the mountains of Switzerland, with rail access allowing excursions across the country.

Barmaids, Chambermaids, Waitresses to work from 8½ hours, 5 days a week. Salary approx. £690 per month. Minimum period of work 2½ months from May/June to September/October. Accommodation provided. Knowledge of German required.

Applications, with a photo, from April to the above address.

HOTEL ALPENBLICK: Oberdorf, CH-3812 Wilderswil, Switzerland (☎+33-828 3550; fax +33-828 3551). The hotel is situated in the Ferienort Wilderswil near the Jungfrau. It has an excellent reputation for the high standard of its cooking, and a friendly, co-operative and cosy atmosphere.

Cook to prepare meals for the à la Carte restaurant and also prepare the menu and meals for half-board hotel guests. Good cooking abilities, and the ability to cope with the stresses of a busy restaurant are prerequisites.

Waiting Staff to serve breakfast, evening meals and light afternoon snacks. Applicants should have a sound knowledge of German, experience of waiting on tables and a well groomed appearance.

Housekeeper to clean the hotel and restaurant and to look after children; the applicant should have a love of order and a way with children.

All posts pay £940 gross per month, for 45-48 hours per week; board costs c.£190 and lodging c.£90 per month. Period of work is from early June to mid September, with the minimum period of work being 2-3 months. All staff should speak German.

Applications are accepted from October onwards, addressed to Richard Stöckli at the above address.

HOTEL BAHNHOF: CH-8201 Schaffhausen, Switzerland (☎52-624 19 24; fax 52-624 74 79).
Hotel Staff (2) for housekeeping and work in the dining room. Wages up to £1,500 per month. 8 hours per day, 5 days per week. Knowledge of German required. Minimum period of work 4 months between 1 June and 30 September.

Applications from the spring to Arnold P Graf at the above address.

HOTEL BELLEVUE: CH-3901 Simplon-Pass, Switzerland (☎027-979 1331; fax 027-979 1239).
Secretary to work on reception desk and take care of all correspondence. Knowledge of German, French and Italian essential. Good secretarial and hotel experience required.
Chambermaid. Knowledge of German, French and Italian an advantage.
Waiters/Waitresses (4). Must have experience in similar work. Knowledge of some German, French and Italian required. Suit trainee wishing to widen experience.

Wages on application. Free board and accommodation provided. Minimum age 18 years. Minimum period of work 2 months during the summer season.

Applications from January to the above address.

BEST WESTERN HOTEL BERNINA SAMEDAN: CH-7503 Samedan, St Moritz, +Switzerland (☎081-852 12 12; fax 081-852 36 06; e-mail hotel-bernina@bluewin.ch; website www.hotel-bernina.ch). The Hotel Bernina is a traditional hotel for holiday-makers (in summer: hiking, biking and mountain climbing) with 100 beds, an à-la-carte Italian restaurant, bar, park, tennis courts and sun-terrace.
Porters, Waiters/Waitresses (3) with experience in hotel/restaurant work. Wages about £1,400 per month. To work 42 hours per day, 5 days per week. Minimum period of work is three months between June and October. Board and accommodation is available at a cost of £250 per month. Must have previous experience and knowledge of German.

Applications to Th. Bonjour, Director at the above address until May at the latest.

BURGENSTOCK HOTELS & RESORT: CH-6363 Bürgenstock, Switzerland (☎+41-41-612 9910; fax +41-41-612 9901; e-mail human.resources@buergensto ck-hotels.ch). Luxury standard 5-star hotels 20km from Lucerne, open from April to October.
Chef de Rang (15), Commis de Rang (10), Kitchen Staff (15) for a la carte and banquet catering and service, all applicants should have high standards, previous experience and should speak German. Wages from £980 per month according to experience.
Bar Staff (3) should have previous experience of bar work, wages by negotiation according to experience.

Chambermaids (10) wages from £960 per month.

Staff work a 45 hour week, with the period of work running from April to October, with dates of work varying according to position. Board and lodging is available at a cost of c.£160 and £77-£155 respectively. Staff speak German, English or French.

Applications are invited from November onwards to Frau Regine Bartsch, Human Resources Manager at the above address.

HOTEL CASA BERNO: CH-6612, Ascona, Switzerland (☎091-791-3232; hotel@casaberno.ch; www.casaberno.ch). This four star hotel is situated above Ascona, with magnificent panoramic views.
Kitchen/Office Staff. (2) No special qualifications nor languages necessary.
Laundry Staff for light work/ironing. No special qualificatons necessary, nor languages.

For both positions, the minimum period of work is 2 months between 15th March and 31st October. Board and accommodation available for approx. £310 per month. Wages are approx. £1,100 per month.

Apply to Pierre Goetschi, the Director, at the above address.

HOTEL CLUB: 71 rue du Parc, CH-2300 la Chaux-de-Fonds, Switzerland (☎041-32 914 15 16; fax 041-32 914 15 17).
Bar Assistant to serve drinks and attend to customers; training will be given.
Trainee Receptionist to welcome clients, take reservations, operate the telephone switchboard and computer, run the front office, and help serve breakfasts when things are quiet.
Breakfast Assistant to prepare a buffet breakfast, serve tea and coffee and generally clean up.
Chambermaids for general cleaning duties in all parts of the hotel, work in the laundry and to perform general errands.

Wages approx. £920 per month. To work a 42 hour, 5 day week; working hours will vary according to need. Board and lodging available for around £100 per month. Period of work by arrangement between July and August and December and January. Applicants who can speak French are preferred; knowledge of Swiss-German, German, French, English and/or Italian would be advantages. The hotels' clients tend to be businessmen so efficiency of service is of importance.

Applications to Madame J. Koegler, Director, at the above address at any time; due to large number of applications only candidates who might be hired will receive replies.

CONTINENTAL PARKHOTEL: CH-6900 Lugano, Switzerland (☎91-966-11-12; fax 91-966-12-13). This holiday hotel set in a sub-tropical park, overlooks Lake Lugano and the mountains.
Waitress £700 net or more, depending on previous experience, per month. 45 hour, 5 day week. Free board and accommodation provided. Season from 1 April to 30 October. Knowledge of German or experience of hotel work necessary to see to get a working permit (citizens of EU only).

Applications to E. Fassbind at the above address.

HOTEL CRISTALLO: Poststrasse, CH-7050 Arosa, Switzerland (☎081-377 2261; fax 081-377 4140).
Waiter/Waitress (1-2). £1,500 per month. Must have previous experience. Staff work about 9 hours per day, 5 days per week. Board and accommodation provided

at £300 per month, deducted from gross salary. Knowledge of German essential. Minimum period of work 12 weeks between the middle of June and the end of September.

Applications to the above address in March and April.

HOTEL FORNI: Marzio Forni, CH-6780 Airolo, Switzerland (☎91-869 12 70; fax 91-869 15 23; e-mail: INFO@forni.ch).
Kitchen Staff and Waitress to serve in the bar and restaurant. Must be presentable. Approximately £1,000 per month. To work 9 hours per day, 5 days per week. Board and accommodation available for £340 per month.

Applications to the above address.

BERGHAUS GFELALP: CH-3718 Kandersteg, Switzerland (☎+41-33-6751161). This hotel is situated in Kandersteg, an area of outstanding beauty, and renowned for its hiking possibilities.
Waiting and Chamber Staff: required between 15th July and 15th September, to work 45 hours per week over 5-6 days. The posts are available as either 2 female or 2 male jobsharers, or one male/female working full time. Job sharing would mean both employees working at weekends with one free during the week to travel or go sightseeing. Wages are £405 approx. per month and free accommodation is provided. Employees must be able to speak German.

To *apply* write to Fam Schärer at the above address.

GRAND HOTEL BELLEVUE: CH-3789 Gstaad, Switzerland (☎033-748 31 71; fax 033-724 21 36).
Waiting Assistants (2). Wage approx. £900 per month. To work 42 hours per week, with board and lodging available for around £285 per month. Period of work by arrangement between Christmas/New Year and July/August. Applicants should speak German, English and French.

Applications to Mr Ferdinand D. Salverda, General Manager, at the above address.

THE HIKING SHEEP GUEST HOUSE: Villa La Joux, CH-1854 Leysin, Switzerland (tel/fax +41(0)24-494 3535; e-mail hikingsheep@leysin.net; www.leysin.net/hikingsheep). A guesthouse in the Swiss French Alps nestled beside forest and snow-capped mountains, looking towards the Trient Glacier and the Mont Blanc massif.
General Staff required to assist in the running of the guest house. Should speak basic French and English; speaking German would be an asset. Applicants must be outgoing, friendly, flexible and trustworthy. To work 4-5 hours a day 7 days per week, all year round; minimum period of work 1 month. Board and lodging are provided.

Applications may be made at any time of year to Gérard at the above address.

HOTEL HIRSCHEN: Passhöhe, CH-9658 Wildhaus, Switzerland.
Counter Assistants/Waiting Staff (1/2) to serve hotel guests at mealtimes, present buffets, wash glasses, prepare coffee, breakfast etc. Wages approx. £1,100 per month. 9-9½ hours work per day, 5 days per week. Board and lodging provided. Minimum period of work 3 months between June and October. Knowledge of German and previous experience of hotel work essential.

Applications to S. Walt at the above address from February.

JOBS IN THE ALPS (EMPLOYMENT AGENCY): 17 High Street, Gretton, Northants NN17 3DE (e-mail info@jobs-in-the-alps.com; www.jobs-in-the-alps.com).

Waiters, Waitresses, Porters, Kitchen Porters and Housekeepers (200 in the winter, 150 in summer) for good Swiss hotels, cafés and restaurants at mountain resorts. Wages of circa £500 per month for a 5-day week with free board and accommodation. Knowledge of French and/or German required for most positions. Experience is not essential, but a good attitude to work and sense of fun are definite requirements. Periods of work: June to mid-September (minimum period three months including July and August), or December to April.

Applications should be sent by 30th April for Summer and 30th September for Winter.

HOTEL JUNGFRAUBLICK UND BEAUREGARD: Haupstrasse, CH-3803 Beatenberg, Switzerland (☎41-33 841 15 81; fax 41-33 841 20 03).

Waiting Staff. Wages £825 per month, approximately. To work 8½ hours per day, 5 days per week. Board and lodging available for £270 per month. Period of work at least 4 months from June to October or November. Knowledge of German required. Applicants should be reliable workers who can take pleasure in their work.

Applications to Herr Heinrich at the above address.

HOTEL LANDHAUS: CH-7299 Davos Laret, Switzerland.

Waitress for general dining room duties. £500-£600 per month. Preferably with previous experience and some knowledge of French and German.

Stillroom Maid for general and buffet duties. £150-£180 per month. Some knowledge of French and/or German an advantage.

8½ hours per day, at least 5 days per week. At the height of the season a 7 day week may be worked. Free board and accommodation. All applicants must be available for the whole of the period 1 July to mid September and be over 18 years old.

Applications with recent photograph and international reply coupon from April to the above address.

HOTEL MEIERHOF: CH-7260 Davos-Dorf, Switzerland (☎41-81 416 82 85; fax 41-81 416 39 82; e-mail: info@meierhof.ch; applications kathrin.frey@meierhof.ch; www.meierhof.ch). Traditional and charming mountain resort-hotel with 80 rooms, set in the heart of the village next to all the attractive sport and leisure facilities of Davos.

Waiter/Waitress £900 per month, for a 44 hour week, 9 hours per day. Board and accommodation provided. Knowledge of German essential. Must be able to start work on the 15 June.

Applications in March and April to Mrs Kathrin Frey, at the above address or e-mail.

HOTEL MEISSER: CH-7545 Guarda, Switzerland (☎81-862-21-52; fax 81-862-24-80). A medium-sized hotel, 2½ hours from Zurich, led by a young dynamic team.

Service Workers (1-2) Wage about £775 per month. Should have relevant experience.

General Workers (1-2) Wage around £775 per month.

Both positions involve 8-9 hours work a day, 5 days per week. To work from 15 June to 31 August or as contracted. Board and accommodation are available, the cost to be deducted from wages. Ability to speak German and English is important; knowledge of German, French or Italian would also be useful.

Applications are invited to Benno Meisser at the above address from January onwards.

HOTEL MOND: Dorfstrasse 1, CH-6375 Beckenried, Switzerland (☎+41-620 1204; fax +41-620 4618; e-mail info@hotel-mond.ch; www.hotel-mond.ch). The 'Mond' hotel was built in 1870. Since then it has been owned and run by the same family. The hotel has 60 beds, 2 restaurants and a bar and is located at Beckenreid, on the edge of Lake Lucerne.

Buffet Assistants to serve drinks.

Waiting Staff to serve in a la carte restaurant.

Wages approximately £1,250 per month gross. To work 8-9 hours per day, 5 days per week. Period of work from the beginning of June to the end of September: minimum period of work 2 months. Applicants must speak German.

Applications to Monica Egli-Amstad at the above address before the end of January.

HOTEL MOTEL KRONE: CH-3074 Berne-Muri, Switzerland.

Assistant Waiter. Some waiting experience and a little German essential.

Buffet Assistant. To prepare snacks and drinks. Some knowledge of German essential.

Dishwasher (1), Kitchen Porter (1). No previous experience required but a little German is required.

All staff work 9 hours per day, 5 days per week, probably on split shifts. Board and accommodation is provided free of charge. All applicants should be available for at least 2½ months, between 18-25 years of age and EU members.

Applications as soon as possible to Herrn Bachler at the address above.

MOTEL-RESTAURANT MON ABRI: 3658 Merligen, Switzerland (☎033-511380; fax 033-513671).

Temporary Waiting Assistant to work in a good standard *a la carte* restaurant. Wage according to turnover, with a minimum of £950 per month. To work 8 hours per day, 5 days per week. To work shifts either from 7am-3.30pm or from 3.30pm-midnight, each with a 30 minute meal break. Accommodation available for approx. £130 per month. Minimum period of work three months. Applicants should be friendly and speak English and German; knowledge of French would be an advantage.

Applications to Fam. C. Rijke-Wyler at the above address in April and May.

MOTOTEL POSTILLON: CH-6374 Buochs, Switzerland.

Waiting Staff to work in a busy restaurant on a motorway. Approximately £940 per month. To work 8½-10½ hours per day, 5 days per week. Board and accommodation available for £95-£115 per month approx. Knowledge of German and English is necessary.

Applications to Rene Ulrich, Director, at the above address.

PARKHOTEL BAD RAGAZ: CH-7310 Bad Ragaz, Switzerland.

Waiting Staff (2), General Assistants (2). Wages by arrangement. 42 hours per 5 day week. Minimum period of work 5 months between April and October. Board and accommodation available for around £200 per month. Applicants should speak German and have some previous experience.

Applications to the Manager at the above address as soon as possible.

PARK HOTELS WALDHAUS: CH-7018 Flims-Waldhaus, Switzerland (☎+41-81-928 4848; fax 81-928 4858; e-mail info@park-hotels-waldhaus.ch; www.park-hotels-waldhaus.ch). The Park Hotels Waldhaus have 140 rooms and 20 junior suites and apartments.

Assistant Waiters/Waitresses: must have previous experience of serving and speak German and French or Italian.

Swimming Pool Attendant to care for the pool, pool bar and information kiosk as well as to do cleaning work. Must speak German and either French or Italian.

Net wages approximately £900 per month, with board and lodging provided for approx. £300 per month.

Applications, with a photograph, should be sent to the above address from February; *only applicants from EEA countries will get work permits for Switzerland.*

RESIDENCE AND BERNERHOF HOTELS: CH-3823 Wengen, Switzerland.
Waiters/Waitresses, Buffet Assistants, Laundry Maids, General Assistants. Monthly salary payment. Staff work 9 hours per day, 5 days per week. Accommodation (30) days. Meals: lunch/dinner (no breakfast) for 22 days. 2 hotel restaurants; à-la-carte, and pizzeria. Guests almost always English, German, US, and Swiss. In the centre of Wengen. Period of work from December to April, and June to October. Knowledge of German required; knowledge of French an advantage.

Applications to Rudolph Schweizer at the above address.

RESTAURANT BLAUES ROSSLI: CH-3668 Utzigen, Switzerland.
General Assistants (2, preferably girls) to help clean rooms, serve in the restaurant and help at the counter coffee bar, wash dishes, help with the laundry. To work 5 days per week. Salary approximately £400, net, per month. Board and accommodation provided free of charge. Minimum period of work 8 weeks, although preference will be given to those who can work for the whole season, April to October. Knowledge of German preferable.

Applications to Mrs Kilchör at the above address at any time.

HOTEL RIGIBLICK AM SEE: Seeplatz 3, CH-6374 Buochs, Switzerland (☎41-41-624 4850; fax 41-41-620 6874; e-mail info@rigiblickamsee.ch; www.rigiblickamsee.ch). A 4-star hotel and restaurant on the lakeside.
Trainee Assistant (Waiter/Waitress), Trainee Chef to work 44 hours, 5 days a week. Wages approx. €1800 (£1,260) per month. Period of work May/June-August/September. Board and accommodation provided for €600 (£420) per month. *Applicants must hold an EU passport* and have a very good knowledge of German.

Applications as soon as possible to the above address.

ROMANTIK HOTEL SÄNTIS: CH-9050 Appenzell, Switzerland (☎0041-71 788 11 11; fax 0041-71 788 11 10; e-mail: romantikhotelsantis@bluewin.ch; www.romantikhotels.com/Appenzell). A traditional family-run 4-star hotel in one of the most beautiful areas of Switzerland; Appenzell is in the German-speaking region. The staff are mostly young people of various nationalities.
Waiter/Waitress, gross salary approx. SFr 3000 per month. To work 9 hours per day, 5 days per week. Board, accommodation available for SFr 540 per month. Minimum period of work is 4 months between June and October. Applicants must have experience and speak German. Temporary residence permits are only available for EU/EFTA nationals.

Applications to Stefan A. Heeb at the above address.

ROMANTIK HOTEL SCHWEIZERHOF: CH-3818 Grindelwald, Switzerland (☎033-853-22-02; fax 033-853-20-04; e-mail info@hotel-schweizerhof.com..
The Schweizerhof, a truly traditional hotel in Grindelwald, world famous holiday and winter sports centre at the foot of the Eiger in the Bernese Oberland.
Chambermaids (4-5) to clean rooms and do laundry.
Maintenance Assistants (3) to carry out general maintenance tasks on house and in garden.
Assistant Cooks (2) to assist in the kitchen with preparation and washing-up.
Laundry Assistants (2)
Wages about £1,400 per month. To work a 42-hour 5-day week. Period of work is from 1 June to 15 October. Board and accommodation is available at a cost to be arranged. Knowledge of German is required.
Applications to the above address between January and March at the latest.

SCHWEIZER HOTELIER-VEREIN: Monbijoustrasse 130, Postfach, CH-3001 Bern, Switzerland (☎41-31-370-43-33; e-mail hoteljob.be@swisshotels.ch; www.hoteljob.ch). The 'Swiss Hotel Association' has around 2500 hotels and restaurants as members.
General Assistants from EU and EFTA countries to work in hotels in German-speaking Switzerland. Wages approximately £1,100 per month. Duties include helping with cooking, service and cleaning. Wages by arrangement. To work 8 hours and 25 minutes per day, 5 days per week. Period of work 3-4 months between June and September.
Board and accommodation available at a cost of approximately £325 per month. Good knowledge of German essential. Please note that jobs in the French and Italian speaking parts of Switzerland can not be arranged. Applicants must possess valid passports etc. A registration fee of approximately £30 is payable.
Applications accepted all year round.

SEEHOTEL WILBERBAD: CH-6062 Wilen am Sarnersee, Switzerland (☎041-662 70 70; fax 041-662 70 80; e-mail wilerbad@tic.ch; www.wilerbad.ch).
Waiter/Waitress (1-2) for lido and terrace restaurant. Must speak fluent German. Wages of around £450 per month. All staff to work 8½ hours per day, 5 days a week. Board available at approx. £110 per month; accommodation in a double room costs approx. £58 per month. Minimum period of work 3 months.
Applications in the autumn to Herr Bruno Odermatt, Director, at the above address.

HOTEL SONNE: CH-9658 Wildhaus, Switzerland (e-mail beutler-hotels@bluewin.ch; www.beutler.hotels.ch).
Waiters/Waitresses (3). £700, net, per month. Good knowledge of German required.
Buffet Staff (2). £600, net, per month. Good knowledge of German required.
Staff work 8½ hours per day, 5 days a week. Board and accommodation available at £216 per month. Minimum period of work 10 weeks. Winter season December to March and Summer season July to October.
Applications as soon as possible to the proprietor, Paul Beutler, at the above address.

TRUMMELBACH FALLS: Gletscherwasser-Fälle, CH-3822, Lauterbrunnen, Switzerland.
Restaurant Assistant to work in the self-service restaurant at the entrance to the

falls. The position calls for an all-rounder as duties include assisting behind the counter, operating the cash register, clearing tables and cleaning.

Elevator Operator/Restaurant Assistant to operate a funicular lift inside a mountain, taking people to see the waterfalls. Time to be divided between operating the lift 2-3 days per week and working in the restaurant.

Wages of £800-£900 per month for working a 5 day week. To work approximately 8-10 hours a day with a half hour lunch break. Applicants must speak fluent English and some basic German; knowledge of French would be an advantage. Must hold an EU passport and be aged at least 22.

Applicants should *send* a full CV and a passport photo to Herr Urs von Almen at the above address by January.

HOTEL WALDHAUS: CH-7514 Sils-Maria, Engadin, Switzerland (☎081-838 5100; fax 081-838 5198; e-mail staff@waldhaus-sils.ch; www.waldhaus-sils.ch). A five-star family hotel with up to 70% regular guests from all over the world.

General Assistants (2) to play an extensive role in service for the guest-rooms, lounge and terraces, and to see to the welfare of 220 guests as well as taking responsibility for their meals, under the direction of a superior. Wages £715-£858 per month. Must have knowledge of German, and the ability to take pleasure in working for guests.

To work 8-9 hours per day, 5 days per week. Minimum period of work is 3-4 months in the summer or winter seasons. Food and accommodation are available at the following prices; a double-room costs about £70 per person per month.

Applications are invited up until mid-March for the summer season, or mid-August for the winter, and should be sent to Irene Ryser, Personnel Manager, at the above address.

HOTEL ZUM WEISSEN ROSSLI: CH-6487 Goschenen, Switzerland (☎+41-886 80 10; fax 886 80 30).

Waiting Assistants, Buffet Assistants, Chambermaids. Wages and hours of work by arrangement. Board and lodging provided. Period of work by arrangement, minimum contract of 6 months. Good knowledge of German required. *Work permits cannot be obtained for applicants from eastern Europe*.

Applications to the above address 8 weeks before the desired beginning of work.

Sports, Couriers and Camping

CANVAS HOLIDAYS LIMITED: East Port House 12 East Port, Dunfermline, Fife KY12 7JG (☎01383-629018; fax 01383 629071; www.canvasholidays.com). Canvas Holidays are looking for enthusiastic individuals who enjoy camping and a real challenge. Main positions available include:

Campsite Couriers. Varied responsibilities, but largely responsible for the cleaning and preparation of customer accommodation, welcoming and looking after customers on-site, helping with any problems that might arise and organising activities for children and adults. Variable working hours.

Package includes tented accommodation, medical insurance, full uniform and return coach travel and from UK port of entry. Period of work from end March to October.

Applications are invited from September to Nina, Karen or Sandy to the above address.

EUROCAMP: Overseas Recruitment Department (Ref SJ/04) (☎01606-787525). Eurocamp is a leading tour operator in quality self-drive camping and mobile home holidays in Europe. Each year the company seeks to recruit up to 1,500 enthusiastic people for the following positions:

Campsite Courier: job involves cleaning and preparing customer accommodation, providing assistance, acting as an information service and performing some administrative duties. Couriers need to be flexible to meet the needs of the customer to provide them with excellent service. Minimum age 18 years. Applicants should be independent with plenty of initiative and relish a challenging and rewarding position. They should also possess a friendly and helpful personality. Previous customer service experience would be an advantage. Applicants should be available to work from April/May to September.

Children's Courier: work involves organising a wide range of exciting activities for children aged 4-13. Applicants should possess initiative, imagination and enthusiasm along with good safety awareness. Previous childcare experience is essential. Minimum age is 18 years and applicants should be available from April/May to September. Languages are not a requirement but would be an advantage (in particular German). Successful candidates will be asked to apply for an Enhanced Disclosure.

Senior Couriers: required to work alongside a team of Campsite Couriers and organise their daily workload, as well as carrying out the normal day to day duties of a Campsite Courier. Applicants should have good language skills and experience of leading a team.

Site Managers: required to lead a large team of Campsite Couriers, organising their daily workloads and ensuring they provide the very best customer service. Applicants should be 21 or over, have proven managerial experience, excellent communication skills and language ability.

Comprehensive training is provided together with a competitive salary, insurance, return travel and accommodation. Applications are accepted from September/ October and *can only be accepted from UK/EU passport holders*. Interviews will be conducted in Hartford, Cheshire between October and April.

Applicants should apply online at www.holidaybreakjobs.com or telephone 01606 781525 for an Application Pack.

SWISS TRAVEL SERVICE: 55-59 High Road, Broxbourne, Herts, EN10 7DT (☎01992-456250; fax 01992-448855; e-mail swiss@bridge-travel.co.uk; www.swisstravel.co.uk). Swiss Travel Services is a UK market leader for holidays to Switzerland with over 50 years experience. Posts are available both in summer and in winter.

Resort Reps (20) required to meet and greet clients, liaise with suppliers and sell tickets for excursions. Ability to speak German, Italian or French would be advantageous.

During the summer season the minimum period of work is 4 months between 1 April and 1 October; generally working from 8:30am to 7:30pm 6 or 7 days a week. Board, accommodation and a wage of around £400 per month are provided.

Applicants should be at least 21 years old, have good client handling skills and experience of dealing with older people.

Applications can be made through the above website and are invited from EU and EFTA nationals or those who have obtained permission to work in Switzerland.

VENTURE ABROAD: Rayburn House, Parcel Terrace, Derby, DE1 1LY (☎01332-224-951; 01332-22-49-60; e-mail charlottel@rayburntours.co.uk; ww w.ventureabroad.co.uk). Venture Abroad organise package holidays for scout and guide groups to the continent. They arrange travel and accommodation and provide representatives in the resort.

Resort Representatives (2-3) to work in Belgium and Switzerland; checking in groups, dealing with accommodation enquiries, organising and accompanying local excursions etc.

Applicants should be practical, resourceful and calm under pressure. Speaking German an advantage. To work six days a week, flexible hours. Five weeks minimum work from June to August.

Applications to the above address.

Work with Children

THE HAUT LAC INTERNATIONAL CENTRE: CH-1669 Les Sciernes, Switzerland (☎+41-26-928 4200; fax +41-26-928 4201; e-mail admin@haut-lac.com; www.haut-lac.com). The Haut Lac Centre is a family run business organising language and activity courses for an international clientele. A high client return rate is due to the Centre's work and play philosophy.

Language Teachers; French (6), English (3), German (2) to take four 40 minute classes (Monday, Tuesday, Thursday, Friday) and one 40 min. study per day, supervise one test per week and have two days off per week. Candidates should have a degree and a TEFL qualification or equivalent, or be studying for a Language or Teaching degree.

Sports Activity Monitors (6) to organise and run a wide variety of sports and excursions. One day off per week.

Maintenance Person to carry out garden upkeep, decorating tasks and repair work, should have previous experience.

House Staff for Cleaning Work.

Wages for all positions are from £100 per week according to qualifications and experience. Board and accommodation are included as is laundry. Staff work 45-54 hours per 5-6 day week. Period of work mid-June until mid-August, with a minimum requirement of 4 weeks work.

Applicants should speak English, French or German, and *applications* are invited at any time to the above address.

ROMANTIK HOTEL SANTIS: CH-9050 Appenzell, Switzerland (☎+41-71-788 1111; fax +41-71-788 1110; e-mail romantikhotels.a.e.ntis@bluewin.ch; www.romantikhotels.com/Appenzell). A traditional family-run 4-star hotel in one of the most beautiful areas of Switzerland, Appenzell is in the German-speaking region. The staff are mostly young people from around the world.

Waiter/Waitress; wage approx. £1,025 per month. To work 9 hours per day, 5 days per week. Board and accommodation available for approx. £221 per month. Minimum period of work 4 months between June and September. Applicants must have experience and speak German. Work permits are only available for EU/EFTA nationals.

Applications to Stefan A. Heeb at the above address.

VILLAGE CAMPS INC: Personnel Office Dept. 815, 14 Rue de la Morâche, 1260 Nyon, Switzerland. (☎+41 22 990 9405; fax +41 22 990 9494; e-mail personnel@villagecamps.ch; www.villagecamp.com). Village Camps has been organising educational and activity camps for children from all over the globe for over 25 years with a serious commitment to client and staff alike.

Specialists and General Counsellors required for outdoor education, orienteering, leadership training, nature/environmental studies, swimming, archery, tennis, outdoor education, soccer, arts and crafts, mountain biking, gymnastics and drama etc.
Qualified Instructors in rock climbing, canoeing, mountain leading, watersports.
Language Teachers for English, French and German classes.
Nurses/Medical Staff: must be qualified RSN or equivalent.
Kitchen and **Domestic Staff** (EU passport holders only for these domestic positions)
Drivers
Junior Staff: for the Day Camp only (No accommodation included).

The Outdoor Education Programme occurs from May to June in Switzerland and France and in the autumn, August to October in Switzerland. The Summer Residential and Day Camps occur from June to August in Switzerland, UK, Holland, France and Austria. Room and board, accident & liability insurance and a generous allowance are provided. All staff must be over 21. Much is expected of staff but the rewards are generous. Experience working with children is essential and knowledge of a second language is an advantage. Motivated staff are required for short seasonal positions.

Visit the above website for more information or *contact the Personnel Department* at the address above for an application pack.

Voluntary Work and Archaeology

GRUPPO VOLUNTARI DALLA SVIZZERA ITALIANA: CP 12, CH-6517 Arbedo, Switzerland (☎079-3540161 (NATEL) 091-8574520 (office); fax 071-6829272; e-mail Fmari@vtx.ch).
Volunteers (15 per camp) to take part in work camps in Maggia, Fusio and Borgogne **helping mountain communities, cutting wood, help the aged, in the orchards, etc.** 4 hours work per day. Board and accommodation available. Minimum period of work one week between June and September.

Applicants should speak Italian, German or French. Minimum age, 18.

Applications to the above address. Volunteers must be able to present valid documents and a residence permit.

INTERNATIONALE BEGEGNUNG IN GEMEINSCHAFTSDIENSTEN eV: Schlosserstrasse 28, D-70180 Stuttgart 1, Germany (☎0711-6491128; fax 711-6409867).
Volunteers to attend international youth workcamps in Switzerland. Typical projects might include **restoring an old castle, environmental protection, children's playschemes and media projects.** Each workcamp consists of a group of about 15 people aged 18-30 from all over the world living and working together for the public benefit.

There is a registration fee of approximately £55; food and accommodation are provided free on the camps. The annual programme is published in March.

Applications to the above address.

INTERNATIONALE UMWELTSCHUTZ STUDENTEN: IUS-AWSR, Postfach 1, CH-9101 Herisau, Switzerland (tel/fax 071-351 5103).
International Student Exchange Placements for voluntary work during the summer.
Volunteers aged between 18 and 28 to help on mountain clearing and conservation projects. The projects last 10-20 days in the Alps around Davos, Zermatt and

Engelberg. The work involves **clearing rubbish from ski slopes and footpath networks and repairing footpaths.** Volunteers receive pocket money of £2 per day and accommodation is offered in tourist camps offering traditional Swiss food.

Volunteers must meet their own travel costs, and obtain health, accident and third-party insurance before arriving. A registration fee is also required and details of that are in the application form. In addition to being in good physical condition applicants should be surefooted with some mountain experience. The nature of the work is such that applicants must be German speakers, willing to participate in camp life and over 18.

Further details and an *application form* are available from IUS at the above address.

MOUNTAIN FOREST PROJECT: STIFTUNG BERGWALDPROJEKT: Hauptstrasse 24, CH-7014 Trin, Switzerland (+41 81-630-4145; fax +41-81-630-4147; e-mail info@bergwaldprojekt.ch; www.bergwaldprojekt.ch). An organisation of workcamps for volunteers from 18 to 80, working in the mountain forests of Switzerland, Austria and Germany.

Volunteers: 15-20 places per week available in over 60 camps per year. **Work involves reforestation and forest maintenance, building footpaths for access and fences.** No experience is necessary. Camps run from April to October. Volunteers may stay for one week per year. Free board and lodging is provided. Volunteers should have a basic knowledge of German.

Programme details for 2004 will be available from January and *applications* will be accepted from then onwards. Apply online if possible.

Au Pairs, Nannies, Family Helps and Exchanges

PRO FILIA: 51, rue de Carouge, 1205 Geneva, Switzerland (tel/fax 022-329 84 62).

Au Pairs can be placed with families in the regions of Switzerland and Geneva for stays of a minimum of 12 months. The office is manned from 8.30am-11am Monday-Friday and from 2.30-5pm on Wednesday. For further details *contact* the above address.

Central and Eastern Europe

Armenia

The chances of finding paid summer work in the Armenia are slim. In addition to the entry below, the voluntary organisations in the *Worldwide* chapter may be able to find placements.

ARMENIAN CENTER FOR INTERNATIONAL COOPERATION: 161 Bashinjaghyan Street, Apt. 19, Yerevan, Armenia (☎+374 1 35 50 83; fax +374 1 52 70 11; e-mail: aci@datacomservice.com or armaci@e-mail.com).
Short-term Volunteers (80) required for July and August for reconstruction, environmental and social work. 5 hours per day, Monday to Friday. Board and lodging are provided. No special qualifications are needed. Must be aged 17-35 years.
Applications to Edward Balayan, President of ACI Armenia, at the above address or e-mail.

Belarus

Short-term voluntary work in Belarus can be obtained for UK nationals through the International Voluntary Service, UNA Exchange, Youth Action For Peace and Concordia; US nationals need to contact Service Civil International or CIEE; see their entries in the *Worldwide* chapter for details. The following organisation can also act as an advisory service for those interested in finding voluntary work in Belarus.

ATM BELORUSSIAN ASSOCIATION OF INTERNATIONAL YOUTH WORK: P.O. Box 64, 220119 Minsk, Belarus (☎0172-278183; fax/☎0172-222714).
Volunteers (150) for workcamps in Belarus in different fields including ecology and various social issues. Volunteers from abroad come to the Belorussian workcamps every year to take part in activities and study programmes, or to help with office work, or to lead the camps and help with the co-ordination of the summer exchange. Applicants of any nationality are welcome and will be assisted with visas, etc.
No special skills are needed, apart from Russian language skills for some of the programmes. German and English are the other camp languages. The minimum age limit is 18 years and there is no upper limit. Disabled applicants welcome, but they must contact the organisation prior to application. The usual length of placement is three or four weeks between June and September, although some volunteers can be placed for two to four months. Volunteers must pay an application fee, but during the workcamp they are provided with free food, accommodation and health insurance. Accommodation is provided in student hostels.
For further information *contact* the above address.

Croatia

The chances of finding paid summer work in Croatia are not that great though its tourist industry is burgeoning, but following organisation does offer offer paid employment.

Work at Sea

SETSAIL HOLIDAYS: The Business Centre, 140 Station Road, Redhill, Surrey, RH1 1ET: (☎01737-764-443; fax 01737-765-985; e-mail boats@setsail.co.uk; www.setsail.co.uk). Setsail Holidays are a specialist tour operator providing flotilla sailing and bareboat charter holidays to Greece, Turkey and Croatia.

Skippers, Hostesses and Engineers organising, operating and running flotilla sailing holidays. The skipper, hostess and engineer work together to co-ordinate and run the flotilla which can consist of up to twelve yachts. Should have sailing experience and qualifications and the ability to work well with people. First Aid qualifications would be useful. Accommodation is provided on the 'lead yacht'. Minimum period of work, seven months.

Applications to John Hortop at the above address.

Voluntary Work

ECO-CENTRE CAPUT INSULAE-BELI: Beli 4, 51559 Beli, Island of Cres, Croatia (☎+385-51-840-525; +385-51-840-525; e-mail caput.insulae@ri.tel.hr; www.caput-insulae.com).

Conservation Volunteers to help with a variety of projects including the **conservation of the Eurasian griffon vulture; cleaning and feeding griffons in the bird sanctuary, repairing dry stone walls, saving small ponds, interpretation centre, picking olives and helping local shepherds.**

Applicants should be healthy, able to swim and speak English. Minimum age 18. To work a minimum of one week between 15th January and 15th December. Volunteers have to pay a volunteer fee, travel expenses to and from Croatia, and food expenses. Accommodation is provided.

Apply to the address above.

The Czech Republic

The chances of finding paid summer work in the Czech Republic and Slovakia are low, but voluntary work can be arranged for British people by International Voluntary Service, UNA Exchange, Youth Action For Peace and Concordia; the CIEE helps to place Americans as does Service Civil International (see the International Voluntary Service entry). Details of the above organisations can be found in the *Worldwide* chapter.

RED TAPE, VISAS & WORK PERMITS

Visa Requirements: A visa is required by British nationals and citizens of many other countries when travelling to the Czech Republic for non-tourist purposes. Those unsure about whether they require a visa should check with their nearest

Czech consulate. When applying for a visa, applicants must be able to present a passport valid for at least 15 months (or 9 months for a short term traveller) from the date of issue of the visa, two passport-sized photographs, a document proving the purpose of the stay (e.g. a work permit or a Long Term Residence visa) confirmation of available accommodation, proof of health insurance and proof that they have sufficient funds to cover their living expenses in the country.

Residence Permits: A new Residency Law came into force in 2000 making it necessary to apply for a long-stay Czech visa before arrival in the country. Full details are available from the Czech Embassy in your country (in Britain phone 020-7243 1115/fax 020-7243 7988 or in the USA www.czech.cz/washington). Anyone who intends to work or for any other reason stay in the Czech Republic for longer than 90 days must obtain the visa in advance. Necessary documents include a work permit issued by the employer, proof of accommodation, etc. all presented in the original or a notarised copy.

Work Permits: Must be obtained by your future employer from the local employment office *(Urad práce)*. They will need a signed form from you plus a photocopy of your passport and the originals or notarised copies of your education certificates. Work Permits will only be granted where the employer can prove that they cannot find a suitable Czech candidates to carry out the job. All of this takes at least three months.

Teaching and Language Schools

ITC - INTERNATIONAL TEFL CERTIFICATE: Kaprova 14, 110 00 Praha 1, Czech Republic (tel/fax (420 2) 2481-4791; fax 0420-224-81-75-30; wes@itc-training.com; www.itc-training.com) US voice-mail ☎1-800-915-5540; US fax 1-877-682-6515).

ITC-International TEFL Certificate offers the internationally recognized 120 hour TEFL Certificate course in Prague, Barcelona and Madrid. More than 1,800 students have graduated from ITC. Sessions held year-round on a monthly basis. Course is designed for those with little or no teaching experience. Tuition is US$1,500 and includes registration, course manual, **Immediate Job Guarantee in Eastern Europe**, lifetime job guidance assistance worldwide, and city orientation walk and welcome dinner. Housing options available.

Applications to the above address.

Voluntary Work

BRONTOSAURUS MOVEMENT: Brontosaurus Council CR, Bubenska 6, Praha 7, Czech Republic 170 00 (☎42-2 667 102 45).

Volunteers (2,000 per year) to take part in **environmental summer workcamps** around the Czech Republic. The Movement is an independent body co-ordinating the efforts of local groups which must be applied to directly.

Contact Jan Dusik, International Co-ordinator, enclosing an International Reply Coupon for a copy of the list of summer camps open to foreigners.

CONCORDIA: Heversham House, 20-22 Boundary Road, Hove, East Sussex BN3 4ET (☎01273-422218; fax 01273 421182; e-mail info@concordia-iye.org.uk; www.concordia-iye.org.uk).

Concordia offers young people aged 16-30 the opportunity to take part in international volunteer projects, lasting 2-3 weeks, from June to September. The work is community based and ranges from **nature conservation, renovation,**

construction and social work including children's playschemes and youth work. Volunteers pay a registration fee of £85 and fund their own travel. Board and accommodation are free of charge.

For further information *write* enclosing an s.a.e. to the International Volunteer Co-ordinator at the above address.

KMC: Karoliny Svetle 30, 110 00 Prague 1, Czech Republic (tel/fax +420-2222-20347; e-mail kmc@kmc.cz; www.kmc.cz).
Volunteers (25) to take part in various work camps lasting approx. two weeks each in the Czech Republic between June and September. Typical projects might involve **gardening, cleaning and renovation work in centres for handicapped children, castles or zoo gardens, or taking part in ecological projects in the mountains.** Board and lodging provided free of charge; to work 6-7 hours per day, Monday-Friday. Applicants should be aged 18-30.

Applicants should apply through partner voluntary organisations in their own country: in Britain these are UNA Exchange in Cardiff (☎02920-223088; www.unaexchange.org) and Concordia in Hove (☎01273-422218; www.concordia-iye.org.uk): in the US contactCIEE (www.councilexchanges.org) or Volunteers for Peace (☎802-259 2759; www.vfp@vfp.org).

Hungary

In addition to the opportunities listed below there are also opportunities for voluntary work arranged by Youth Action for Peace, International Voluntary Service and UNA Exchange for UK nationals, and for US nationals through Service Civil International: see the *Worldwide* chapter for details.

Voluntary Work

BIOKULTURA/WWOOF: Eszter Szonyi, Biokultura Egyesulet, Hungarian Association for Organic Farming, 1024 Budapest, Kitaibel Pu 4, Hungary.
Volunteer Farm Workers needed: **placements on organic farms and gardens** in Hungary can be arranged by the Biokultura Association, The Hungarian Association of Organic Growers, in co-operation with WWOOF. Work can include weeding, animal husbandry and helping with the harvest.

Applicants must speak German, English or French; knowledge of Russian might be useful. It is recommended that applicants arrange insurance for themselves and have an anti-tetanus injection. Those interested should contact the address above.

Latvia

The following organisation can help people to find employment in Latvia. In addition UK nationals can arrange voluntary work there through International Voluntary Service, Youth Action for Peace or UNA Exchange and US nationals through Service Civil International (see the *Worldwide* chapter for details).

RED TAPE, VISAS & WORK PERMITS

Visa Requirements: Visas - Required, but NOT by the following for stays of up to 90 days: holders of Latvian, Estonian & Lithuanian passports, citizens of (and holding a passport valid for two months from arrival) Andorra, Austria, Belgium, Croatia, Czech Rep, Denmark, Estonia, Finland, France, Germany, Greece, Hungary, Iceland, Ireland Rep, Italy, Japan, Liechtenstein, Lithuania, Luxembourg, Malta, Netherlands, Norway, Poland, Portugal, Slovakia, Slovenia, Spain, Sweden, Switzerland, the United Kingdom, United States.

Residence Permits: In order to obtain a residence permit for Latvia an applicant must submit an application form, a photocopy of a valid travel document and an invitation certified by the Department of Migration and Citizenship Affairs. If an applicant intends to work in Latvia, an invitation approved by the State Labour Department must be obtained. For assistance obtaining residency permits, special visas or work permits call the visa section of the Citizenship and Migration Board, Raina 5, ☎721 94 24, fax 782 03 06.

INTERNATIONAL EXCHANGE CENTRE: 89 Fleet Street, London EC4Y 1DH (☎020-7583 9116; fax 020-7583-9117; e-mail outbounder@btconnect.com; www.isecworld.co.uk). The International Exchange Center works to promote positive, enjoyable cultural exchanges. Overseas work is offered in various countries for various types of work. See website for details. Non-students welcome. No language requirement.

English Teachers to work on EFL teaching programme. English teachers are placed at language schools, summer language centres in Latvia, Russia and Ukraine. Some teaching experience/qualifications desirable. Placement fee of £100. Students must arrange their own medical insurance and visas must notify IEC of their arrival dates at least one week before arrival.

Applications must be submitted at least 3 months before the earliest program start date for those wishing to be placed through IEC and 1½ months for those wishing to find their own job.

Poland

Teaching work in Poland can be found with the organisations listed below. In addition, voluntary work in Poland can by arranged through Youth Action for Peace, UNA Exchange and International Voluntary Service for British people, and the CIEE and Service Civil International for Americans: see the *Worldwide* chapter for details.

RED TAPE, VISAS & WORK PERMITS

Visa Requirements: EEA nationals and those from the USA do not require visas to enter Poland but their stay is limited to anything from 14 to 90 days depending on country of origin, and 180 days for British citizens. Note: there are several types of visa obtainable such as visitors, transit and business; for more details contact your nearest Embassy or Consulate of the Republic of Poland.

Work Permits: A work visa (Visa 06) must be applied for in your country of origin. Original or notarised copies of your degree diploma and TEFL Certificate (if applicable) must be presented along with a promisory work permit from your future employer to the Polish Consulate in your country of residence. The Consulate then issues a residence visa. After arrival the residence visa and interim work permit are taken to the regional employment office *(Wojewòdzki Urzad Pracy)* to obtain a proper work permit. The handout from the Polish Consulate entitled 'Visas for Teachers' sets out the procedures and states that the current cost of the multi-entry residence visa is £104. Ring the Polish Embassy for details (020-7580 0475; www.polishworld.com/polemb).

Language Schools

ANGLO-POLISH UNIVERSITIES TEACHING PROJECT. APASS UK NORTH: 93 Victoria Road, Leeds LS6 1DR (☎(emergency only) 0113 2758121, 8-10am/4-6pm; fax 020-7498 7608). The Polish Ministry of Education invites applications for paid posts as **English Language Instructors** in their English language summer schools. Payment is subject to qualifications and experience. Placements are either for four or eight weeks in July/August. The students are from grammar schools, roughly of the same age and ability.The course will be two and a half hours English instruction in the morning (mainly conversational) followed by only two hours recreational activities either in the afternoon or evening. Weekends are free.

Accommodation and food are provided free, as well as leisure/sporting facilities (swimming, walking, barbecue, horse riding, discos, visits to places of interest etc. Some placements include a weekend trip to Prague. After three weeks out at the summer school, a week's 'grand tour of Poland' is organised; visiting Warsaw, Krakow, Auschwitz and the Tatra Mountains-all expenses paid by the Polish host. Applicants of all ages from 16+ are welcome (16-17-year-olds need written parental permission), as are parents with children (maximum two) aged 10+.

For a comprehensive information pack, please *send* a 45p stamped, A4 self-addressed envelope plus a £3 postal order to the above address.

THE ENGLISH SCHOOL OF COMMUNICATION SKILLS (ESCS): Attn. Personnel Department, ul. Sw. Agnieszki 2/Ip, 31-068 Kraków, Poland (tel/fax 0048 12 422 85 83; e-mail personnel@escs.pl).
Teachers of English (60) wanted for full-time positions at ESCS schools in: Kraków, the cultural heart of Poland; Tarnów, where the locals are reputedly the friendliest people in Poland; Nowy Targ, where they take their skiing seriously; Myslenice, the best of both worlds, close to the big city and in the beautiful countryside; and Katowice, the rock 'n' roll capital of Poland.

Period of work from October to June. Job involves teaching English to Polish students of all ages. Salary according to experience and qualifications. Applicants must hold an EFL methodology certificate and have a degree level education. ESCS holds EFL training courses in September.
Summer School (15) same as above for July and August.
Summer Camp (6) TEFL teachers wanted. Job involves teaching English for 4-8 hours per day to Polish students of all ages in an informal atmosphere at the beautiful Polish seaside. Duties include participating in sports events (baseball) and other activities. Accommodation, food and travel to and from Krakow provided. Minimum age 21. Applicants should be educated to degree level, with bright, confident personalities and be enthusiastic about sport.

Applications to the above address.

Russia

While there are occasional opportunities for finding paid temporary work in Russia it is still easier to find voluntary than paid work there. In addition to the opportunities listed below British people should contact Youth Action for

Peace, International Voluntary Service, UNA Exchange and Concordia while Americans should contact the CIEE and Service Civil International; for details see the *Worldwide* chapter. The Russian state body 'Goskomtrud' is responsible for the hiring of manpower from abroad. The address of the Department is: The Goskomtrud of Russia, 1 Square Kuibysheva, 103706, Moscow, Russia.

INTERNATIONAL SCIENTIFIC PROJECTS: Laboratory of Geoarchaeology (Institute of Geology, Acad. Sciences, Kaz), State Institute for Scientific Research and Planning on Monuments of Material Culture (Min. Culture Kaz), Tole Bi 21, Room 31, 480100 Almaty, Kazakhstan (☎+7-3272 914386; fax +7-3272 917931; e-mail ispkz@nursat.kz).

Volunteers for archaeological fieldwork, to take part in four programmes of summer fieldwork based mainly on geoarchaeological survey and documentation. Under instruction from specialists from several kazakh institutes, volunteers will receive training in steppe archaeology, paleoecology, methodology, aerial surveying and documentation. Programme costs are between US$250-300 (£175-£210 approx.) per week, in return volunteers will be provided with food and accommodation.

For more details *contact* Renato Sala or Jean-Marc Deom at the Institute or consult the following fieldwork opportunities webpagesL www. archaeological.org/ webinfo.php or www.cincpac.com/afos/testpit.html.

INTERNATIONAL EXCHANGE CENTRE: 89 Fleet Street, London EC4Y 1DH (☎020-7583 9116; fax 020-7583-9117; e-mail outbounder@btconnect.co m; www.isecworld.co.uk). The International Exchange Center works to promote positive, enjoyable cultural exchanges. Overseas work is offered in various countries for various types of work. See website for details. Non-students welcome. No language requirement.

Camp Counsellors Programme: Camp Leaders/Activity Instructors/Language Teachers needed to work in children's summer camps in Russia and Ukraine, looking after children aged 8-15 years old. Energetic and friendly personality and a genuine desire to work with kids is essential; specialists in sports, music etc. are especially welcome. Free board and accommodation. Pocket money is low by western standards but is equivalent to the basic wage of local camp staff. Placement fee of £100.

English Teachers to work on EFL teaching programme. English teachers are placed at language schools, summer language centres in Latvia, Russia and Ukraine. Some teaching experience/qualifications desirable. Placement fee of £100.

Work and Study Experience Russia. This programme allows foreign participants to get involved in Russian daily life and culture. Participants are enrolled into 4 week language courses (10 hours per week) based at universities in Moscow, followed by work experience in a company in Moscow and other cities in Russia for a period of 2-4 months. Whenever possible. The programme cost of £240 (US$350) includes the cost of 4 weeks of study and accommodation in a University dormitory room, pick up on arrival to Moscow and a work placement. Salary may be low by Western standards – £34-£138 (US$50-200) per month. Participants can extend their study period while they are in Russia by paying directly to the University £82 (US$120 for 4 weeks of study). Jobs are at entry level positions mainly in hospitality but may be in other areas. Participants can also choose to find a job themselves while studying at language courses: however they need to be aware that unemployment rate is Russia is high. IEC will provide informational support but will not find an actual job for such participants. (If finding own job, the programme costs $330). Students must arrange their own medical insurance and visas must notify IEC of their arrival dates at least one week before arrival.

Applications must be submitted at least 3 months before the earliest program start date for those wishing to be placed through IEC and 1½ months for those wishing to find their own job.

Slovenia

The following organisation organises voluntary work in Slovenia. British people can also find this type of work there through International Voluntary Service or UNA Exchange, while US citizens can apply to Service Civil International; see the *Worldwide* chapter for details.

ZAVOD VOLUNTARIAT: Service Civil International Slovenia, Breg 12 Sl-1000 Ljubljana, Slovenia (☎+386-1-2417620; fax +386-1-2417626; e-mail placement@zavod-voluntariat.sl; www.zavod-voluntariat.si). Voluntariat is a non-profit and non-governmental organisation which co-ordinates voluntary work and international work camps in Slovenia. Voluntariat aims to promote social justice, sustainable development and solidarity through voluntary service.

International Work Camp Volunteers. Voluntariat organises between 15 and 20 work camps in Slovenia every year. Most work camps are held from June to September and last two or three weeks. The main topics of the work camps are: ecology, Bosnian refugees, children and handicapped people. Most work camps do not require any special skills. Accommodation and food is provided.

Long and medium-term voluntary work: projects of LTV and MTV are based mostly in Ljubljana and they include: refugee projects, projects for youngsters from underpriviledged backgrounds and projects for elderly people. Voluntariat also offers long and medium-term voluntary work abroad.

Applications should be made through the applicant's nation branch of SCI.

Turkey

Opportunities for paid work in Turkey normally involve either teaching English or working for a tour operator. There are opportunities for volunteer work with the organisations listed below or through UNA Exchange, Youth Action for Peace, International Voluntary Service and Concordia for British citizens, or the CIEE and Service Civil International for Americans; see the *Worldwide* chapter for details.

Please note that those who enter Turkey as tourists with or without a tourist visa are not permitted to take up employment in the country.

RED TAPE

See the website www.turkconsulate-london.com/visa for up-to-date information.
Visa Requirements: All British, Australian, US, Canadian and Irish nationals can obtain a 3 months/multiple-entry visa at their point of entry to Turkey. New Zealand citizens do not need visas for stays of up to 3 months as tourists. Any UK national entering Turkey is advised to have a minimum of 6 months validity on their passports from the date of their entry into Turkey. In the UK up-to-date details of visa and permit requirements can be obtained by telephoning 09068-347348 (calls cost 60p per minute).

> **Residence Permits:** If you wish to reside in Turkey longer than the normal period allowed to tourists you need to apply for a residence visa. After obtaining the visa, you are required to register with the local police headquarters within a month following the arrival in Turkey in order to get a residence permit.
>
> **Work Permits:** a contract of employment by the private sector is required before application to the Turkish Consulate General is made. A letter of approval from the Undersecretariat for the Treasury is also required from those who will be employed as technical staff in the private sector. Prospective English teachers must have a degree and TEFL certificate. Should the employer be related to the tourism business, a letter of approval should be obtained from the Turkish Ministry of Tourism before visa application. Permits must be applied for and obtained before departure for Turkey. Applicants should allow at least 8 weeks for their permit application to be processed. Employment is only likely to be offered to those with special qualifications. Visa fees range from £38 to £80. If a work visa is granted the holder is required to register with the local police within a month of their arrival and obtain a residence permit.
>
> **Au Pair:** work permits are required.
>
> **Voluntary Work:** work permits are required.

Sports, Couriers and Camping

MARK WARNER: telephone 020-7761 7300 (24 hour) or 020-7761 7340 for childcare recruitment.

Managers, Accountants, Receptionists, Watersports Instructors, Tennis and Aerobics Instructors, Chefs, Bar Staff, Nannies, Handymen, Nightwatchmen and more are required to work in hotels in Turkey during the summer from April to November. Wages from £50 per week plus full board, medical insurance, travel expenses and free use of watersport and activity facilities. Some reserve staff also needed throughout the season. Requirements for languages, age, experience, qualifications etc. vary according to the job applied for. *For further details*, please call the Resorts Recruitment Department on the above number.

SAVILE TOURS: 47 Charlbert Street, St. John's Wood, London NW8 6JN (☎020-7722 2986; fax 020-7586 4859; e-mail info@saviletours.com; www.saviletours.com). Savile Tours is an upmarket tour operator specialising in holidays to Turkey and Northern Cyprus.

Overseas Representatives (3-4) to escort clients between airport and accommodation and assist them during their holidays. Pay negotiable depending on experience. Previous experience preferred. Working hours are variable and the minimum period of work is 6 months from May to October.

Apply immediately to Ali Barchman at the above address.

Work at Sea

SETSAIL HOLIDAYS: The Business Centre, 140 Station Road, Redhill, Surrey, RH1 1ET: (☎01787-764-443; fax 01787-765-985; e-mail boats@setsail.co.uk; www.setsail.co.uk). Setsail Holidays are a specialist tour operator providing flotilla sailing and backboat charter holidays to Greece, Turkey and Croatia.

Skippers, Hostesses and Engineers to organise, operate and run flotilla sailing holidays. The skipper, hostess and engineer work together to co-ordinate and run the flotilla which can consist of up to twelve yachts. Should have sailing experience and qualifications and the ability to work well with people. First Aid qualifications would be useful. Accommodation is provided on the 'lead yacht'. Minimum period of work, seven months.

Applications to Paul Stonehouse at the above address.

Voluntary Work and Archaeology

CONCORDIA: 20-22 Boundary Road, Hove, East Sussex BN3 4ET (☎01273-422218; fax 01273 421182; e-mail info@concordia-iye.org.uk; www.concordia-iye.org.uk).

Volunteers aged 16-30 are needed for international volunteer projects lasting 2 weeks from July to September. Work is mainly on **construction and manual projects in villages.** Basic food and accommodation are provided. Volunteers pay a registration fee of £85 and organise their own travel and insurance.

Send a stamped addressed envelope to the above address for further information.

GSM YOUTH SERVICES CENTRE: Bayindir Sokak, No.45/9 Kizilay, 06450 Kizilay-Ankara, Turkey (☎+90-312-417-11 24/417-29-91; fax +90-312-425-81-92; e-mail gsmser@superonline.com).

GSM organises around 20 workcamps throughout Turkey in co-operation with the local municipalities and universities. The projects, usually taking place in towns or on campus sites, can involve **environmental protection, restoration and/or festival organisation.**

The age limits are: 18-28 in all of the projects. The projects last for 2 weeks from July until the end of September. Volunteers work 5 hours a day, weekends are free with organised excursions available. Board and lodging are provided in dormitories, small hotels/pensions, camp houses or with families. Volunteers pay their own travel costs and pay a contribution fee of approx. £45.

Applications through partner organisations including Concordia, Quaker International Social Projects and the United Nations Association (Wales): see the *Worldwide* chapter for details.

Au Pairs, Nannies, Family Helps and Exchanges

ANGLO PAIR AGENCY: 40 Wavertree Road, Streatham Hill, London SW2 3SP (☎0208-674 3605; fax 0208-674 1264; e-mail anglo.pair@btinternet.com; www.angloau-pairs.co.uk). The agency has its own office in Istanbul to offer support to those placed in Turkey.

Nannies (50 or more) to work 40-45 hours per week with babies and young children in Turkey. Weekends normally off. Wages £150-£250 per week if qualified or £100 or more per week if unqualified, with accommodation provided and other living expenses covered. Placements are either for the summer (May-October) or at any time of year. Applicants must be native English speakers and normally aged 20-35. Unqualified nannies must have experience in child care.

Au Pairs (50 or more) for summer and year round placements in Turkey; applicants from overseas also placed in the UK. Pocket money of £45-£65 per week plus living expenses and accommodation. Duties include childcare and light housework 25-35 hours per week. Applicants should be aged 19-27 and should have some childcare experience.

Applications to Mrs Kim Kirtley at the above address.

GENCTUR Istiklal Cad. Zambak Sok. 15 / 5 80080 Istanbul, Turkey (☎ +90 212 249 25 15 - 243 41 31; fax +90 212 249 25 54; e-mail workcamps.in@genctur.com; www.genctur.com). Contact Person : (Mr) Zafer Yilmaz, Workcamps Coordinator. Genctur is Turkey's leading youth and student travel organisation. Their main activities are international voluntary workcamps in Turkey and in Northern Cyprus. Camps last 2-3 weeks.

Project volunteers   for mostly manual work including **repairing and painting schools, digging water trenches, constructing schools or health care centres, gardening and environmental development works or social schemes such as helping to handicapped people or practising English with children.** Projects take place mostly in small villages and towns where the traditional way of life can be seen and contact with the local is offered. Full board and accommodation is provided. Camp language is English. There are also one French speaking and one Japanese speaking camp each year. Age group is 18 and over.

Applications are only accepted through the partner organisations below:
GREAT BRITAIN

   UNA Exchange, Temple of Peace Cathays Park CARDIFF CF10 3AP; ☎+44 (0)2920-223 088; fax +44 (0)2920-665 557; e-mail : unaexchange@btinternet.com.

   Quaker Voluntary Action, Friends Meeting House, 6 Mount Street, Manchester M2 5NS E-mail: qva@quakervolaction.freeserve.co.uk (www.qva.org.uk); tel/fax +44 (0)161-819 16 34

   Concordia,-UK 2nd Floor, Heversham House 20-22 Boundary Road. Hove BN3 4ET UK; tel/fax +44 (0)1273-422 218; e-mail: gwyn@concordia-iye.org.uk.

   IVS-GBS Old Hall, East Bergholt Colchester CO7 6TQ; ☎44 +(0)1206.298215; fax +44 (0)1206.299043; e-mail: ivs@ivsgbsouth.demon.co.uk; www.ivs-gb.org.uk.

   IVS-GBN, Castlehill House, 21 Otley Road, Headingley GB Leeds LS6 3AA; ☎44.1132.304600; fax: + 44 (0)1132-304610; e-mail: ivsgbn@ivsgbn.demon.co.uk; www.ivsgbn.demon.co.uk .

   IVS-SC, 7 Upper Bow, Edinburgh EH1 2JN; tel:+44 (0)1312-266722; fax +44 (0)1312-266723 e-mail ivs@ivsgbscot.demon.co.uk; www.ivsgbn.demon.co.uk .

   YAP-UK, 8 Golden Ridge, Freshwater, Isle of Wight 9040 9LE; ☎+44 (0)1983-752557; fax +44 (0)1983-756900; e-mail yapuk@ukonline.co.uk .

Ukraine

Apart from the voluntary work available in the Ukraine through the Latvian-based International Exchange Centre (see chapter on Latvia), short-term voluntary work can be arranged for UK nationals through Concordia, International Voluntary Service and UNA Exchange. US citizens can arrange placements through the CIEE and Service Civil International. Voluntary work can also be obtained through the organisation listed below.

UNION FORUM: Lychakivska St. PO 5327; Lviv-10, Ukraine, 79010. (☎/fax +38 0322 726934; e-mail info@union-forum.org; www.union-forum.org).
Union Forum is an NGO, nonprofit organisation involving youth in international exchange programmes since 1990. Outbound programmes include international work experience and training, and seasonal agricultural work, selecting and sending students abroad.
Short-term Volunteers are needed for inbound programmes including summer short-term projects, for those aged between 18 and 30 years of age. Projects

include reconstruction and environmental work during July and August. No special qualifications are required. Board and accommodation are provided free of charge.

Applications should be made to Inga Vorobyova, Co-ordinator at the above address.

YOUTH VOLUNTARY SERVICE: 11/60 Lystopadna, LVIV, 290034, Ukraine (tel/fax 00-380-322 423658).
Volunteers (15) required to take part in short term social projects (2-3 weeks) from late June until the end of August. To work 5 hours a day, Monday-Friday. Board and accommodation provided.

Applications through national organisations or directly to the above address.

Yugoslavia

Short-term volunteer projects in Yugoslavia can be arranged for British citizens by Youth Action for Peace and in Serbia by UNA Exchange. See their entries in the *Worldwide* chapter for more details. The following organisation offers opportunities to work in Yugoslavia.

GALINDO SKOLA STRANIH JEZIKA (SAVA CENTAR & VOZDOVAC): Milentija Popovica 9, 11070 Novi Beograd, Yugoslavia (☎11-311 4568; fax 11-455785; e-mail galindo@net.yu). The first private language school in the country, located in Novi Beograd's congress and shopping centre. Excellent working atmosphere, with students from pre-school to executives.
English Teachers (3) to work with Yugoslavian children, adolescents and adults. Minimum wage approximately £280 per month, working 6 or 7 hours per day, 5 days per week.

Applicants should be enthusiastic and responsible, and have a BA in English and TEFL, TESL or TESOL qualifications. Knowledge of some Serbo-Croatian would be an advantage. *Applications* should be sent to Nada Gadjanski at the above address.

Africa and the Middle East

Egypt

Chances of finding a paid summer job in Egypt are slight but there may be possibilities in the tourist industry for example in the diving resort of Dahab. Otherwise opportunities for temporary work are normally restricted to voluntary work.

Teaching and Language Schools

INTERNATIONAL HOUSE: International Language Institute Heliopolis, 2 Mohamed Bayoumi Street, Off Merghany Street, Heliopolis, Cairo, Egypt (☎202-291295/418 9212; fax 202-415 1082; e-mail ili@idsc.net.eg; www.ihworld.com).

Teachers of English (6) required to teach intensive English courses to adults and young learners aged 5-15. Applicants should be Cambridge/RSA or CELTA qualified and preferably have experience of working with young learners. 20-25 hours of work per week between June and September, minimum period of work 6 weeks. Wages c.£600 per month with free accommodation. Depending on the length of contract worked there is a bonus of a percentage paid towards the cost of the flight to Egypt, e.g. 50% for 12 weeks worked, up to a limit of £380.

Applications to the above address from February.

Voluntary Work and Archaeology

WIND SAND & STARS: 6 Tyndale Terrace, Islington, London, N1 2AT (☎020-7359 7551; e-mail office@windsandstars.co.uk; www.windsandstars.co.uk). Wind Sand & Stars is a small specialist company that organises a wide range of journeys and projects within the desert and mountain areas of South Sinai.

Participants for work on an annual **environmental, scientific, historical expedition operated during August in the desert and mountains of Sinai**. There is a fee attached for travel to the area. All applicants must be over 16 years of age.

*Applicants should *contact* the above address any time.

Ghana

Voluntary work for Britons in Ghana can be organised by Concordia, UNA Exchange and Youth Action for Peace. A summary of their work is listed along with their addresses in the *Worldwide* chapter. The organisations below also offer opportunities to work in Ghana.

Voluntary Work and Archaeology

AFRICA TRUST NETWORKS: Beaufort Chambers, Beaufort Street, Crickhowell,Powys NP8 1AA or Africatrust Bureau, PO Box KS 14727, Kumasi, Ghana, West Africa (UK tel/fax 01873-812453; e-mail info@africatrust.gi or ghana@africatrust.gi; www.africatrust.gi). The organisation helps at an orphanage in Kumasi, and SOS village at Asiakwa and a Conservation Project in the Rain Forest at Bawdie and four rural village schools. Their mission is 'Building Trust Through People'.

Volunteer tropical field workers needed for **help with disadvantaged young people in Ghana.** Fairly long hours. Minimum period of work of three months. Work is available September through July. Accommodation provided. Mainly Graduates with relevant skills/experience taken on.

Applications should be made online to Dr Kofi Kwansah-Filson DVM at the above website www.africatrust.gi. Interviewing, selection and pre-departure briefings take place in the UK – London or Wales.

FIOH/WWOOF GHANA: P.O. Box TF 154, Trade FairCentre, Accra, Ghana (tel/fax 23321-716091; e-mail kingzeeh@yahoo.co.uk). WWOOF is concerned with organic farming and FIOH runs tree planting and environmental projects. Both organisations require a large number of participants for their annual WORKCAMPS. Their schools help train children from poor families, participants get to experience traditional and proverbial Ghanaian hospitality. The founder is a former school teacher who has founded four international organisations in Africa.

Voluntary farm workers to **work on both organic and traditional farms in Ghana. Work includes weeding with a hoe or cutlass and harvesting of food and cash crops including maize, cassava, oranges, cocoa etc.** Volunteers with experience of organic farming especially welcome.

Volunteers to **work in a bicycle repair workshop** currently being set up; no wage paid at present but there is the possibility of pocket money in the future. Two volunteers needed every six months. No particular qualifications are necessary, but applicants should be have experience of repairing bicycles.

Other schemes are also operated such as: summer workcamps on which volunteers work on construction conservation projects and tree planting activities in rural areas; placement schemes for qualified teachers are also organised. Practical lessons in traditional African drumming and dancing are available too.

For further information *send* two international reply coupons to Mr Kenneth Nortey-Mensah, Co-ordinator, at the above address.

RURAL UPGRADE SUPPORT ORGANISATION (RUSO): P.O. Box C1, 11066 Tuma, Ghana (☎+233 21 513149; e-mail benxzola@africanus.net)

RUSO is a non-political, non sectarian and non-governmental organisation that employs volunteer humanitarian action to empower local communities and contribute grass-roots solutions to rural challenges of providing **healthcare, education and small scale business management, cultural exchange and social development**. It is a unique service organisation registered in Ghana on September 6th 1999 to help the rural people from different cultures gain a new understanding of each other in the spirit of sharing ideas by working together toward a common goal.

About 35 foreign volunteers (usually active and retired professionals, and students) work side-by-side with the permanent staff of RUSO in the fields mentioned above. Volunteers for **fish farming** project also required; must have knowledge of fish farming.

Refer to the website: www.interconnection.org/rap/ for details of volunteer costs. *Apply* direct or through the website.

SAVE THE EARTH NETWORK: Save the Earth Network, PO Box CT 3635, Cantonments-Accra, Ghana, West Africa ☎ 233-21-667791; e-mail ebensten@yahoo.com; eben-sten@hotmail.com). Save the Earth Network is an organisation dedicated to promoting sustainable development, agroforestry, environmental conservation and cultural exchange through voluntary work in Ghana.

Volunteers to **teach English language and mathematics in primary and junior secondary schools for under-privileged communities. Caring for orphans, destitutes and abandoned children** in foster homes and orphanages, **assisting in giving free basic education to street and financially disadvantaged children and HIV/AIDS education. Reforestation and environmental conservation, agroforestry, organic farming, primary health care and community development programmes.** Volunteers mostly work alongside staff and volunteers from the local community. Special skills, professional qualifications or previous experience is not essential, however, some of the volunteers may undergo a short (one week) training in Ghana, prior to the volunteering work.

Volunteers work four or more hours a day. Period of work 4 weeks to a year or longer. There is a monthly fee for participation, which covers board and lodging with local families: $475 (4 weeks); $775 (8 weeks) and $1,075 (12 weeks). Payment is made a day after beginning in Ghana. Volunteers must be aged 18 or above.

Other programmes run by the same organisation are Visitor/Cultural Exchange Programme and General Tour Programme.

VOLUNTARY WORKCAMPS ASSOCIATION OF GHANA (VOLU): PO Box 1540, Accra, Ghana (☎233-21-663486; fax 233-21-665960).

VOLU organises workcamps in the rural areas of Ghana for international volunteers. Tasks involve mainly manual work; **construction projects, working on farm and agro-forestry projects, tree planting, harvesting cocoa and foodstuffs, working with mentally retarded people, teaching, etc.** Around 1,500 volunteers are needed for workcamps at Easter, Christmas and from June to October. Volunteers can stay throughout each period.

No special skills or experience are required but volunteers should be over 16 years old and fit to undertake manual labour. Volunteers pay their own travelling costs and an inscription fee of approximately £120 but accommodation and food are provided at the camps. VOLU supplies offical invitations to enable volunteers to acquire visas before leaving for Ghana.

Applications to the above address.

VOLUNTEER GHANA/TEACH IN GHANA: BUNAC, 16 Bowling Green Lane, London EC1R 0QH (☎020-7251 3472; fax 020-7251 0215; e-mail volunteer@bunac.org.uk).

BUNAC runs a *Volunteer Ghana* programme which enables recent graduates aged under 27 to spend between three and six months working and travelling in West Africa. Placements range from teaching positions to development projects to administrative roles. Departures are in January, July and October.

BUNAC also runs a *Teach in Ghana* programme, which arranges teacher placements in secondary schools in Ghana between September and July. Applicants should have some teaching experience and preferably a teaching qualification (for example, PGCE, QTS or BEd). There is one departure at the end of August.

Placements on these programmes are unpaid and participants will be expected to make a small weekly contribution towars living costs.

For further details about these programmes *contact* BUNAC at the above address or visit www.bunac.org.

Israel

A foreigner wishing to take up paid work in Israel must find a job and hold a work permit (obtained by his or her employer) before entering the country. A special visa exists for volunteers, and fortunately for those who wish to find a place on a kibbutz or moshav once they are in the country it can in some circumstances be obtained after arrival; see below for details. However it is usually preferable to arrange a kibbutz place before leaving for Israel.

There are some opportunities for paid employment in the tourist industry, especially around the resort of Eilat on the Red Sea and the Old City in Jerusalem. However, most people who wish to work in Israel for a few months choose to work on kibbutzim or moshavim. These are almost wholly self sufficient settlements which take on volunteers for a normal minimum of eight weeks. The main difference between the two is that the property is shared on a kibbutz, while most houses and farms are privately owned on a moshav. So on one volunteers work and share the farm tasks with permanent staff, while on the latter they are paid and there is less communal spirit. However, the whole kibbutz system is set to undergo some potentially dramatic changes as plans are in hand to transfer kibbutzim from state to private ownership. It is very possible that the kibbutz system will eventually disappear, or become more like the moshavim movement in which private ownership of land is the norm.

On a kibbutz the work may consist of picking olives, grapes or cotton in the fields, domestic duties, or factory work; on a moshav the work is agricultural. In return for a six day week volunteers receive free accommodation, meals, laundry and cigarettes. Volunteers are normally given pocket money on kibbutzim, while on a moshav a small wage is paid but the working hours are liable to be longer. Other programmes available on kibbutzim include Kibbutz Ulpan (which is intensive Hebrew study) and Project Oren Kibbutz Programmes (which is intensive Hebrew study, as well as travel and study of Israel).

The addresses in the *Kibbutz* section below who help people who want to arrange work on a kibbutz are based in London. Americans can contact Kibbutz Program Center at 21st Floor, 633 Third Ave., New York, NY 10017 (☎1-800247 7852 or 212-318-6130; fax 212-318-6134; e-mail kibbutzdsk@aol.com or ulpankad@aol.com); volunteers need to bear in mind that with this organisation they must be prepared to make a commitment of at least six weeks. There are many other placement offices around the world: Israel's diplomatic missions should be able to advise on the nearest one to you.

The following organisation may be able to place people who are actually in Israel. In recent years the authorities have been discouraging volunteers from travelling to Israel on one way tickets without having a written assurance of a place on a kibbutz, and with insufficient money for their fare home: the official line is that volunteers must have a return ticket and a reasonable sum of money (around £150/$225) in their possession when they enter the country. Contact the Kibbutz Program Centre: Volunteers Department; 18 Frishman Street, 3rd Floor, Cr. Ben Yehuda ☎ Aviv 61030 (☎03-524-6156 or 03-524-8874; fax 03-523-9966; e-mail kpcvol@inter.net.il; www.kibbutz.org.il); it is open 9am-2pm, Sunday-Thursday.

The centre advises people who do not pre-arrange a place before entering Israel that there might be a wait of days or even weeks before one is found, especially in the summer. However in the current political circumstances, there is a general shortage of foreign volunteers. All volunteers must be available for a minimum of 2 months, be between the ages of 18 and 35, speak a reasonable level of English and be in good mental and physical health.

The other major form of voluntary work in Israel consists of helping with archaeological excavations, often of Old Testament sites. The minimum stay for volunteers is normally two weeks. In the majority of cases volunteers must pay at least £15/US$25 a day for their expenses on a dig. British citizens wishing to find voluntary work in Israel can obtain placements through Concordia.

Those wanting to know more about not only work on kibbutzim and moshavim, but also all other forms of short-term work in Israel should consult the book *Kibbutz Volunteer* (see the *Useful Publications* chapter).

Placing an advertisement in the English language paper *The Jerusalem Post* may also lead to an offer of a job. They can be contacted at the *Jerusalem Post* Building, P.O. Box 81, Romena, Jerusalem 91000 (fax 2-377646).

RED TAPE, VISAS & WORK PERMITS

Visa Requirements: to work in Israel you must have a Foreign Worker's Visa for Israel which has to be arranged before arriving in Israel. This is the only visa that allows a visitor to work (other than for voluntary work e.g. kibbutz) in Israel. For volunteer work a work visa is not normally required prior to arrival by citizens of the UK, USA and some Western European countries.

Residence Permits: on entering the country, a visitor is likely to be given permission to stay for up to three months. Permission for a longer stay should then be obtained from the Ministry of the Interior, Hakirya Ruppin Road, no.2, Jerusalem.

Work Permits: your prospective employer should obtain the necessary permit from the Ministry of the Interior in Israel. You should have the permit with you when you enter the country.

Voluntary Work: a B4 Volunteer Visa is required of participants doing voluntary work (which includes kibbutzim and moshavim). The fee is NIS675 ($20) which covers 3 months. If you have pre-arranged your stay before arrival and have a letter of invitation you can obtain the B4 at the point of entry: otherwise, you can obtain it within 15 days of beginning voluntary work, provided you obtained the position through official channels. The B4 can be renewed only once.

Kibbutzim and Moshavim

KIBBUTZ PROGRAMME CENTER: 18 Frishman St. (corner of Ben Yehuda St.), ☎Aviv 61030, Israel (☎03-524 8874/03-524 6156; fax 03-523 9966; e-mail kpc@vollinter.co.il; www.kibbutz.org.il). The Kibbutz Programme Center is the only office officially representing all the 250 kibbutzim. The center is responsible for their volunteers and provides for them from arrival until they leave the kibbutz.

Kibbutz Volunteers required all year round, to work 7-8 hours per day over a 6 day week. Period of work 2 months (minimum) to 6 months. Volunteers receive full board and accommodation, free laundry and £60 pocket money per month. Volunteers are also entitled to three free days of their choice days per month.

Volunteers need to pay a registration fee of £40, and be able to converse in English. To apply contact the centre with details of your name and date of birth, date of arrival, passport number and a covering letter describing yourself.

Applications are accepted all year round, but apply at least one week in advance of your arrival in Israel.

KIBBUTZ REPRESENTATIVES: 16 Accommodation Road, Golders Green, London NW11 8EP (☎020-8458 9235; 020-8455 7930; e-mail: enquiries@kibbutz.org.il). Has sent volunteers to Kibbutzim for over thirty years; offer full orientation, flexible of group or individual placement, and post departure care.
Working Visitors to learn the way of kibbutz life and its various aspects. Minimum stay 8 weeks; maximum stay 8 months. Accommodation, food, entertainment and occasional short trips arranged free in return for working 8 hours a day, 6 days a week, with a 3-day break in addition each month. Age 18-45 years. Medical certificate and two character references required. Informal interview and full orientation given, plus choice of group or individual travel.
Working Hebrew Scheme: as above but with chance to learn some Hebrew, with a 36 hour working week and 12 hours per week of Hebrew lessons; the course lasts for 3 months. Places are limited. Cost £175 plus approx. £10 for books.
Send s.a.e to above address for application forms and further information.

Voluntary Work and Archaeology

DEPARTMENT OF CLASSICAL STUDIES: ☎Aviv University, Ramat Aviv, ☎Aviv, Israel (fax 3-6406243; e-mail: fischer@post.tau.ac.il; www.tau.ac.il/~yavneyam). Since 1992 five seasons of archaeological excavations have been carried out at the ancient port site of Yavneh Yam, with the help of hundreds of volunteers from about ten countries, offering them an unique possibility of both reconstructing the past and encountering the complexity of modern Israeli society. The participation fee of £470 for two weeks includes a full board accommodation at the modern Youth Village 'Ayanoth', a lecture series on archaeology, geography and history of the Holy Land, field trips, a wonderful swimming pool, the blue Mediterranean...
Volunteers (up to 40) needed to take part in **archaeological excavations**. Volunteers are recruited for two-week periods in July and August; it is possible to stay for more than one period. Volunteers must pay for their own food and accommodation (cost around £470 per two week period). Applicants should speak English, French or German: previous archaeological experience is an advantage but not essential.
For further details *contact* Prof. Moshe Fischer at the above address.

ELI SHENHAV: JNF: 11 Zvi Shapira Street, ☎Aviv, Israel.
Volunteers (17) to work on an **excavation of a Roman theatre** three miles from Caesarea, a Roman Theatre in Shuni. Working hours are from 5.30am-noon, 5 days per week. Minimum period of work 1 week in July and August. Board and accommodation provided for around £10 per day.
For further details *contact* Eli Shenhav at the above address.

FRIENDS OF ISRAEL EDUCATIONAL FOUNDATION 'BRIDGE PROGRAMME': P.O.Box 7545, London NW2 2QZ (fax 020-7794 0291; e-mail info@foi-asg.org). A British foundation established to promote an understanding of the geographies, histories, cultures and peoples of Israel, and to forge working links between the UK and Israel.
Scholarships are offered to 12 British applicants per year to enable them to take part in **kibbutz work and community action and do some teaching in a developing town.** The scholarships cover travel, insurance, board and lodging: there is no pay.

5-6 hours per day, 6 days per week between February and August. Applicants should be resident in the UK, prepared to work hard and to show initiative.

Applications, enclosing a stamped addressed envelope or an International Reply Coupon, must be made to the above address by 1 July for the following year.

ISRAEL YOUTH HOSTEL ASSOCIATION: c/o Youth Travel Bureau, 1 Shezer Street, P.O. Box 6001, Jerusalem 91060, Israel (☎972-2-655 84 00: fax 972-2-655 84 32; e-mail: iyha@netvision.net.il; http://youth-hostels.org.il).
Volunteers interested in **working in a youth hostel in Israel** should write to the hostels directly.

Apply to hostels directly: a list of youth hostels is available from the association at the above address.

UNIPAL: BCM Unipal, London WC1N 3XX (tel/fax 01227-272590; e-mail unipal1@hotmail.com). Written enquiries preferred. Unipal (Universities' Trust for Educational Exchange with Palestinians) runs a summer programme of **teaching in the West Bank, Gaza and Lebanon**.
Volunteers to teach children, aged 12-15 from mid-July to mid-August. Volunteers must be native English speakers, based in the UK and at least 20 years old. Cost approx. £380.

Closing date for *applications* is the end of February.

WEIZMANN INSTITUTE OF SCIENCE: P.O.Box 26, Rehovot 76100, Israel (fax 972-8-9344492; e-mail greta1.rosenberg@weizmann.ac.il; www.weizmann.ac.il/acadsec/students.shtml).
Undergraduate Research Students to join a research project involving the Life Sciences, Chemistry, Physics and Mathematics and Computer Science. A small stipend is provided. Projects last for between 10 weeks and 4 months in the summer. Applicants must have finished at least 1 year at university and have some research experience.

Application forms are available on the Internet at the Weizmann Institute homepage (www.weizmann.ac.il/acadsec/students.shtml) and should be sent to the Academic Affairs Office the Summer Program for undergraduate students, at the above address; they must arrive by 31 December, of each year.

YOUTH TRAVEL BUREAU: 1 Shazer Street, P.O. Box 6001, Jerusalem 91060, Israel (☎972-2-655 84 00: fax 972-2-655 84 32; e-mail: iyha@iyha.org.il; http://youth-hostels.org.il). Can help groups of Youth Hostel Association members to participate either in archaeological excavations for a minimum period of 2 weeks, or help individuals volunteer in the hostels (for room and board and pocket money) for a minimum of 2 months.

Apply to the above address for details.

Kenya

Chances of finding a paid summer job in Kenya are minimal, but there are opportunities to participate in voluntary work with the following organisations. In addition, Concordia and UNA Exchange can place British, and Service Civil International, American nationals in voluntary work in Kenya: see the *Worldwide* chapter for details.

KENYA VOLUNTARY DEVELOPMENT ASSOCIATION: PO Box 48902, GPO Nairobi, Kenya (tel/fax 254-02-225379, or 254-02-247393; e-mail kvdakenya@yahoo.com).

Volunteers to work on projects in remote villages aimed at improving amenities in Kenya's rural and needy areas, working alongside members of the local community. The work may involve **digging foundations, building, making building blocks, roofing, awareness campaigns etc.** Short-term camps take place in January, April, June, July, August, November and December, and there are normally 20-25 volunteers per camp with six hours of work per day, six days per week. The long-term programmes take place all year round, entailing placements of three or more months, in Kenyan communities on a professional basis as social workers, agriculturalists etc.

Accommodation is normally provided in school classrooms or similar buildings; foreign participants are expected to adapt to local types of foods, etc. The camps normally last for 2 or 3 weeks. Minimum age 18. There is a registration fee to be paid on arrival, of approximately £130/£220 for July and August.

For *further details* send three International Reply Coupons to the Director at the above address.

TAITA DISCOVERY CENTRE: The Tsavo Kasiagu Wildlife Corridor, PO Box 48019, Nairobi, Kenya, (☎254-2-331191 or 254-2-222075; fax 254-2-330698 or 254-2-216528; e-mail tsavo@savannahcamps.com / eaos@africaonline.co.ke; www.savannahcamps.com/tdc). Surrounding the unique Mount Kasigau are a number of relatively small and isolated rural communities. With the assistance of The African Wildlife Foundation's programme, these communities have committed themselves to participating in a conservation project to retain the unparalleled biodiversity of the region and preserve its currently untouched landscape.

Volunteers (max 20 at any time) live in basic conditions in the village, and are left to complete their chosen projects independently, although support is available 'on request' and in an emergency.

Community Service Projects Teachers needed for art, music, sport and drama.

Community Based Micro Enterprises Projects to develop the use of edible and useful plants of the bush, develop herbal remedies, develop a Bonsai tree enterprise. There are also projects in elephant dung paper and products, and aquaculture, sericulture and apiculture enterprise.

Conservation Data Collection Volunteers to take part in data collection, inventories of invertebrates, birds, plants, etc. Volunteers also needed for ecological plot sampling and behavioural studies of birds.

Other Projects include putting oral accounts of the Taita people onto paper, rural health programmes, primary school infrastructure development, economic studies and the development of alternative fuels.

Projects costs start at US$177 per person per week, plus the cost of getting to/from Tsavo. Minimum stay 4 weeks. In each week, volunteers will spend 5 nights working on community projects from their base at the Kasigau Bandas. The concept here is that the biggest threat to wilderness and wildlife in Africa is that of local people. Conservation is not only about looking after animals - but is also about changing attitudes, habits and concepts of the local people. By addressing the communities needs we should inherently affect the various conservation issues. Then for the balancing 2 nights per week volunteers can if they wish go over to The Taita Discovery Centre for a bit of recreational game viewing, and possibly participate in the wildlife conservation and research activities.

Contact the above address for further details.

Madagascar

Opportunities for paid temporary work in Madagascar are rare. The following organisation can arrange voluntary placements there.

AZAFADY: Studio 7, 1A Beethoven Street, London W10 4LG (☎020-8960 6629; fax 020-8962 0126; e-mail mark@azafady.org; www.madagascar.co.uk).
Azafady is a registered UK charity and Malagasy NGO working to alleviate poverty, improve well-being and preserve beautiful, unique environments in southeast Madagascar. Has an award-winning team that works alongside rural communities on integrated conservation and development projects helping communities to build a better future for themselves.
Pioneer Madagascar is a ten-week volunteer scheme, run by Azafady, departing four times a year in January, April, July and October. Pioneers gain first hand experience of frontline development and conservation work. Volunteers live work and travel in one of the most beautiful and remote parts of southeast Madagascar. Living under canvas with basic facilities, the types of projects that pioneers will be involved with include: **building wells to provide clean water which helps protect villagers from cholera, monitoring endemic and endangered lemur species; assisting with GPS and other data-collection for forest management plans or establishing community market gardens and beehives to improve nutrition and provide villagers with alternative incomes.**

As part of the scheme, volunteers are asked to raise through fundraising a minimum donation of £2000. This goes directly to support Azafady's charitable work, with only a small portion used to cover the volunteers' food, safe water, in-country travel, orientation and language training. Full support and advice is given to applicants on fundraising, international travel, visas, insurance and medical preparations before the expedition. Groups of 10-15 pioneers are accompanied by dedicated staff whilst in Madagascar. Pioneer is open to people over 18 of reasonable fitness. No special qualifications needed, but enthusiasm and flexibility to take part in ongoing projects is essential.

For more information and an *application form* visit www.madagascar.co.uk or call the London office.

Morocco

Work permits are necessary for employment in Morocco: they are generally only given to people who speak French and/or Arabic, and have some particular skill or qualification that is in demand (e.g. teaching or IT).

There are, however, possibilities of seasonal work in the expanding tourist industry, especially around the resorts of Agadir, Marrakesh and Tangier. Several European holiday companies operate in Morocco and employ summer staff. Knowledge of French will normally be expected: this is also the language most likely to be used in voluntary workcamps, although English should be understood.

In addition to the voluntary opportunities listed below, Concordia, International Voluntary Service, Youth Action for Peace and UNA Exchange can help UK nationals, and the CIEE and Service Civil International Americans, find voluntary work in Morocco: see the *Worldwide* chapter for details. Students can arrange places in work camps listed.

RED TAPE, VISAS & WORK PERMITS

Visa Requirements: a visa is not required by citizens of most Western European countries, Australia, Canada, New Zealand and the United States if they are entering Morocco as tourists for up to 3 months.

Residence Permits: those planning a stay of over three months must register with the police and be able to provide evidence of how they are supporting themselves.

Work Permit: any foreigner taking up paid employment in Morocco must have a valid work permit: this will be obtained by the prospective employer from the Ministry of Labour (or by applying directly to the Ministry of Labour if self-employed). Work permits (*Contrats de Travail*) can be obtained while in Morocco if a job is found.

Au Pair: not customary.

Voluntary Work: a foreigner does not need a work permit or special visa in order to take part in an organised voluntary work project in Morocco providing (a) the scheme lasts for less than three months and (b) the work is unpaid.

Voluntary Work

LES AMIS DES CHANTIERS INTERNATIONAUX DE MEKNES: PO Box 8, 50001 Meknes, Morocco (fax +212-5-517772; e-mail acim-b@hotmail.com). International non-profit making organisation.

Volunteers and professionals are needed to take part in work camps throughout Morocco from July-August. Minimum period of work 3 weeks. The aim of A.C.I.M is heightening **awareness of conservation projects through workshops, guided tours, lectures, courses and architectural and archaeological workcamps.** Activities are aimed at 17-35 year olds. Volunteers are insured by the organisation when they are in the camp.

Applications to Zouhir Ouzzine, General Secretary, at the above address.

ASSOCIATION DES CHANTIERS DES JEUNES (ACJ): B.P. 171, Salé Medina, 11005 Morocco (tel/fax +212 3785; e-mail acj.ong.maroc@caramail.com).

Founded in 1967, ACJ is a not-for-profit organisation that works to safeguard the environment, incorporates youth into the social and cultural life of the area, development of the rural regions, restoration of monuments, to institute peace and cooperation between people without distinction of their religion, race or colour.

ACJ places about 400 volunteers annually. The types of work done by volunteers include assisting with **children's activities, restoration of monuments, maintenance work, etc**. There are also courses in ceramics, and other Moroccan handicrafts and language. Volunteers should be over 18. Workcamps last from one to three weeks and participants are from many countries. Volunteers pay a participation fee which covers board and lodging. There are about 90 volunteers per camp.

Apply direct to ACJ at the above address.

CHANTIERS SOCIAUX MAROCAINS: BP 456, Rabat, Morocco (☎07-79 13 70).

CSM organises workcamps in Morocco which concentrate on **projects intended to benefit the local community.** About 300 volunteers a year are involved, spending two or three weeks of the summer on the sites with fellow workers from many European and African countries.

Applicants should be between 18 and 30 years old, and in good health. Food and accommodation are provided, but the volunteer is responsible for all his or her personal expenses.

Those interested can either *apply through* their national branch of the CCIVS (which is International Voluntary Service in Britain), or directly to the President at the above address.

MOUVEMENT TWIZA: A.M.T, 23, Rue Echiguer Hammandi, Hay Salam B.P. 77, 15000 Khemisset, Morocco.

Mouvement Twiza organises weekend and summer work camps for volunteers in Morocco. It recruits about 500 volunteers per year to participate in a range of **socio-cultural activities including work in the slums and in schools and construction work.**

Applicants of any nationality are accepted, but volunteers must speak French and English, and preferably be outgoing and sociable. The minimum age limit is 18 years of age, and applicants must be healthy, willing and able. Volunteers are required in the summer for a maximum of three weeks. Accommodation is provided but pocket money is not.

Those interested should *write to the above address*.

Nigeria

Opportunities for paid temporary work in Nigeria are rare. The following organisation can arrange voluntary placements there.

NIGERIAN CONSERVATION FOUNDATION (NCF): Lekki Conservation Centre, Km 19, Lagos-Epe Expressway, PO Box 74638, Victoria Island, Lagos, Nigeria, West Africa (☎+234-1 2642498; fax +234-1 2642497; e-mail ncf@hyperia.com; www.ncf-nigeria.org).

NCF promotes **conservation through the management of protected areas,** advocacy, research and education. Volunteers not only assist in these areas but with **publications, communications and fund-raising** too. The period for which the volunteer stays and time of year is flexible. Command of English is essential; knowledge of a Nigerian language and/or French is a distinct advantage. Volunteers must be in good health. A monthly allowance adequate for sustenance is provided but volunteers must pay their own accommodation costs.

NCF produces a variety of publications a list of which can be found on their website.

Applications to the Principal Manager – Education Unit at the above address.

VOLUNTARY WORKCAMPS ASSOCIATION OF NIGERIA:, G.P.O. Box 2189, Lagos, Nigeria (☎01-821568).

VWAN organises workcamps centred on community projects for youths of different cultural backgrounds and nationalities throughout Nigeria. Between 120 and 150 volunteers per year participate in the workcamps; the work is mainly unskilled manual labour. This includes **bricklaying, carpentry, sport, games, excursions, debates and discussions.** VWAN also undertakes short and medium term programmes in the year.

Applicants of any nationality are welcome, but a knowledge of English is required. Volunteers must also be physically fit. The usual length of placement is between one and two months (i.e. July to September). Volunteers must pay a registration fee of approx £130 while feeding, board and lodging are provided for selected volunteers throughout the duration of the camps.

There is a charge of $20 for an application form, brochure and placement for the camps. Only applications received with the prescribed fee before the month of May will be treated each year.

Applications to the Secretary General at the above address.

Sierra Leone

The following organisation can arrange voluntary placements in the Sierra Leone.

PA SANTIGIE CONTEH FARMER'S ASSOCIATION (PASCOFAAS): PMB 686 Freetown, Republic of Sierra Leone, West Africa (☎+232-22 228568; fax +232-22 224439; e-mail cbau@Sierratel.SL).

PASCOFAAS is centred around Makarie and over 20 neighbouring villages in the Bombali district, and was founded in 1982 to promote increased agricultural productivity for food production and income generation in order to improve the living conditions of its approximately 2,000 members with special attention to women, children and young people.

Activities undertaken include agriculture, the planting of rice and trees, construction of houses, roads and so on. Opportunities open to volunteers include **secretarial work** in the head office, **agricultural and construction work and training local people in different skills**.

All nationalities may apply as long as they speak English. They are required all year round for periods of two weeks to two years. Up to 20 international volunteers are taken on at a time. Preference will be given to volunteers who are willing to help programmes either financially or with materials. The minimum age is 17. Expenses and pocket money are not paid but accommodation is provided. The Association also supplies information to anyone interested in farming in rural areas of Sierra Leone.

For *further details* about this or the voluntary work, contact Andrew Conteh, the Director, at the above address.

South Africa

The government is (understandably) not keen to hand out work permits to Europeans and other nationalities when so many of their own nationals are unemployed. Work permits are granted only in instances where South African citizens or permanent residents are not available for appointment or cannot be trained for the position. The weakness of the rand has lead to a 'brain drain' out of the country and positions exist for professionals.

Most people who do casual work have only a three-month tourist visa, which must be renewed before it expires. A 90-day extension can be obtained from the Department of Home Affairs in Johannesburg or Cape Town for a fee. After you have done this a few times, the authorities will become suspicious.

One solution to the problem is to consider BUNAC's work and travel programme in South Africa. Full-time students and recent graduates under the age of 27 may be eligible for a 12-month working holiday permit (see entry).

Voluntary work is organised for British citizens in South Africa by UNA Exchange and Youth Action for Peace. See their entries in the *Worldwide* chapter for details. Work can be found in South Africa through the two organisations below.

FOREIGN PLACEMENTS CC: P.O. Box 912, Somerset West 7129, South Africa (☎04457-7677; fax 04455-32680).
The agency Foreign Placements can arrange **short-term casual work** in South Africa as well as contracts for **medical staff and skilled workers.**
For details *contact* the above address.

WORK SOUTH AFRICA/VOLUNTEER SOUTH AFRICA: BUNAC, 16, Bowling Green Lane, London EC1R OQH (☎020-7251 3472; fax 020-7251 0215; e-mail volunteer@bunac.org.uk; www.bunac.org).
BUNAC administer the *Work South Africa* programme that enables students who are to graduate this year and who are aged under 27 to take up legally any job anywhere in South Africa: BUNAC can provide help in arranging work on arrival. Many participants work in hotels and restaurants or in jobs within the tourist industry. Many also take up shop-based or office work or community developmental work. The work visa is valid for up to 12 months and departures from the UK are in July, October. BUNAC arranges flights, visas, insurance and the first six nights' accommodation.
BUNAC has also offers the new placement programme, *Volunteer South Africa,* which enables applicants with suitable skills to become involved with volunteer projects in one of four main areas: the environment; tourism; education; and social welfare. Placements last for two months and accommodation and meals are included in the programme fee: participants may then stay for another month in South Africa travelling. Departures are available on a year-round basis.
For further details *contact* BUNAC at the above address or visit their website www.bunac.org.

Voluntary Work and Archaeology

CONCORDIA: Heversham House, 20-22 Boundary Road, Hove, East Sussex BN3 4ET (☎01273-422218; fax 01273-421182; e-mail info@concordia-iye.org.uk; www.concordia-iye.org.uk).
Concordia's International Volunteer Programme offers 20-30 year olds the opportunity to join an international team of volunteers working on community-based projects ranging from **nature and wildlife conservation, restoration and construction, to art/culture and social projects including work with adults or children with special needs, children's play schemes and teaching.** Projects last for 2-4 weeks and run year round.
Generally no skills or experience are needed, although Concordia runs a preparation weekend for applicants. Volunteers pay a registration fee of approx. £250 depending on the country and fund their own travel. Board and accommodation are free of charge.
For more information *write to the above address* enclosing an s.a.e., or e-mail.

SANCCOB – THE SOUTH AFRICAN NATIONAL FOUNDATION FOR THE CONSERVATION OF COASTAL BIRDS: P.O. Box 11116, Bloubergrant 7443, Cape Town, South Africa (☎+27-21-557 6155; fax 21-557 8804; e-mail sanccob@netactive.co.za; www.sanccob.co.za).

Volunteers required to help with the cleaning and rehabilitation of oil-soaked coastal birds. The main tasks involve **keeping the hospital clean (scrubbing pools and pens), feeding the birds and checking that the centre is prepared for a major oil spill.** The coastal waters of South Africa are a major shipping route and oil pollution is a recurrent problem, the main bird types dealt with are African penguins, gulls, gannets, tern and cormorants.

Volunteers must be willing to work in hard conditions with wild and difficult birds. Help is given with finding Bed & Breakfast accommodation and volunteers must meet their own living costs (approx. US$30-40). The period May-October is the busiest but spills can happen at any time, the minimum stay is two weeks and applicants must be at least 16 years old.

To apply contact SANCCOB at the above address.

Tanzania

In addition to the following entry, Concordia and UNA Exchange can offer short-term volunteer projects to Britons wishing to work in Tanzania for a few months, while Americans may be able to apply through Service Civil International; their entries in the *Worldwide* chapter give more details.

VOLUNTEER AFRICA: PO Box 24 Bakewell Derbyshire DE45 1TA (www.vo lunteerafrica.org). Providing support to a community-based organisation working in the Singida and Tabora Regions of Tanzania, VolunteerAfrica is run entirely by volunteers to keep down running costs.

Volunteers to spend one, two or three months **living and working alongside villagers on locally initiated projects such as the building of new schools or village health centres.**

The cost of participating during 2004 is up to £2,500 which consists of £650 for training, food, accommodation and travel costs in Tanzania, £1,000 towards the cost of the projects, a maximum of £250 towards UK administration costs and approximately £600 for flights and insurance.

Applicants must be aged 18 or over when they are due to travel overseas and *applications can only be made through the organisation's website.*

Togo

Apart from obtaining a voluntary work place through UNA Exchange (see *Worldwide* chapter for details), the following organisations can provide voluntary work opportunities in Togo.

JEUNESSE EN ACTION: S/C WWOOF-TOGO, B.P. 25 Agou Nyogbo, Togo (☎+228-471030; fax +228-471012; e-mail wwooftogo@hotmail.com). Jeunesse en Action is a non-profit making organisation, aiming to bring young people together while carrying out reforestation and conservation work.

Volunteers required for **workcamps** in Togo, between July-August and August-September. Camps cost approx. £60 which covers board and lodging. Volunteers must speak French.

Applications are invited all year, although for the summer camps the deadline for applications is 30 June; to obtain further information send two International Reply Coupons to S. Y. Agbeko at the above address; information on these camps can also be obtained from MOACTIMO, Annie Jossaume le Bessin, F-50510 Cerences, France (fax +33-2-33 51 94 30).

WWOOF-TOGO: B.P. 25 Agou Nyogbo, Togo (☎+228-471030; fax +228-471012; e-mail wwooftogo@hotmail.com).
Part of the worldwide organisation of organic farms WWOOF-TOGO can provide information on organic farms in Togo and West Africa, in return for two International Reply Coupons.
    Contact the above address.

Uganda

The following organisation can arrange voluntary placements in the Uganda.

UGANDA VOLUNTEERS FOR PEACE (UVP): P.O. Box 3312 Kampala, Uganda (☎+256-77 402201; fax +256-41 349203; e-mail uvpeace@yahoo.com).
UVP works towards peace, development and much needed solidarity in Uganda. It organises international **work camps** in January, March, April, June, August, October and December for 3-week periods. Age limits 15-35 years. Languages required: English, Swahili and French. Accommodation is provided free. There is a participation fee of US$200 and international membership costs US$100 per year.
    Further details from the above address.

The Americas

Canada

The employment of foreigners in either short or long term work in Canada is strictly regulated. Even with Canada's relatively strong economy (unemployment currently at 8%), it is illegal to work in Canada without a work permit; with some exceptions, a job must be obtained from outside the country, and even then the employer will face difficulty in obtaining permission to employ you unless they can show that they are not depriving a Canadian citizen or permanent resident of the job.

Anyone seeking employment in Canada should write directly to Canadian employers before arrival to enquire about employment prospects. Information on jobs in Canada can also be obtained by reviewing Canadian newspapers or trade journals, which are available at larger newsagents. Addresses of potential employers can also be found in the *Canadian Trade Index* or the *Canadian Almanac and Directory*, both of which can be found at large libraries.

Teachers from British Commonwealth nations may be able to arrange exchange placements by contacting The League for the Exchange of Commonwealth Teachers, Commonwealth House, 7 Lion Yard, Tremadoc Road, London SW4 7NQ (☎020-7819 3938; fax 020-7720 5403; e-mail emily-ann.bowden@lect.org.uk; www.lect.org.uk).

To work legally in Canada, you must obtain a Work Permit from a Canadian High Commission or Embassy before you leave your home country. The Canadian government offers in the neighbourhood of 17,000 Work Permits each year to full-time students to work temporarily in Canada. Participants in the official work exchange must be aged 18-30 years and must have proof that they will be returning to a tertiary level course of study on their return to the UK.

Interested students should check the website www.canada.org.uk/visa-info or obtain the general leaflet 'Student Temporary Employment in Canada' by sending a large s.a.e. with a £1 stamp and marked 'SGWHP' in the top right-hand corner to the Canadian High Commission (Immigration Visa Information, 38 Grosvenor St, London W1K 4AA; 09068-616644 60p a minute). Students who already have a job offer from a Canadian employer may be eligible for 'Programme A'. They can apply directly to the High Commission in London for a Work Permit (reference 1102) which will be valid for a maximum of 12 months and is not transferable to any other job.

The other and more flexible possibility is to obtain an Open Work Permit through BUNAC (see Worldwide). BUNAC's *Work Canada* programme offers about 1,500 students (including gap year students with a university place and finalists with proof that they will return to the UK) the chance to go to Canada for up to a year and take whatever jobs they can find. Students on this programme can depart at any time between February and December. The great majority of participants go to Canada without a pre-arranged job and spend their first week or two job-hunting.

Concordia arrange voluntary placements in Canada, and UNA Exchange can organise voluntary work in French-speaking Quebec; the CIEE can arrange voluntary work in Canada for Americans. For details of all these see the *Worldwide* chapter.

RED TAPE, VISAS & WORK PERMITS

Visa Requirements: citizens of the United Kingdom and most other countries in Western Europe, of UK dependent territories, Australia, New Zealand, the United States and Mexico do not normally require a visa for a visit to Canada. Citizens of other countries may need to obtain one. No matter what the length or purpose of the proposed stay, permission to enter and remain in Canada must be obtained from the Immigration Officer at the port of entry. If the purpose is any other than purely for a tourist visit to Canada, you should consult the Canadian High Commission or Embassy abroad before departure.

The length of stay in Canada is decided at the port of entry. Normally entry is granted for six months.

Work Permit: authorises an individual to work 'at a specific job for a specific period of time for a specific employer'. It must be applied for before arrival. Some details of the Work Permits available through BUNAC (16 Bowling Green Lane, London EC1R 0QH; ☎020-7251 3472; www.bunac.org.uk) are given above.

Student General Working Holiday Programs : see www.canada.org.uk. are open to full-time students aged 18-30 from the UK, Ireland, Sweden and Finland. Citizens of the latter four countries can apply directly to the immigration section of their local embassy, providing a letter of university acceptance and a letter confirming return to studies or proof that they have completed their studies within the previous 12 months and sufficient funds must be proven for voluntary work). Citizens of the UK, Ireland, Sweden and Finland can also make applications through local organisations: these are BUNAC for the UK (see above); CIMO PO Box 343 Hakaniemenkatu 2 SF 00531, Helsinki (www.cimo.fi) for Finland; and The International Employment Office, Kristinegatan 21, SE 791 60 Falum, Sweden (☎46 23 93700) for Sweden.

General Working Holiday Program: Irish non-students aged 18-35 may be eligible for a 12-month working holiday permit. All enquiries from Irish citizens should be directed through USIT (9 Aston Quay, O'Connell Bridge, Dublin 2; ☎+353 1 677 8117).

Student Work Abroad Program (SWAP) is available to full time students aged 18-30 from Australia and New Zealand and is co-ordinated through STA (travel) offices in Australia and New Zealand. Prospective SWAP applicants must contact the STA office for information on the programme for that year.

Voluntary Work: a special category of work permit covers voluntary work which takes about two to four months to process if you have found a placement through a recognised charitable or religious organisation.

Agricultural Work

WILLING WORKERS ON ORGANIC FARMS (CANADA): 4429 Carlson Road, Nelson, British Columbia, Canada VIL 6X3 (tel/fax 250-354 4417; e-mail ; wwoofcan@shaw.ca; www.wwoof.ca). Hundreds of young people, from 30 different countries, every year go 'wwoofing' in Canada. Hosts available from the east to the west coast of Canada.

Volunteers to work on 450 organic farms in Canada ranging from small homesteads to large farms. Duties include general farm work and may include going to market, working with horses, garden work, milking goats, etc. No pocket money but board and lodging provided free of charge. Opportunites may be available all year round. Minimum age 16. Only EEA nationals with valid tourist visas need apply.

Applications, enclosing c.$30 (cash) for postage for a farm list and description booklet, should be sent to the above address.

Voluntary Work and Archaeology

FRONTIERS FOUNDATION/OPERATION BEAVER: 2615 Danforth Avenue, Suite 203, Toronto, Ontario, Canada M4C 1L6 (☎416-690-3930; fax 416-690-3534; e-mail frontiersfoundation@on.aibn.com; www.frontiersfoundation.org). Frontiers Foundation is a non-profit voluntary service organisation supporting the advancement of economically and socially disadvantaged communities in Canada and overseas.

Volunteers are recruited from across the world to serve in native and non-native communities across Canada for a variety of **community construction and recreation projects.** The organisation works in partnership with requesting communities in low-income rural areas. Projects help to provide and improve housing, to provide training and economic incentives and to offer recreational/educational activities in developing regions.

Volunteers must be 18 or older and available for a minimum period of 12 weeks. Skills in carpentry, electrical work and plumbing are preferred for construction projects; previous social service and experience with children are sought for recreational/educational projects. The greatest need for volunteers is in June, July and August. Group size is usually between 2 and 8.

All accommodation, food and travel, within Canada is provided. Travel to and from Canada is the responsibility of the volunteer. Accommodation is normally provided by the community; volunteers must be prepared to live without electricity, running water or roads in some communities. Long term placements of up to 18 months are possible provided that the volunteer's work is deemed satisfactory after the initial 12 week period.

Application kits and information are available from the above address; please provide 3 International Reply Coupons; once an applicant has sent in application forms there can be a delay of 3-12 weeks as references come in and possible placements are considered. Acceptance cannot be guaranteed.

Other Employment in Canada

INTERNSHIP CANADA PROGRAMME: CIEE (Council on International Educational Exchange) 52 Poland Street, London W1F 7AB (tel: 020-7478 2020; fax 020-7734 7322; e-mail infouk@councilexchanges.uk; www.ciee.org.uk). Assisting over 1500 students undertake practical training in North America each year, CIEE is a worldwide organisation helping people develop skills and acquire knowledge for working in a multicultural, interdependent world.

The programme enables students who hold *British or Irish passports* to complete a period of work experience of up to one year in Canada. Minimum age 18. Applicants must be enrolled in full-time further or higher education (HND level or above) or a recent graduate within 12 months of finishing, or a gap year student with an unconditional offer of a university place. Before applying applicants must have secured a full-time work placement in Canada directly related to their studies.

Programme costs start at £200 for a two month stay and particpants must have CIEE insurance cover for the length of their stay. Official documentation and assistance with visa application are provided, as are orientation materials covering taxes, housing, Canadian culture and transportation; plus 24-hour emergency assistance with any problems whilst in Canada.

Applications can be made at any time of year, but should be made at least two months before the desired date of departure.

KING'S ENGLISH LANGUAGE SCHOOLS: 58 Braidley Road, Bournemouth, Dorset BH2 6LD, UK (☎01202-293535; fax 01202-293922; e-mail info@kingsschool.co.uk/info@kingsschool.uk.com; www.kings-group.co.uk). Leading English language schools in Canada, Thailand and England.
English as a Foreign Language Teachers. Suitable qualifications will be expected.

Applications should be made to Danielle Watts or the Marketing Department at the above address.

WORK CANADA: BUNAC, 16 Bowling Green Lane, London EC1R 0QH (☎020-7251 3472; e-mail canada@bunac.org.uk).
There are approximately 1,500 places on the Work Canada programme for full-time students (degree, HND, NVQ 4/5 or those in a gap year with a confirmed place for the following Autumn). The Work Authorisation is valid for one year and enables participants to work and travel anywhere in Canada. You can apply either with
    (1) a definite job offer plus $600 support funds
    (2) a letter of sponsorship from a Canadian citizen plus support funds of $600, or
    (3) $1,000 support funds only.
Approximately 90% of participants go to Canada without a pre-arranged job and take an average of six days to find one. BUNAC also offers advice on job-hunting, various travel deals and on-going support services whilst in Canada.

For *further details* contact the above address or visit the website www.bunac.org.

Colombia

The following organisation has vacancies for suitably qualified employees in Colombia.

CENTRO COLOMBO AMERICANO: Cra. 45 No. 53-24, Medellín, Colombia (☎574-513-4444; fax 574-513-2666; e-mail lshem@colomboworld.com; www.colomboworld.com).
TEFL Teachers (140) in the programme, preference of nationality: U.S., Canadian or British. Six US/UK teachers hired. Other countries also welcome, conditions may vary. Applicants must have BA or MA (Education, Language teaching, TESOL, TEFL or related qualifications). Teachers are employed on one-year contract (renewable), 30 contact hours per week including Saturdays. English for children and adults. Salary: 1,500,000 2,200,000 pesos (£445-£535 approx.) per month, plus round trip ticket and all visa expenses paid. Assistance in finding housing. Pre-service and in-service training provided. Medical benefits and Spanish lessons provided.

Candidates should *apply directly to the school*, selection is made through references and phone interview. Send CV and three letters of recommendation to Lai Yin Shem, Academic Director.

Costa Rica

Under Costa Rican law it is illegal for foreigners to be offered paid work, but the organisations listed in this chapter offer voluntary work. US nationals may be able to obtain voluntary work through the CIEE allowing for yearly changes in their project planning. Britons may find opportunities arranged by UNA Exchange.

AGROPECURIA BALVE S.A.: Am hohlen Stein 54, D-58802 Balve, Germany (tel/fax +49-2375 21 70).
or Finca Bella Vista, Raizal Colorado de Abangares, Guanacaste, Costa Rica (☎+506-6780464; fax +506-6780467; e-mail: balvesa@racsa.co.cr; http: /homepages.compuserve.de/RicaUrlaub).
Volunteers are needed to help run and work on a tropical ecological farm in Costa Rica. Typical work duties include **small-scale agriculture, gardening, construction, carpentry, fishing and maintenance work.** Relevant skills and experience are useful, but not essential, though it is recommended that volunteers have some basic knowledge of Spanish. An interest in ecology and biological farming is a plus. Applicants over 16 years are accepted. The minimum stay is one month, and there is no upper limit.

Volunteers are expected to pay $100 a week to cover food and lodging in rooms usually rented to tourists. Wages cannot be paid, but volunteers can enjoy a lot of privileges like use of the swimming pool, horse or cycle riding, excursions, and working and living with Costaricans to learn Spanish rapidly. Those wishing to learn Spanish whilst they are there are encouraged to apply.

Those interested should *contact* Rudolf Micknass, President, at the above address, preferably by e-mail. Alternatively, contact Am Hohlen Stein 54, D-58802 Balve, Germany (tel/fax 0049 2375-2170). Please note only Spanish speakers should telephone the Costa Rica number.

IYOK AMI: P.O. Box 335-2100, San José, Costa Rica, Central America. (☎+506-387-2238 or +506-254-1822 (Spanish is preferred); fax 506-771-200 or 506-223-1609; e-mail iyokbosque@yahoo.es or ciprotur@rasca.co.cr; www.ecotourism.co.cr/iyokami).
An extensive private reserve that includes both tropical cloud and tropical rain forests, and an Indian reserve. These wild areas have been set aside to protect flora, fauna and water resources, and also to serve as areas of scientific and research study.
Volunteers' help is needed to **build and maintain trails** and for **reforestation, help with labelling and transplantation of flowering plants around the trails, making topographical and pictorial maps of the area, constructing signposts, teaching English in schools, protecting and stimulating the Quetzal bird reproduction.** Volunteers also help with the **classification of plants, birds and fungi,** and other work depending on the volunteer's interest and specialist knowlege.

Volunteers will receive a free daily hour of basic Spanish teaching. Anyone is welcome to apply. Iyok Ami is a private organisation that receives no funding and so volunteers pay $650 per month, to cover board, laundry and accommodation (overlooking the forest, the Irazu, and Turrialba volcanoes). Volunteers are expected to work five hours per day, Monday to Friday. Weekends are free for visiting other places (the beach etc.).
Applications to the above address.

RAINFOREST CONCERN: 27 Lansdowne Crescent, London, W11 2NS (☎020-7229 2093; fax 020-7221 4094; e-mail info@rainforestconcern.org; www.rainf

orestconcern.org). Rainforest Concern is a non-political charity dedicated to the conservation of vulnerable rainforest. They invite support for the sponsorship of acres of tropical rainforest and encourage volunteers to help out with research and reserve maintenance.

Turtle Monitors (20) for Costa Rica and Panama. The chief purpose of the programme is to protect the leatherback turtle. The work includes protecting the beach from egg-collecting poachers, monitoring and tagging turtles and cleaning trails. Hours of work are 8pm-4am, on a variable number of days per week, between mid-March and the end of August. Minimum period of work is 1 week. Board and lodging is provided at a cost of $116/£63 per week. No special skills are required, although Spanish would be helpful, but applicants must have a sincere interest in conservation, be over 18 and generally fit.

Applications can be sent to the above address at any time of year.

VOLUNTEER COSTA RICA: BUNAC, 16 Bowling Green Lane, London EC1R OQH (☎020-7251 3472; e-mail enquiries@bunac.org.uk).
This placement programme run by BUNAC allows participants to spend 3-6 months working as a volunteer in Costa Rica. Placements can be in areas such as **agriculture, conservation, small business development or teaching**. Accommodation is provided as part of the programme fee however participants will be expected to make a contribution towards their food costs. Applicants are expected to speak Spanish confidently to an intermediate level and must be either a current university level student or a graduate aged 18-32.

For *further details* contact BUNAC at the above address or visit www.bunac.org.

Cuba

The following organisation recruits people for a working holiday scheme in Cuba.

THE CUBA SOLIDARITY CAMPAIGN: c/o Red Rose Club, 129 Seven Sisters Road, London N7 7QG (☎020-7263 6452; fax 0207-561 0191; e-mail office@cuba-solidarity.org.uk; www.cuba-solidarity.org.uk, www.cubaconnect.co.uk). The CSC is a national membership organisation which campaigns against the US Blockade. Membership is open to all. CSC's aim is to promote friendship and solidarity between Cuba and the UK. People are encouraged to join CSC and take part in a wide range of activities.

Volunteers to take part in a scheme in Cuba involving 3 week's work on a self-contained camp near Havana. The work involves building and agricultural work. 4½ day working week, with transport to Havana provided during time off and excursions arranged on Sundays. There are many opportunities to meet Cubans, and a number of optional educational visits and lectures. Two work brigades are organised each year, one in the summer and one in the winter.

Participants must cover their own travel costs and make a contribution for accommodation, food and travel (approximate cost £800). The Campaign organises the necessary visa.

Contact the above address for application deadlines and further information.

Ecuador

As well as the following organisations, Concordia, UNA Exchange and Youth Action for Peace offer short-term International Volunteer Projects to Britons in Ecuador, while the CIEE can do the same for US citizens. See their entries in the *Worldwide* chapter for more details.

BENEDICT SCHOOLS OF LANGUAGES: PO Box 09-01-8916, Guayaquil, Ecuador (☎593-4-2444418; fax 593-4-2441642; e-mail benecent@telconet.net).
TEFL Teachers: (15) required for several schools in Guayaquil (Urdesa, Centro, Garzota, Centenario, Entrerios). Applicants should ideally be British, American, Canadian or Irish, hold a teaching certificate or college degree and be proficient in English.

Minimum period of work 6 months (two courses), although the school prefers it if teachers can stay at least 10 months. Help is given with finding accommodation and the salary is US$4.50/$5.00 per hour.

Applications accepted and work available all year round, to *apply* contact Mercedes de Elizalde, General Director at the above address.

FUNDACION GOLONDRINAS/ THE CERRO GOLONDRINAS CLOUDFOREST CONSERVATION GROUP: c/o Calle Isabel La Catòlica N24-679, Quito, Ecuador (☎593-2-2226 602; e-mail manteca@uio.satnet.net (subject: volunteer); www.ecuadorexplorer.com/golondrinas).
Volunteers required to help conserve 25,000 hectares of highland cloudforest on the western slopes of the Andes. The project's work involves the introduction of **sustainable agro-forestry techniques, soil conservation, research and the reintroduction of tree species.** Volunteers will be involved in these activities in two field sites; some general labouring also required.

Minimum stay 1 month. Some experience of horticulture/permaculture, and advanced Spanish are prerequisites, and a contribution to costs of c. $310 per month. Special financial arrangements will be made by the group for those with advanced skills in gardening, agro-forestry, permaculture and those who wish to stay more than 3 months.

Volunteers accepted all year round, but contact Fundacion at least 2+ months in advance of desired dates of placement. Volunteers must arrange their own travel, visas and field kit.

For details of work and kit requirements *contact* the above address.

RAINFOREST CONCERN: 27 Lansdowne Crescent, London, W11 2NS (☎020-7229 2093; fax 020-7221 4094; e-mail info@rainforestconcern.org; www.rainf orestconcern.org). Rainforest Concern is a non-political charity dedicated to the conservation of vulnerable rainforest. They invite support for their sponsorship of acres of forest and encourage volunteers to help out with research and reserve maintenance.
Volunteers for **reforestation/ trail maintenance and the establishment of organic agriculture** (18) required at any time. The work involves an element of monitoring and of physical labour, such as reforestation or compiling species lists, depending on the projects being undertaken at the time. Two of the current projects are in the cloud forests of western Ecuador (minimum period of work 3 days) and one is in the lowland Amazon rainforest (minimum period of work 7 days). Hours of work are flexible, and places are available all year-round. Board and lodging is provided at a

cost of $19 and $20 per day. No special skills are required, although Spanish would be helpful, but applicants must have a sincere interest in conservation, be over 18 and generally fit.

Applications can be sent to the above address at any time of year.

Mexico

Paid employment is difficult to find in Mexico and must be approved by the Mexican Government before a visa will be issued to enter Mexico. Permits are generally issued to people who are sponsored by companies in Mexico. Visitors entering Mexico as tourists are not permitted to engage in any paid activities under any circumstances.

There are a growing number of opportunities for voluntary work in Mexico. British applicants can find voluntary work in Mexico through Concordia, UNA Exchange or Youth Action for Peace, US nationals through the CIEE; see the *Worldwide* chapter for details.

AMERICAN FRIENDS SERVICE COMMITTEE: 1501 Cherry Street, Philadelphia, Pennsylvania 19102, USA.
Volunteers to work in remote rural villages in Mexico **improving and constructing schools or other community facilities and to help with agricultural projects.** Work generally lasts for 7 weeks from early July to late August. Applicants should be 18-26 years old and speak Spanish. Limited scholarships available some years. Participants are responsible for their own travel costs and must make a contribution of around $400 to cover orientation, food and accommodation and health and accident insurance

For details *American applicants* should write to the above address enclosing an international reply coupon before 1st March; *European applicants* should apply directly to SEDEPAC, Apartado Postal 27-054, 06760 Mexico DF, Mexico (fax 52-5-584 3895; e-mail sedepac@laneta.apc.org)

Please note that no paid jobs are available in Mexico or US through the AFSC or SEDEPAC.

BUSCA (BRIGADA UNIVERSITARIA DE SERVICIOS COMUNITARIOS PARA LA AUTOGESTION): Casa de la Cultura Raul Anguiano, Parque Ecologico Huayamilpas, Yaqui esq. Nezahualcoyotl s/n, Colonia Ajusco Huayamilpas, Mexico, D.F. 04390 Mexico (tel/fax 525-6 66 47 71; e-mail busca@laneta.apc.org.).
Volunteers to work with young local people in indigenous communities in Mexico **on development projects concerned with areas such as health, education, human rights, the environment, community work etc.** Volunteers live and work in teams of five or six people. No pocket money is paid, and participants must pay a fee of approx. £310 towards costs of food, accommodation and transport inside Mexico. Minimum period of work 7 weeks between 25 June and 15 August. Volunteers should be aged 18-26, must have a good knowledge of Spanish and be willing to share and exchange experiences.
Volunteers are also required to join 20 Mexicans in a 2,000 km bicycle journey across Mexico which has the objects of promoting the bicycle as a form of transport and raising funds for community development projects. Volunteers must raise sponsorship of $0.50 per km and need at least a basic knowledge of Spanish. Should be aged 17-27.

Participants must pay for their own travel to and from Mexico. *Applications* should be sent to the above address between January and May 1st.

Peru

The following organisations have vacancies for paying volunteers/suitably qualified employees in Peru.

KIYA SURVIVORS: 38 Hove Park Villas, Hove, East Sussex BN3 6HG (☎01273-721092; fax 01273-732875; e-mail jansampson@tiscali.co.uk; www.kiyasurvivors.org).
Kiya Survivors is a registered Peruvian charity set up to **help special needs children in Peru** for whom there is virtually no help. Volunteers aged from 18-80 are needed for placements of two, four or six months' duration starting in September, January and May. Cost ranges between £900 and £2,700, depending on the length of stay. On average a full placement of four months costs £2,350 and includes return flight to Lima valid for year, two nights in Lima, transfer to project, six-week Spanish course, accommodation in a volunteer family house or home, a two-day Inca trail and trip around the Sacred Valley; a horse-riding excursion and tourist ticket with access to all local ruins and museums. Volunteers buy their own insurance and food. The volunteer house has cooking facilities and local markets provide cheap fresh food.
  Contact Jan Sampson at the above address or e-mail.

TAMBOPATA JUNGLE LODGE: P.O. Box 454, Cusco, Peru (tel/fax +51-84-245695; e-mail tplcus@terra.com.pe; www.tambopatalodge).
Nature Guides to lead nature walks for tourists and accompany them during their stay at a jungle lodge in the rainforest of Southern Peru within the Tambopata National Reserve. Working hours required may be any time between 4am and 8pm, as the tour programme dictates. Those taken on will be qualified students and scientists. The exchange programmes are: people who participate in 20 days per month of guiding will receive in exchange return air travel between Lima or Cusco and Puerto Maldonado per 90 days and £100 per month, or guide 10 days per month and receive in exchange a return air ticket for each 90 days worked and the remainder of the month free for research, etc. Applicants can also combine these two programmes.
  The minimum stay is 180 days at any time of year. Applicants will ideally stay for six months, have a background in nature studies, speak English and Spanish; knowledge of French and German would be an advantage. Those interested should contact the above address including a curriculum vitae.

USA

Despite a slowing economy, relative to most other countries the USA has low unemployment and there is still a strong demand for workers to fill a wide variety of specialized summer jobs. Opportunities for summer work in the United States are so numerous that apart from those listed below, there are thousands covered in detail by a separate publication ***Summer Jobs in the USA 2004*** which lists thousands of vacancies in resorts, theatres, hotels, ranches, business, national parks, etc. throughout the USA; it also gives details on the different work visas necessary for any non-American citizen wishing to work in the USA. This book is published in the USA at $18.95 by Peterson's Guides (PO Box 67005, Laurenceville, NJ 08648-4764) and is available in Britain in good bookshops for £12.99 or (plus £1.75 postage) direct from Vacation Work (www.vacationwork.co.uk).Vacation Work also offers from Petersons the book *Internships 2004* (US price $26.95), a guide to career-related jobs for students in the USA. The UK price is £18.99 plus £3 postage.

Placing an advertisement in an American paper may lead to the offer of a job. The New York Times (www.nytimes.com) is published by A.O. Sulzberger, of 229 West 43rd Street, New York, NY10036. It has a UK office at 66 Buckingham Gate, London, SW1 6AU (☎020-7799 2981/7592 8325).

Au pairing in the US differs from au pairing in Europe since the hours are much longer and, if the au pair comes from the UK, there is no language to learn. The basic requirements are that you be between 18 and 26, speak English, show at least 200 hours of recent childcare experience and provide a criminal record check.

Voluntary work in the USA can be arranged through the Winant-Clayton Volunteer Association (entry below), Youth Action for Peace, UNA Exchange, Concordia, International Voluntary Service, the CIEE, and Service Civil International. See the *Worldwide* chapter for details.

RED TAPE, VISAS & WORK PERMITS

Visa Requirements: since the introduction of the Visa Waiver Program, the tourist visa requirement is waived in the case of 28 nationalities, including British and Australian citizen passport holders. Nationals of the 29 VWP countries may enter the U.S. for up to 90 days for tourism or business, provided they meet all of the regulations for visa free travel. Note: Certain travellers are not eligible to travel visa free, for instance those who have been arrested and/or convicted of an offence.

The Rehabilitation of Offenders Act does not apply to U.S. visa law. For a full list of the 29 visa free countries, including the criteria which must be met to travel visa free, and further information on those not eligible to travel under the VWP, contact your nearest Embassy or Consulate, or visit the Department of State's website at http://travel.state.gov.

Anyone entering the United States to work requires the appropriate work visa. Under no circumstances can a person who has entered the U.S. as a tourist take up any form of employment paid or unpaid.

Residence Permits: Anyone seeking to take up permanent residence in the U.S. requires the appropriate immigrant visa. In general immigration is family or employment based. For further information, contact your nearest Embassy or Consulate, or visit the Department of State's website as above.

Work Permits: Anyone taking up temporary employment, whether paid or unpaid, requires the appropriate work visa. There are a number of possible visas for temporary workers, au pairs, exchange visitors and cultural exchange visitors. Most of the opportunities listed in this chapter are covered by the J-1 Exchange Visitor visa, which is arranged by the organisations with entries. Employment-based H-2B visas are available through major employers of seasonal workers (as in ski resorts) only after the employer receives Labor certification from the Department of Labor (which takes 3-6 months).

Au Pair: J-1 visa available through officially approved exchange visitor programmes overseen by the Public Affairs Division of the Department of State. The au pair placement programme allows thousands of young Europeans with childcare experience to work for American families for exactly one year on a J-1 visa. They apply through a small number of sponsoring organisations (the au pair agencies) which must follow the guidelines which govern the programme, so there is not much difference between them. They will issue the IAP-66 applcation form which is sent to the Visa Branch of the US Embassy.

Voluntary Work: Individuals participating in a voluntary service program benefitting U.S. local communities, who establish that they are members of and have a commitment to a particular recognised religious or non-profit charitable organisation may, in certain cases, enter the United States with business (B-1) visas, or visa free, if eligible, provided that the work performed is traditionally done by volunteer charity workers, no salary or remuneration will be paid from a U.S. source other than an allowance or other reimbursement for expenses incidental to the stay in the United States, and they will not engage in the selling of articles and/or solicitation and acceptance of donations. Volunteers should carry with them a letter from their U.S. sponsor which contains their name and date and place of birth, their foreign permanent residence address, the name and address of their initial destination in the U.S., and the anticipated duration of the voluntary assignment.

Camp America
campamerica.co.uk

10,000 summer jobs in the U.S.A.
10 weeks travel time
Free flights, food & accommodation
Visa application support
Great C.V. builder

*Whatever your choice of work,
from summer camps to winter resorts,
Camp America has a work and travel
adventure for you.*

For your free brochure:
campamerica.co.uk
tel: 020 7581 7333

Industrial and Office Work

TREKAMERICA: PO Box 159, Rockaway, NJ, 07866, USA (☎001-973-983-1144; fax 001-973-983-8551; e-mail info@trekamerica.com; www.trekamerica.com). A small group adventure camping tour operator offering treks throughout North

America's National Parks and Indian lands.

Sales Representatives (1-2) to work inside and outside an office. Duties involve handling incoming calls, orientation for clients, greeting participants. Past sales experience and travel experience in the States is preferred. Must be friendly, and willing to do public presentations. To work 40-45 hours per five day week. Minimum of two months' work between July and September. A wage is provided but no accommodation. The successful applicant may be entitled to a free tour. No other languages required.

Applications to the above address.

Summer Camps

CAMP AMERICA: Dept. SJA, 37A Queen's Gate, London SW7 5HR.
Camp America is looking to recruit Youth Leaders/Specialist Counsellors to work on American summer camps for 9 weeks from June. The work could include childcare and teaching of specialist activities such as sports, music, arts and drama.

Applicants are offered free London-New York return flight, board and lodging at camp, J1 Cultural Exchange Visa, pocket money and up to 2 months' independent travel. Anyone who applies must be 18+ and free from June to September.

Applications to the above address.

CAMP COUNSELORS USA: UK Offices: Green Dragon House, 64-70 High Street, Croydon CR0 9XN (☎020-8688 9051; e-mail Inquiry@ccusaweusa.co.uk; www.ccusa.com) and 27 Woodside Gardens, Musselburgh, nr. Edinburgh EH21 7LJ (☎0131-665 5843; e-mail 101355.257@compuserve.com; www.ccusa.com). US Office: 2330 Marinship Way, Suite 250, Sausalito CA 94965, USA.
Camp Counselors USA is a high quality programme that places young people at American Summer Camps. Counselors are only placed at camps that have a good reputation with CCUSA. Each year CCUSA staff inspect the camps and interview Counsellors, so that improvements can be made if necessary. CCUSA require people with sports and/or arts and crafts qualifications or willing to assist with the physically and mentally handicapped.

In addition CCUSA require well motivated young people who are willing to be role models for the camps (to look after the children whilst they are at camp). In the coming year Camp Counselors will also be recruiting support staff, who must be full time students. All applicants must be available for interview in Europe.

For further information *contact* the above addresses.

Be a Camp Counselor in an American Summer Camp

If you are:
19-28 years of age
Available from at least June 15 to August 25
Patient with a good sense of humour
Adventurous and enjoy the outdoors
Able to be away from home for more than 9 weeks

We offer you:
Free round-trip to USA (open return ticket)
All Visa administration
After Camp travel
Pocket money

the best Summer of your life!

Write for an application today

CCUSA
CAMP COUNSELORS USA

CCUSA
27 Woodside Gardens
Musselburgh EH21 7LJ
TEL: 0131 665 5843
www.ccusa.com

or

CCUSA
Green Dragon House
64-70 High Street
Croydon CR0 9XN
TEL: 020 8688 9051

CAMPOWER: Dept. SJA, 37a Queen's Gate, London SW7 5HR.
Camp America is looking to recruit students to work on American summer camps or resorts for 9 weeks from June. The work might be in the kitchen or laundry or involve driving or general maintenance; it represents an ideal camp alternative for those not wishing to work directly with children.

Applicants are offered free London-New York return flight, board and lodging at camp, a J1 Cultural Exchange Visa, pocket money and up to 2 months' independent travel. Applicants must be students aged at least 18 and free from June to September.

For details *contact* the above address.

KAMP: BUNAC, 16 Bowling Green Lane, London EC1R OQH (☎020-7251 3472; fax 020-7251 0215; e-mail: camps@bunac.org.uk).
KAMP is a low cost fare-paid programme for summer camp staff who are not afraid of two months' work in an ancillary capacity. Working in the kitchen and maintenance areas, staff do not look after children and have access to many of the camps' facilities during time off.

BUNAC places applicants, arranges the special work/travel visa, flight and travel to camp. In addition, participants are given free board and lodging at camp, a salary and up to six weeks of independent travel afterwards. The programme is open to those who are currently enrolled at a British university, studying full time at degree (or advanced tertiary or postgraduate) level, and gap year students with an unconditional offer of a university/college place to return to. The programme fee was £62 in 2003.

Applications to the above address.

SUMMER CAMP USA: 16 Bowling Green Lane, London EC1R 0QH (☎020-7251 3472; fax 020-7251 0215; e-mail: camps@bunac.org.uk).
A low-cost, non-profit camp counsellor programme run by BUNAC (the British Universities North America Club), placing over 5,000 people in US summer camps. Provides job, work papers, flights, salary, board and lodging, and a flexible length of independent holiday time after the 9 week work period.

Applicants must be aged 18-35, have experience of working with children *and be living in the UK at the time of making their application.* The programme fee was £62 in 2003.

For details contact the above address or visit the website www.bunac.org.

Voluntary Work and Archaeology

ANDY'S ORGANIC: PO Box 1729, Pahoa, HI 96778, USA (☎808 937-9806; e-mail andysorganic@hotmail.com). A certified organic farm striving to become a school for tropical agriculture, specialising in yellow ginger, Thai ginger and turmeric but also growing diverse tropical crops. The farm is located in a rural and beautiful agricultural area on Hawaii's largest island. Tide pools, hot ponds, a small lake and a healing centre where one can take yoga classes can be found nearby.
Voluntary farm hands with extensive experience who wish to deepen their understanding of sustainable agriculture in the tropics. Farm work includes **planting, cultivating, harvesting, washing and packing as well as other tasks that may arise.** Apprentices are required to work 20 hours a week in exchange for room and food from the garden, and are expected to contribute to community chores as well. Applicants should be prepared to stay for one to three months.

Applicants can apply to the above address at any time. Please enclose postal and e-mail address and a résumé would be helpful.

GIBBON CONSERVATION CENTER: P.O. Box 800249, Santa Clarita, CA 91380 (☎661-296 2737; fax 661-296 1237; e-mail gibboncenter@earthlink.net; www.gibboncenter.org). This non-profit organisation houses the largest group of gibbons in the Western Hemisphere. It is devoted to the study, preservation, and propagation of this small ape.

Voluntary **primate keepers** (up to 3 at any one time) to work with gibbons at the centre. Duties include **preparing food and feeding, changing water, cleaning enclosures, observing behaviour (if time permits), entering data into computer (Apple Mac), maintaining grounds** etc. To work from approx. 6.30am-5pm, 7 days a week; opportunities for time off depend on the number of volunteers. Volunteers must make their own travel arrangements and buy their own food locally; accommodation is provided.

Applicants must be aged at least 20, well motivated, love animals, be capable of retaining unfamiliar information, get along with a variety of people, be in good physical condition and able to work outside in extreme weather conditions. They will need to have the following medical tests: stool cultures, ova and parasite stool test, standard blood chemistry and haematology, tuberculosis (or written proof from a doctor certifying that they have been vaccinated against tuberculosis) and Hepatitis B. Also required are vaccinations against tetanus (within the last 5 years), rubella, measles and Hepatitis B (if not already immune).

Applications to Deb Domres Volunteer Co-ordinator at gibbonvolunteers@earth link.net or ☎303-584 0371 or to the above address.

THE INTERNATIONAL VOLUNTEER PROGRAMME: La Société Française de Bienfaisance Mutuelle, 210 Post Street, Suite 502, San Francisco, CA 94108, USA (☎415-477-3667; fax 415-477-3669; www.ivpsf.com). Founded in 1991 this cultural and volunteer exchange programme sends applicants from Britain or France to the USA.

Volunteer **exchange staff** required for six weeks in California, to work in a range of **placements such as hospitals, homeless shelters, and the offices of not for profit organisations.** Places of work are located throughout California. Programme fees of £900 (UK applicants)/€1500 (French applicants) cover round trip flights, board and lodging and transport to and from the airports to the places of work.

Further information can be obtained by *contacting* Rebecca Jewell, Programme Director at the above address.

KALANI OCEANSIDE ECO-RESORT: RR 2 Box 4500, Pahoa, Beach Road, Hawaii 96778 (☎+808 965-7828 (business) +800 800-6886 (registration); fax +808 965-0527; e-mail kalani@kalani.com; www.kalani.com). Kalani Oceanside Eco-Resort is a non-profit inter-cultural conference and retreat centre located on an island with twenty acres of pristine land, surrounded by tropical forest and the Pacific Ocean.

The retreat centre operates with the assistance of approximately 20 resident volunteers who **help to provide services to the guests of the Resort.** To participate in the programme volunteers must stay a minimum of three months. In exchange for thirty hours of volunteer time per week participants receive mainly vegetarian meals, shared lodging, and a week long vacation during the three-month placement. Opportunities for volunteering exist in food service, grounds/maintenance, and housekeeping. The cost of the Resident Volunteer Programme is $900/£610 for the three-month term. Volunteers must be at least 20 years old and in good health;

experience in the area for which the applicant volunteers is preferred.

Application form and free brochure are available from the above address.

WINANT-CLAYTON   VOLUNTEER   ASSOCIATION   (WCVA):   179 Whitechapel Road, London E1 1DU (☎020-7375 0547; fax 020-7377 2437; e-mail wcva@dircon.co.uk). WCVA operates an annual exchange of volunteers between the UK and USA. It hopes to promote friendship and understanding between the two countries as well as to provide valuable life experiences.

Volunteers (20) for **work with the homeless, the elderly and children, psychiatric rehabilitation, drug rehabilitation and helping on HIV/AIDS programmes.** Placements are largely in New York and Eastern States. Pocket money, board and accommodation provided while working, but volunteers must pay for their own air fare and other travel expenses. However, some bursaries are available for volunteers from Ireland and East London. Period of work 8 weeks from the middle/end of June to the beginning of September, followed by a two/three week period for independent travel.

Applicants must be UK passport holders. No particular qualifications are essential, but previous experience of voluntary work is useful.

For further details send a large s.a.e. to the above address; *applications* must be received by mid-January as interviews are held in February.

WWOOF HAWAII (Willing Workers on Organic Farms): 4429 Carlson Road, Nelson, British Columbia, Canada V1L 6X3 (tel/fax 250-354-4417; e-mail wwoof/ hawaii/can@shaw.ca; www.wwoofusa.com). US youths and hundreds of people from all over the world go 'wwoofing' every summer. Farm Hosts are available in most states and on four of the Hawaiian islands.

Volunteer experiences range from small homesteads to large farms. **Duties include general work, milking goats etc.** Pocket money is not usually provided, but board and lodging are provided free of charge. Opportunities may be available all year round. Minimum age of sixteen. If not a US citizen, *only EEA nationals with valid tourist visas* need apply.   US membership is $30 and Hawaii membership is $15 plus postage. Cash or cheques (made payable to John Vanden Heuvel) are accepted. WWOOF will then send you the booklet of host farms.

Applications can be made online, or send full name, mailing address and registration fee.

UNIVERSITY OF CALIFORNIA RESEARCH EXPEDITIONS PROGRAM: University of California, Davis, USA (☎503-752 0692; www.urep.ucdavis.edu). Carries out **animal studies, arts and culture, geology, archaeology and environmental studies with the assistance of volunteers.** No previous experience required for volunteering.

Applications should be made the above address.

Other Employment in the USA

INTERNATIONAL EXCHANGE CENTRE: 89 Fleet Street, London EC4Y 1DH (☎020-7583 9116; fax 020-7583-9117; e-mail outbounder@btconnect.co m; www.isecworld.co.uk). The International Exchange Center works to promote positive, enjoyable cultural exchanges. Overseas work is offered in various countries for various types of work. See their website for full details.

Work and Travel in the USA Programme: Choice of various entry-level jobs around the US in cities, resorts and national parks. From ride operators at amusement parks to waitresses in Cape Cod. Working hours around 40 a week, pay $5.25+ per hour. Subsidised accommodation arranged. Applicants must be university students aged 18+. Enthusiasm and commitment the key to great time. The programme runs from May-July.

To *apply* contact the above address.

INTERNSHIP USA PROGRAMME: CIEE (Council on International Educational Exchange), 52 Poland Street, London W1F 7AB (tel: 020-7478 2020; fax 020-7734 7322; e-mail internusa@councilexchanges.org.uk; www.ciee.org.uk). Assisting students to find work in America each year, CIEE is a worldwide organisation helping people develop skills and acquire knowledge for working in a multicultural, interdependent world.

This scheme enables students and recent graduates to complete a period of course-related work experience/training for a period of up to eighteen months in the US, with an optional travel period preceding or following placement. Minimum age 18. Applicants must be enrolled in full-time further or higher education (HND level or above) or be a recent graduate. Participants must find their own training placements, related to their course of study, and either through payment from their employer or through other means, finance their own visit to the United States.

Participants pay an administrative fee of £270 with £30 increments for each additional month of stay. The CIEE provides the legal sponsorship required to obtain the J-1 visa, as well as orientation materials covering issues such as social security, taxes, housing, American culture and transportation; plus 24-hour emergency assistance with any problems whilst in the United States and comprehensive insurance. The CIEE's website (www.councilexchanges.org.uk) provides support for finding internships in the USA.

Applications can be made at any time of year, but should be made at least six weeks before desired date of departure.

LORRAINE BUSHELL: 5 Parklands, Blossomfield Road, Solihull B91 1NG (☎07973 886979; e-mail lorraine@au-pairs4u.com; www.au-pairs4u.com; www.100s-aupairs.co.uk). Based in Birmingham, Lorraine works with InterExchange USA providing university students, graduates and young professionals opportunities to train in USA under the J-1 Visa with a company in their field of study. Career Training and Development Programmes offer two types of programme. The International Student Internship Programme and the International Practical Training Programme. The programme applies to graduates from the Britain, Ireland and the rest of the EU.

Applications to the above address.

PORTALS OF WONDER: 212 East 83rd St – £4D, New York, NY 10028, USA (☎212 861-1638; e-mail helpers@ portalsofwonder.org or sandra@portalsofwonde r.org; www.portalsofwonder.org).
Artistic Helpers and Performers for a company engaged in programs, exhibitions and training for the performing arts – illusion, comedy, song and dance.

Applications should be made to Sandra Nordgren at the above e-mail address.

WORK AMERICA: BUNAC, 16 Bowling Green Lane, London EC1R OQH (☎020-7251 3472; fax 020-7251 0215; e-mail: workamerica@bunac.org.uk).
Work America is a general work and travel programme open to students through BUNAC. The programme enables participants to take virtually any summer job in the US and provides the opportunity to earn back living and travelling costs. A

special work and travel visa allows students to work and travel from June to the beginning of October.

BUNAC provides a Job Directory, which is packed with jobs from which to choose and arrange work before going. The programme is open to those who are currently enrolled at a British University or college studying at degree (or advanced tertiary or postgraduate) level and gap year students who have an unconditional offer of a university place to return to at the end of summer. The programme fee was £89 in 2003. Early application is strongly advised.

Visit www.bunac.org for more details.

WORK & TRAVEL USA: CIEE (Council on International Educational Exchange), 52 Poland Street, London W1F 7AB (☎020-7478 2020; freephone 0800 731 9076; fax 020-7734 7322; e-mail: infouk@ciee.org.uk). CIEE is a worldwide organisation placing people in casual work, internships and teaching positions across the world. This scheme enables full-time students to work and travel anywhere in the USA from early June to mid October. CIEE's website (www.councilexchanges.org.uk) has a searchable database of thousands of jobs in the USA. Assistance with finding jobs and job lists are also provided at the comprehensive arrival orientation. Students choose their flight dates and can fly into New York, Chicago or San Francisco.

Minimum age 18. Applicants must be enrolled in full-time higher education, be a recent graduate or on a gap year. The programme includes flights, insurance, job listings, travel information, pre-departure orientation materials, first night's accommodation and practical orientation on arrival, visa service, and 24 hour emergency assistance with any problems while in the United States.

Apply from January to June.

WORK EXPERIENCE USA: c/o Camp Counselors, UK Offices: Green Dragon House, 64-70 High Street, Croydon CR0 9XN (☎020-8688 9051; e-mail Inquiry@ ccusaweusa.co.uk; www.ccusa.com) and 27 Woodside Gardens, Musselburgh, nr. Edinburgh EH21 7LJ (☎0131-665 5843; e-mail 101355.257@compuserve.com; ccusa.com). US Office: 2330 Marinship Way, Suite 250, Sausalito CA 94965, USA. Camp Counselors' Work Experience USA work and travel programme is a US government authorised programme which runs between June and September. Applicants for this programme must be full time students between the ages of 20 and 28.

The only work limitations are that you cannot work as a domestic help or as a nanny; other than that the sky's the limit and the job is arranged before you leave the U.K. Wages will generally be at entry level and equivalent to those of Americans doing the same work.

For further information *contact* the above address.

Au Pairs, Nannies, Family Helps and Exchanges

AU PAIR IN AMERICA: 37 Queen's Gate, London, SW7 5HR; (tel: +44 (0)20 7581 7350; e-mail: info@aupairamerical.co.uk; www.aupairamerica.co.uk).

Au Pair in America offers you the choice of three programmes to America: Au Pair in America, Au Pair Extraordinaire and EduCare in America. The Au Pair in America package includes free return flights to New York from London and other destinations word wide, medical insurance (candidates must contribute $100 toward medical insurance), a month travel period and a four-day orientation course near New York covering first aid, culture shock and what is expected in general childcare. Au Pairs receive a weekly payment of $139.05 and a $500 study allowance in exchange for up to 45 hours of childcare a week, plus room and board. If you have a childcare qualification and are at least 20 years old with two years of recent childcare experience under your belt, you could earn $200 per week as an Au Pair Extraordinaire. EduCare has fewer childcare hours and a $1000 study allowance and is available for those of you interested in a taste of US college life.

Au Pair in America and Au Pair Extraordinaire require a $400 'good faith deposit' that is payable when you are matched with a host family, and candidates will be reimbursed their deposit after completing the 12 months and the study component of the programme. To participate you must be aged 18 – 26 and have a driving licence. You will be invited to meet a local interviewer to complete the application process. Au Pair in America's US office will match you with a family based on your experience, interested and skills.

Contact the above address for further details.

CHILDCARE AMERICA/AU PAIR IN AMERICA: Childcare International Ltd., Trafalgar House, Grenville Place, London NW7 3SA (☎020-8906 3116; fax 020-8906 3461; e-mail: office@childint.co.uk; www.childint.co.uk).
Au Pair and **Nanny** stays in the USA. Childcare America offer a visa-supported one year stay to applicants aged 18-26 with good childcare experience. Applicants must drive. Families provide full round trip air fare, medical insurance and part time college course plus two weeks' paid holiday. Salary up to $200 per week for qualified nannies and a minimum of $139.05 per week for au pairs. Choose from a wide range of approved families from across the USA. Four days orientation is provided in the USA. Full local counsellor support is provided to introduce friends and give guidance with every aspect of the stay.

Applications to the above address.

EDUCARE AMERICA: Childcare International Ltd., Trafalgar House, Grenville Place, London NW7 3SA (☎020-8906 3116; fax 020-8906 3461; e-mail: office@childint.co.uk; www.childint.co.uk).
The Educare Program offers the opportunity to work and study in the United States. It provides the opportunity for young people aged 18-26 to spend a year in the States caring for school-aged children for 30 hours a week while attending an American college. Families provide full round trip air fare, medical insurance, two weeks paid holiday and a salary of $105 per week. Full local counsellor support. Driving licence essential.

For programme information *please contact* the above address.

Asia

Bangladesh

The following organisation offers the opportunity of voluntary work in Bangladesh.

BANGLADESH WORK CAMPS ASSOCIATION (BWCA): 289/2 Workcamp Road, North Shajahanpur, Dhaka-1217, Bangladesh (☎+880-2-9358206/9356814; fax +880-2-956 5506/5483; e-mail bwca@bangla.net; www.mybwca.org).
Bangladesh Work Camps Association (BWCA) promotes international solidarity and peace through organising community development, which takes the form of national/ international workcamps for volunteers in rural and urban areas of Bangladesh. The projects organised include **environmental and health education, literacy, sanitation, reforestation, community work, development and construction, etc.** Volunteers work 30 hours a week on placements, which last from 1 to 6 weeks from October to February. A RTYP (Round The Year Programme) is also available to medium-term volunteers staying for a minimum period of three months. At least 30 volunteers a year are recruited onto one of the three international workcamps and 20 volunteers through RTYP.
Volunteers ages 18-35, must be able to speak English, be adaptable to any situation and be team-spirited. Accommodation and simple local food is provided but volunteers must pay all other expenses including insurance and travel.
Applications to BWCA three months in advance of scheduled Camp/Programme date. Applications must come through a BWCA partner organisation in the applicant's country; if this is not possible individual, direct applications may be accepted and should be accompanied by a payment of US$25. Apply in the first instance for the address of the nearest partner organisation.

China

British nationals can find voluntary work in China through the UNA Exchange see the *Worldwide* chapter for details. The following organisations offers the opportunity to work in China.

EARTHCARE: GPO Box 11546, Hong Kong, China (☎+852-25780434; fax +852-25780522; e-mail care@earth.org.hk; www.earth.org.hk).
Earthcare, a local Chinese charity, aims to promote the concepts of benevolence and compassion in traditional Chinese teaching to establish a green lifestyle, environmental conservation, humane education and the protection of animals. About 150-200 volunteers are recruited annually to help in the following areas: **fundraising, computer/data processing/maintenance, administration, clerical work, campaigning, animal care/treatment, publishing/printing, photography and filming, multimedia design and application, public relations and education.**

Campaigns include: banning bear farming and advocating herbal alternatives to animal derived remedies in Chinese medicines. Minimum period of voluntary work is two weeks at any time of year. Applicants must be able to speak English, any knowledge of Cantonese would be a bonus. Very simple accommodation can be provided but all other expenses must be met by the volunteer.

Applications to the above address.

ENGLISH FIRST: 36-38 St Aubyns, Hove, East Sussex BN3 2TD (☎01273-201431; fax 01273-746742; e-mail recruitment.uk@englishfirst.com). English First is part of EF Education, which specialises in language teaching and educational travel. EF recruits and interviews English teachers in the UK, to work in its 45 English schools spread throughout China.

English Language Teachers (40) to teach English to children, teenagers and university students. 40 hours a week with 24 contact teaching hours, 6-days a week. Will involve working in the morning and the evening as well as at weekends. Pay of $530 per month plus board, lodging, insurance, working visa, and flight allowance of up to $1,000. Must have TEFL/TESL Certificate. Minimum period of work is two months.

Apply from January to the above address.

TEACH IN CHINA: CIEE (Council on International Educational Exchanges), 52 Poland Street, London W1F 7AB (☎020-7478 2020; fax 020-7734 7322; e-mail: infouk@councilexchanges.org.uk; www.ciee.org.uk). Sending more graduates to China than any other organisation, CIEE is a worldwide organisation helping people develop skills and acquire knowledge for working in a multicultural, interdependent world.

Teach in China offers an opportunity for graduates to spend 5 or 10 months teaching English in a university, college or school in China. There is no age limit, and teaching/TEFL qualifications are not required in order to apply. Successful applicants attend a one week training course on arrival in Shanghai; focusing on learning Chinese, understanding Chinese culture and giving an insight to TEFL. Host institutions in China provide private accommodation (usually a teacher's apartment on or near the campus), and a monthly salary which is generous by Chinese standards. Participants are responsible for paying their outward air fare and programme fee to CIEE to cover the costs of arranging the placement, processing all paperwork required for visas and work permits, visa fees, the training centre and 24 hour emergency support while in China. Return fare is paid by the host institution on completion of a 10 month contract.

CIEE sends participants on this programme in late August and early February in accordance with the Chinese semester system, and *applicants* are encouraged to return forms and application materials at least 3 months beforehand in order to ensure that a suitable placement is found. US applicants should apply to the CIEE in the US (for address see the *Worldwide* chapter).

India

Despite its vast size India offers few opportunities for paid temporary work, particularly for those without any particular skill or trade to offer an employer: there are untold thousands of Indians who would be delighted to do any unskilled job available for a wage that would seem a pittance to a westerner. Anyone determined to find paid employment there should explore the possibility of working for tour operators who specialise in organising holidays to India, and they would normally only consider applicants who are familiar with the country.

There are, however, a number of opportunities for taking part in short-term voluntary schemes in India. One of the most famous is *Mother Teresa's Missionaries of Charity* in Calcutta which takes on part-time volunteers to care for and feed orphaned children, the sick and dying, mentally or physically disabled adults and children or the elderly at its children's home in Calcutta (Shishu Bhavan, 78 A.J.C. Bose Road), in the Home for Dying Destitutes at Kalighat and other houses run by the Missionaries of Charity in Calcutta and other Indian cities, but no accommodation can be offered. To register, visit the Mother House at 54A A.J.C. Bose Road, Calcutta 700 016. Further information is also available from their London office at 177 Bravington Road, London W9 3AR (020-8960 2644).

Council: International Volunteer Projects and Service Civil International can place Americans on voluntary schemes in India, and Concordia and UNA Exchange can offer similar placements for Britons: see the *Worldwide* chapter for details. Please note that as is normal with short-term voluntary opportunities, those taking part must pay for their own travel expenses, and will often be required to put something towards the cost of board and lodging.

RED TAPE, VISAS & WORK PERMITS

Visa Requirements: a tourist visa is required by all non-Indian nationals entering India for a visit as tourists.

Residence Permits: those planning a stay of over 3 months must register with the Foreigners Regional Registration Office within 14 days of arrival and be able to provide evidence of how they are supporting themselves. It is not possible to change a tourist visa to a long stay visa within India.

Employment Visas: any foreigner taking up paid employment in India must have a valid work permit before they enter the country: they should apply to the nearest Indian consulate, enclosing a copy of their contract.

Au Pair: not customary.

Voluntary Work: details of the voluntary work to be undertaken should be sent to the Indian consulate when applying for a visa at least 2 months in advance as they have to be forwarded to India. If you do want to attach yourself to a voluntary organisation for more than three months, you should aim to enter India on a student or employment visa (see Indian Embassy website www.hcilondon.org).

BHARAT SEVAK SAMAJ (BSS): Nehru Seva Kendra, Gurgaon By-pass Road, Mehrauli, New Delhi 30, India; ☎+91 11 66644761,6642215.

The Samaj was founded by Shri Jawahar Lal Nehru, the first Prime Minister of India, as a non-political national platform for mobilising people's spare time, energy and resources for development and reconstruction. It has a network of branches all over the country, with a membership of over 750,000, 10,000 members working on projects, and about 20 foreign volunteers helping each year. Any person who offers his services for a minimum of two hours a week can become a member of the Samaj.

Its normal programme includes the **organisation of urban community centres in slum areas, night shelters, child welfare centres, nursery schools, training camps for national reconstruction work, family planning camps and clinics, and publicity centres. The work also encompasses relief and reconstruction work**

after natural calamities, such as famine, drought, cyclones and earthquakes as well as the construction of houses for the Schedule Caste (lower caste) and tribes and low cost latrines in villages.

Both skilled and unskilled workers are welcomed. Foreign volunteers, who can serve for between 15 days and three months, should be prepared to live in simple accommodation and respect local customs and traditions. They must finance their own stay, and it is preferred that they speak English.

Applicants should contact the General Secretary at the above address for further details; IRCs should accompany all letters.

DAKSHINAYAN: c/o Siddarth Sanyal, A-5/108 Clifton Apartments, Charmwood Village, Eros Gardens, Surajkind Road, Faridabad 121009 (☎0129-525 3114 or 525 3165, cellphone 9811192133; e-mail dakshinayan@vsnl.com).

Volunteers to work with a registered trust engaged in **providing education and medical assistance to tribes in the Rajamhal Hills and the surrounding plains.** The project requires two volunteer health workers, who should be qualified/trainee doctors or nurses, to provide first aid, dispense medicines and train village women in health work. Any number of unskilled volunteers aged at least 18 are also needed to help on other development projects. Volunteers normally work 4-6 hours a day, 6 days a week for between 4 weeks and 6 months. Help is needed throughout the year. No expenses are paid and individuals are expected to contribute approx. £3 per day for food and a one-time fee of approx. £30 for processing applications and other administrative charges.

All applicants must be at least 18 years old, socially sensitive and willing to work in remote locations. Living conditions on most rural development projects are very basic. Knowledge of Hindi an advantage. Participants must arrive in Delhi in the first week of the month for orientation and placement.

Applications, at least 30 days in advance of desired departure date, to Siddharth Sanyal, Executive Trustee, at the above address; please enclose an international postal coupon.

DORE: (Devoted Organisation for Reforming Environment), 196-b Khari Bazar, Ranikhet 263645, Dish, Almora (Uttaranchal), India (☎+91 5966-20458).

DORE recruits 15-25 volunteers a year to help in the areas of **natural resource management, child health and education, socio-economic development of rural villages, introduction of appropriate technology, and eco-tourism** in India. Volunteers can stay from one to six months but preferably in the summer. No special skills or qualifications are required but practice in very basic Hindi conversations is advisable for the comfort of the volunteer. All expenses (accommodation, food, airfares, etc.) must be met by the volunteer.

Applications to the Secretary at the above address.

JAFFE INTERNATIONAL EDUCATION SERVICE: Kunnuparambil Buildings, Kurichy, Kottayam 686549, India (fax 91-481-430470; e-mail jaffeint@sify.com).

Voluntary teachers to teach in summer schools all over India. Subject areas include: Beauty Therapy, Creative Writing, Cooking, English, French, Gardening, Journalism, Music, Painting, Photography, Travel and Tourism. Due to foreign currency restrictions, no salary is paid but free board and lodging is provided. Hours of work are flexible; minimum 3 hours a day, Monday to Friday. Volunteers required from 1 April to 31 May; minimum period of work 4 weeks. Applicants must have at least an undergraduate degree in the subject of specialisation and proficiency in the English language.

Applications from 1 January to the address above.

JOINT ASSISTANCE CENTRE: G-17/3, DLF City, Phase 1, Gurgaon, Haryana-122002, India (☎+91-124-6352141 or 6353833; fax 0091-124-6351308; e-mail: jacindia@mantraonline.com). JAC offers a unique opportunity of an exciting and challenging nature carrying out humanitarian works in close unison with local agencies as well as the UN and other international groups.

Volunteers can join 'learn while you travel' scheme and perform various jobs for a voluntary action group (registered as a charity) concerned with furthering disaster preparedness through training programmes, exhibitions and seminars. It also has cultural schemes, fund raising, camps, digs, workcamps and related publications. **Tasks include helping with office work, editing, writing, teaching, social work, joining youth workcamps, helping run seminars and giving demonstrations and lectures, etc.** on first aid, camping, trekking, rock climbing etc. There are opportunities for learning natural cures (chromopathy), yoga, meditation, Indian language and about Indian life philosophy through cheap travel and visits to several other projects through the JAC travel scheme.

Any number of volunteers are accepted, but for specific projects, to suit personal applicant profile, volunteers must be able to work for a minimum of three months. Working hours are 8 hours a day and 5 days per week with free days or weeks by mutual arrangement. Simple but safe and secure accommodation is provided in a rural camp style in huts or tents, in the slum or rural areas. Longer term placements in other projects according to skills/interests are also arranged. Three day long orientation programmes about India, its history, culture and thought, are organised every month. Students wanting to do internships or study and research in any field can also be accepted.

No special qualifications required but some experience of first aid, typing or scouting would be helpful. Minimum age 18 years. Help is needed from volunteers for periods of from 4-26 weeks, around the year. Participants are required to send a processing fee of £30 with their application. They must then contribute a further £100 for the first month to cover food, accommodation, administration, and airport pickup).

Contact Narendra Kumar Jain, Convener, at the above address for application forms, enclosing 3 International Reply Coupons for reply by Air Mail.

NOMAD TRAVEL: (☎01707-659510; e-mail cathy@nomadtravel.co.uk; www.nomadtravel.co.uk). Help is needed on the West Bengal/Sikkim borders, in the foothills of the Himalayas, approximately three hours from Darjeeling. This is a small clinic set up in Karmi Farm to help the indigenous population with day to day health care and child care. Funds are raised in the UK to pay for nurse, board and lodging and pharmaceuticals.

Volunteer Nurse/Doctors to help in rural communities. The clinic currently caters for 210 families from the surrounding area. There is also outreach work. Situated in the foothills of the Himalayas, transport is all on foot. The main illnesses are skin disorders, chest problems, dehydration, childhood illnesses. Midwifery plays a big part. People turn up at the clinic any time night or day. However, there are long spells when it is quiet. Minimum period of work for applications – 6 weeks. Work is available all year round. Comfortable accommodation and organic food provided.

Applications should be made to Cathy Goodyer on the above details at any time.

RURAL ORGANISATION FOR SOCIAL ELEVATION: Social Awareness Centre, Kanda Bageshwar 263631, Uttarancahal,, India. R.O.S.E. is a small charity, based in a beautiful location at the foot of the Himalayas. It provides volunteers with the opportunity of experiencing true rural Indian life while providing education and improving local sanitation and health care facilities.

Volunteers (1-10) to carry out work in rural areas including teaching English to children, construction, poultry farming, environmental protection, agricultural work, recycling paper to make hand-made greetings cards, office work, compiling project proposals, reports and health care. Groups of volunteers can be organised into work camps lasting 10 to 30 days, but individuals are also welcome to apply. Volunteers work 5 hours a day, five days a week. Accommodation in a family house provided in addition to three delicious meals a day. Volunteers must pay their own travel costs and about £4 a day towards board and lodging costs, administration and R.O.S.E's school expenses.

Applications should be addressed to Mr Jeevan Lal Verma at the above address. Please enclose 3 international reply coupons and a large envelope.

Japan

The range of short-term casual jobs open to Westerners in Japan is extremely limited, even with unemployment in Japan having rapidly fallen in recent years. However, longer-term opportunities do exist, particularly in the area of teaching English: it has been estimated that 11% of all Japanese people attend English 'conversation classes'. A native English speaker therefore possesses a marketable skill if he or she has a degree; experience or qualifications in teaching English as a foreign language are added advantages.

For further information on teaching work in Japan see *Teaching English Abroad*. Anyone who is serious about wanting to spend some time in Japan should read *Live and Work in Japan*, a thorough guide for anyone hoping to live and work there. See the *Useful Publications* chapter for details of these books.

CIEE and Service Civil International can help US residents, as can Concordia, Youth Action for Peace, UNA Exchange and International Voluntary Service UK residents, to find short term voluntary work in Japan; see their entries in the *Worldwide* chapter for details.

RED TAPE, VISAS & WORK PERMITS

Visa Requirements: nationals of the UK, USA, Ireland, Germany, Switzerland and Austria can visit Japan as tourists without a visa for up to 3 months and extend this to 6 months. Most other nationalities can visit for up to 3 months, as long as they have a return or onward ticket and sufficient funds.

Work Permits: A position must be secured and working visa obtained before you enter the country. Applicants for working visas must submit their application to the Consulate in person. If the person obtains a certificate of eligibility from Japan a visa can be issued in three days.

Working Holiday Visas. Holders of British, Australian, Canadian and New Zealand passports can apply for working holiday visas: these must be applied for at the Japanese Embassy of their home country. The rules are generally the same, but full details can be obtained from the nearest Japanese Embassy or consulate. For British citizens, working holiday visas may be granted provided they are:

    (1) British citizens resident in the United Kingdom;
    (2) intend primarily to holiday in Japan for a period of up to one year from date of entry;

(3) aged between 18 and 25 years inclusive at time of application, except where the competent authorities of the Government of Japan agree to extend the limitation upwards to 30 years;

(4) unaccompanied by children or spouses, except where the spouse also possesses a working holiday visa;

(5) in possession of a valid passport, return travel ticket or sufficient funds to purchase such reasonable funds for normal maintenance purposes during the initial part of the proposed stay in Japan;

(6) in good health;

(7) willing to leave Japan at the end of their stay;

(8) able to confirm that they have not previously been issued with such a visa.

There is a non-refundable processing fee for a working holiday visa (£6 in the UK). 400 Working Holiday Visas are available to British citizens between April and the following March, applications are accepted from the 17th of April. To apply one each of the following must be supplied to the Japanese Embassy or Consulate-General in addition to a valid British passport: visa application form, a 35mm x 45mm photograph, a typed CV or personal history, a proposed itinerary for the first six months in Japan to include details of any prearranged employment, a typed reason for applying, evidence of travel tickets/reservations and evidence of funds (for ticket holders this is £1,500, confirmed reservation holders £2,500). Application forms and explanatory material can be obtained from the Japanese Consulate-General in London or Edinburgh.

There is a support organisation – the Japanese Association for Working-Holiday Makers with offices in Tokyo, Osaka and Kyushu (Tokyo office: Sun Plaza 7th Floor, 4-1-1 Nakano, Nakano-ku, Tokyo 164-8512, Japan; ☎03-3389-0181) which can be found on-line: www.jawhm.or.jp.

Japanese Working Holiday visas are single entry, so if you have to leave Japan for any reason you must obtain a re-entry permit from the competent immigration authorities before leaving. Travellers who stay in Japan longer than 90 days have to register with the local municipal office, and keep them informed of any subsequent change of address. They can also register with their embassy or consulate on arrival or later during their stay but this is not obligatory, merely advisable. For clarification of these points and news of any changes in the regulations please contact the nearest Japanese Embassy or consular mission.

Voluntary Work: new since May 2003 is a Volunteer Visa Scheme which allows British nationals to undertake voluntary work in Japan, working for charitable organisations for up to a year. Work should be unpaid but pocket money and free board and lodging are permitted. Details and application forms are available from the Consulate General of Japan in London (101-104 Piccadilly, W1J 7JT; ☎020-7465 6565) and Edinburgh (2 Melville Crescent, EH3 7HW; ☎0131-225-4777).

Teaching and Office Work

THE JAPAN EXCHANGE AND TEACHING (JET) PROGRAMME: JET Desk, Embassy of Japan, 101-104 Piccadilly, London WIJ 7JT (☎020-7465 6668/6670; e-mail: jet@embjapan.org.uk). The JET programme is a Japanese governmental scheme. Graduates from thirty-nine countries are recruited annually to assist Japanese English teachers in secondary schools or to work in local government offices, for a period of one year. In 2003 over 6,000 graduates worldwide took up positions in high schools throughout Japan on this programme; over 650 of them from Britain. Participants receive remuneration of 3,600,000 yen (equivalent to

£23,000) per year and a return air ticket to Japan, orientation programmes are provided both pre-departure and post-arrival, as well as assistance with finding accommodation.

JET applicants in the USA should contact the Embassy of Japan at 2520 Massachusetts Avenue NW, Washington DC 20008 (☎202-939-6772). Graduates from Australia, Brazil, Canada, China, France, Germany, Ireland, Israel, Italy, New Zealand, Mexico, Peru, Portugal, the Republic of Korea, the Russian Federation and Spain should contact the Japanese Embassy in their country of origin.

Application forms are available from early October each year and UK applicants must return them to the JET Programme Desk at the above address by the 5th December deadline. Successful applicants will depart for Japan in late July 2004.

OSHIN SHIZEN JUKU (NEW NATURE SCHOOL): Tsurui-Mura, Akan-Gun, Hokkaido 085-1207 Japan (☎0154 642821).
Volunteers (up to 4) required: kind, honest, responsible and enthusiastic applicants wanted to teach English to Japanese people. Free food and accommodation are provided, in return for **teaching and gardening** work, minimum period of volunteering 6 weeks. Hours and programme vary from day to day but there is plenty of time for recreation. An interest in learning Japanese is encouraged. Applicants with an international driver's licence essential.

Applicants also needed for six month paid contracts. For those who can make a contract to stay and teach for six months (with working holiday visa – Australia, New Zealand, Canada, UK and France) the school provides a monthly allowance of 20,000 to 50,000 yen.

Applications with photo to Hiroshi Mine, Manager, at the above address.

Korea

The following organisation has recently started recruiting British applicants for voluntary work in Korea.

CONCORDIA: Heversham House, 20-22 Boundary Road, Hove, East Sussex BN3 4ET (☎01273-422218; fax 01273-421182; e-mail info@concordia-iye.org.uk; www.concordia-iye.org.uk).
Concordia's International Volunteer Programme offers 18-30 year olds the opportunity to join an international team of volunteers working on community-based projects ranging from nature and wildlife conservation, restoration and construction, to art/culture and projects that are socially based including work with adults or children with special needs, children's playschemes and teaching. Projects last for 2-4 weeks and run mainly in the summer months.

Generally no skills or experience are needed, although real commitment to a project is a must. Volunteers pay a registration fee of approx. £85 depending on the country and fund their own travel, Board and accommodation are free of charge. For more information write enclosing an s.a.e., or e-mail.

Nepal

Nepal is one of the most promising destinations for young people who want to spend a few months as a volunteer in a developing country. People who find voluntary openings in Nepal may face a visa problem. The first tourist visa will be issued for 60 days (£20 single entry and £55 multiple entry from the Nepalese Embassy in London – near Notting Hill Gate tube station). Processing takes a few days. A tourist visa can be extended from the Department of Immigration and Pokhara Immigration Office for a total of 120 days. An additional 30 days visa may be granted on reasonable grounds from the department.

Over the course of a visa year, a tourist cannot stay in Nepal more than cumulative 150 days. People who overstay their visas have in the past been fined heavily or even put in prison. More information is available at www.nepembassy.org.uk. An impressive range of non-governmental organisations makes it possible for people to teach in a voluntary capacity. Although volunteers must bear the cost of travel and living expenses, the cost of living is very low by western standards.

Concordia, UNA Exchange and Youth Action for Peace can arrange short-term voluntary work placements in Nepal. See their entries in the *Worldwide* chapter for more details. The following organisations are also looking for volunteers to work in Nepal.

NEW INTERNATIONAL FRIENDSHIP CLUB NEPAL: (NIFC-Nepal) PO Box 11276, Maharajgunj, Kathmandu, Nepal (☎+977-1 427406/429176; fax +977-1 429176; e-mail nifc@mos.com.np; www.geocities.com/nifnepal). Friendship Club Nepal is a small Nepali-run NGO organising regular workcamps to assist rural communities. A long-term project in Chitwan district will establish a co-operative farm demonstrations.
Volunteers are required to participate in both research and physical workcamps. Research work usually involves investigating and **writing a report on the development situation** (health, education, environment or agriculture etc.) in a rural area. A physical workcamp might involve **construction or agriculture**. **Teacher** also needed for schools.

Volunteers should be aged between 17 and 65. Proficiency in English is essential. Working hours are approximately 36 hours, a six day week. Workcamps last 15 days, medium-term placements 2-6 months. No wages or fare paid but basic Nepali style board and lodging provided. Work camp fee US$150; medium-term volunteers should contribute US$150 per month. Registration fee US$30. Volunteers should arrange their own travel, visa and insurance.

Recruitment throughout the year; preferably *apply at least 2 months in advance* of intended departure date enclosing CV.

GRAHUNG KALIKA: Walling Municipality, 2 Bartung, Syangja, Nepal. A non-governmental organisation set up in 1996 in a remote area of Nepal (about 260km west of Kathmandu) to improve the teaching of English to primary school children. Volunteers required for short and long term placements (minimum stay 4 weeks) to **teach English, develop western farming practices and help raise awareness of issues and practices for healthy childbirth.** No teaching experience necessary; volunteers must adopt a practical and creative approach and be able to muck in with the local community. Apart from the opportunity for first hand experience of Nepalese rural life, volunteers can enjoy mountain trekking, white-water rafting and sightseeing in the Himalayas.

Volunteers should be aged at least 17 and will need to pay a registration fee of $20 (£13 approx), their own travel and insurance costs, as well as contributing approx. £40 towards the project's costs. Board and lodging are arranged by the project at a rate of £30 per month. *Applications* should be made at least one month in advance of the proposed visit to Nepal, especially in June-July when the monsoon closes many project schools. An information sheet giving further details of the project can be obtained by writing by registered post (enclosing an International Reply Coupon) to the above address.

Enquiries to Mr Dol Raj Subedi, P.O. Box 11272, Kathmandu, Nepal (☎+977-1-532674; (e-mail ptarasubdei@hotmail.com; mahendracom@hotmail.com).

INSIGHT NEPAL: P.O. Box 489, Male Patan, Pokhara, Nepal (☎+977-61-30266; e-mail insight@fewanet.com.np; www.insightnepal.org). Insight Nepal was established with a view to providing an opportunity to those who are interested in gaining a unique cultural experience by contributing their time and skills for the benefit of worthwhile community service groups.

Volunteer **Teachers** (15) **to teach various subjects in primary, secondary and vocational schools in Nepal**. To work 5 to 6 hours per day, 5 or 6 days per week. Insight Nepal organises homestays for the volunteers, and the host family provide accommodation and two meals per day. Work available all year round.

Applicants should be aged between 18 and 60 and be educated to at least A level standard. Experience of teaching is advisable but not essential. Applicants with games, sporting and artistic skills preferred. Short-term volunteer placements also can be arranged upon request.

Applications to the above address.

PEOPLE'S WELFARE COMMITTEE: G.P.O. 12137, Kathmandu, Nepal (fax 0977-1-412997; e-mail jbardewa@wlink.com.np)

Volunteer **agriculturalists** (5 per month) and volunteer **teachers** (10 per month) **to teach English in primary schools** needed to work for 60 hours per month.

For further details *send* an International Reply Coupon to Mrs Srijana Bardewa at the above address.

SAVE THE WORLD: P.O.Box 5947, Kathmandhu, Thamel, Nepal (☎+977 1 222939; fax +977 1 4250319; e-mail savetheworldnepal@hotmail.com; www.sav etheworldnepal.org)

STW works to raise public awareness for peace, human rights and sustainable development activities. Detailed information is provided on the website. 6-8 volunteers are taken on annually to work in the areas of **education, health and environment** related social organisation. Volunteers are normally recruited for three months and are provided with food and lodging.

Apply direct to the VWOP address below.

VOLUNTARY WORK OPPORTUNITIES IN NEPAL: GPO Box 11969, Kathmandu, Nepal (fax +977 1 416144; e-mail vwop2000@hotmail.com).

VWOP is a voluntary programme which liaises between international volunteers and the schools/organisations which provide voluntary jobs and opportunities in urban and remote areas of Nepal, including **teaching in schools, being involved in environmental, health, agriculture and research programmes**. Volunteers may also arrange and implement their own ideas/programmes/activities, which directly help the local community. We also help those who intend to invest in education, livestock, health, the environment, research etc. in rural areas of Nepal.

Qualifications and experience are not essential except for environmental and health programmes. Volunteers who wish to can have first hand experience of living and working with local village people. Volunteers are invited to participate in cultural activities and will have the opportunity to explore other parts of Nepal where they can engage in trekking, white water rafting, sightseeing etc.

Volunteers stay with a local family during placement sharing their home, food and amenities. Volunteers pay some amount for food accommodation and organisation fee. Fees are US$20 (application), US$50 (administration) and US$50 per month (host family).

Application forms from the above address .

Thailand

In addition to the conservation project listed below Concordia, UNA Exchange and Youth Action for Peace offer British volunteers the chance to work in Thailand.

Teaching and Language Schools

KING'S ENGLISH LANGUAGE SCHOOLS: 58 Braidley Road, Bournemouth, Dorset BH2 6LD, UK (☎01202-293535; fax 01202-293922; e-mail info@kingsschool.co.uk/info@kingsschool.uk.com; www.kingsgroup.co.uk). Leading English language schools in Canada, Thailand and England.

English as a Foreign Language Teachers. Suitable qualifications will be expected.

Applications should be made to Danielle Watts or the Marketing Department at the above address.

TEACH IN THAILAND: CIEE (Council on International Educational Exchanges), 52 Poland Street, London W1F 7AB (☎020-7478 2020; fax 020-7734 7322; e-mail: infouk@councilexchanges.org.uk; www.ciee.org.uk). Sending more graduates to Thailand than any other organisation, the CIEE is a worldwide organisation helping people develop skills and acquire knowledge for working in a multicultural, interdependent world.

Teach in Thailand offers an opportunity for graduates to spend 5 or 10 months teaching English at a school in or around Bangkok. There is no age limit, and teaching/TEFL qualifications are not required in order to apply. Successful applicants attend a one-week training course on arrival in Shanghai focusing on the language and culture and giving an insight to TEFL. Host institutions provide private accommodation (usually a teacher's apartment on or near the campus), and a monthly salary which is generous by local standards. Participants are responsible for paying their outward air fare and a programme fee to CIEE to cover the costs of arranging the placement, processing all paperwork required for visas and work permits, visa fees, the training centre and 24-hour emergency support while in Thailand. Return fare is paid by the host institution on completion of a 10-month contract.

CIEE sends participants on this programme in late October and early May in accordance with the Thai semester system, and *applicants* are encouraged to return forms and application materials at least 3 months beforehand in order to ensure that a suitable placement is found. US applicants should apply to CIEE in the USA (for address see the *Worldwide* chapter).

Voluntary Work

THE WILD ANIMAL RESCUE FOUNDATION OF THAILAND: 235

Sukhumvit Soi 31, Bangkok 10110, Thailand. (tel/fax (662) 261-9679; e-9570, 2261-9672; fax: 2662-0898; war@war-thai.org; www.warthai.org). The Foundation is dedicated to the protection and provision of welfare to all wild animals in need and operates two sanctuaries in the south of Thailand. The Gibbon Rehabilitation Project was set up in 1992 and deals exclusively with Gibbons many of which have been rescued from situations of abuse and cruelty. The aim of the project is to release selected gibbons from the sanctuary into the wild and to provide on-going care to those who through their association with humans are now unfit for release.

The second sanctuary in the province of Ranong provides a home to all wild animals common to Thailand which have suffered at the hands of humans. The project is still under development but already houses many gibbons, a large colony of macaques and many other species.

At both projects, volunteers are involved in the **day-to-day operation of the unit including food preparation, cage cleaning and maintenance, assisting with health inspections, behavioural observation and informing of the work of the Foundation to people who call at the visitors' centre.**

Volunteers should be in good physical condition and be able to live and function in field station conditions. Enthusiasm and an ability to live and work with people of different cultures are essential. The minimum stay period is three weeks.

For current placement rates and opportunities, please contact preferably by e-mail.

SEA TURTLE PROJECT PHRATHONG ISLAND: CHELON, Viale val Padana 134B, I-00141 Rome, Italy (☎+39-06-8125301; e-mail chelon@tin.it). CHELON an Italian based research group, works to obtain in-depth knowledge of the biology of marine turtles and aid their conservation. They work in collaboration with the Marine Biological Centre in Phuket.

Volunteers to help researchers studying Olive Ridley, Green, Leatherback and Hawksbill turtles in the south of Thailand between December and May. Volunteers will assist in **gathering data on nesting behaviour, tagging turtles for observation and taking part in raising conservation awareness among tourists and local people**.

The presence of volunteers helps deter poaching of turtle eggs and young as well as involving the local community in the project. The work often involves long walks patrolling the three beaches to estimate the number of nests and the species of turtle nesting there. Visits to villages are used to involve the locals and to collect information on trade in turtle eggs, and talks given in the evenings at the Golden Buddha Beach resort increase understanding of turtle conservation amongst tourists.

Volunteers are accommodated in huts at the Golden Buddha beach resort, this and meals at the resort clubhouse are covered by the registration fee of £375, per two weeks. The minimum stay is two weeks, but volunteers can stay longer subject to approval. Travel and insurance expenses are met by the volunteer.

Contact CHELON at the above address for further information and an application form.

South Korea

The following organisation can provide opportunities for voluntary work in South Korea.

KOREAN INTERNATIONAL VOLUNTEER ASSOCIATION (KIVA): 11th Floor Sekwang B/D, 202 Sejong-ro, Chongro-gu, Seoul, South Korea 110-050 (e-mail: info@kiva.or.kr; volunteer@kiva.or.kr; www.kiva.or.uk)

KIVA organises international voluntary work placements throughout Korea. One of these placements requires about four native English speakers to **teach children English in an orphanage** in Seoul. The aim of the orphanage programme is to act not only as a learning experience for the children but for the volunteer as well, as knowledge of the respective different cultures is exchanged between teacher and child. Placements last a minimum of four weeks. Volunteers need to be emotionally stable and have a good sense of humour. Simple board and lodging is provided but volunteers need to fund their own airfares and other expenses.

Applications four weeks in advance of programme commencement to the above address.

Sri Lanka

The following organisation can provide opportunities for voluntary work in Sri Lanka.

SAMASEVAYA: National Secretariat, Anuradhapura Road, Talawa NCP, Sri Lanka (☎+94-25 76266; +94-25 76266; samasev@sltnet.lk).

Samasevaya works towards peace through organising development **programmes in self-reliance, education, environmental conservation, children's development, women's development, nutrition and health**. About 10 volunteers a year are recruited to assist with the work on these projects. Minimum age 18 and volunteers must be in good health and prepared to work in rural areas. Placements are available all year round and normally last one month but this period can be extended. Simple accommodation is provided and volunteers are requested to pay US$90 per month for their food; all other expenses, including entry visa (visas can be extended once in Thailand if necessary) must be met by the volunteer also.

Applications to the National Secretary at the above address.

Australasia

Australia

The short length of this chapter does not bear any relation to the vast range and number of temporary opportunities available in Australia: there are many with unemployment falling to a level of 6.2%. However, there are a few factors to bear in mind when considering Australia as a destination for a summer job. The first factor is the reversal of seasons: the Australian summer takes place in what is winter to much of the rest of the world and so jobs on their fruit harvests and at the peak of their tourist industry occur at the wrong time of year for anyone hoping to find work between July and September. There is also the financial factor: the cost of a return ticket to Australia makes going there for a paid job for just a few weeks very uneconomic – even though in real terms the cost of getting to Australia is at its cheapest ever the cost is still such that it makes better financial sense to stay for months rather than weeks.

Luckily for the foreigner, Australia has a reciprocal working holiday scheme with certain countries that can ease the formalities for those going there to pick up casual work. Some guidelines for those hoping to do so are given below, but working holidays in Australia are covered in greater depth in, *Work Your Way Around the World* (see *Useful Publications* section), in the information available from Australian High Commissions and Embassies or through the Australia Government Immigration Website at www.immi.gov.au. A third point to consider is that Australia is one of the most popular destinations for working travellers, and the limited number of visas means that you need to begin the application process well in advance of your intended travel: 57,000 people apply for visas every year and the processing usually takes at least 5 weeks. The fee at present is £70. It is important to remember that your Working Holiday Maker visa can only be obtained in your country of origin, you cannot apply for a WHM visa once you are in Australia.

Although Australia now has a declining unemployment rate, job-seekers must be prepared to devote time and energy to the job hunt. One tip is to look for work away from the big cities, where other new arrivals from overseas may be competing for the same jobs. A valuable source of rural jobs is Employment National (EN), the government's privatised job agency. Enquiring in one office will allow you to uncover harvest work near one of the more than 200 other offices across the country. Employment National encourage working holidaymakers to contact their specialist fruit and crop-picking department on 1300-720126 or to check their website (www.employmentnational.com.au) which has details of the EN offices all over the country and the types of work that these may offer.

The fruit harvests of Northern Victoria employ a massive 10,000-12,000 people in the Australian summer (January –March). The city of Shepparton is in the Goulburn Valley, about two hours north of Melbourne with easy accessibility via rail or bus services. From Sydney, catch a train to Albury and from there take the bus to Shepparton. Information can be obtained from the Northern Victoria Fruitgrowers' Association Ltd. (NVFA), PO Box 612, Mooroopna, Vic 3629

(03-5825-3700; fax 03-5825-5029; e-mail administrator@nvfa.com.au and The Victorian Peach and Apricot Grower's Association (VPAGA) PO box 39 Cobram, Vic (03-5872-1729; fax 03-5871-1612). When sending for the information leaflet *Guide to Your Working Holiday* from NVFA you **must** include an International Reply Coupon (IRC) obtainable from the post office, to ensure a reply. Additional information relevant to the fruit harvest in the Goulburn Valley can also be obtained from the NVFA website www.nvfa.com.au. Go to 'Harvest Labour' on the menu. There is also a National Harvest Hotline number of 1300 720 126. This number gives the option of states and areas within Austalia where current seasonal work is available. By following the prompts, callers are able to obtain accurate updated information to a particular area or are able to speak directly with a person in a particular area.

Searching the web for employment leads is especially productive in Australia. There are dozens of routes in to finding out about job vacancies. A wide search can be done by looking at Employment under Google's regional directory at http://directory.google.com/Top/Regional/Oceania/Australia/. Before leaving home, you might like to register (free) with www.gapwork.com which is updated regularly and lists employers who hire working holidaymakers. The relatively new www.jobsearch.gov.au is a government source of information with details of the National Harvest Trail. One of the best sites is a free service by the Wayward Bus Company (www.waywardbus.com.au/seaswork.html) which has an index of actual employers, hostels and pubs recommended for job-seekers and agents. EN's website has useful links (www.employmentnational.com.au).If in Queensland check the adverts in *Queensland Country Life* magazine (www.queenslandcountrylife.com). The magazine also has an online jobs guide (www.jobsguide.com.au). Some properties also function as holiday ranches and they often take on domestic staff and guides.

A publication called **Workabout Australia** shows areas where fruit picking and other seasonal work is available. It also gives times, transport information, accommodation information, contacts for jobs on arrival; a British edition of this book will be published by Vacation Work (www.vacationwork.co.uk) in March 2004 at £10.99.

Hard-working travellers can earn A$100 a day doing harvest work, although AS$9 an hour would be more typical. The cost of living in Australia is a lot lower than in Britain so those wages go further than it sounds if you convert them into sterling at the current rate (£1 is worth A$2.84 at the time of writing).

Anyone who is serious about earning their way over a long period by fruit picking should consider obtaining the small format specialist booklet Fruit Picking around Australia which is available in Australia for A$10 from Pickpack (11 Coral St, Saunders Beach, Queensland 4818; payable to L. Hutchinson) or from campsites and bookshops in the relevant areas. Details can be found on www.cix.co.uk/~yama.fruit.

Some city-based employment agencies deal with jobs in outback areas, primarily farming, station, hotel/motel and roadhouse work. In Western Australia Pollitt's (13th Floor, 251 Adelaide Terrace, 13th Floor, Perth 6000; ☎08-9325 2544) who said that experienced farmworkers and tractor drivers are paid £4.50-£5 (A$12-$14) an hour for 10-12 hour days, seven days a week at seeding time (April to June) and harvest time (October to December). Housekeeping, nannying and cooking positions are available for two to three months at a time throughout the year. The standard wage is £105 (A$300) a week after board, most of which can be saved. For work in outback roadhouses and hotels, previous experience in kitchen, food and beverage service is essential to earn £140 (A$400) a week after lodging. The three-month commitments enable travellers to experience the regional country towns while saving most of their earnings.

In urban areas the usual range of jobs exists (bar, restaurant, office and factory work) available through the many private employment agencies such as Bligh, Adecco and Drake Personnel. It is also worth investigating tourist areas such as the coastal and island resorts of Queensland for jobs in hotels, restaurants, etc. especially during the Australian winter from June to October.

One of the best sources of job information for working holidaymakers in Australia is the extensive network of backpackers' hostels, some of which employ young foreigners themselves and all of which should be able to advise on local possibilities. One such is Brook Lodge Backpackers (3 Bridge Street, Donnybrook, WA 6239; ☎08-9731 1520; e-mail info@brooklodge.com.au; www.brooklodge.com.au) in Western Australia, which provides accommodation and can arrange hourly or weekly contract seasonal work including seasonal work in the apple harvest between November and May. Details of lodges like this can be found on the internet at http://backpackingaround.com, a website set up by backpackers which carries job and visa information as well as links and info on accommodation around Western Australia. Another useful source is the work exchange called Workstay Australia which is based in Western Australia and can be found at www.workstay.com.au. There is a membership fee and members are guided to a network of hostels when work is available. The group HNH Travellers Australia (Gabba Guesthouse, 18 Withington St, East Brisbane, Queensland 4169; ☎+61-7-3411-5955; www.hnh.net.au) primarily arranges accommodation for paying clients with host families, though it can also arrange fruit-picking in some areas. They offer a Travellers Discount Card for Aus $5 which will enable travellers a 10% discount at restaurants along with corporate car hire rates etc.

Either before you leave or once you are in one of the major cities, get hold of the free 200-page booklet *Australia & New Zealand Independent Traveller's Guide* published by the London-based travel magazine *TNT* (14-15 Child's Place, London SW5 9RX; ☎020-7373-3377; www.tntmagazine.com); send an A5 80p s.a.e. It includes a section on work and some relevant advertisements as well as travel advice.

Most newspapers advertise jobs on one or two days each week - varying from paper to paper and state to state. The *Sydney Morning Herald* is based at 201 Sussex Street, Sydney, NSW 2000 (www.smh.com.au). *The Australian* can be contacted at 46 Cooper Street, Surrey Hills, NSW 2010, and *The West Australian* at Newspaper House, 50 Hasler Road, Osborne Park, Western Australia 6017.

Copies of the above newspapers, plus information and application forms for visitor and working holiday visas may be obtained in the UK from the High Commission's designated agent, Consyl Publishing. For an application form and a free copy of *Travel Australia*, a newspaper aimed at those planning a working holiday in Australia, write to Consyl Publishing, 3 Buckhurst Road, Bexhill on Sea, East Sussex TN40 1QF (☎01424 223111; e-mail consylpublishing@btconnect.com; www.consylpublishing.co.uk); enclose an A4 stamped addressed envelope bearing at least 66p worth of stamps.

RED TAPE, VISAS & WORK PERMITS

Tourist Visa Requirements: All intending visitors require either a visa stamped in their passport or an Electronic Travel Authority (ETA) which is a paperless visa. Tourist visas are issued for 6 or 12 months. ETAs are obtained through airlines, travel agents or specialist visa agencies. An ETA is valid for 12 months and covers multiple entries into Australia for no more than three months each. Private visa agencies and delegated travel agencies can issue an ETA over the phone for varying fees, usually between £10 and £25. Major airlines may offer a free ETA service if you purchase an air ticket through their reservations offices. Three of the many agencies are Visas Australia Company (PO Box 1, Nantwich, Cheshire CW5 7PB; 01270 626626; www.visa-australia.co.uk) and Australian Visas Ltd (PO Box 170, Ashford, Kent TN24 0ZX; 01233 211800) and www.ausvisa.iborders.com (01270 626626). Those with ETAs and visitor visas are not permitted to work.

Working Holiday Visas The Australian Government operates a working holiday scheme for passport holders of the following countries: United Kingdom, Republic of Ireland, Canada, Germany, Japan, Republic of Korea, Malta, Netherlands, Norway, Sweden and Denmark. To be eligible for the granting of a 12 month, non-renewable working holiday visa you must satisfy the following criteria: be aged over 18 and under 31, have no dependent children have not previously entered Australia on a working holiday visa or applied for one, intend to travel and holiday in Australia with the option of taking incidental work to supplement your holiday funds but are prohibited from working for one employer for more than a total of three months, are in possession of reasonable funds (currently £2,000 in the UK and €3,200 in Europe) for normal maintenance purposes for the initial part of the proposed holiday period and sufficient for airfare.

The allocation of the annual quota of visas starts in July; once the total has run out, applications are not considered until the start of the next round, so the best time to apply is in the northern summer. There is a non-refundable processing fee for a working holiday visa, currently £65 in the UK (subject to change). Current information is available by calling the Australian Immigration and Citizenship Information Line on 09065-508900 (calls are charged at £1 per minute).

During those 12 months of the visas validity you may leave and re-enter the country as many times as you wish. Full details are available on the Australian Immigration website www.australia.org.uk. Britons should apply in plenty of time to the High Commission in London (Australia House, Strand, London WC2B 4LA) or in the north to the Australian Consulate in Manchester (Chatsworth House, Lever St, Manchester M1 2DL; 0161-228 1344) or online to www.immi.gov.au.

The first step is to get the working holiday visa application form from a specialist visa agent or Consyl Publishing (as above) or from www.australia.org.uk or from Australia Outlook, 3 Buckhurts Hill, Bexhill on Sea, East Sussex, TN40 1QF (send an s.a.e). The second step is to save at least £2,000 (€3,200) since you will have to submit bank statements with your application.

John Mahon of Visa Australia Company arranges visas for working holidays in Australia (14 Anglesea Street, Temple Bar, Dublin 2; ☎01 6795452; fax 01 6795459; e-mail sales@australianvisas.ie) and Visa Australia, PO Box 1, Nantwich, Cheshire CW5 7PB (☎01270-626626; fax 01270-626226; e-mail john@visas-australia.com; www.visas-australia.com). Visa Australia Company also arrange travel insurance and specialises in gap year insurance on the website www.coverworks.com.

Agricultural Work

RJ CORNISH: RMB 2024, Cottons Road, Cobram, Victoria 3644, Australia (☎+61 (0)3 58 72 10 54; e-mail info@rjcornish.com; www.rjcornish.com). RJ Cornish and Co is a family-owned and operated business and is one of Australia's

largest producers of apples, pears and canning peaches.
Fruit Pickers (approx. 200). Weather and crop permitting work is 6 days per
week 7.30am to 4pm. Australian Workers Union rates paid per bin harvested.
Accommodation (dormitory) and meals (except on Saturdays) are provided for A$
110.20 per week. Campsite and caravans also available for charge. Work period is
from late January to mid-March. Please see website for further details.

Apply in December to Doug McKean at the above address or e-mail.

OUTBACK STAFF: P.O. Box 8042, Allenstown, QLD 4700, Australia
(☎+61-7-49-274300; fax +61-7-4922-6923; e-mail outstaff@rocknet.net.au;
www.rocknet.net.au/~outstaff). Outback Staff is an Australia-wide rural employment
agency; they have jobs for farmers, tractor drivers, cotton workers, cooks and
seasonal staff; and provide on-going support and back-up during your time working
in Australia. The experience of working within the primary industries overseas aims
to broaden your knowledge of technology and work practices.
Farm Staff: numerous vacancies for personnel to operate farm machinery, drive
tractors/harvesters, or work on irrigation schemes. Wages start at around £4-£5 per
hour, applicants must have an agricultural background.
Cooks, Housekeepers, Nannies to work on outback farm stations. Wages between
£120-£160 per week. Applicants should have experience with cooking housework
and childcare.

All positions work 8-10 hours a day over a 5 or 7 day week. Farm workers are
required all year, while cooks are needed between February and October. Minimum
period of work two weeks. Board and lodging is usually included, but this depends
on the location. Applicants should speak English.

Applications are invited at any time to the above address.

TORRENS VALLEY ORCHARDS: P.O. Box 1659, Gumeracha, SA 5233,
Australia (e-mail tvo@hotkey.net.au; www.tvo.com.au). Farm business that has used
a lot of student and backpacker workers over the last 16 years particularly during the
cherry harvest. He has had German, English, Japanese, Korean and French people,
the majority of them female. Provides hostel type accommodation for travellers.
Owner Tony Hannaford says that anyone who stays at TVO should be quick, polite,
clean and look after the facilities provided. He organises trips to barbecues, football,
beach etc. The farm is 30 minutes from Adelaide on the local bus run. As well as
picking, there is a lot of fruit packing work.

Apply to Tony Hannaford at the above mail or e-mail address.

VISITOZ: Springbrook Farm, MS188, Goomeri, 4601 Queensland, 4601 Australia
(fax 0061-741-686-155; e-mail info@visitoz.com; www.visitoz.org).
VISITOZ offers an introduction to Australia for those with Working Holiday Visas.
All those entitled to Working Holiday Visas find work in rural Australia as tractor
drivers, stockworkers, horse riders, hospitality workers, on cattle and sheep stations,
and mothers' helps and teachers. There are generally around 200 vacancies to choose
from and employment is guaranteed. Wages vary according to the job being done,
working hours, the State and the age of the worker; earnings are generally around
£140 per week with free board and lodging but have been known to reach around
£500 per week.

Staff are needed around the year but working holiday regulations limit the time
with any one employer to 3 months. Applicants must be aged 18-30 and all are
assessed and/or trained for the job required. Participants in the scheme must pay for
their own air fare, visa costs and the Visitoz training fee of £595 which also covers

being met at the airport on arrival, 3 days jet lag recovery, 5 days on the training farm and help with the red tape once in Australia.

For further details contact *Dan and Joanna Burnet* at the above address by fax or e-mail; there are also two UK contacts; William on 07966-528664 or wdtb@aol.com, and Jules on 07771 992 352.

WILLING WORKERS ON ORGANIC FARMS (AUSTRALIA): RSD Buchan 3885, Victoria, Australia (☎+61-03-5155 0218; fax +61-03-5155 0342; e-mail wwoof@wwoof.com.au; www.wwoof.com.au).
WWOOF Australia offers the chance to learn about organic farming and Australian culture by giving practical help on over 1500 farms and properties around Australia. Jobs may range from weeding to building. Applicants should note that WWOOF **is not a source of paid employment**, but food and accommodation is provided in exchange for 4-6 hours work per day. Positions available all year.

Write for a brochure, or send £23 if single (£27 for a couple), for the list and insurance.

Sports, Couriers and Camping

THREDBO RESORT CENTRE: Kosciusko Thredbo Pty Ltd, P.O. Box 92, Thredbo, NSW 2625, Australia (☎+61-2-6459 4100; fax +61-2-6459 4101; e-mail r ecruitment@thredbo.com.au; www.thredbo.com.au). Thredbo is Australia's premier ski resort, with a season from mid-June to the end of September. They employ over 600 staff in winter, and have a ski village population of over 4,200.
Ticket Sellers (5) to sell ski lift and ski school products. Applicants should have cash handling, accurate balancing and computer skills/experience. Wages £650 per month.
Ski Hire Staff (8) to fit customers with skis and snowboards and hire out clothing and equipment. Should have some cash handling experience and be willing to work split-shifts. Wages £750 per month.
Lift Attendants (8) to assist customers on and off the ski lifts and t-bars, and checking tickets. Should be willing to work outdoors in all weathers, and able to pay attention to safety requirements: training in safety will be given. Wages £780 per month.
Food and Beverage Staff (10) should have passed Australian 'Responsible Service of Alcohol Course' and have previous experience of busy establishments.

Hours of work vary between 28-38 per week according to position. The period of work is from around 1 July to 28 September (depending on snow), with a minimum period of work of 12 weeks. Board and lodging is available for a cost of £45 per week.

Applications to the above address are invited from January and close in mid-April, with interviews in Sydney in early May.

Voluntary Work and Archaeology

AUSTRALIAN KOALA FOUNDATION: Level 1, 40 Charlotte Street, Brisbane, QLD 4000, Australia (☎+61-7 3229 7233; fax +61-7 3221 0337; e-mail research@ savethekoala.com; www.savethekoala.com.
The Australian Koala Foundation (AKF) is a non-profit, non-government funded, conservation organisation whose central aim is the **conservation of Australia's unique koala habitat.**

Volunteers can also assist with **general office duties**, especially during the major public awareness and fundraising campaign – Save the Koala – held in July each year. Field trip participation costs begin at AU$1,000 per week, depending on location. Applicants should advise the AKF of any specialist areas of expertise or interest they may have. Minimum age 18. Volunteers for office duties are generally required from March to October each year.

Contact Lorraine O'Keefe, General Manager, Administration and Finance, at GPO Box 2659, Brisbane, QLD 4001, Australia, to discuss the voluntary opportunities available. Also check out the website for upcoming fieldtrips.

BOB WHITWORTH: 100 Deserio Road, Cedar, Pocket, Gympie, Queensland, Australia (☎07-54-886-147; e-mail forest@spiderweb.com.au)
Volunteer **farm workers** to work as part of the WWOOF scheme. Bob Whitworth also offers accommodation in a converted dairy, and in a small self-contained hut in a forest clearing (with wood stove, single bed and desk). The farm is surrounded by hills, a rainforest, and a creek. He invites visitors all year round (one or two at a time) of any nationality. *Applicants* must speak some English. Accommodation is offered and usually food, although some visitors make a contribution.

Contact the above address for details.

CONSERVATION VOLUNTEERS AUSTRALIA (CVA): Head Office, PO Box 423, Ballarat, Victoria 3353, Australia (☎+61-3-5333 1483; fax +61-3-5333-2166; e-mail info@conservationvolunteers.com.au; www.conservationvolunteers.com.au). Conservation Volunteers Australia is Australia's largest practical conservation organisation. CVA welcomes everyone who is enthusiastic about the outdoors and hands-on conservation. Volunteers are part of a team of 6 to 10 people under the guidance of a CVA team leader. Projects undertaken by CVA include: **tree planting, native seed collection, endangered flora and fauna surveys, constructing and maintaining walking tracks in national parks.** Projects are run in every state and territory of Australia throughout the year and include some of Australia's most beautiful locations. CVA offers overseas volunteers the Conservaton Experience six weeks package. Volunteering with CVA costs £8.50 (A$23) a night which includes all meals, project related travel and accommodation.

For more information *visit* the website or e-mail or write to CVA.

CHRISTIAN WORK CAMPS AUSTRALIA: P.O. Box K164, Haymarket, NSW 2000, Australia.
Volunteers to take part in work camps, which are held for two to four weeks each January and July. The camps are currently held in New South Wales, the Northern Territory and Far North Queensland. Volunteers must pay camp registration fees of approximately £23; additional expenses may include food and accommodation at a further £23, approx. per week. Volunteers are responsible for their own travel costs.

For information on forthcoming projects *send* an International Reply Coupon to the above address.

Other Employment in Australia

CAMP COUNSELORS USA: UK Offices: Green Dragon House, 64-70 High Street, Croydon CR0 9XN (☎020-8688 9051; e-mail Inquiry@ccusaweusa.co.uk; www.ccusa.com) and 27 Woodside Gardens, Musselburgh, nr. Edinburgh EH21 7LJ (☎0131-665 5843; e-mail 101355.257@compuserve.com; ccusa.com).
Work Experience Down Under is a high quality programme that helps young people to work and travel in Australia or New Zealand for up to 12 months.

For details *contact* the above addresses; US citizens should *contact* CCUSA/ Work Experience Down Under, 2330 Marinship Way, Suite 250, Sausalito, CA 94965; e-mail downunder@ccusa.com.

WORK AUSTRALIA: BUNAC, 16 Bowling Green Lane, London EC1R 0QH (☎020-7251 3472; e-mail downunder@bunac.org.uk).
BUNAC offers a work and travel scheme to Australia for up to a year. The package includes a round trip flight, group departures, organised stopover on outward journey, a working holiday visa, 2 nights' accommodation in Sydney, and orientation with guidance on jobs, housing, health, taxes, etc. plus back-up services. Departures from the UK are from June to March; participants in BUNAC's US programmes (Work America, Summer Camp USA, KAMP) can take a flight from California usually in late September.

Applicants must be aged 18-30 inclusive, *citizens of the UK, Ireland, Holland, Sweden, Denmark, Norway or Canada*, and will need to be able to show that they have reserve funds of at least £2,000. Programme costs were between £1,500 and £1,800.

For further details *contact* Work Australia at the above address.

WORK AND TRAVEL AUSTRALIA PROGRAMME: CIEE (Council on International Educational Exchange), 52 Poland Street, London W1F 7AB (☎020-7478 2022; fax 020-7734 7322; e-mail: infouk@councilexchanges.org.uk; www.ciee.org.uk). CIEE is a worldwide organisation placing people in casual work, internships and teaching positions across the world.
This programme allows participants to travel in Australia, taking up work along the way to support themselves. CIEE offer assistance at every stage, from obtaining the visa, to helping find work and accommodation in Australia. Ongoing services include mail receiving and holding, 24 hour emergency support, and access to office facilities and free internet at their resource centre in Sydney.

This programme is open to British, Canadian, Dutch and Irish passport holders resident in the UK, aged 18-30, who have not been on a working holiday to Australia before. Programme fee starts at £320 (and rises in increments for every month's additional stay) and includes all services and 2 night's accommodation. Visa valid for 12 months from entry to Australia. Wide variety of work available, for up to 3 months per position.

Applications to the above address.

WORK & TRAVEL AUSTRALIA: CIEE (Council on International Educational Exchange), 3 Copley Place, Suit A, Boston MA 02116; 1 –888-268-6245 e-mail info@councilexchanges.org; www.councilexchanges.org). The US address of the worldwide organisation placing people in casual work, internships and teaching positions across the world.
This is the equivalent to the above programme for *US citizens* aged 18-30; it allows employment in Australia for up to four months at any time of year, with the possibility of an additional tourist visa. The scheme includes documentation, assistance in finding work and housing through Council's Sydney office, orientation etc.

For further details call 1-88-COUNCIL (toll-free) for a brochure or see www.councilexchanges.org.

New Zealand

New Zealand offers many opportunities just as its massive neighbour Australia does. The downside is that visas and work permits are necessary for any form of paid employment in New Zealand, the only exception being for Australians. These should normally be obtained before entry to the country, and a job offer must be held at the time of application.

The UK Citizens' Working Holiday Scheme allows Britons aged 18-30 to do temporary jobs in New Zealand for up to 12 months. The allocation has steadily risen and now stands at 8,000 working holiday visas which are granted annually on a first come first served basis starting September 1st. Information can be obtained from the New Zealand Immigration Service, Mezzanine Floor, New Zealand House, 80 Haymarket, London SW1Y 4TE (fax 020-7973 0370) in person, by phone on 09069-100100 (charged at £1 per minute) or via the internet at www.immigration.govt.nz.

To apply you need the right Application for Work Visa form, your UK passport, the fee of £30, evidence of a return ticket and evidence of NZ$4,200 (about £1,200). Sponsorship from a New Zealand citizen is not considered an acceptable substitute for proof of funds. Applications for the working holiday visa must be lodged in the UK. Other working holiday schemes are open to Irish, Canadian, Japanese and Malaysian nationals who must apply in their country of nationality. You do not need a job offer when applying as the scheme allows you to pick up temporary work while holidaying in New Zealand.

The expense of getting to New Zealand, together with the fact that wages are significantly lower than in Australia, means that many people who visit New Zealand to work are more concerned with the cultural than the financial aspects of their trip. Opportunities vary from region to region depending on the local employment situation.

Worth reading is the *Independent Traveller's Guide – Australia & New Zealand* published bi-monthly by *TNT Magazine* which runs to around 200 pages of information, ideas and advice about travelling in Australia and New Zealand. To obtain a copy send an A4 S.A.E. (70p) to: TNT Travel Guides, TNT/Southern Cross, 14-15 Child's Place, Earl's Court, London SW5 9RX (☎020-7373-3377; www.tntmagazine.com).

If you want to place an advertisement stating that you are looking for work the *New Zealand Herald* is published by Wilson and Horton Ltd, P.O. Box 32, 46 Albert Street, Auckland (☎9-379 5050; fax 9-373 6410; www.wilsonandhorton.co.nz).

RED TAPE, VISAS & WORK PERMITS

Visa Requirements: New Zealand has Visa Waiver agreements with 30 countries so citizens of the UK, Ireland, USA and most European countries do not need a visa for bona fide tourist or business visits of up to 3 months (6 months for UK citizens). On arrival, visitors must have valid passports, return tickets and evidence of sufficient funds (about £300 per month of stay). Renewals of permits will be considered to allow stays of up to a maximum of 12 months: approval is not automatic.

Residence Visas: People wishing to reside permanently in New Zealand can make a prior application to a New Zealand overseas post, or can apply while on a temporary permit in New Zealand.

Work Visas & Permits: Recent changes to immigration rules make it possible for people on working holidays to apply to extend their stay or even for residence without having to leave the country. Applicants with skills in demand may apply for a new work permit option that will be valid for up to six months at one of the seven Immigration Service offices in New Zealand. Permission may be given if there are no local residents available to take up the work offered.

American students are eligible to apply for a six-month work permit from the CIEE or BUNAC USA to work between April 1st and October 21st. CCUSA at 2330 Marinship Way, Suite 250, Sausalito, CA 94965 (1-800-999-CAMP; out bound@campcounselors.com/ www.campcounselors.com/australia.html) runs a three-month work experience programme (June to September).

Au Pair: Not customary. Work permit required.

Voluntary Work: Work permit required.

However, it should be noted that the above rules are liable to sudden change; all visas, including visitor visas, are charged for. There is a charge for all permit applications. For further information, check the New Zealand Immigration Service website (www.immigration.govt.nz).

Agricultural Work

FARM HELPERS IN NEW ZEALAND: 16 Aspen Way, Palmerston North, New Zealand (tel/fax +646-355-0448; e-mail fhinz@xtra.co.nz; www.fhinz.co.nz).
FHINZ is a voluntary group of over 180 farms throughout New Zealand who offer free farm stays to visitors in exchange for 4-6 hours help per day. Board and lodging is provided in the family home in return for daily farm work dependent on season and type of farm. No experience is necessary and all equipment is provided. Most farms will collect visitors from the nearest town at no cost, and return them after the stay, which can be from 3 days to several months, depending on the needs of the farm. Visitors need to each have a membership booklet (revised every month), with full details of all the farms, the family and what kinds of work visitors will be helping with. These are $25 each, valid for one year and available either by mail order or through some agents. For more information *contact* the address above.

WWOOF: P.O. Box 1172, Nelson, New Zealand (tel/fax 03-5449890; e-mail wwoof@wwoof.co.nz; www.wwoof.co.nz).
Volunteer Farm Labourers for unpaid work on organic properties including orchards, nurseries, farms etc. in New Zealand. It must be stressed that these positions are unpaid, and that participants must pay for their own travel expenses; they do, however, receive free food and accommodation. Positions are available at any time of year. WWOOF runs 650 farms around New Zealand. Applicants must be aged over 16 and must not be from countries whose nationals need special invitations to enter New Zealand.

For further information *write to* Jane and Andrew Strange at the above address enclosing £12 membership fee.

Voluntary Work

INVOLVEMENT VOLUNTEERS NEW ZEALAND: P.O. Box 153, Helensville, New Zealand (☎64-94-207859; fax 64-94-207858).
Involvement Volunteers is an organisation that places volunteers in the areas of **social work, conservation, farming and education**. Board and lodging is sometimes provided free of charge but at other times a small fee is charged. Minimum period

of work 2-6 weeks all year round. Knowledge of English is required. There is a fee for placement.

Contact the above address for further details.

Other Employment in New Zealand

BUNAC: 16 Bowling Green Lane, London EC1R 0QH (☎020-7251 3472; fax 020-7251 0215; e-mail downunder@bunac.org.uk; www.bunac.org).

BUNAC offers a work/travel scheme entitled *Work New Zealand*, which enables participants to spend up to one year working and travelling in the South Pacific. The programme is open to all students and non-students aged 18-30 *who hold a British or Irish passport*. Choose any type of job, anywhere in New Zealand. The package includes group departures, a round trip flight, stop over in Bangkok, two nights' accommodation and orientation with guidance on jobs, housing, health and taxes. Support services and resource centre are available throughout the stay.

For further information *contact* BUNAC at the above address or through their website www.bunac.org.

WORK AND TRAVEL NEW ZEALAND PROGRAMME: CIEE (Council on International Educational Exchange), 52 Poland Street, London W1F 7AB (☎020-7478 2022; fax 020-7734 7322; e-mail: infouk@councilexchanges.org.uk; www.ciee.org.uk). CIEE is a worldwide organisation placing people in casual work, internships and teaching positions across the world.

This programme allows participants to travel in New Zealand, taking up work along the way to support themselves. CIEE offer assistance at every stage, from obtaining the visa, to helping find work and accommodation. Ongoing services include mail receiving and holding, 24 hour emergency support, and access to office facilities and free internet at their resource centre in Auckland.

This programme is open to British, Canadian and Dutch passport holders resident in the UK, aged 18-30, who have not been on a working holiday to New Zealand before. Programme fee starts at £320 (and rises in increments for every month's additional stay) and includes all services and 2 night's accommodation. Visa valid for 12 months from entry to New Zealand. Wide variety of work available, for up to 3 months per position.

Applications all year round, at least 8 weeks before planned departure for New Zealand.

WORK & TRAVEL NEW ZEALAND: CIEE (Council on International Educational Exchange), 3 Copley Place, Suit A, Boston MA 02116; 1 –888-268-6245 e-mail info@councilexchanges.org; www.councilexchanges.org). The US address of the worldwide organisation placing people in casual work, internships and teaching positions across the world.

This is the equivalent to the above programme for *US citizens* aged 18-30; it allows employment in New Zealand for up to six months between April 1st and October 31st. The scheme includes documentation, assistance in finding work and housing through Council's partner organisation in New Zealand, orientation etc.

For further details call 1-88-COUNCIL (toll-free) for a brochure or see www.councilexchanges.org.

Useful Publications

ARCHAEOLOGY ABROAD: 31/34 Gordon Square, London WC1H 0PY; fax 0207-383-2572; e-mail arch.abroad@ucl.ac.uk; www.britarch.ac.uk/archabroad Publishes bulletins in April and November, which list a wide range of archaeological fieldwork opportunities worldwide. Fieldwork Awards are available to help subscribers with their expenses. For details send an s.a.e..

CAREERS EUROPE: Onward House, Baptist Place, Bradford, BD1 2PS (☎01274-829600; e-mail europe@careersb.co.uk; www.careerseurope.co.uk). Careers Europe is the UK Euro Guidance Centre for International Careers and produces *Eurofacts* and *Global Facts* which are a series of international careers leaflets, and *EXODUS* which is a database of international careers information. This information is available via UK careers offices and other careers libraries.

CHRISTIAN VOCATIONS: St. James House, Trinity Road, Dudley, DY1 1JB (☎01384-233511; fax 01384-233032; e-mail info@ChristianVocations.org; www.ch ristianvocations.org). Christian Vocations provides advice and information regarding a wide range of short or long-term opportunities with Christian organisations both in the UK and overseas. These are also posted on their website.
Publishes the *Short-Term-Service Directory*, a comprehensive source of information about short-term service options with a Christian emphasis in the UK and abroad, at a cost of £5.25 plus £1.75 post & packing (overseas postage is extra). For further details and information on their other publications and services contact them at the above address.

CO-ORDINATING COMMITTEE FOR INTERNATIONAL VOLUNTARY SERVICE (CCIVS): UNESCO, 1 rue Miollis, F-75732 Paris Cedex 15, France (☎+33-1-45-68-45-36; e-mail ccivs@unesco.org; www.unesco.org/ccivs). CCIVS is an international non-governmental organisation created in 1948 under the aegis of UNESCO to promote and coordinate voluntary work worldwide. CCIVS has 140 member organisations present in more than 90 countries.
 Publishes *How to be a Volunteer* in Europe, Africa, Asia and America a guide and useful address book, costing €2.5 or 7 International Reply Coupons. Other specialised publications include *Volunteering in Conflict Areas* (€5), and *How to Present a Project* (€5), postage included.
 CCIVS does not recruit volunteers directly so would be volunteers should contact CCIVS member organisations in their own country.
 For a full list of publications, please send your request to the above address with one IRC or see their website.

ISCO PUBLICATIONS: 12A Princess Way, Camberley, Surrey GU15 3SP (☎01276-21188; www.isco.org.uk). ISCO is an educational charity providing careers and higher education advice to students and independent schools. Publications through ISCO CareerScope are available to all educational establishments.
ISCO produce a booklet entitled *Opportunities in the GAP Year*, price £6.95 (plus postage costs of £1.00 on orders up to £10.00), that gives advice to those with a spare year between leaving school and going to University; for details please contact ISCO at the above address. They also issue the magazine *CareersScope* which has

numerous articles on career fields and developments.

JOBCENTRE PLUS: International Job Search Advice, Jubilee House, 33-41 Park Place, Leeds LS1 2RE; Job Centre Plus produce a series of fact sheets for each of the countries in the European Economic Area, entitled 'Working in...' followed by the name of the country. They provide general information in sections headed Finding Work, Accommodation, Education and Useful Addresses and are available at the Jobcentre Plus offices or the website www.jobcentreplus.gov.uk.

OVERSEAS JOBS EXPRESS: 20 New Road, Brighton, Sussex BN1 1UF (☎01273-699777; fax 01273-699778; e-mail editor@overseasjobsexpress.co.uk; www.overseasjobsexpress.co.uk).
A fortnightly newspaper for international job hunters covering more than 30 categories of work, from seasonal opportunities to permanent/contract work. Contains details of current vacancies and feature articles on work abroad, travel, migration etc.

PETERSON'S GUIDES: P.O. Box 67005, Laurenceville, NJ 08648-4764 (www.petersons.com). Leading publishers of books on employment and education in the US.
Summer Jobs for Students 2004; ($18.95). Covers opportunities in the US in detail. Available in the UK as *Summer Jobs USA* (see Vacation Work below). Also see under Vacation Work below. *Internships USA.* ($26.95). A guide to career-related employment in the US.

VACATION-WORK: 9 Park End Street, Oxford OX1 1HJ, (☎01865-241978; fax 01865-790885; www.vacationwork.co.uk), publishes or distributes the following titles in the UK.
Summer Jobs for Students USA 2004; (£12.99). Covers opportunities in the US in detail. Published by Peterson's Guides in the US.
Work Your Way Around The World (£12.95). Contains invaluable information on all the ways to find temporary work worldwide, both in advance and when abroad.
Taking a Gap Year (£11.95). A comprehensive guide for anyone planning a year off before or after college.
Workabout Australia (£10.99), the first UK edition of a complete guide to finding seasonal work in Australia.
Working in Tourism – The UK, Europe & Beyond (£11.95). New edition for 2004 of the comprehensive guide to short and long-term work in the booming tourist industry.
Working on Cruise Ships (£10.99) a complete guide to both short and long term work afloat.
Working in Ski Resorts – Europe & North America (£11.95). Includes details on both how to arrange a job with a British based ski operator and how to find a job after arriving in a ski resort. New edition 2003.
The International Directory of Voluntary Work (£11.95). A comprehensive worldwide guide to both residential and non-residential voluntary work.
The Au Pair and Nanny's Guide to Working Abroad (£11.95). Explains how to get domestic work abroad, including a guide to agencies and country by country guides.
Teaching English Abroad (£12.95). Covers both short and long term opportunities for teaching English abroad for both qualified and untrained teachers.
Internships USA 2004: (£18.99). Published by Peterson's Guides in the US ($26.95),

it lists over 50,000 opportunities for short term career-related work throughout America.

THE WORLD ATLAS OF WINE: by Hugh Johnson and Jancis Robinson (£24.50 from Amazon.co.uk); although primarily aimed at the wine-lover, this large book provides useful information on the location of vineyards around the world for those looking for work picking grapes. It may be available for consultation at public libraries. Mitchell Beazley, the publisher, also produce a number of other more pocketable books covering the wine regions of specific countries.

WORLD SERVICE ENQUIRY: 237 Bon Marché Centre, 241-251 Ferndale Road, London SW9 8BJ (☎0870-770-3274; fax 0870-770-7991; e-mail wse@cabroad.org.uk; www.wse.org.uk).
World Service Enquiry provides expert, impartial information and advice about working or volunteering overseas in the Third World. Information is available for both skilled and unskilled people seeking overseas placements. *The Guide to Volunteering for Development* is updated every year and a copy can be seen on the website. The Guide outlines ways to be involved in development issues and lists hundreds of agencies that take volunteers in the UK and overseas on short-term placements. WSE also provides career guidance and Opportunities Abroad, a job list; further details on the website above.

Vacation Work Publications

	Paperback	Hardback
Summer Jobs Abroad	£10.99	£16.95
Summer Jobs in Britain	£10.99	£16.95
Supplement to Summer Jobs Britain and Abroad *published in May*	£6.00	-
Work Your Way Around the World	£12.95	-
Workabout Australia	£10.99	-
Taking a Gap Year	£11.95	-
Taking a Career Break	£11.95	-
Working in Tourism – The UK, Europe & Beyond	£11.95	-
Working in Aviation	£10.99	-
Kibbutz Volunteer	£10.99	-
Working on Yachts and Superyachts	£10.99	-
Working on Cruise Ships	£10.99	-
Teaching English Abroad	£12.95	-
The Au Pair & Nanny's Guide to Working Abroad	£12.95	-
The Good Cook's Guide to Working Worldwide	£11.95	-
Working in Ski Resorts – Europe & North America	£11.95	-
Working with Animals – The UK, Europe & Worldwide	£11.95	-
Live & Work Abroad – A Guide for Modern Nomads	£11.95	-
Working with the Environment	£11.95	-
The Directory of Jobs & Careers Abroad	£12.95	-
The International Directory of Voluntary Work	£11.95	-
Buying a House in France	£11.95	-
Buying a House in Spain	£11.95	-
Buying a House in Italy	£11.95	-
Live & Work in Australia & New Zealand	£10.99	-
Live & Work in Belgium, The Netherlands & Luxembourg	£10.99	-
Live & Work in France	£10.99	-
Live & Work in Germany	£10.99	-
Live & Work in Italy	£10.99	-
Live & Work in Japan	£10.99	-
Live & Work in Saudi & the Gulf	£10.99	-
Live & Work in Scandinavia	£10.99	-
Live & Work in Scotland	£10.99	-
Live &Work in Spain & Portugal	£10.99	-
Live & Work in the USA & Canada	£10.99	-
Drive USA	£10.99	-
Scottish Islands – The Western Isles	£12.95	-
Scottish Islands – Orkney & Shetland	£11.95	-
The Panamericana: On the Road through Mexico and Central America	£12.95	-
Travellers Survival Kit Australia & New Zealand	£11.95	-
Travellers Survival Kit Cuba	£10.99	-
Travellers Survival Kit Lebanon	£10.99	-
Travellers Survival Kit Madagascar, Mayotte & Comoros	£10.99	-
Travellers Survival Kit Mauritius, Seychelles & Réunion	£10.99	-
Travellers Survival Kit Mozambique	£10.99	-
Travellers Survival Kit Oman & The Arabian Gulf	£11.95	-
Travellers Survival Kit South America	£15.95	-
Travellers Survival Kit Sri Lanka	£10.99	-

Distributors of:

Summer Jobs in the USA	£12.99	-
Internships	£18.99	-
World Volunteers	£10.99	-
Green Volunteers	£10.99	-
Archaeo-Volunteers	£10.99	-

Vacation Work Publications, 9 Park End Street, Oxford OX1 1HJ
☎ **01865-241978   Fax 01865-790885**

Visit us online for more information on our unrivalled range of titles for work, travel and gap years, readers' feedback and regular updates:

www.vacationwork.co.uk

SOUTH TYNESIDE LIBRARIES
WITHDRAWN FROM STOCK